Interrelatedness in Chinese Religious Traditions

Bloomsbury Studies in World Philosophies

Series Editor
Monika Kirloskar-Steinbach

Comparative, cross-cultural and intercultural philosophy are burgeoning fields of research. Bloomsbury Studies in World Philosophies complements and strengthens the latest work being carried out at a research level with a series that provides a home for thinking through ways in which professional philosophy can be diversified. Ideal for philosophy postgraduates and faculty who seek creative and innovative material on non-Euroamerican sources for reference and research, this series responds to the challenges of our postcolonial world, laying the groundwork for a new philosophy canon that departs from the current Eurocentric sources.

Titles in the Series
Andean Aesthetics and Anticolonial Resistance, by Omar Rivera
Chinese Philosophy of History, by Dawid Rogacz
Chinese and Indian Ways of Thinking in Early Modern European Philosophy,
by Selusi Ambrogio
Indian and Intercultural Philosophy, by Douglas Berger
Toward a New Image of Paramārtha, by Ching Keng
African Philosophy and Enactivist Cognition, by Bruce B. Janz
Interrelatedness in Chinese Religious Traditions, by Diana Arghirescu

Interrelatedness in Chinese Religious Traditions

An Intercultural Philosophy

Diana Arghirescu

BLOOMSBURY ACADEMIC
LONDON • NEW YORK • OXFORD • NEW DELHI • SYDNEY

BLOOMSBURY ACADEMIC
Bloomsbury Publishing Plc
50 Bedford Square, London, WC1B 3DP, UK
1385 Broadway, New York, NY 10018, USA
29 Earlsfort Terrace, Dublin 2, Ireland

BLOOMSBURY, BLOOMSBURY ACADEMIC and the Diana logo are
trademarks of Bloomsbury Publishing Plc

First published in Great Britain 2022
This paperback edition published 2024

Copyright © Diana Arghirescu, 2022

Diana Arghirescu has asserted her right under the Copyright, Designs and
Patents Act, 1988, to be identified as Author of this work.

For legal purposes the Acknowledgements on p. vi constitute an
extension of this copyright page.

Series design by Louise Dugdale
Cover image © Olga Kurbatova/Getty Images

All rights reserved. No part of this publication may be reproduced or transmitted in
any form or by any means, electronic or mechanical, including photocopying,
recording, or any information storage or retrieval system, without prior
permission in writing from the publishers.

Bloomsbury Publishing Plc does not have any control over, or responsibility for, any
third-party websites referred to or in this book. All internet addresses given in this
book were correct at the time of going to press. The author and publisher regret any
inconvenience caused if addresses have changed or sites have ceased to exist, but
can accept no responsibility for any such changes.

A catalogue record for this book is available from the British Library.

Library of Congress Cataloging-in-Publication Data

Names: Arghirescu, Diana, author.
Title: Interrelatedness in Chinese religious traditions : an intercultural philosophy / Diana Arghirescu.
Description: First edition. | London, UK ; New York, NY, USA : Bloomsbury Academic,
Bloomsbury Publishing Plc, 2022. | Series: Bloomsbury studies
in world philosophies | Includes bibliographical references and index.
Identifiers: LCCN 2022036569 (print) | LCCN 2022036570 (ebook) |
ISBN 9781350256859 (HB) | ISBN 9781350256897 (PB) |
ISBN 9781350256866 (ePDF) | ISBN 9781350256873 (eBook)
Subjects: LCSH: China–Religion–Philosophy. | China–Religion–History. | Qisong,
1007-1071–Criticism and interpretation. | Zhu, Xi, 1130-1200–Criticism and interpretation.
Classification: LCC BL1802.A74 2022 (print) |
LCC BL1802 (ebook) | DDC 200.951–dc23/eng20221024
LC record available at https://lccn.loc.gov/2022036569
LC ebook record available at https://lccn.loc.gov/2022036570

ISBN: HB: 978-1-3502-5685-9
PB: 978-1-3502-5689-7
ePDF: 978-1-3502-5686-6
eBook: 978-1-3502-5687-3

Series: Bloomsbury Studies in World Philosophies

Typeset by Newgen KnowledgeWorks Pvt. Ltd., Chennai, India

To find out more about our authors and books visit www.bloomsbury.com
and sign up for our newsletters.

Contents

Acknowledgements vi

Introduction: Intercultural philosophical approach and cultural presuppositions 1

Part 1 Western Theories and Cultural Presuppositions: An Intercultural Perspective

1 Classical theories of Western philosophy of religion (Durkheim and Weber): An analysis of their presuppositions from a Chinese perspective 25
2 Contemporary theories of Western religious studies and philosophy of religion (John Hick, Ninian Smart, Jonathan Z. Smith): An analysis of their presuppositions from a Chinese perspective 75

Part 2 Chinese Cultural Presuppositions: Ethical Interrelatedness in Song Dynasty Philosophico-Religious Traditions

3 Ethico-spiritual interrelatedness: The meaning of ethico-religious practice in the Chan scholar-monk Qisong's writings 113
4 Ethico-organic interrelatedness: The meaning of ethico-religious practice in the Neo-Confucian scholar Zhu Xi's writings 131

Part 3 Ethical Interrelatedness

5 Ethical interrelatedness: An interpretive theory for Chinese religious traditions 159

Part 4 Contemporary Sinological, Philosophical and Buddhological Approaches to Chinese Religious Traditions

6 A comparative perspective: Similarities and differences 187

Conclusion 223

Notes 229
Bibliography 249
Index 257

Acknowledgements

I developed this interpretive study during an extended period of research in 2020 and 2021. I am most grateful to the Université du Québec à Montréal – my academic home – for support during this period. The research grants permitted me time free of teaching and administration.

First, I would like to thank my family for their endless support throughout the project. Sincere gratitude to my long-time friend Professor Kirill Ole Thompson from National University of Taiwan, who offered important insights. I also owe him a debt of gratitude for his editorial help. Special thanks to the three anonymous reviewers of my initial project, whose valuable feedback and constructive reviews helped shape this book into its final form. Obviously, any remaining faults of this work are entirely mine.

My thanks go to Colleen Coalter, editor (Philosophy), for believing in this project from the beginning and for guiding me through the book's various stages of development. My deepest appreciation and thanks are extended to editors Monika Kirloskar-Steinbach and Leah Kalmanson for their encouragement and helpful comments. A special thanks to Suzie Nash, editorial assistant, for support in this work.

Montréal, Université du Québec à Montréal
November 2021

Introduction: Intercultural philosophical approach and cultural presuppositions

1 Introduction: An intercultural philosophical approach

The study of religions is essential to understanding other cultures as well as to building a sense of belonging in a multicultural world. It supports openness to diversity and intercultural dialogue. This book offers a philosophical hermeneutics of 'Chinese religions' (in particular, Song dynasty Neo-Confucianism and Chan Buddhism), which envisages them as an interrelated group of interlocutors and partners in world interreligious and intercultural dialogue. As the focus of this work is on Song dynasty thought (Chan and Neo-Confucian) and ethical interdependency as one of their major common features, it sets aside the Daoist tradition which has its own interest and is less concerned with social interrelationships. The present hermeneutical reflection might be described as a philosophical practice as well as a method. It aims to meet 'otherness' not within the historical as in the Western interpretive tradition (i.e. through exercising a historical understanding of the thought of another historical epoch) but within the intercultural (i.e. through a comparative interpretation of the Chinese and Western cultural presuppositions).

In particular, as already mentioned, it focuses on a comparative understanding of translations of Song dynasty texts from two major traditions, Confucianism and Chinese Chan Buddhism. This interpretive process has two comparative dimensions: intracultural – unveils and interprets the exchanges and connections between Confucianism and Chan during the Song dynasty (960–1279); and intercultural – discusses Chinese and Western cultural presuppositions based on philosophical translations of classical Chinese works.

This book is the fruit of two of my experiences as a sinologist armed first with a background in Western philosophy but also with specializations in Song dynasty thought and culture and (Western) hermeneutical philosophy. The first experience is related to teaching courses on philosophy of religion as well as Chinese thinking and spirituality regarded as 'non-Western' thought and spirituality – that is, from a comparative and intercultural perspective (Western and Chinese as non-Western) to students enrolled in (Western) philosophy and in science of religions programs; the second experience is related to undertaking philosophical and interpretive translations of Song dynasty Neo-Confucian and Chan Buddhist texts.[1]

I define intercultural dialogue as dialogue focusing on reciprocal transformative exchanges and learning between cultures. Unlike the cross-cultural and transcultural projects which look for contrasts and resemblances across cultures considered as case studies and then compare these case studies in order to forge new definitions, concepts, theses and principles, intercultural dialogue is aimed, first and foremost, to develop new relations between cultures through deep, mutual understanding and thus promote mutual intellectual, ethical and spiritual growth. I suggest that, for transformative and formative understanding and growth to occur in the course of such intercultural dialogue, the effort to reciprocally realize and interpret the implicit cultural presuppositions, core values and beliefs, that is, the deeper elements of culture rooted in each of the participant cultures, is necessary. A general observation is that the standard transcultural and cross-cultural studies deal with comparisons at the level of external or peripheral elements of culture: explicit forms of behaviour, environment, sociopolitical organization, moral codes, rituals, aesthetics and so on.

Teaching in these fields, doing philosophical translations and carrying out hermeneutical studies using these translations have made me concretely aware that 'comparative religion' or the comparative study of religions is an entirely Western academic discipline, premised on Western cultural preconceptions and consequently rather ill-equipped to address Chinese religiousness or religious experience. In fact, the founding fathers of this field of study were 'liberal Christians', and as early as 1858, Max Müller (1823–1900) defined this 'science of religion' and 'history of religion' as 'the wonderful way by which the different families of the human race have advanced toward a truer knowledge and a deeper love of God'.[2] Such a classic definition clearly illustrates the boundaries of this scholarly area. It also implies the need to develop adequate tools for analysis and interpretation in order to approach non-Western ways of thinking and spiritualities like the Chinese in more sensitive and accurate ways, in other words, without distorting them through the prism of fixed Western cultural assumptions like the above-mentioned notion of God. Obviously, these premises constitute the bedrock upon which this domain was built, and they can be traced back to the Age of Reason. To adopt Jonathan Smith's words, 'The academic study of religion is a child of the Enlightenment. This intellectual heritage is revealed in the notion of generic religion as opposed to historical, believing communities.'[3] Laurie L. Patton, too, highlights this Western perception of 'religion' as a system of ideas and beliefs, arising from the influence of the 'Enlightenment understanding of religion as analogous to a kind of scientific system of beliefs'.[4]

I notice, too, that university students often use such Western devices (theories) based on implicit Western cultural presuppositions, as they are trained to do, when they set out to 'analyse' various Chinese realities (philosophical, religious, cultural, sociopolitical, economic, etc.). Manifestly, in this process, the specific cultural assumptions of the latter are obscured, and the final study usually becomes misleading because it necessarily misses the very roots of a non-Western, cultural or religious reality.

For this reason, it is useful, as a first step, to unveil and examine in Part 1 (Chapters 1 and 2) the Western presumptions at work within the framework of religious studies.

In this way, one becomes aware of their presence at the very core of analytical tools often assumed to be impartial and universal. Such awareness hopefully could, in turn, motivate the development of new analytical tools, relevant, in this case, to Chinese studies and based on the Chinese cultural suppositions. The work of translation unfolded in Part 2 (Chapters 3 and 4) makes several implications obvious: that the very foundation upon which each type of thinking is built is formed by specific cultural presuppositions; the latter animate culturally specific thought processes which are embedded in languages and texts; the uncovering of such premises is transformative and formative, broadens one's horizon through infusing oneself with cultural sensibility; the usefulness of becoming aware of the tension between Western and Chinese (non-Western) assumptions in every intercultural translation or communication.

This book suggests that, largely because of its background in Western assumptions, the above-mentioned scholarly field lacks malleable theoretical tools which could be tailored to suit the needs of an authentic intercultural analysis and interpretation of Chinese thinking and spirituality, without deforming them through the prism of Western cultural presuppositions. Consequently, the starting point of the present study of Chinese and Western spiritualities and ways of thinking, as well as their underlying cultural suppositions, is the following assumption: the major bearer of these specific characteristics of each of these ways of thinking is the language. I argue that, more precisely, in this particular case, it is the written language, that is, the texts, and its particular structure – the Western phonetic writing versus the Chinese graphs – that provide the fundamental underpinning for the peculiar coherence of each of the two ways of thinking and for their cultural presuppositions.

2 Religion and Chinese religions

The present work employs the conventional term 'Chinese religions', which is a general label used in the domain of studies of religion(s). However, here this designation has a distinct meaning, unconcerned to align itself with the inadequate Western theoretical foundations of this Western discipline – that is, a distinct definition of the concept of religion but one that resonates suitably with the very essence of Chinese culture. For reasons to be set out below, in the present context, 'Chinese religions' is equivalent to Chinese 'philosophico-religious' or 'ethico-religious' thought. It should be noted from the outset that unlike the West that makes a clear distinction between religion and philosophy, the Chinese sphere does not decouple them.

The Latin noun 'religion' is a Western notion with two possible etymological sources, as Derrida reminds us: *relegere*, from *legere* ('harvest, gather': we understand that to mean attentively read and examine the ultimate essence of God), and *religare*, from *legare* ('to tie, bind': religious obligations to the law of God). The former identifies the Ciceronian tradition continued by W. Otto, J. B. Hollman and Benveniste; the latter goes from Lactantius and Tertullian to Kobbert, Ernout-Meillet and Pauly-Wissowa.[5] This double etymology of the term reveals a number of major cultural assumptions embedded in the meaning of the Western concept of religion, which will be examined in detail in the Chapter 1: belief or faith in God – a source of dualistic dichotomies, such as between sacred and profane, ordinary life and religious life, hence the need to promote contact with the sacred; obligation to reread His word. Therefore, there is ceaseless focus on explanation and understanding of the unknowable, as well as on ultimate explanations of the world, and the law or commandments of God as humanity's bond – so recognition of an obligation of debt between man and God and so on.

In religious studies, this originally Latin notion of religion itself went through a process of universalization. As Derrida notes

> *Religion* circulates in the world, one might say, like an *English word* <*comme un mot anglais*> that has been to Rome and taken a detour to the United States. Well beyond its strictly capitalist or politico-military figures, a hyper-imperialist appropriation has been underway now for centuries. ... From here on, the word 'religion' is calmly (and violently) applied to things which have always been and remain foreign to what this word names and arrests in its history.[6] (italics in original)

His observation also applies to the particular field of interest of this work, which sets out to demonstrate that 'Chinese religious traditions' are somehow a vague and distorting label that names things which remain foreign to what the Western word 'religion' names and subsequently proposes a constructive and interpretive remedy in Part 3 (Chapter 5).

The Chinese term for religion has its own graphic etymology as well. The latter offers a good illustration of distortions in meaning resulting from a transcultural translation. *Zongjiao* 宗教 is a Chinese neologism innovated in Japan to translate the Latin word 'religion'. Its verbatim translation means 'the teachings of the ancestors'. It resonates with the broad Chinese term *jiao* 教, 'to teach' or 'teaching': it designates any kind of teaching, instruction and education, and of course, it also includes the so-called three teachings (*san jiao* 三教), namely, what one would call the main philosophico-traditions of China: Confucianism, Daoism and Buddhism. Xu Shen 許慎 (58–148 CE), the author of the first historical dictionary of Chinese graphs, the Han dynasty *Shuowen Jiezi* 說文解字, explains the oldest meanings not of what we call words in the sense of alphabetic words but of graphs. According to him, as a graph, the character *jiao* 教, teaching, depicts a young disciple *zi* 子 in an inferior position (see the graph 教), who receives what comes from above, that is, from the master.[7] Note that according to this graphic etymology of the term 'teaching', the Chinese understanding of religion does not embody the idea of the belief in God, bond or obligation, debt between man and God (*religare*) or the effort of reading and understanding of the divine essence (*relegere*). Instead, as will be discussed in this work, it concretizes a live process of orderly exchange, an interactive practice of teaching and learning between disciples and master, sages and ancestors, between living individuals and between individuals and the 'traces' (graphs, i.e. written texts, classics) of those who lived before. Chinese religions as teachings thus focus on the interrelatedness between individuals as transformative foundation, ethical and spiritual guidance for everyday living. Moreover, as mentioned above and illustrated throughout the book, this Chinese perception of teaching does not separate the philosophical from the religious as the Western culture does.

A further question arises: What is the content of the above-mentioned notion of teaching in the context of 'Chinese religions', that is, in this study's definition, of Confucianism and Chinese Buddhism? In a broader sense, as Part 2 will spell out, it is the constant, everyday practice that allows oneself to transform into an ethically interdependent individual, one who sincerely carries for the others as one carries for oneself. The nature of this training is equally and indiscriminately what translates into both the Western notions of 'philosophical' and 'religious'. In an enlightening paragraph, Masao Abe suggestively describes the difference between this philosophico-religious character of the East Asian religions and the Western concept of religion. He makes direct reference to the Chan tradition, but, as will become evident in Chapters 4 and 5, his consideration is also relevant to what might be called mature Confucianism, that is, Song dynasty Neo-Confucianism:

> In the West, philosophy and religion are generally understood as two different entities: the former is a human enterprise for understanding humans and the universe based on intelligence or reason, whereas the latter is faith in divine revelation. … In the East, especially in Buddhism, philosophy and religion are not two different entities. Since Buddhism is originally not a religion of faith in a transcendent deity but a religion of awakening to the true nature of self and others, *praxia* and *theoria*, to use Western terms, are interfused and undifferentiated.[8]

When approaching the so-called Chinese religions, it is necessary to pay attention to the originally Western tools of interpretation and be cautious of any move that might misrepresent and misunderstand the Chinese religions in our interpretation. The objective of this work is to elaborate a sensitive theoretical device and thus make a significant contribution to enriching such global intercultural exchanges. It is aimed to incubate a critical, nuanced and balanced redefinition of multiculturalism, religious pluralism and diversity in the contemporary world. This important incubation process will be one that calls for everyone's collaboration, including key actors like civil society as well as the governmental and academic sectors. Note that, for now, multiculturalism and diversity are largely defined in a simplistic, Western-centric, dualistic way: Western and non-Western. Obviously, the implicit idea of the ascendancy of Western culture and of the self-proclaimed universality of its values inhabits this dualist vision. The latter can be viewed as a living remnant and limiting legacy of the Christian Western Enlightenment and era of colonization. Yet, it does not come just from the Age of Reason. As Gadamer recalls, this universalizing Western orientation has deeper roots in the very beginnings of the West. These cultural origins could be seen as an original Enlightenment. Let us not forget that the background to the modern Enlightenment is described as the 'Renaissance' or rebirth of Greek and Roman antiquity.[9]

3 Cultural presuppositions: Chinese and Western

3.1 A hermeneutical and intercultural perspective

The preliminary reflection above highlighted some specific meanings and cultural assumptions embedded in the etymologies of the Western word 'religion' and of the Chinese graph for teaching. It introduced a central notion of this text that invites here a preparatory clarification: cultural presuppositions. To that end, in what follows, I take as my initial inspiration the concept of presupposition or 'fundamental, enabling prejudice' of the hermeneutical school of thought and infuse it with new meaning in a different, this time intercultural sense. Gadamer sees the fundamental, enabling prejudices as the element of tradition in our historical-hermeneutical activity. They fulfil the meaning of 'belonging' and forge the 'horizon of our present'.[10] In Ricoeur's terms, the prejudices represent a 'component of the understanding, related to the historically finite nature of the human being',[11] in other words, 'the anticipation structure of the human experience' (ce qu'on appelle préjugé exprime la structure d'anticipation de l'expérience humaine).[12] In the following paragraph as well, what Gadamer has in mind is our belonging as contemporary Westerners to a historical tradition and a peculiar present, from which we seek to understand the otherness of the past from which we come – that is, for example, Greek thought:

> We started by saying that a hermeneutical situation is determined by the prejudices that we bring with us. They constitute, then, the horizon of a particular present, for they represent that beyond which it is impossible to see. But now it is important to avoid the error of thinking that the horizon of the present consists of a fixed set of opinions and valuations, and that the otherness of the past can be foregrounded from it as from a fixed ground. In fact the horizon of the present is continually in the process of being formed because we are continually having to test all our prejudices. An important part of this testing occurs in encountering the past and in understanding the tradition from which we come. Hence the horizon of the present cannot be formed without the past. There is no more an isolated horizon of the present in itself than there are historical horizons which have to be acquired. Rather, understanding is always the fusion of these horizons supposedly existing by themselves.[13]

In order to develop an intercultural hermeneutics (Chinese/Western) about cultural, not historical assumptions (such as those defined by Gadamer in the paragraph above) and their functioning, I take inspiration from the works of Gadamer and Ricoeur. They both approach prejudices from an intracultural (Western) and historical perspective. In contrast, the present study regards the different cultural presumptions or prejudices (Western and Chinese) as defining a distinct hermeneutical situation: our encounter and mutual exchange with the so-called Chinese religions within the textual context of translations. The book focuses on a precise horizon of understanding that is not historical but cultural, that is, it does not refer to the intracultural encounter between a Western individual's particular present and his past, as in Gadamer's Western situation, but rather to her intercultural encounter with Chinese culture, thought and religions. This meeting is beneficial, not only because it allows us to interculturally test and realize how our Western opinions and valuations prevent us from clearly seeing the Chinese philosophico-religious realities so that we entertain misapprehensions but also because it is only in this hermeneutical situation, sensitized to prejudices, that our horizon of understanding really opens itself to learning from the Chinese cultural field.

As a consequence, this opening is transformative. The hermeneutical encounter in which we find ourselves proves to be not merely an intellectual interpretation of the culturally other aimed at satisfying our curiosity but a true learning situation. The latter involves the Chinese horizon of religions not as an intriguing object to investigate facing the subject-investigator (as in the typical Western act of comprehension) but as a teacher. This instructor teaches the Westerner about difference, helping us recognize our prejudices that hinder our understanding of the other. It educates us to identify and go beyond that Enlightenment universalist way of thinking.

The latter belongs to the so-called scientific domain. It is predicated on the presupposition that all humans possess the same characteristics and considers as negligible the specificity of each culture's foundations. This is to say it insists that other cultures could and should be interpreted in terms of the same theoretical categories as Western tradition. The following appreciation of the French sociologist and sinologist Marcel Granet (1884–1940), disciple of Émile Durkheim and fine expert of the ancient Chinese world, echoes, for instance, the universalist view of his time:

> There is no question that the progress and the diffusion of the scientific spirit are related in the West to the existence of languages all of which are, to varying degrees, instruments of analysis that make it possible to define and classify, that teach to think logically and also, make it easy to transmit the fully elaborated, clear and distinct thinking. However, I do not think that the Chinese language, as is written or spoken, has even to a lesser extent, any of those qualities of the great European languages. ... The problem that came up for the Chinese seems to me to be this: to start working right away in order to transform the spoken language, thus making it susceptible to support a phonetical transcription; to make from it a new language which is not influenced by the written language which could gradually escape monosyllabism, and where the usage of derivation and grammatical forms could be set up.[14]

There are reverberations of this Enlightenment spirit in the following reflection of Robert Neville, as well: 'I shall argue here that Confucianism needs to expand its family of discourses in four related areas. It needs a contemporary metaphysical discourse, a contemporary discourse in philosophical cosmology in connection with science, a contemporary discourse about human nature and experience, and a contemporary discourse of social theory.'[15] It is noteworthy that the Enlightenment spirit is not a thing of the past but a central pattern of thinking of our time.

The purpose of the intercultural hermeneutical situation centred on presuppositions is to critically integrate dimensions of the scientific spirit and to go beyond it: beyond knowledge sharing and exchange, to make room for the culturally other, acquire awareness of and deference towards the one who is culturally different. In other words, to learn from the latter new possibilities for living, connecting with people and things and preventing causing harm to them. In Gadamer's words, it teaches us something we don't know we don't know: that 'the prejudices and fore-meanings that occupy the interpreter's consciousness are not at his free disposal. He cannot separate in advance the productive prejudices that enable understanding from the prejudices that hinder it and lead to misunderstandings.'[16] Consequently, this study focuses on the Chinese assumptions while dealing as well with Western productive and hindering prejudices of the analyst that come into play while interacting with the Chinese religions.

Gadamer builds his hermeneutical situation around the intracultural issue of one's 'belonging' (Ricoeur's concept of 'appartenance') to one's tradition or cultural world. In the intercultural situation I am building in this book, I also find inspiration in another concept – Ricoeur's theme of 'distancing' (distanciation), which he develops in the footsteps of Gadamer and in the same area of the historical tradition. Here I transform this notion and develop a different hermeneutical function of distancing: one concerned with an intercultural context. Obviously, in this new circumstance, distancing presupposes one's participative belonging, not as the precedence of being in the world (préséance de l'être-au-monde)[17] but as the precedence of belonging to one's distinct culture. In other words, being in the world is, first and foremost, being part of a distinctive culture.

Furthermore, this concept of intercultural distancing provides the reason why I choose Chinese philosophico-religious texts and their Western hermeneutical translations as the textual medium for intercultural communication. The Western translation of the Chinese written document is the place where the mediation occurs and inherently embodies the dynamic and creative correlation between both intercultural distancing and cultural belonging. In this case, the conscious effort of intercultural distancing through a hermeneutical translation sensitive to cultural presuppositions means neither to alienate or estrange nor to make the unfamiliar familiar but a willingness to open oneself to different cultural assumptions, to de-centre one's own knowledge, to learn to look at something from multiple standpoints. Such an effort is not only creative but also transformative and provides a further impulse in the process of human growth.

The following paragraph of Ricoeur, who also advocates for interpretive mediation through the text, appears to me enlightening in this sense, and moreover, not merely in a historical context, but in an intercultural situation, as well, in which the distancing is particularly resonant:

> Interpreting is to bring nearer the distant (temporal, geographical, cultural, spiritual). In this regard, the mediation through the text is the model of a distancing which would not be simply alienating, as the *Verfremdung* that Gadamer combats in all his work, but would be authentically creative. The text is par excellence, the medium of a communication in and by the distance ('le support d'une communication dans et par la distance').[18]

The above paragraph paradigmatically reflects the perspective and approach that the present intercultural analysis, focused on Song dynasty thought and spirituality, embraces. The study works from the assumption that the best way for the foreigner to understand and learn from the classical Chinese religions is by approaching their salient philosophico-religious texts. Because this foreigner (Western, non-Chinese, contemporary Chinese) is situated at a cultural, spiritual and temporal distance from the classical works, each one of these dimensions of the foreigner's distancing bears multiple presuppositions, different from those of the Chinese religions. For this reason, the way to understand them is through an interculturally Chinese-Western interpretation, mediated through philosophical translation. I agree with Ricoeur that the most suitable medium for this kind of mediation is the written text. All the more because, as will be demonstrated later, in our specific case, it is the written text, the graphs and not the spoken word that best embodies the Chinese cultural depth and the functioning of its context-related meaning.

3.2 A mediation through written texts and philosophical translations: Coming to meet classical Chinese 'religiousness'

In the field of the philosophy of religion, there are voices like that of Robert Cummings Neville who advocate for a pragmatic (American tradition, Charles S. Peirce's (1839–1914) semiotic theory) approach to religious experience in general, regardless of its particular cultural characteristics: for 'interpreting engagement of real things in the world'[19] instead of interpreting texts. This engagement with things, Neville points out, is guided by interpretations that employ signs.[20] Seen from the perspective of the specificity of cultural presumptions, his paradigm of engaging with things, not texts, seems problematic when applied to the Chinese sphere. Note that in Peirce's interpretive context, the reality means objects, and his theory of signs is a 'philosophy of representation' based on the division of observer and observed. Starting from logic as the science of the necessary laws of signs, the theory of signs he proposes remains, however, connected with Ferdinand de Saussure's (1857–1913) model and the Western cultural presupposition of the convention of language, as signs detached from the reality. The following excerpt from Peirce, cited by Neville,[21] clearly illustrates quite a few Western paradigms – the centrality of the observer of the reality; the human mind, and ideas as external, outside reality; the reality as objects to be engaged by the human observer; and the functioning of the Western perception of representation of these objects through signs:

> A sign, or *representamen*, is something which stands to somebody for something in some respect or capacity. It addresses somebody, that is, creates in the mind of that person an equivalent sign, or perhaps a more developed sign. That sign which it creates I call the *interpretant* of the first sign. The sign stands for something, its *object*. It stands for that object, not in all respects, but in reference to a sort of idea, which I have sometimes called the ground of the *representamen*. (Peirce, Collected papers, vol. 2, par. 228; italics in original)

The present comparative Chinese/Western study on classical Chinese religious traditions is based on an exploration of their cultural presuppositions. One of the assumptions that this investigation uncovers is that the human observer is not central but integrated within the course of events of the reality and interdependent with these interconnected events as reality. Moreover, these events that the reality is made of are animated by a specific dynamism which is alien to the Western 'reality as independent objects', logically embraced by Peirce. His theory is meant to be universal, 'objective' and unaware of the multiple meanings of the reality of things, according to unique cultural backgrounds. The reality of the relations between things and human in this non-Western sphere – the study argues – is grounded otherwise.

This book aims to demonstrate that in the specific case of the Chinese philosophico-religions, due to the distinct nature and cultural role of the written text and graphs, as discussed further on, an effective way to come to meet the 'Chinese religious traditions' is through gaining access to the suppositions that constitute their foundations. It is precisely by way of the hermeneutical translation of texts that such access is made possible. At that deep level, through examining the meanings of graphs, through the mediation of the written texts, of their philosophical translation sensitive to cultural prejudices – the Chinese and the Western – one is able to actually discover the cornerstone of the Chinese religiousness – that is, the Chinese cultural assumptions – and to comprehend their functioning. The theory I am proposing consists precisely in identifying and examining these presumptions.

It is noteworthy that the above-mentioned contrast texts/real things is also a Western cultural presupposition and therefore extremely pertinent in the Western context in which the phonetic alphabetical writing is a convention. Plato discusses this convention in *Phaedrus* 274c and the disadvantages of writing by evoking a dialogue between Thoth, the Egyptian god of writing, and the king of gods. In the words of Derrida, this writing is 'redoubling of the sign, sign of the sign; significant of the phonic significant' (écriture comme redoublement du signe, comme signe de signe; signifiant du signifiant phonique).[22] In Western culture, an area based on alphabetic writing – a system of signs that represent the words and sounds using separated phonemes – it seems appropriate to go beyond the writing convention in order to investigate the 'real things in the world'.

However, these dichotomies texts/real things are not replicated in the Chinese arena. Here, the role and functioning of the written language are fundamentally different from the artificial, invented conventions which constitute the Western writing. The Chinese graphs are not at all a tacit agreement between the members of a language community, something similar to the Western language recognized by Saussure as being both 'a social product of the language faculty and a set of necessary conventions that have been adopted by the social body to permit the exercise of this language faculty in individuals.' (Mais qu'est-ce que la langue? ... C'est à la fois un produit social de la faculté du langage et un ensemble de conventions nécessaires, adoptées par le corps social pour permettre l'exercice de cette faculté chez les individus).[23]

The Chinese written language emerges from the process of divination. As discussed later in this work, divination is not a mere search for omens, for special signs of good or bad luck, but a procedure of decryption of the course of things. The French sinologist Léon Vandermeersch (1928–2021) defines the aim of divination as 'the explication of the hidden meaning of the event-driven conjuncture into which is inserted the conjuncture concerning which the divination is called in'.[24] The characters emerge from the annotations of diagrams at the end of this procedure of divination. The writing is thus manipulated as a revealing instrument of the latent course of events, and the graphic etymology of each character/diagram explains it not as an artificial convention – as is the case for the Western writing – but as a tracing indicative of, in Vandermeersch's edifying terms, 'the particular event-driven conjuncture whose cosmological structure the diagram reveals' (la conjoncture événementielle particulière dont il révèle la structure cosmologique).[25] For this reason, among others discussed in the following chapters, it would appear that it is entirely appropriate to privilege the encounter with the textual milieu when building an intercultural encounter with the Chinese religions rather than the 'engagement with things'.

3.3 A basic premise of this study: Re-evaluation of the Western Enlightenment presuppositions

As a consequence, the present study offers an analysis of some Chinese cultural presuppositions starting from interpretive translations of the selected Neo-Confucian and Chan philosophico-religious texts. In this context, it first enquires into the suitability for this domain of the analytical tools with which the Western discipline of religious studies provides us. In Part 3, it proposes a new hermeneutical tool for understanding the Chinese philosophico-religious reality that emerges from this examination and is built on the notion of interrelatedness. Part 4 considers it in relation to other sinological, philosophical and Buddhological approaches specifically designed for the Chinese cultural context.

This endeavour rests on one basic premise: the assumption that in order to allow new interpretive ideas to emerge in the sphere of the intercultural analysis and exchange, there is a need to constantly identify, re-evaluate and, in some instances, remove from the construction of some of our theoretical tools – particularly those of the study of religions – some tacit Enlightenment assumptions, for example, the idea of universal categories. This presumption and the comparative effort it requests are part of the theory I am proposing. Gadamer particularly urges us to question 'the universality of the scientific Enlightenment and its consequences'.[26] I would describe this premise as a critical recovery of the Enlightenment-rooted analytical tools or theories.

In a similar vein, Hall and Ames also stress that this Western standard is not only inadequate but also harmful when used to evaluate non-Western cultures:

Central to our beliefs as Anglo-European [let's replace this limited label used by Hall and Ames with the term Westerners] heirs of the Enlightenment is the conviction that the scientific rationality emergent at the beginnings of the sixteenth century names a universal norm for assessing the value of cultural activity everywhere on the planet. This expression of our provincialism has arguably been more harmful than those insular attitudes that harbor less evangelical motives.[27]

Much earlier, Heidegger in his encounter with a Japanese interlocutor in the celebrated essay 'A Dialogue on Language: Between a Japanese and an Inquirer', published at the end of the fifties, was already denouncing the inevitable distortion of the 'East Asian nature of Japanese art' by the presuppositions embedded in the 'European' language. Similarly, he was referring to the continuous destructive effect of the very 'reason' and technical rationality celebrated by the European Enlightenment on other cultures, specifically on East Asian culture:

> J: The incontestable dominance of your European reason is thought to be confirmed by the successes of that rationality which technical advances set before us at every turn.
> I: This delusion is growing, so that we are no longer able to see how the Europeanization of man and of the earth attacks at the source everything that is of an essential nature. It seems that these sources are to dry up.[28]

Several decades later in 1994, Gadamer expressed similar views. Invited to participate in a small discussion group led by Jacques Derrida and Gianni Vattimo in Capri on the theme 'religion in our world', just a few years before his death at the advanced age of 102, Gadamer first remarked that the selection of the participants was one-sided, as everyone came from the Latin world and he was the only German, the only Protestant. In addition, he considered particularly problematic the absence of any representative of Islam and the fact that no woman was present. An early student of Heidegger and an influential philosopher in his own right, Gadamer whose life spanned the entire twentieth century warned that the capitalism and industrialization inspired by Puritanism (as Max Weber taught us) have transformed in a 'religion of the global economy'. I suggest that, when he deplores this gradual erosion of Western religiosity and its transformation into the present breakneck global quest for economic development, he implicitly conveys that it is because of its specific nature and legacy of the Enlightenment that the Western religious impetus gradually transformed itself into a non-religious pursuit – economy.

Heidegger was decrying the cultural destruction wreaked by Western language, rationality and technology – 'of everything that is of an essential nature', where 'everything' seemingly means philosophy, religion, other ways of thinking and spiritual paths. Like Heidegger, Gadamer warns about the overwhelming threat posed by the present technological development of Western civilization. In contrast with his teacher, he focuses on the connection between applied science and weapons and stresses something infinitely greater and more appalling than the destruction of ways of thinking other than the Western: the possible destruction of life, of humankind and of all living things because of weapons technology and atomic technology. He also reminds that this progress in science and technology has already grown into an 'independent power that is simply out of our control'.[29] For this reason, he urges contemporaries to find and follow what he calls a 'corrective approach'. For the philosopher, the latter can be achieved through education, through a comprehensive practice meant to sociopolitically educate humankind. In his view, this amounts to critically engage with the past of the Western Enlightenment tradition, to surpass its

Introduction

major presupposition – he clearly pinpoints it, that of the rupture between nature and culture, and therefore work to restore their lost equilibrium:

> The power of destruction which technology places in the hands of men – weapon technology in general and atomic technology in particular – have made, for the first time a topical issue from the question of mankind, the question that the survival of mankind on this planet raises. What kind of corrective approach, of social and political education of mankind ('démarche correctrice, d'éducation sociale et politique de l'humanité') should be taken in order for us to be able to create a new equilibrium between nature and culture?[30]

As discussed earlier, the first assumption of this book focuses on a critical engagement with the Enlightenment cultural presuppositions underlying the discipline of science of religions. This attempt can be viewed as a 'corrective approach' in keeping with the aforesaid words of Gadamer and as a kind of response to his call. Furthermore, to combat this direct threat to the life of humankind and of all forms of natural life that has resulted as a by-product of the steady implementation of the Enlightenment principles since the seventeenth century, the philosopher who expanded the field of philosophical hermeneutics also exhorts us to resolutely and consistently look for remedies to this critical situation in non-Western cultures, that is, for other ways to envisage the world, for new ways of doing things, besides the Western Enlightenment-rooted way. In this manner, Gadamer draws attention to the inevitable flaws that have arisen out of the strengths of the Enlightenment. Note, too, that he sees the West's continuing anchorage in the Enlightenment principles as an expression of the West's unconscious provincialism. As such, Gadamer not only highlights our duty to embark on a quest of critical recovery of this past but equally suggests what the nature of this process should be. In his view, the latter needs to be an educative process, through which the West must 'learn to think on a large scale', especially with respect to religions; in other words, one might say, to rise out of its universalist provincialism, open itself up to other cultural and religious worlds and sincerely learn from them. This book aims to contribute to his reflexion:

> We must however learn to think on a large scale when, under the title 'the religion and the religions,' we are trying to take humanity's destiny into account and to take stock of its future. We must equally be committed to address the question whether other religious worlds and other cultural worlds could eventually contribute to the universality of the Enlightenment science and of its consequences a response other than the one of the religion of global economy. The world will possibly find another response about which we still have no idea.[31]

In this essay 'Dialogues in Capri', Gadamer makes explicit reference to the Far Eastern civilizations among other possible cultures capable of teaching the West 'to think on a large scale', in order to correct the deficiencies of the Western Enlightenment heritage and remedy the critical and dangerous situation that the whole of humanity is currently faced with. He focuses our attention on the East Asian virtues as one form of non-Western qualities among others from which we could learn, and which we might begin to rely on in an effort 'to take over the European science and technique' and bridge the failures of the current situation of the world caused by the Western-rooted 'religion of global economy':

> Think, for example, of the Far Eastern civilizations, those of China and Japan, amongst others: it is through taking completely different paths from ours that these people have developed virtues which are very familiar to us, such as personal discipline, vitality, and diligence, qualities that precisely allow to master the European science and technique.[32]

As discussed earlier, the separation between nature and culture is a specific issue to which Gadamer refers in one of the preceding paragraphs. This idea merits closer examination in the present context. The philosopher stresses the current worldwide imbalance between nature and culture and the urgent need for humanity to take a corrective approach in order to create a new balance for them. It is noteworthy that this idea of their initial disconnection in ancient Greek thought, which has finally taken the form of a de facto critical disconnection on a planetary scale, is, in fact, a Western cultural presupposition: the dualism involving the dichotomy between nature – the living reality, considered as independent of culture – and human activity and history. If 'culture' in the Western sphere means human thought (remember the Enlightenment thinker Pascal's vision of the human as a thinking reed, the weakest of nature), the essential meaning of 'nature' is suggested by the Greek verb φύω – to grow in the vegetal world – and the Latin *nascor* – to be born and live: in Maurice Merleau-Ponty's edifying words, 'There is nature wherever there is a life that has a meaning, but where, however, there is no thought; hence, the kinship with the vegetal: it is nature that has a meaning, without that meaning having been laid by the thought.'[33] Nature is also bestial, potentially dangerous, as are human beings in the state of nature. Plato and Aristotle make a distinction between the rational human being and the beast. Furthermore, in the dualist Judeo-Christian intellectual tradition, the animals are living beings ranked under the humans' dominion. In the famous fragment 347, ed. Brunschvicg of his *Pensées* (trans. W. F. Trotter), Pascal equates human (i.e. culture) with human thought, morality and dignity and clearly distinguishes them from 'universe' (i.e. nature) devoid of thought and morality:

> Man is but a reed, the most feeble thing in nature, but he is a thinking reed. The entire universe need not arm itself to crush him. A vapour, a drop of water suffices to kill him. But, if the universe were to crush him, man would still be more noble than that which killed him, because he knows that he dies and the advantage which the universe has over him; the universe knows nothing of this. All our dignity consists then in thought. By it we must elevate ourselves, and not by space and time which we cannot fill. Let us endeavour, then, to think well; this is the principle of morality.

What is the Chinese culture's response to the question of the relationship between human and nature? Unlike the Western sphere, the Chinese world does not conceive the original relationship between nature or reality and culture or human education in terms of dissociation and opposition. Instead, it perceives them as continuous, closely linked and interdependent, human nature being an intrinsic part of nature's organism, and the order or law of nature as essentially moral and a model to be followed by the humans.

Like all Chinese characters, the graph *wen* 文 – that means culture but above all means character (sinograph) and written text – is polysemic, and its multiple meanings are context-related. Xu Shen in his first century CE Han dictionary of Chinese graphs provides us with the first interpretation of this graph and its context-related connotations. The character *wen* 文 is a drawing of lines that cross one another, therefore intertwining traces. Xu Shen recounts in a very short phrase what one could call the Chinese myth of writing. Xu tells the story of Cang Jie 倉頡, the legendary historian, with two sets of eyes, of the emblematic founder of the Chinese civilization and culture hero, the Yellow Emperor (ca. 2600 BCE). In order to record major events, he created the characters. By observing with his two sets of eyes everything that moved in the sky (the tracks of the flying birds and celestial bodies) and on the earth (tracks of the animals' paws), in other words, the visible footprints of all movements, the appearances-configurations of these continuous life processes, it is said that he created the written characters according to the various types (earthly and heavenly) of visible forms of these natural images-phenomena (*xiang xing* 象形). These are what is called culture, *wen* 文 (初造書契依類象形故謂之文).[34]

Let us further interpret the core idea of Xu's explanation: culture means written graphs, which are the visible forms of the processual images of phenomena (*xiang xing* 象形). An aside here: in this context one may recall Peirce's Western paradigm of the sign discussed earlier (see Section 3.2). In the Chinese context, in the *Classic of Changes*' interpretations of the hexagrams, this visible form of an image from which the graph is derived has a particular meaning, completely different from the representational meaning of its Western counterpart. Thus, these characters-images are not reproductions of static objects, their reflections in the mirror, but visible forms bearing an invisible dynamism that animates the things in a procession of transformation, inchoate things seen as interrelated elements in a continuous course of events. Accordingly, the apparently static visible image (the graph) is just the track of the things in passing, in constant flux, what remains as visible traces of an invisible dynamism continuously present within each element of the reality. The nature of this dynamic invisible present within the graph is not only organic but also ethical and spiritual. The *Classic of Changes* in its commentaries on the trigrams, hexagrams and their images and meanings deals in detail with these dimensions of the invisible dynamism working through the microcosm (human) and macrocosm. It is noteworthy that Xu's definition of the graphs corroborates their archaeological explanation rooted in divination outlined above. Both accounts suggest the intrinsic and inseparable relationship between nature and culture, whereby the latter means becoming aware of the early, quasi-invisible signs of the transformative dynamism of the reality, including society. One could define this ceaseless activity as the functioning of a spontaneous ethico-spiritual law-order of heaven and earth. Part 2 of this book offers a detailed interpretation of the ethical and spiritual features of this efficacy simultaneously at work in human and non-human reality. It connects culture and nature at a profound level. As discussed in the present chapter, both teachings, Confucianism and Chan Buddhism, train and equip the individual to reach a deep state of nature and constantly dwell in it.

This Chinese etymological detour provides further confirmation of Gadamer's intuition that in order to find a new balance between nature and culture, we must learn from non-Western cultures, including the East-Asian (Sinicized) cultures. The Chinese culture and its religions could serve as an experienced teacher, able to help the Western world: first, become aware of the limits and deficiencies of some of its cultural presuppositions reinforced during the Enlightenment – such as the antagonism between nature and culture; second, develop the ability to surpass dualisms, for instance, to envisage nature and culture differently, so as to realize and preserve their interrelatedness.

After this preliminary presentation of the first basic premise of this work – that is, the need to identify certain tacit Enlightenment assumptions present in the construction of our theoretical tools and re-evaluate them – let us introduce one of its major consequences. This concerns the inadequacy of the articulation Western/non-Western. As a matter of fact, the necessity identified above to question and set aside the universalist assumption of the Enlightenment stems from the fact that this binary Western/non-Western, in other words, Western-centric perception, makes diversity and interreligious as well as intercultural dialogue not only difficult but outright impossible. Ample evidence of this is the present rise of Western extremism in our Western societies. I can adduce recent specific examples from Canadian society, and I am sure that other Western countries, including our American neighbours, with whom we have a long shared history, can also recognize this trend in their own societies: the distrust for the Black Lives Matter movement; attacks on Muslim families and Muslim women; the perception of Native Americans as aliens who should 'go back' where they came from; the recent shocking discoveries of thousands of unmarked graves of Indigenous children near the mandatory residential schools run by the Catholic Church from 1828 to 1997, where the children were sent, deculturized and forcibly assimilated into Euro-American culture; threats against members of the Asian community after the outbreak of the global pandemic; and so on. John Berthrong also points out that 'North American and European racism is hardly a thing of the past as far as feelings about Asians go.'[35] Of course, this dualistic Western/non-Western framework has a lot to do not only with an unfortunate result of the historical legacy of the Age of Reason and colonial Enlightenment but also with the perennial issue of power relationships. Thus, one can see that a similar dualistic position, but this time Sinocentric – Chinese (Han) and non-Chinese (Uighurs, Tibetans, etc.), Sinicized and non-Sinicized – is taken up in the contemporary Chinese society.

Starting from the premise set out above, this study suggests that one powerful cultural tool that might be effective in raising awareness about the responsibility of everyone to acknowledge, counteract and remedy the corrosive effects of the imbalance of power (Western/non-Western, Sinicized/non-Sinicized, etc.) is to promote multicultural and multireligious sensibility through education. One of the keys to achieving that goal is through expanding and upgrading the Western academic space (the field of science of religions included) and its area of multicultural, intercultural and transcultural studies, and this beyond the still predominant principles and concepts based on Western-centred, Enlightenment ideals and values.

This book suggests that the new approach would consist in developing understanding and awareness about cultural differences through comparatively investigating the different backgrounds of cultural presuppositions (Chinese and Western). It is worth emphasizing that the latter trigger culturally dependent ways of thinking. Cultivating through education the ability to become aware of these differences and to understand them enables one to get past the Western cultural presupposition of Enlightenment universalism – source of unidimensional dialogue – and address the culturally other, foster appreciation and respect not only what makes us unique but also the diversity of people around us. It bears repeating that one can acquire such a sensitivity to diversity only through a never-ending process of repetitive learning. The comparative philosophical work proposed here contributes to this endeavour by placing the accent on illustrating and interpreting the specificities of the cultural presumptions of Chinese spirituality when compared with those of the Western counterpart. To this end, it develops not a universalizing interpretive framework but rather a specific one, sensitive and responsive to the peculiarities related to China's culture and written language.

4 Justifying the choice of the textual context: Song dynasty interaction between Neo-Confucianism and Chan Buddhism

In the light of the above considerations, at this preliminary stage, it is necessary to provide further detail about the particular textual context within which the present book is undertaking its task of comparative, intercultural and interpretive evaluation of Chinese and Western cultural presuppositions. This includes some major Song dynasty philosophico-religious works. Its frame of reference comprises eleventh- and twelfth-century texts that can be viewed as sites of extremely rich ethical and spiritual exchanges between the Neo-Confucian and Chan Buddhist traditions. These mutual interchanges are important because they occur at a key moment in Chinese cultural history – when both schools of thought are finally ready to interact and connect in profound ways. This Song dynasty interaction has fundamentally reshaped the configuration of Chinese culture (philosophy and religion) from that time to the present. Consequently, I suggest that it is Song dynasty thought that accurately prefigures the new, enriched shape of the Chinese culture and its cultural premises through the long and multidimensional interaction between Confucianism and Buddhism.

This book engages with Song dynasty Neo-Confucian and Chan Buddhist philosophical developments through a comparative and hermeneutical study of the original texts of the Northern Song Chan scholar-monk Qisong 契嵩 (1007–1072) and the Southern Song Neo-Confucian scholar Zhu Xi 朱熹 (1130–1200).[36] I have chosen this period because it represents an era of prodigious cultural and spiritual effervescence and fruitful mutual influences between the two Chinese teachings. Qisong, an eleventh-century influential Chan Buddhist scholar-monk, provides what I call a Confucianized interpretation of Chan Buddhism for his contemporary Confucian scholars. During Qisong's lifetime and early in the following century, the Northern Song Neo-Confucian masters[37] established the School of Principle, or the Cheng-Zhu school. A century after Qisong, the Southern Song Neo-Confucian scholar Zhu Xi compiled and wrote the most influential commentaries on the Confucian anthology, the *Four Books*, which were widely read not only in China but in the sinicized East Asian countries, Japan, Korea and Vietnam as well. The Cheng-Zhu school remains the most prominent Confucian school to this day. Its members fostered a creative philosophical and spiritual renewal of ancient Confucianism, rooted in Mencius's thinking. I will also demonstrate that, despite the Cheng-Zhu school's official rhetorical criticisms aimed at the Buddhist tradition, their ethical philosophy and spirituality incorporate Chan Buddhist elements in an innovative and creative fashion.

Starting from these two Chinese masters, the study discloses 'ethico-spiritual interrelatedness' as a central cultural assumption of the Chinese sphere. Building on this assumption, it proposes an interpretive theory, which it offers as a theoretical tool for the study of Chinese religious traditions. In this context, it also seeks to open a dialogue between the cultural preconceptions of this instrument of analysis and those of the received classical and contemporary theories of religion. Such an intercultural and comparative perspective makes it possible to uncover differences between the various Western and Chinese cultural presuppositions upon which these theories are built. It also argues against the idea that Western thought provides the theory and non-Western domains (Chinese) simply provide contents for study.

Extensive and in-depth studies in 'Chinese philosophy' as well as comparative Chinese/Western studies have been conducted concerning the thought of ancient China and the former Han (ancient Confucianism, Daoism, Legalism, School of Yin and Yang, etc.) by Western sinologists, historians, sociologists and philosophers. These include, among others, Marcel Granet,[38] Benjamin Schwartz,[39] A. C. Graham,[40] David Hall and Roger T. Ames[41] and Robert Cumming Neville.[42] Their examinations of ancient Chinese thought as representative of the entire Chinese tradition in comparative dialogue with Western thought have been an important beginning in the effort of developing the interculturalism that is sorely needed today on a global scale. It is important to continue this undertaking, but it is even more important not to stop at this level.

Consistent with the reasons set out above, the next step will be to consider not the ancient thought but Song dynasty thought as the Chinese interlocutor in our Chinese/Western intercultural dialogue. Ancient Chinese thought does not include the Buddhist presence in the Chinese world. It was roughly at the end of the Tang dynasty that this teaching became a genuinely 'native' Chinese school, an indelible feature of the landscape of Chinese culture. Moreover, in the history of the latter, the Song dynasty is an essential moment: it is during this period that genuine philosophical interaction between Chinese Buddhism and Confucianism commences.

5 Learning now to think on a large scale

As noted above, besides the growing interest in the Song dynasty textual context above and beyond the existing focus on ancient thought, a change in the tone and objectives of these comparative, philosophico-spiritual encounters, Chinese/Western, is essential. One should also consider the universalist approach as only an initial and sympathetic attempt to understand the unfamiliar or the other, the effort to establish connections between elements of an alien culture and some familiar elements of one's own culture deemed as universally recognizable. Following this effort to establish preliminary rapport, the natural next step and continuation of this process of rapprochement of cultures and spiritualities would require a new tone and approach – the natural result of an evolving and mutually nurturing relationship. Gadamer suggests a very fruitful and rewarding attitude that might stop the erosion of multiculturalism which is the effect of the universalist spirit: 'to learn to think on a large scale'. In these pages, this is nothing less than coming to meet the classical Chinese world, envisage it as an instructor, able to teach Westernized humanity new ways of thinking and able to correct the side effects of the dominant heritage of the Enlightenment. Such an attitude could lead to focusing together, interculturally, not monoculturally, on the real problems of humanity and to looking together at ways to overcome them. So far, the usual aim of comparative studies has been to trigger developing transcultural and cross-cultural dialogue. Most of the time, these result from the comparative curiosity and Cartesian spirit of the researcher, fully equipped with investigatory tools, one who wants to truly understand the classical Chinese way of thinking as an object of analysis, only thereby to end up comparing it with familiar characteristics of the Western tradition. The new tone of studies, the above-mentioned one suggested by Gadamer, is supposed to encourage deeper intercultural research in religious studies and stimulate true interculturalism. It is to adopt the attitude of a researcher-student, not that of a researcher-teacher, one who does not merely scrutinize another culture as a master with one's own investigatory techniques but as a student who is open and interested in learning something new from the other tradition and thus constantly adapts their tools.

In 1994, Gadamer expressed his viewpoint on the world situation, on the necessity for humanity to learn to think on a large scale, that is, on the need to globally receive teaching from non-Western cultures and religions, including the Chinese ones. It can be said that, in a sense, his exhortation responds to the call made more than three decades earlier, in 1958, by the four Contemporary New Confucian masters, Mou Zongsan 牟宗三 (1909–1995), Tang Junyi 唐君毅 (1909 1978), Zhang Junmai 張君勱 (1886–1969) and Xu Fuguan 徐復觀 (1902–1982), in their jointly published declaration to the world, *A Manifesto for a Reappraisal of Sinology and the Reconstruction of Chinese Culture* (為中國文化敬告世界人士宣言：我們對中國學術研究及中國文化與世界文化前途之共同認識). In this document they comparatively explain for the Westerners the specificity or the Chineseness of their culture and some differences between the two cultures, the Chinese and the Western.

The importance of the Song dynasty philosophico-religious exchanges has previously been highlighted. It is notable that another pivotal moment in Chinese culture is the contemporary twentieth century when a new era of interaction, with the Western thought this time, has arisen in its landscape. These exchanges are also embodied in the works of the Contemporary New Confucians.

In the fifth section of the *Manifesto*, 'Ethics, Morality and Religious Spirit in Chinese Culture', the four Contemporary New Confucian masters clarify what they consider as a misunderstanding and prejudice held by Westerners. In his examination of the ideas of the Contemporary New Confucians and the question of religion, Lee Ming-huei highlights this major prejudgment exposed in their joint declaration: the Westerners' erroneous view that 'Chinese people only attach importance to everyday-life ethics and morality and lack a religious transcendent feeling. Chinese ethical and moral ideals were considered merely to be concerned with regulating people's external behavior while neglecting the internal dimension of spiritual life. This misunderstanding can be traced back to Hegel's *Lectures on the History of Philosophy*.'[43] This perception of Chinese religiousness is entirely distorted; the Contemporary New Confucian scholars explain and clarify what the Westerners are unable to discern because they examine Chinese culture using strictly Western criteria: 'Since the religious transcendent feelings of the Chinese people and the religious spirit they value have the same cultural roots as the ethics and morality the people cherish, they integrate the religious with the ethical and moral spirit as one inseparable entity.'[44]

One may observe that their viewpoint resonates deeply with Masao Abe's definition, mentioned earlier, of the inseparable cohesion between philosophy and religion in East Asian Buddhist spirituality. As well, it is important to note that, from what I would call the 'interdependent' perspective of Contemporary New Confucians, the Western analytic tendency functions by dissecting and drawing dichotomous distinctions and cannot serve as an effective strategy for achieving intercultural conceptual understanding but indeed is often responsible for fuelling conflict-provoking polarizations. What the Western thinker discerns, since the time of the Greek philosophy, is the dualistic distinctions between ontology and epistemology, transcendent and immanent, being and human knowledge about being, religion and reason and so forth. These basic dichotomies are evaluative and focused on ontological knowledge. As will be demonstrated, in the Chinese world, the stress on interrelatedness is not focused on that type of knowledge but on ethical understanding, particularly on relationship awareness and togetherness ethics, on living together and establishing the sort of ethical harmony that can ground ethical relations. The cherished objective is therefore different in the two cultures.

For this reason, in their *Manifesto*, the Contemporary New Confucians make an evaluation of the Western dichotomy God/science and universal reason, not from the perspective of knowledge but from an ethical perspective, and perceive it less as a celebration of the human individual but primarily as a source and stimulus of multidimensional conflict, as well as the ethical and spiritual disharmony present from small communities to the global village. At the end of the day, what is prevalent for those who dwell in the dualist Western world, is the discord created at the level of communities as the inevitable result of victories of the individual – the dissension between communities of different religions, between weaker and stronger nation states, between working and capitalist social classes, between colonizers and colonized countries:

> The spirit of modern Westerners is connected with the infinite sanctity of their unique God. However, their spirit also relies on universal reason to understand the natural world. During the Renaissance period, the human individual became aware of his own self. All these elements combined resulted in the birth of an awareness concerning individual dignity, and this in turn generated a quest for freedom of the spirit. The reform of religion followed, then nation-states were gradually established, reason was freely used, and thus the Enlightenment movement took shape. Nature and the history of society are understood in their multiple dimensions. Knowledge about nature is used in order to transform society. A certain political and cultural ideal of society is used in order to transform the human world. The ideals of liberty and democracy within the political sphere, liberty and justice within the social domain, and universal fraternity within society are born together. …
>
> Thus, in its rapid and vigorous advancement, modern Western culture faced all kinds of conflicts and problems. The wars of religion followed after the Reformation. The establishment of nation-states was followed by wars, which these states waged against one another. The antagonism between workers and capitalists appeared after the industrial revolution. The imperialist politics that oppressed the weaker nations came after the quest for resources overseas and the exploitation of colonies.[45]

This work is intended to respond equally to both appeals: Gadamer's advice to learn from East Asian religion and the New Confucians' call to discover the Chineseness of the Chinese world.

After presenting in this introduction the central notions of this book – cultural presuppositions – Part 1 proceeds to discuss another main concept – theory. It focuses on the Western theories of religion and on the interpretation of their fundamental assumptions.

In Chapter 1, I comparatively and interculturally explore this notion as well as several classical theories of the philosophy of religion and their cultural foundations.

Part 1

Western Theories and Cultural Presuppositions: An Intercultural Perspective

ized' theory of religion, that is, a theoretical
1

Classical theories of Western philosophy of religion (Durkheim and Weber): An analysis of their presuppositions from a Chinese perspective

As already emphasized, this study is carried out in the theoretical field of the philosophy of religion. Therefore, the introduction addresses – comparatively and interculturally – the meanings and cultural presuppositions of the central notion of religion in its Western and Chinese contexts. This preparatory analysis that continues in the following chapters serves as the starting point in discovering and illustrating the fundamental traits that make up the identity and specific character of the Chinese religion(s), as well as how they differ from their Western counterparts. These traits are subsequently used to design a 'customized' theory of religion, that is, a theoretical tool that suits the Chinese cultural context without misrepresenting its distinct assumptions.

Next, this chapter and Chapter 2 address a complementary Western term – 'theory' – directly linked to the notion of religion and focus on the differences between its Western and Chinese presuppositions (see Section 2), as illustrated by an intercultural analysis of several classical and contemporary theories of religion. Concretely, Section 3 examines this concept in two Western classical interpretations. In this work focusing on the theory of religion, I chose to concentrate on them as not only they are both social theorists and significant contributors to the fields of philosophy of religion and religious studies but also they have something in common with the ambiance of the Chinese religions outlined above: Émile Durkheim's (1858–1917) for his interest in social life and Max Weber's (1864–1920) for his parallel between ascetic Protestant ethics and Chinese ethics. The exercise of placing their Western presumptions at the centre will allow us to see the particularity of the Chinese context in a new light.

But before addressing Durkheim's and Weber's ideas on religion, in order to better identify the specificity of their Western assumptions, yet viewed from the outside, from the point of view of the Chinese culture, this chapter commences with a preamble that takes us on a journey to the core of Chinese philosophico-religious thought, away from the Western way of thinking. I suggest that it is against this foreign backdrop that the Western habits of thinking operating in the two above-mentioned theories of religion are best displayed.

1 Preamble: Major assumptions of the Chinese philosophico-religious traditions

In the introduction, I have interculturally interpreted the difference between the meanings of the idea of religion in Western and Chinese cultures from an etymological perspective. My finding was that in both Western and Chinese cultures, the terms for religion are culturally sensitive designations, based on particular presuppositions. Consequently, it would be misguided to attempt to produce a general, culturally neutral definition of religion, based solely on Western analytical skills and indifferent to specific cultural assumptions. Such an approach would inevitably lead to both intercultural misapprehension and the concealment of peculiar features of non-Western (Chinese) religiousness. Arguments were given in the introduction that demonstrated the need to elaborate a theory as a particular methodological tool for the investigation of Chinese philosophico-religious traditions, based on distinct Chinese premises.

Let us recall several previously noted (see the introduction) foundational features of religion in the Western perspective: first, the belief or faith in the transcendent God, existing apart from the ordinary human reality and not subject to its limitations. This proves to be the source of such related dichotomies as sacred/profane, ordinary life/religious life, religion/philosophy and transcendent/immanent.

In contrast – as will be seen in detail in the next section and the later chapters – the Chinese world embraces what might be called religion as part of one's everyday life, a state of mind as well as a continuous quotidian ethical practice intrinsically related to the tradition's philosophical thought. The philosophico-religious continuum consists of a collaborative and transformative teaching/learning between master (ancestors, exemplary individuals, written works of the sages of the past, included) and disciple. At its heart lies the fusion (lack of separation) between what, in the Western context, is known as the inner self and the outer world, the mundane and the transmundane, the transcendent and the immanent. To illustrate, let us now leave the place to the textual context of the Song dynasty perception of religion.

1.1 Song dynasty textual context: Chan scholar-monk Qisong (1007–1072) and Neo-Confucian scholar Zhu Xi (1130–1200)

As mentioned, this book examines Chinese philosophico-religious traditions in the context of Song dynasty culture. More specifically, the study will be focused on texts written by two representative thinkers of the period. The first is the eminent eleventh-century Northern Song Chan monk Qisong of the *Yunmen* 雲門 sub-school of Chan. In fact, it was one of the five main Chan schools (*Yunmen*, *Guiyang* 潙仰, *Linji* 臨濟, *Caodong* 曹洞, *Fayan* 法眼) of the Song dynasty. A connoisseur of the Confucian classics, Qisong belongs to a distinct group termed 'scholar-monks'. Huang Chi-chiang provides an overview of the main activities of the *Yunmen* lineage monks during the Northern Song. He argues that they were responsible for the consolidation of Chan Buddhism at that time and moreover developed a new form of Chan known as 'literary Chan' (*wenzi* Chan文字禪), which includes poetries and essays (Huang

1986: 115–40). Robert Gimello attempts to highlight the polemical character of the Chinese term in the context of Song dynasty Chan history by offering the more assertive translation: 'lettered Chan'. Gimello's rendition captures the combination of spiritual discipline with literacy and learning as the distinctive feature of this 'conservative' type of Chan practised by adherents of the *Yunmen* school, as distinct from the 'unlettered' or anti-intellectual Chan of other schools (Gimello 1992: 381). In this book, I propose the denomination 'Confucianized Chan' to emphasize, first, the novelty and hybrid nature of the Chan scholar-monk Qisong's philosophico-religious work and, second, its deep-rooted sense of belonging to Song dynasty culture. The latter might be defined as a Confucian culture with a genuinely native Chinese Chan Buddhist dimension. Another argument in favour of the label 'Confucianized Chan' is the important fact that Qisong wrote his original interpretation of Buddhism not in a typical Buddhist style but in the Confucian *guwen* 古文 scholarly style, to explain Buddhism more efficiently to his Confucian contemporaries. Using *guwen*, he also makes extensive implicit and explicit references to the Confucian classics.

The second thinker, the Southern Song scholar Zhu Xi, needs no introduction. His works, especially his Neo-Confucian commentaries on the *Four Books*, are at the very heart not only of Chinese culture but of all East Asian cultures from the twelfth century to this day. In order to highlight the coherence and particularity of Song dynasty cultural premises and ethico-religious thought, I have chosen to construct a dialogue between these two thinkers whose works, in my view, best encapsulate the spirit of their epoch and of the classical Chinese way of thinking.

1.2 'Chinese religious traditions': Song dynasty views on learning

When speaking of 'Chinese religious traditions' as learnings, first and foremost, a preliminary question emerges: What are these learnings and processes of change through learning all about? Importantly, they are not focused on externals, apart, different and separate from oneself, or the differentiation between the sacred and the profane of Western religion. Broadly speaking, Qisong's and Zhu's learnings both embody a way of life based upon a continuous ethical concern and effort to develop and preserve a deep connection between oneself and others in daily life. However, as will be elaborated below, this ethical practice is premised on one's realization of the metaphysico-spiritual substratum of reality. A distinguishing feature of Chinese Song dynasty thought, that is, of the Neo-Confucian and Chan Buddhist traditions, which one does not find in the Western context, is the idea that *profoundly connecting with oneself, nourishing one's ethical, metaphysical, and spiritual substratum, means in fact becoming aware of one's connection with all others at a non-substantial, profound level*. One's inner awareness of the Neo-Confucian principle of coherence (*li* 理) or authentic nature (*xing* 性) as well as of Chan's original heart-mind (*ben xin* 本心) or original nature (*ben xing* 本性), achieved through dedicated work on oneself, is what ipso facto nurtures an individual's outer world and enriches their everyday human interactions. One discovers that their innermost self is not purely individual, isolated from everything à la Descartes; on the contrary, it is one's authentically good nature, the same in everyone, that interconnects the individual, at a subtle level, that is, ethically, spiritually and metaphysically, with all others. At the heart of both of these Song dynasty ethico-religious traditions lies this simultaneously inner and outer practice. They each offer a *dao* 道 or pathway to be followed – in other words, a way of carrying out this constant practice concurrently and continuous with and within one's everyday activities and interactions.

Let us begin with an introductory depiction of Song ethico-religious thought. I offer that, given this understanding, the parochialism and over-specificity of the bedrock assumptions underlying Western religion become vividly apparent vis-à-vis this foreign framework. Qisong defines Chan for lay practitioners as the conjunction between the way of humans (*rendao* 人道) and the way of spirit (*shendao* 神道). The first way refers to the teaching about precepts and good actions. These moderate, from the outside, human behaviour and the emotions/desires which determine their behaviour (*zhi qi wai* 制其外). The second refers to a subtle and spiritual level of the practice of precepts and good actions: it concerns inwardly touching people's heart-minds (*gan qi nei* 感其內) with the teaching of karmic resonances, thus transforming them and their everyday behaviour[1] (Qisong, *Yuanjiao*, 0650b20-5). The Chan scholar-monk focuses on the two basic ways, which correspond to the Buddhist vehicles of the human and of heaven or nature. As mentioned above, these paths are not for the devout members of the religious community but for lay Buddhists, one might say, members of Confucian society. The latter are attached to emotions and cannot remove their desires. Therefore, the teaching focuses on emotions/feelings (*qing* 情) and trains individuals to become aware of the good and bad sides of their emotions/feelings. This practice aims to moderate the emotions, not so the practitioners can finally abandon them but so they can transcend the emotions while still following them (以世情膠甚而其欲不可輒去。就其情而制之。... 佛行情而不情耳。).[2]

The heart of Qisong's Chan teaching concerns the inner practice and shaping of affections, as intrinsically linked to one's outer ethical actions in social intercourse. In the paragraph 0648c25 of the essay *Yuanjiao* (*Inquiry into the Teachings*) included in his collection *Fujiao bian* (*Essays on Assisting the Teaching*), the scholar-monk reveals the subtle interdependence and mutual causality generated by emotions/feelings, and he specifies what one needs to cultivate (*xiu* 修) by controlling their good and bad sentiments, according to (Chan) Buddhist learning and dedicated practice:

> The ten thousand things have nature and emotions. Since ancient times until today there is death and there is life. Yet, from the beginning, death, life, nature, and emotions cause each other. Death is certainly caused by life; life is certainly caused by emotions; the emotions are certainly caused by the nature. The emotions are the reason why the ten thousand things are continuously submerged in the life and death cycle. Only the sages endowed with their great clairvoyance see the causes before this life and instruct people about what will come after death. They show them what they are going to achieve after death and teach (*jiao* 教) them what they should cultivate now. Therefore, with their *dao*, they guide the people how to rid themselves now of the false emotions of their actual life, this will certainly assist them to achieve something in the next life. 萬物有性情。古今有死生。然而死生性情。未始不相因而有之。死固因於生。生固因於情。情固因於

性。使萬物而浮沈於生死者。情為其累也。有聖人者大觀。乃推其因於生之前。示其所以來也。指其成於死之後。教其所以修也。故以其道導天下。排情偽于方今。資必成乎將來。³

According to Qisong, the purpose of the teaching is to transform people through education so they can renew themselves and become good: in other words, to do good actions rooted in a spiritual substratum, which is further discussed below.⁴

The Neo-Confucian Zhu Xi also focuses on practice, on the teaching of sages that guide people to cultivate (*xiu* 修) their particular pathways (*dao*). Cultivation, in his view, has a clear connotation, which complements that of Qisong: the Confucian sage uses his own outstanding qualities, with which he was endowed by heaven, and evaluates how people can regulate (moderate) their inner and outer behaviour (修，品節之也。),⁵ depending on their specific qualities received from heaven. Accordingly, he teaches them how to cultivate themselves. One's behaviour includes one's emotions and desires, as well as conduct in social affairs and interactions. The Confucian teaching of the sage includes different categories of regulations that everyone is to follow, like the rites, music, punishments and rules of governing.⁶ While the Chan teaching takes into account the interrelatedness between people's present, past and future lives when evaluating what has to be cultivated now in the context of society, the Confucian focuses on individuals' present actual life and needs of cultivation.

In his article *Yuanjiao* 原教 (*Inquiry into the Teachings*), Qisong comparatively illustrates this difference between the two teachings:

> All teachings are similar to the crossing of a river. It is the same water, but one may pass over a deep ford with clothes on, or a shallow ford with the clothes rolled up to one's knees; it has shallow and deep areas. In Confucianism, what the sage governs is a lifetime [this world, this society]. In Buddhism, what the sage governs goes beyond a lifetime [this world, this society]. 諸教也亦猶同水以涉而屬揭有深淺。儒者聖人之治世者也。佛者聖人之治出世者也。⁷

In his commentary to the ancient *Zhongyong*, the Neo-Confucian Zhu also makes reference to 'the way of the humans' (*rendao* 人道), as the learning to work on oneself, to eliminate the selfish temptations coming from the outside, so as to uncover and realize in oneself one's original goodness (以去夫外誘之私，而充其本然之善).⁸ At a later stage, one is apt to transform this awareness of inner goodness in something concrete, good actions (先明乎善，而後能實其善者，賢人之 學。由教而入者也，人道也。).⁹

Like the Chan scholar-monk Qisong, the Neo-Confucian thinker focuses on the emotions and their control. Furthermore, in his interpretation of the *Analects of Confucius*, Zhu highlights the negative sentiments one needs to control as the selfish desires and inclinations which arise in one's pursuit of personal advantage, interest and profit. Self-benefit is the desire inherent in each individual's feelings (利者，人情之所欲。).¹⁰ In Western culture, the inner is hermetically sealed from the outside world. Unlike this view, in the Chinese world (both Confucians and Buddhists), what is highlighted is the porousness between inside and outside, in fact, the continuity between one's self and the external world. Accordingly, in Zhu's paragraph quoted above, one's personal desires and pursuit of profit do not come from the inside, wherein dwells the original goodness or the authentic nature bestowed by heaven, but rather from one's exchanges with the outside. One's initial inner Neo-Confucian practice is focused on eliminating the selfish desires, to gain access to one's original goodness, a metaphysical substratum, later to be expressed in outer practice, that is, concrete good actions and ethical behaviour and relations. As evidenced in the following quote, Qisong's account from a hundred years earlier resonates with Zhu's: the Chan monk stresses that the emotions keep individuals in a state of confusion (*huo* 惑). However, while Zhu presents the feelings and the authentic nature in a metaphysically dualist light, albeit organic under further specification, the Chan monk highlights their spiritual non-duality. Broadly speaking, whereas the metaphysical view pertains to an intellectual quest, the spiritual evades the analytical and logical. In the essay *Guang yuanjiao* 廣原教 (*Extensive Inquiry into the Teachings*), also included in his anthology *Fujiao bian* (*Essays on Assisting the Teaching*) written in Confucian *guwen* style, the Chan monk explains:

> The emotions emerge from the human nature, the human nature lies hidden within the emotions. If the nature is hidden, then the perfectly real *dao* is lost. For this reason, the sage makes the nature the content of his teaching and trains people about their nature. The movements of the world originate from the emotions. To remove the state of confusion of human beings requires rectifying their (awareness of) their nature. 情出乎性。性隱乎情。性隱則至實之道息矣。是故聖人以性為教而教人。天下之動生於情。萬物之惑正於性。[11]

In conclusion, each of the Song teachings (Chan or Neo-Confucian) and their corollaries – the learnings – consists in making constant, daily efforts to become aware and thus able to follow as a guide something profoundly present inside oneself: one's inner goodness, the capacity to understand what a good action is, how to maintain and strengthen one's relationships with others by performing such good actions. The Chan scholar-monk Qisong emphasizes that both teachings have a common goal, which he defines with originality as 'making people good [that is, willing to perform good actions] (*wei shan* 為善)': 'The teachings provided by sages are different (*bu tong* 不同); however, they are identical in that they make people good (而同於為善也).'[12]

To better illustrate the ethical context of the term 'good' (*shan* 善), let us look at the etymology of the graph. It means not only morally good, positive and profitable, right conduct but also 'becoming friends' and 'being on good terms'. Xu's Han dictionary presents the etymology of the graph to disclose its meaning in light of its graphic composition: after a dispute (*yan yan* 言言), the situation became good, favourable 羊 (*xiang* 祥). Good is not an abstract notion but is equivalent to joyfulness, good omen, prosperity and propitious outcome. Thus, the ambiance of the meaning of this term for good suggests the dynamism of a timely or well-timed process with a beneficial result. In the *Book of Rites*, *Liji* 禮記, the same character *xiang* 祥, which is an element (radical or unit) of the character good (*shan* 善), designates the offerings presented to a deceased parent at the beginning of the second and third years of bereavement.

Through this *xiang* 祥 element, spiritual and religious dimensions are evident in this graph that designates the good through multiple references to the connection between the living and their ancestors re-actualized at the moment of family rituals, the good omen and prosperity as concrete results of the functioning of this spiritual relationship. Good *shan* also signifies harmonious communitarian relationships: allusion to the idea of being on good terms, stopping quarrels, as that which is of good omen brings prosperity and joyfulness.

In ancient Chinese (Daoist) thought, the natural order of reality is perceived as spontaneously good, moral: 'the highest good is like water' (上善若水), says Laozi's paragraph 8.[13] The allusion to organic life is implicit here, too. For this reason, Confucius has confidence in one's natural ability to distinguish the individuals who are well behaved, to perceive them as role models and to choose to emulate them (*ze qi shan* 擇其善) – as he clearly expresses in *Analects* 7:21.[14] It is noteworthy, however, that the good in Song philosophico-religious thought is not only an ethical concept but it also has a metaphysico-spiritual profundity. We shall explore this in the following.

The ethico-religious in Qisong's Chan thought is embodied in the spirit of humans (*shen* 神). In his essay *Yuanjiao*, the Chan monk explains that this does not refer to the phantoms and spirits of heaven and earth (the traditional Confucian understanding of the character) but to the very spiritual essence of the human (*jing shen* 精神), the heart-mind (*xin* 心), one's perfect and original spiritual goodness, beyond the ordinary dichotomy good and bad. However, even this spiritual goodness needs to be cultivated through the constant daily life ethical practice of the teaching: 'If the individual cultivates his spiritual essence,' Qisong explains, 'he fulfills his duties well. During his life he receives back good fortune; at his death, his spirit ascends to purity' (謂人修其精神善其履行。生也則福應。死也則其神清昇。).[15]

As to Zhu Xi's Neo-Confucian thought, its ethico-religious dimension is expressed in the requirement to make sure that one remains continuously aware of one's moral quality (*de* 德). The latter does not merely refer to one's actions and interactions but includes a profound awareness of being in relationship with others at a deep level, that of the initial goodness received from heaven-nature. This constitutes the metaphysical substratum of humans, which is the same in everyone but remains inaccessible to most people without effort: 'Keeping the moral quality in one's heart-mind means to preserve in one's heart-mind the goodness with which one is naturally endowed' (懷德，謂存其固有之善。).[16]

It is notable that both Song dynasty thinkers highlight in a clear and unequivocal manner the ethical as core of the two Neo-Confucian and Song Chan traditions and as the highest concrete objective of their practical teachings. However, I suggest that this is a special type of ethical, let us call it ethico-religious for now, which has no equivalent in Western culture: it has two intrinsically and organically related, inseparable and not separated (as in the Western dichotomy, mundane/supramundane, transcendent/immanent) constitutive levels. The Western separation embodies a division that permanently needs to be overcome. One could sketch out the Chinese ethical as having two coexisting and inseparable levels of depth but not as being constituted of two elements: 'ethical as metaphysical or spiritual corporeality' and the 'performative ethical'. In other words, the subtle and spiritual level of the ethical – the ethical's subtle body (*ti* 體), and the social level of the ethical – the concrete functioning (*yong* 用) of this subtle body, as observable in the social interaction of everyday life. The spiritual body supports and enables its actualization through concrete functions: everyday life relationships and actions.

1.3 'Ethico-organic' religiousness: Song dynasty views on metaphysico-spiritual corporeality

The analysis unfolded in the previous subsection reveals two specific dimensions of the so-called Chinese religions (here represented by Qisong's and Zhu Xi's works): they are understood as learnings, consisting in making constant, daily efforts to become aware and thus able to follow as a guide the inner goodness present inside oneself, hence maintain and strengthen one's relationships with others by performing such good actions; Chinese religions (Neo-Confucianism and Chan Buddhism) focus on a particular form of ethico-religious that has two levels of depth, that is, 'ethical as metaphysical or spiritual corporeality' and the 'performative ethical'.

The next part will further detail the significance of this ethico-religious dimension in Qisong's and Zhu's works. Suffice it to say at this juncture that in this interrelation between ethical as metaphysical or spiritual corporeality and ethical as social functioning, the accent is not on the descriptive, on understanding (what is ethical?) as in the Western duality transcendent/mundane, which requests the precise definition and clear specification of its terms. The 'organic' Chinese ethical – that is, metaphysico-spiritual corporeality/performative ethical – is focused on how to concretely employ that subtle corporeality of the ethical in society, on how it factually changes and improves the daily life functioning of human interactions.

A word about the meaning of the body (*ti* 體). In light of its graphic etymology, in the context of the articulation body *ti* 體/functioning *yong* 用, the body is often translated as essence or principle as opposed with the application or function. I must draw the reader's attention to how such a translation could be misleading because it transfers this two-levelled organic reality – the Chinese ethical – into the familiar Western paradigmatic ontological disconnect: intellect as separated from physicality; abstract, conceptual, ideal or divine essence as primordially set apart from concrete being. Here, the subtle level of the ethical is considered as corporeality. The latter is not the form of an object but a dynamic processive entity that supports its continuous functionality. Unlike the common Western use of the concept of body as a set of material parts constituting the organism, the Neo-Confucian body is the emblem not of the material but of the metaphysical. It is the living spiritual structure on which its concrete movement – everyday ethical interactions in society – is founded, the spiritual corporeality that fuels and enables its functioning at the sociopolitical perceptible level.

The graph for body (*ti* 體) contains the stylized body *gu* 骨, ordered biotic assembly of bones and muscles as scaffolding the vital functioning of the body: an articulated skeleton that strengthens the body and frames the attached muscles, permitting unlimited variations in movement. The range of movement enabled by this spiritual as body is the dynamic ethical that orders society and human relationships. The concrete ethical in this perspective is the trace of a movement of ordering, similar to the ordering movement of life, not the application of abstract rules and norms. It is the harmonious spiritual as body that allows for efficacious ethical relationships within the community. The metaphysical corporeality is thus primordial, that is, of first importance; it is indispensable and essential because there could be no concrete ethical relationships without this spiritual corporeality and outside it. It contains within itself the interdependence and inseparability of what in the Western world is envisaged as a separation between the sacred and the profane, between the metaphysico-spiritual and the tangible. Another major difference is that within this Western articulation of two elements, the perceptible is the primordial one. Durkheim's following note, for instance, illustrates this presupposition of the scientific thought of Enlightenment: 'what defines the sacred, is the fact that it is added on the tangible' (car ce qui définit le sacré, c'est qu'il est surajouté au reel).[17] In Song dynasty thought, the focus is on the metaphysico-spiritual corporeality, without which no authentic ethical functioning is possible. In the next part, we explore Qisong's and Zhu's interpretations of this two-levelled 'organic' ethical. They complement and complete each other.

In his *Tanjing zan* 壇經贊 (*Encomium of the Platform Sutra*) 0346c27,[18] Qisong expresses the cohesion between the two levels as the non-duality between the subtle root *ben* 本 (i.e. spiritual corporeality *ti* 體) and its concrete traces (*ji* 迹) (i.e. functionality *yong* 用). The first can also be described as the intangible spirituality referred to as Great Vehicle 大乘 or Buddhist *dao* 道 which, in Chan, is the heart-mind (*xin* 心), 'the supernatural heart-mind transmitted by the buddhas' (佛所傳之妙心也)[19], the empty and soundless corporeality (*mo ti* 默體).[20] The heart-mind as empty and soundless corporeality suggests an infinite, all-embracing silent space, devoid of any specific characteristics or particular sounds of its own; empty and soundless, that is, encompassing all things, not as spatial structure but as a subtle, spiritual and non-dual network of interdependence: an intangible 'heart-mind connected with all things' (*xin tong* 心通)[21] (Qisong, *Guang yuanjiao*, 0654c28-2, in the collection *Fujiao bian* (*Essays on Assisting the Teaching*)). The traces (*ji* 迹) imply its concrete realization or great functioning (*da yong* 大用), that is, the tangible teaching (*jiao* 教) of the sages, aimed at cultivating people's heart-mind (*xiu xin* 修心) and their nature (*xiu xing* 修性).

The articulation of subtle corporeality and ethical functionality also lies at the core of Zhu's Neo-Confucian ethical metaphysics, or in contemporary Confucian thinker Mou Zongsan's 牟宗三 (1909–1995) terms, Zhu's moral metaphysics (道德的形上學). The Chinese metaphysics (*xing shang* 形上) signifies 'beyond forms' (things having perceptible appearance), but it indicates something that remains within and inseparable from forms, as their nourishing substratum or invisible feeder root. It is quite interesting that, in the following paragraph, Mou Zongsan envisages the Neo-Confucian highest level of perfection as a form of Chinese universality – other than the Western universality – which cannot grow without taking heaven into account:

> There are individuals for whom metaphysics 形上學 is annoying, and heaven 天 is annoying. They state that the starting point of the Confucian school is the study of daily social interaction. The latter is the reason why humans share a common heart-mind *xin* 心 and the heart-minds share a common principle *li* 理. The

Confucian school aims at universality. This image is not inaccurate. It is true that the Confucian school develops this side and this is why it focuses on 'the method of attaining the highest level of perfection and following the path of the *zhongyong* (中庸).' One can focus on this dimension, but in doing so, one cannot eliminate heaven.[22]

According to Zhu Xi (*Zhongyong zhangju* 1, in *Zhuzi quanshu* ((*The Collected Works of Master Zhu*) ZZQS 6: 33), like a body of any kind, a healthy metaphysical body needs to be looked after, to be taken good care of, 'to be firmly established' (*li* 立) in oneself. The graphic etymology of *li* 立 suggests a man standing upright on the ground. Firmly establishing the metaphysical corporeality is one dimension of Neo-Confucian learning/practice (*jiao* 教). If one's metaphysical corporeality is not equally looked after through learning and practice, it cannot assume its functions, in other words, one cannot follow one's path, that is act well (*xing* 行) and put this profound corporeality into practice. Inevitably, the presence within individuals of a deformed, malformed or damaged metaphysical body (or feeder root) would make it impossible for society to function ethically. The latter represents the second, social dimension of the practice of the 'Chinese religious traditions', inseparable from the individual one. The metaphysical is thus perceived not as abstract but as a subtle living body that needs to be constantly nourished through learning, maintained, firmly established, in order to enable it to function. The graphic etymology of 'acting well, behave, move, follow a path' *xing* 行 indicates a walking man, taking long strides, alternatively moving his legs forward. In Zhu's terms, 'Even if the metaphysical corporeality and functioning of the *Dao* are different, as to stillness and movement, one must first firmly establish the metaphysical corporeality so that afterward its functioning is possible through motion. Therefore, in reality, these are not two separate things' (是其一體一用雖有動靜之殊，然必其體立而後用有以行，則其實亦非有兩事也。).[23] What does it mean to say they are not two separate things or features of the practice? It means they are mutually reinforcing: once one has firmly established one's metaphysical corporeality within oneself, keeping it functioning continuously, that is, preserving one's ethical behaviour in everyday interaction, becomes easy to maintain, effortlessly. And conversely, the effort to respect and take care of others in daily life, to perform right actions, contributes to making the establishment of the metaphysical corporeality within oneself become easy. In addition, the salience of metaphysical corporeality is Zhu's Neo-Confucian understanding of ethical practice is underwritten by the principle of coherence *li* 理, a morally metaphysical principle, or authentic nature *xing* 性 bestowed by heaven to everyone. I suggest the translation 'principle of coherence' for the term *li* 理 as etymologically justified: the Latin *cohaerentia*, 'organic order, structure', emphasizes the quality of constituting a unified whole, and the Latin *principium*, 'source, foundations', has a moral resonance – foundation of behaviour, moral habit, exactly as does *li*. This notion is further developed in Chapter 4, Section 2.2.

The ethical functionality of this metaphysical corporeality is concretized through the movements of vital breath (*qi* 氣)[24] as bodied forth in the human emotions (*qing* 情) – that is, expressions of the daily relationships and interactions in society. The good functioning of the metaphysical corporeality refers not only to individuals who train themselves to keep their vital breath harmonious as exemplary persons (*junzi* 君子) but also to a harmonious society. 'Harmony' (*he* 和) is the term that designates this flawless ethical functioning and has the following precise connotations: impartial, unbiased, disinterested, non-complacent (see Zhu, *Lunyu jizhu* 2:14 in ZZQS, vol. 6). Zhu describes it:

> To realize harmony means: one's heart-mind is not divisive, nor excessive on either side. Complacency means to flatter everybody. Mister Yin[25] said: 'The exemplary individual places behavioral rectitude above all; it is for this reason that he is not complacent. The petty individual places his interest above all; in such a case how could he realize harmony?' 和者，無乖戾之心。同時，有阿比之意。尹氏曰:「君子尚義，故有所不同。小人尚利，安得而和?」[26]

He also highlights in the following terms the incomprehensible – from a Western perspective – fusion between the ethical and the organic:

> Master Cheng said: 'The exemplary individual cultivates his inner self in order to provide the people a peaceful life. He is constantly self-vigilant and for this reason everyone lives in peace. When all individuals from the top down are but one, their conduct is imbued with respectful vigilance, then heaven and earth are naturally in place, the ten thousand beings are naturally growing and developing, all vital breath is in harmony and the four quintessences [heaven, earth, humans, all beings] are replete.' 程子曰:「君子脩己以安百姓，篤恭而天下平。帷上下一於恭敬，則天地自位，萬物自育，氣無不和，而四靈畢至矣。」[27]

This is what configures religious practice in classical Chinese culture as illustrated in the Song dynasty Chan and Neo-Confucian traditions: constant, ordinary, socio-ethical practice fuelled by its metaphysico-spiritual corporeality. Without the body, there would be no functioning of life; by the same token, without metaphysico-spirituality, there would be no everyday social ethics. These paragraphs underscore the unity and consistency of Qisong's and Zhu's body/functioning *ti* 體/*yong* 用 as emblem of the two-levelled ethical. On their view, in order for everyday ethics to be possible, for it to function efficaciously, that is, fulfil its harmonizing social and organic role, there must be a metaphysico-spiritual body of the ethical that sustains the ethical life and triggers the ethical movements of socio-organic reality, exactly as feeder roots stimulate buds to open and grow. The phenomena of life constitute the bonding of these two levels of the ethical – subtle corporeality and its perceptible, socio-organic functioning.

If Qisong stresses their spiritual non-duality beyond any ontological status (see Section 3.1), Zhu postulates their organic inseparability, the fact that they belong not to different ontological levels but to the same, single, interdependent, ordered reality, at once organic, metaphysical and ethical. According to Zhu, in order of importance, the metaphysical is of the utmost priority and importance:

Question: As soon as there is principle, there is also the vital breath; one should not distinguish between which one comes first and which comes later; is this not so? Answer: Basically, it is principle which comes first; however, this is not to say that, if today principle appears, tomorrow vital breath will appear; nevertheless, the first has to be distinguished from the later; if ever, for instance, mountains, waters and earth were to be swallowed up, principle would always remain.[28]

The preceding paragraphs are illuminating with respect to another cultural presupposition of this Song dynasty two-levelled ethical: the fact that the spiritual or metaphysical corporeality discussed above is to be found not only deep inside the individual (i.e. the original heart-mind whether as the Chan Buddha-nature or as the Neo-Confucian principle of coherence) but simultaneously everywhere. Hence, natural reality is not primarily envisaged as tangible things as in the Western space but as an omnipresent ocean or environment, spiritual (Chan) or metaphysical (Neo-Confucian), from whence emerge all concrete things and events. As a result, the deep ethico-organic interrelationships among all things and events are the direct consequence of the ubiquitous presence of this metaphysico-spiritual body which supports and carries everything.

This account of the Song dynasty 'ethico-organic' order rooted in metaphysico-spiritual corporeality may suggest that this type of configuration resembles the Western metaphor of 'organism'. This holds especially true for Zhu's Neo-Confucian view. Still, a thorough exploration of the graphic etymology of the character body *ti* 體 as an essential preliminary step in the process of intercultural translation of the philosophico-religious paragraphs translated above reveals that its underlying cultural assumptions are very different from those of the Western organic and organicism. The latter focus, among others, on the idea of the assemblage composed of structured elements and consequently on the separation between body/organism and soul/spirit/consciousness. I just mention in passing Bergson's conception, for instance. According to him, it is experience that shows the existence of a certain relationship between the body and the soul or consciousness – he calls it solidarity. He perceives this connection as an 'insertion of the spirit within the material' and examines what he calls a progressive materialization of the consciousness.[29] Note here the focus on the effort to connect the two disjointed body and spirit, to explain the structure of assemblage of organs and their functions, the insertion of the spirit within material which suggests the prominence of the latter. By comparison, the Song dynasty offers a completely different emphasis: on the metaphysical and spiritual all-pervasive ocean from whence emerge tangible things and events.

Another essential difference between the two different perceptions of organism is the absence of any ethical connotation in the Western perception of organic life, or of something resembling metaphysico-spiritual corporeality. I agree with Hall and Ames that an explanation of Zhu's 'organicist thinking' should not start from the Western metaphor of 'organism':

> This continuity between humanity and the world also leads to the singular importance of certain metaphors in the definition of relational order within a

Chinese world. One model frequently cited in explanation of the Confucian order is that involving the Western metaphor of 'organism'. This model is influential in some measure because of Joseph Needham's employment of it. But Needham's use of the term organicism is a peculiar one, discussed most fully by reference to Leibniz's theory of monads and Whitehead's philosophy of organism. Additionally, Needham brings in the organismic theories of Plato and Aristotle with analogies of microcosm and macrocosm, as well as the analogical relationship between the individual and the state. For Needham, the paradigm illustration of organicist thinking among the Chinese is the twelfth-century Neo-Confucian, Zhu Xi.[30]

However, it seems to me that Hall and Ames implicitly suggest that 'organism' has an accepted unambiguous meaning and embedded rationales, fixed once and for all by Western thought, and that this concept is inappropriate or non-transferable to Chinese culture. I suggest that it is possible to decentre our vision and move away from the Western context. This effort could be a preliminary towards training ourselves to practice the new attitude suggested by Gadamer: to learn to think on a larger scale, to learn something from the culturally other. One could thus envisage the denomination 'organicity' as a neutral convention (after all, our alphabetical language *is* a convention), not as already confiscated and captive to the Western cultural space. Such a liberal use of this terminological convention may turn out to be instructive and interculturally enriching. It is always possible to use it as a neutral label, without giving it a unidimensional identity, that is, its meaning as developed by the Western philosophy.

To bring this preamble to a close, an interesting question concerns how organism is perceived in different cultures; what is its relationship with the metaphysical and spiritual? The above analysis defined its cultural particularities in the Chinese space by uncovering its different cultural presuppositions: the fusion of the ethico-organic and the corporeality of the metaphysico-spiritual. The Western organic focuses anatomically on the bodily organs and their functioning together.

This prelude introduces some prominent ethico-religious features of Song dynasty culture and examines the perception of 'religion, philosophico-religious, metaphysical and spiritual' in this sphere as compared with the Western meaning of religion. As noted, it provides a backdrop for the examination of the specific cultural ground of the two Western theories of religion: Durkheim's and Weber's.

This long incursion into the cultural premises of Song dynasty religions unfurled in Section 1 is intended to make us step away from the Western coherence of the notion of religion. After this preamble, the inquiry into the Western presuppositions of the two theories – which is supposed to further enable us to grasp the differences between the foundations of this concept in the two cultural spheres – begins by comparatively examining in Section 2 the Greek meaning of the concept of theory and that of its equivalent in Chinese culture. This intercultural evaluation not only will introduce Durkheim's and Weber's ideas but also will allow me to situate the notion of theory within the framework of philosophy of religion and address two related premises arising from that preparatory relation of comparison and of contrast: first, a certain deformation of the thought process as the major problem plaguing the Western effort to build a universal, culturally indifferent theory of religion as a general analytical tool. Much of this is related to the potential for fallacy which lies behind the application of such a presupposed general analytical tool to investigate, as elaborated above, culturally sensitive and language pre-determined philosophico-religious content. The next issue to tackle is the fact that all the classical theories developed within the framework of philosophy of religion and religious studies emerge from such Western disciplines as philosophy, sociology, anthropology, psychology and so on. Thus, they are inevitably rooted in the specific presuppositions of the distinctively Western culture and religion. The next section uncovers and discusses these assumptions in a comparative way, in relation to those of the Chinese space.

2 Defining theory: An intercultural perspective

2.1 Theory: Western etymology

What, in fact, is theory about? Let us first look at the Western concept of theory θεωρία. Anatole Bailly's (1833–1911) well-known *Dictionnaire grec-français* provides insight into the ancient Western meaning of this term. He identifies several connected meanings it has, centred around the act of seeing, of examining.[31] Bailly traces the earliest use of the term 'theory' to Herodotus (c. 484–c. 425): 'travelling to see the world'. In his *Histories* 1.30, the ancient Greek geographer and historian, tells how Solon (c. 630–c. 560), the Athenian lawgiver and poet, known as one of the Seven Wise Men of Greece, 'left the city of Athens to learn about the customs of the foreign people, and went first to Egypt'. The same general ancient signification of theory as travelling to see the world is also found in Plato (c. 428–c. 348 BCE), *Republic* 556c. In the dialogue *Critias* 52b, the philosopher elaborates on the particular meaning of theory as spectacle, as being a spectator at the theatre, as participant in a solemn religious feast or procession: in other words, the initial meaning of Western word 'theory' relates to cultural and intellectual curiosity, desire to know: travelling to see the world (others) instead of remaining to see the feast. This is indeed what one expects from 'the trading peoples of the Mediterranean' who, as Max Weber points out, rationalized their script into an alphabetical form.[32] Starting from Plato, the word 'theory' acquires a new, figurative sense of contemplation of the spirit, meditation and study (*Laws* 951c, *Republic* 517d). Aristotle (384–322 BCE) develops it further as theoretical speculation, opposed to practice (*Metaph.* 1, 8, 16).

It is noteworthy that, first, all these derivative meanings are built on the binary opposition between theory and practice: viewing/becoming involved in, spectator/participant. In the Western perception, finding a theory means to watch something previously unknown (e.g. the customs of a foreign people) as a viewer, as spectator in order to create its definition, explanation through an intellectual process. Consequently, the signification of theory gradually shifts towards the idea of contemplation and observation, as speculation and speculative research of the spectator. In other words, it points to an abstract and speculative knowledge, independent of practice and its practical applications: something that belongs to the viewer, that is about the viewer's perspective and habits of thinking, and is in a sense self-explanatory. According to its etymology, Western theory expresses the abstract, conceptual point of view of an observer, one who travels in order to see other cultures – an observer, a spectator and not a participant – so one must be able in this way to comparatively build one's own intellectual understanding of them. The historian of religions Jonathan Z. Smith highlights what I would call this Western paradigm of spectator, the fact that the theorist's interests constitute the core of a theory, that is, comparisons: 'In the case of the study of religion, as in any disciplined inquiry, comparison, in its strongest form, brings differences together within the space of the scholar's mind for the scholar's own intellectual reasons. It is the scholar who makes their cohabitation – their "sameness" – possible, not "natural" affinities or processes of history.'[33]

Therefore, the accent in this Western perception of theory is first and foremost on the separation between theory and practice – the traveller does not practise in order to understand something completely new but relies on their own way of looking – and second, on the primordial importance of the beholder and their theory. The latter emerges from their speculative capacity to intellectually produce a unifying, explicative theory, applicable to all things that they saw: here one might perceive the initial trace of the universalist tendency of the Western culture. The theory is what the Westerner needs in order to 'systematically' observe the things: something they imagine based on non-participant observation that will enable them to grasp still unknown things. Note in this theoretical vision, the unimportance of a real relationship with the culturally other: what is important is the intellectual knowledge resulting from the visual/intellective encounter, that is, their reasoning skills from which result the definition of things. Based on his investigation of academic research on religion, J. Smith offers the following reflection on the nature of the theory of religion. The reader will notice how his conclusion, which reflects the academic reality, perfectly corresponds to the above account of the Western cultural presuppositions embedded in the etymology of the word 'theory': 'Religion is solely the creation of the scholar's study [i.e. nothing besides meaning, no dialogue between cultures, no transformative education]. It is created for the scholar's analytical purposes by his imaginative act of comparison and generalization. Religion has no independent existence apart from academy.'[34]

In the authentic spirit of Enlightenment, theory is a celebration of the reason of the theorist. In the same vein, Levinas expresses a revelatory and general appreciation of (Western) thought – the Ulysses' itinerary – an idea that could effectively amount to 'theory'. He stresses the fact that this thinking remains committed to 'absorbing any Other into the Same and neutralizing the alterity'. The French philosopher illustrates his ethical view by calling on Greek mythology:

> The philosophy performs as a form in which manifests the refusal to commit to the Other ('le refus d'engagement dans l'Autre'), the wait preferred to action, the indifference toward others, the universal allergy of the early childhood of philosophers. The philosopher's itinerary remains that of Ulysses whose adventure in the world has been nothing but a return to his native island – a complacency in the Same, a lack of knowledge of the Other ('une méconnaissance de l'Autre').[35]

In critically assessing the state of religious studies in universities, J. Smith voices the following reflection – which, in passing, confirms Levinas's suggestion – on academic scholarship on religion and its use of the comparative method. He deplores the fact that, when elaborating a theory of religion which claims to be comprehensive, more often than not, the scholars use comparison in search of similarities – in Levinas's terms, they absorb any difference of a non-Western religion into similarities with Western religion: comparison in religious studies can be viewed as a kind of Ulysses' return trip, so to speak. Again, note that this tendency perfectly embodies not only the Enlightenment legacy but also a Western cultural propensity: 'As practiced by scholarship, comparison has been chiefly an affair of the recollection of similarity. The chief explanation for the significance of comparison has been continuity. The procedure is homeopathic. The theory is built on contagion. The issue of difference has been all but forgotten.'[36]

2.2 Theory and practice: Chinese graphic etymology

What about the signification of theory in the Chinese context? In order to illustrate why Western theories of religion may not be applicable to the Chinese reality – as they are grounded in specific cultural presuppositions such as those uncovered in Section 1 – let us address the meaning of the Chinese counterpart of theory and its fundamental premises. One will discover that the latter are essentially different from the Western ones, focus on different things and assume different meanings: one more reason to take cultural premises into consideration when building a theory for a particular religion.

To this end, a preparatory investigation of the graphic etymology of the Chinese character theory (*lun* 論) – that is, to explain, to discuss, deal with a thesis – might be useful. Xu's *Shuowen* dictionary does not refer to travelling – this can be difficult for a farmer who, unlike the merchant, is carrying on farming operations on fixed lands in accordance with the seasons and with the growth of grains. It focuses instead on the idea of order embodied in this term: *lun* is the expression of a well-ordered thinking, a well-organized argumentation. The interdependence of arguments in the ongoing process of a presentation, that is, their harmonious arrangement in relation to each other according to a particular sequence or pattern, is of central importance in the Chinese idea of theory. The order implies the activity of fine-tuning arguments which can be temporally and spatially interpreted as an ordered sequence of events.

In conclusion, the Chinese theory *lun* 論 intrinsically bears overtones of order. Indeed, the primary meaning of the word in the (Confucian) classic *Record of Rites, Liji*, Chapter 3, *Wangzhi* 王制 (Royal regulations), is actually order, the heaven's order (*tianlun* 天論) or natural law: 'All regulations pertaining to the five punishments must conform to the order (law) of heaven' (凡制五刑必即天論). It is noteworthy that, most of all, this phrase implies the ethical/moral character of the spontaneous, natural order – the paradigm of which is the order of seasons, of organic growth: the above quotation from the *Record of Rites* thus suggests that human society should dispense rewards and punishments in conformity with the model/order presented by the heaven-nature. In other words, the unity of heaven-earth is regulated by the law of life, which, as discussed earlier, is perceived as harmonizing and spontaneously ethical, good. Furthermore, the character *lun* 論 – theory is directly correlated with the character *lun* 倫 – human relationships (their left radicals are different: 言 (discuss) and 人 (human)). The second *lun* also refers to the natural order, the weave of reasoning, moral order as well as ordered human relationships. Arising from the sequence of natural dynamism, the latter fall into five generic categories, based on the family model: between father and son, sovereign and minister, husband and wife, older and younger brothers and friends. All relationships can be integrated into one of these five universal categories, initially family distinctions animated by the spirit of brotherhood. It is important to note that this integrative perspective transforms the merely familial or natural (organic, as Weber calls it, see Section 3.2) into something bigger and different from the simple scope of family unity: this becomes an ethical project about the spontaneously ethical character of the natural law.

Moreover, according to the Han dictionary *Shuowen*, the (right) radical *lun* 侖 of theory 論 comes from the graph *yue* 龠.[37] It has several complementary meanings: performing the rite *yue* 龠 by playing the double flute 龠 (bamboo tubes with three holes allowing the harmonization of all sounds), the instrument used for the ancestral worship cult, for the sacrifice *yue*. In ancient texts of the Western Zhou dynasty (1045–771 BCE), the double flute refers to the celestial double flutes *lingyue* 霝龠 that render all relationships harmonious.[38] Furthermore, the character designating 'celestial', written 霝 and also 靈, carries the connotation of fine rain 雨, in other words, good and beneficial, as well as the meaning spiritual, charged with spiritual capacity. From this example of graphic etymological analysis, it is noteworthy that the characters do not imply fixed and determined significations as in alphabetical languages, but they build what might be called a rich resonance or ambiance of sense and suggest not static things but the processional, interdependent and harmonizing subtle dynamism of reality: the central metaphor of which is the constant cycle of seasons … and one of its major components, the rain. This dynamism embodies a deep level, and for this reason the changes of life (i.e. order of events which can be deciphered through their latent early signs) are essentially ethico-spiritual as well as organic. As will be discussed later, its track is preserved in graphs which originated from the recording of the process of divination.

Those embracing the Western analytical spirit, which employs segmentations, divisions into separate parts in the interest of precision and accuracy, reproach the Chinese for what they see as its grammatical indeterminacy. I heartily agree with Christoph Harbsmeier when he warns that the grammatical suppleness and organic flexibility of the Chinese should not be confused with grammatical looseness or lack of precision:

> Perhaps Classical Chinese, as opposed to Latin, is lexically as well as grammatically a somewhat less rigidly defined, a more openly organic structure in which no morphological straight jacket enforces spuriously clear-cut obligatory divisions where none are required for the efficiency of communication. Chinese grammatical structures are only sufficiently well-defined to articulate meaning, but at the same

time flexible enough not to impose rigid structure where such structure does not serve an articulatory or communicative purpose. ... The Chinese would, then, not only have held an organicist world view. They would also have expressed this world view in a medium of communication which was more supple and less rigid in its articulatory strategies than languages like Latin or Greek. ... Classical Chinese grammar is certainly much more precise than would appear from current descriptions. Organisms are precisely structured subtle things. They are more highly structured than a very advanced rigid device. What I am suggesting is that Chinese is highly structured in supple and subtle ways analogous to those organisms.[39]

In conclusion, from the intersecting graphic etymologies presented above, it is possible to identify some cultural presuppositions that create the ambiance of the Chinese term *lun* 論 – theory, the Chinese homologous of the Western notion of theory. Note that it implicitly carries the meaning of order, as well as of the effort to become aware of the naturally moral order in order to spontaneously respond and heed it. Also, a connotation of this continuous or connected series is the practice and maintenance of harmonious human relationships. Obviously, in this context, harmonious stands for ethical. As discussed in Section 1, Preamble, the celestial order is that of the ethico-spiritual and metaphysical capacities which is represented by the falling of good and beneficial rains. This specific understanding of the metaphysico-spiritual will be further discussed below. The reader now encounters again, in a different but related context, a particular Chinese cultural assumption that was put forward in the introduction: the continuity and inseparability between nature and culture. Society, the human world of culture, is not separate from nature but a part of nature; it can function harmoniously only within nature and in unison with the nature's rhythms. It should be re-emphasized that their working in unison has a major moral/ethical connotation.

Moreover, apart from this presupposition of culture as belonging to nature, the graphic etymology of the Chinese equivalent of theory reveals another implicit fundamental premise: the inseparability of theory and practice; it is far better to assert their identity: in order to become aware and able to follow the moral spontaneous order, one must practise the ordered human relationships. This topic will be explored and developed further in the next section, using translations from Qisong's and Zhu's texts. How can one explain the influence of the presupposition of identity culture/nature on humans' everyday actions and interactions? First and foremost, through their continuous ethical practice, individuals gain access to what might be called a 'theory-practice of the naturally ethical'. The latter refers to one's capacity to foresee or know beforehand the course of the unfolding of the natural ethical order and continuous change of events: that means the ability to detect and ethically interpret, at the very first moment of their appearance, the imperceptible signs of a new change in this continuous process. This quality allows humans to orient their behaviour in advance in an ethical direction, so the course of their social actions and exchanges will maintain and preserve its harmony and goodness for all. When following this theory-practice, the individuals may become aware earlier of unfortunate unfoldings of the course of events, which will materialize if they persist in their unethical behaviour. How do they know what is ethical and unethical? By practising and paying keen attention to the intrinsic relationship between their behaviour and the beneficial or detrimental development of their actions, beginning with the early signs down to their results. Under this mode of attentive practice, all the actions a person conducts are inchoative actions: that is to say, the enterprises include those one undertakes *upon oneself* so as to correct oneself in the unfolding of their actions and in light of the imperceptible signs of change; in this way, the individual may detect and ethically interpret their actions. The rootedness of this theory-practice in the ancient process of divination is undeniable. In light of the detailed analysis given in Section 1, Preamble, it is clear that this knowledge of what should be ethical action in every situation does not come from the beyond, as a supramundane commandment and guidance. But it emerges from the spontaneous functioning of the deep inner metaphysico-spiritual corporeality nourished through Chan or Neo-Confucian theory-practice. Because ethical action arises spontaneously from this internal and deep corporeality, one could call it ethical organicity.

Ethical organicity is further elaborated in Qisong's and Zhu's thought (see Part 2) as a form of spirituality (Chan) and moral metaphysics (Neo-Confucianism). Moreover, it is noteworthy that, as mentioned, this idea of a spontaneous ethical order emerging from the graphic etymology of *lun* 論 theory resonates with the aims and functioning of the process of divination discussed in the introduction. As was stressed above, the undertaking of the scribe-diviner is not an occultic practice of witchcraft. It is a task, based on the scribe-diviner's capacity of subtle observation of the reality as a living organism. This capacity allows them to decipher the early signs of a situation, that is, to detect the imperceptible incipient development of certain events before they come to pass, in accord with the natural ethico-spiritual order that gives life to the reality and preserves it. Vandermeersch suggestively explains that in order to achieve such decipherments, the scribe-diviner uses a technique that is somewhat similar to well logging. Its implementation enables the diviner to obtain the indicative or representative traces of the combination, at a particular time, of an array of cosmic forces which determine the evolution of the conjuncture: this is the properly technical aspect of divination. The divinatory science is the one that guides the interpretation of the diagram, based on extensive cosmological knowledge deepened by the study of the documents preserved by these experts and resulting from previous divination acts.[40] Therefore, at the end of the process of divination, the diviner is able to provide guidance concerning the ethical action that needs to be taken in order to foster favourable results and the unethical action that needs to be avoided in order to avoid or diminish adverse outcomes.

Unlike alphabetic writing, which is rooted in convention and thus introduces a separation between the reality, the abstract words (spoken and written) and the meaning these words embody, the Chinese characters are products of profound observations of the diagrams, which are the effect of the process of divination. Starting from the inspiring interpretation of divination by Vandermeersch, and drawing from the etymology of graphs, I suggest a unique role that the writing and divinatory diagrams play. The latter inchoatively and anticipatorily embody the unfolding process of real phenomena, their traces and trails. Owing to the concern to respect what Vandermeersch calls a graphic parallelism (phenomena/divination diagrams), these footprints give rise to the configurations of the written characters, which are supposed to accurately transpose the traces of the real unfolding of events. As noted, the graph concretizes the track of the natural order, which I highlight, is an ethico-spiritual order that supports and animates the reality. Its early imperceptible signs are embedded in the divinatory diagrams as well as in the sinographs. As will be shown in the next part, the explanation – drawn on the divinatory origin of the Chinese graphs – of the nature and function of this ethico-spiritual natural order is consistent with its Chan and Neo-Confucian interpretations.

In conclusion, several observations concerning the different meanings of the term 'theory' in the Western and Chinese contexts are in order: in the Chinese ethico-religious thought, theory and practice are not separated but organically and inextricably connected; theory does not involve a journey of understanding other religions as spectator but bears a particular meaning, that is, becoming aware and concretely following the natural ethical order, in other words realizing our interrelatedness and learning how to follow it; the root of this natural order (let us call it metaphysico-spiritual corporeality) is spiritual in the Chan tradition and metaphysical in Neo-Confucian thought; moreover, the concrete, everyday reality of the ethical lives of the members of society unfolds due to inner nourishing through learning their spiritual and metaphysical corporeality. It is the latter which enables their concrete ethico-organic functioning and not the other way round. There is resonance or interdependence between cosmic and social reality, between the naturally ethical order and social events and interactions. This interdependence which guides the human world is embodied in the imperceptible presence of the early signs (*ji* 幾) of the dynamics of the events, of the transformation which is about to take place. Although imperceptible, these early signals of an ethically good or bad turn of events are detectable during the process of divination and thus were incorporated in the Chinese characters. As will be discussed later, Qisong discerns these imperceptible first manifestations in the people's emotions, while Zhu in their behaviour. The practice focuses on becoming aware of these indicators at a latent stage in order to ethically correct them before the later, already actualized stages.

Consequently, in this context, the sacred, the profane and their dichotomy as we know it from the Western philosophy of religion do not exist. Instead, this religiousness reflects a subtle metaphysico-spiritual order, naturally ethical, from which emerges the tangible daily life of individuals and of reality. When the course of events unfolds following this order, everyone's life is flourishing.

As this chapter repeatedly pointed out, this excursion into a comparative etymology of the Western idea of theory and the Chinese *lun* 論 theory enables us not only to identify its Chinese assumptions but also to discern more clearly the Western cultural presuppositions embedded in the classic theories of religion(s) in relation to these Chinese presumptions. To that end, the time has come to take a closer look at the classical theories of religion of Durkheim and Weber and their cultural foundations.

3 Classical theories of Western philosophy of religion: Durkheim and Weber

As noted at the beginning of this chapter, I will consider these two classical theories in a particular way – from a Chinese perspective. I selected them – not only because their works laid most of the foundations of the sociology of religion and their influence is of great significance to the development of the science of religions but also in view of the fact that they have much in common with the ambiance of the Chinese religions outlined above: Émile Durkheim's (1858–1917) for his interest in social life and Max Weber's (1864–1920) for his parallel between ascetic Protestant ethics and Chinese ethics.

3.1 Émile Durkheim's sacred and its presuppositions: From a Chinese perspective

The Western polarity between sacred and profane was mentioned earlier as one of the foundational dichotomies of the Western religion. It represents the major conceptual tools of the Durkheimian theory of religion, and this section starts by addressing it. Like a trip back home, the classical Western theorists evaluate religion as a major dimension of the distinctively human life in general and attempt to build its universal definition starting from Western presuppositions and looking for similar, generic characteristics. One recognizes that this search for common features and classifications constitutes a major Western assumption inherited from the Enlightenment era. E. Durkheim's religious sociology (sociologie religieuse), for instance, is clearly based on this premise: 'Because all religions are comparable, because they are all species of the same genus, there are necessarily essential elements that are common to them.'[41] Obviously, for the sociologist, the idea of society is the soul of religion, and the community is the substrate of the religious life (Durkheim 1960: 599–600). At the core of his investigation, which starts with the Australian totemic beliefs, is to be found a primary expectation: that religion understood as beliefs and practices assumes a specific function for and within the community – to reinforce social cohesion.

Unlike the Song dynasty ethico-religious thought which includes a metaphysico-spiritual dimension – the ethical order of karmic resonances, causes and effects, and of the heaven-nature – Durkheim examines religion as a material functionality of the society, a valuable tool designed by society in response to the structural need for cohesion among all groups. Evidently, this generic notion of society does not take into account cultural presuppositions as specific foundations of different societies. Therefore, in his sociological perspective committed to human behaviour and social interaction, the similarity of religions is derived from their common and specific feature, which is not a substantive but a functional one: religion serves as an important instrument for social connection and development. Consequently, he defines religion as 'an eminently social thing' (la religion est une chose éminemment sociale).[42] If so, the fundamental religious representations are collective representations, and the rites 'are ways of behaviour that are born only within the assembled groups and are intended to generate, maintain, or rebuild certain mental states of those groups.'[43]

Furthermore, it is to be noted that he builds this supposed commonality between religions on a major presupposition, clearly inspired by the totemistic principle: the separation between sacred and profane. Nevertheless, one could say that, in a sense, Durkheim's major distinction between sacred and profane as root of the nineteenth-century Western theories of religion is also a derivative of the original separation theory/practice, and of the Platonic distinction between contemplation of the spirit (transcendence), intelligible or pure science versus practical expertise of manufacture and crafts. Durkheim bases his theory on the separation between sacred and profane as two opposed worlds that cannot coexist. In that respect, the French sociologist identifies a 'kind of logical void' (une sorte de vide logique)[44] that separates the sacred from the profane. Jonathan Smith highlights the specific nature of the Durkheimian sacred – it is not intrinsic but consecrated nature; in other words, functional, to repeat the term used above:

> Sacrality is conferred 'by virtue of the sacrament'. We do well to remember that long before 'the Sacred' appeared in discourse as a substantive (a usage that does not antedate Durkheim), it was primarily employed in verbal forms, most especially with the sense of making an individual a king or bishop (as in the obsolete English verbs to sacrate or to sacre), or in adjectival forms denoting the result of the process of sacration. Ritual is not an expression of or a response to 'the Sacred'; rather, something or someone is made sacred by ritual (the primary sense of *sacrificium*).[45]

In Durkheim's words, 'what defines the sacred, is the fact that it is added onto the tangible' (car ce qui définit le sacré, c'est qu'il est surajouté au reel).[46] If we recall the analysis developed in Section 1.3 of what has been described as an ethico-organic religiousness of the Song dynasty manifest as a metaphysico-spiritual corporeality, we realize the difference between the foundations of Durkheim's view and the Song dynasty philosophico-religious thought. Even if, by Durkheim's theory, the Chinese vision embraces community and social relationships, the latter are founded otherwise than upon something like Durkheim's ideas of society, of sacred as society. In what follows, the study provides evidence that refutes the claim to universality of the Durkheimian conception of society. Further references for this argument are to Qisong's spiritual dimension of society and to Zhu's metaphysical (see Chapters 3 and 4).

As a matter of fact, Song dynasty culture also focuses on society, interrelationships and interdependency between individuals, not as the result of representations and rituals as processes of sacration, as in Durkheim, but in a profound ethical and metaphysico-spiritual sense. In other words, they are rooted not in a 'consecrated' social (i.e. declared and made sacred) but in a two-levelled ethical reality as discussed above, embracing at once metaphysico-spiritual corporeality (*ti* 體) and socio-ethical functioning (*yong* 用). It must be stressed that the latter is a special functioning, that is, one embedded in daily life events that are viewed not as conventional ('consecrated') social relationships but as naturally ethical ones, emerging from the intangible corporeality of individuals and the reality carried out by them. In order to uncover the cultural specificity of the Durkheimian articulation between society and religion, the following section elaborates on the meaning of the intangible corporeality in the Chan and Neo-Confucian traditions of Qisong and Zhu Xi.

Unlike Durkheim's separated and consecrated sacred, for Qisong (see the following quotation), the omnipresent, spiritual (*shen* 神) is all-inclusive corporeality or environment (i.e. nothing is apart from it, 無有外) as *dao*; that is, the heart-mind, something he recalls that humans have forgotten for a long time. Therefore, what could be called religious practice or learning in this context means becoming aware of both this habitat and inner depth through the teachings of the Buddhist sage who explains the *dao* and enlightens human beings on their paths, by encouraging ethical everyday interactions and commitments within the community. However, it could be noted that Chan teaching and learning are not only concrete but also non-dual, that is, simultaneously spiritual-intangible and ethical-tangible. This teaching and learning concern this life as well as what lies beyond this life, the past, present, future and so on. It is Chan's non-duality, explains Qisong in his essay *Guang yuanjiao*, that makes it possible for Chan to traverse everything and build subtle bridges that interconnect beings spiritually and ethically within society:

> The heart-mind is the so-called *dao*. Enlightening human beings on *dao* is the so-called teaching. ... *Dao* is the great root of all living beings. The living beings have forgotten their root for a long time. ... The heart-mind does not have an outside, *dao* is always inclusive, therefore there is no thing isolated from *dao*. The sage does not consider *dao* as something personal and does not abandon the beings. Where there is *dao*, there is the sage. It is for this reason that what he teaches traverses the hidden and the manifest, this life and beyond this life. There is nothing that he cannot pass through. Passing through means interconnecting. When interconnected, the beings become corrected and his wish is that all the moral qualities of all the heart-minds are the same as the sage's moral quality. *Dao* is the broadest possible spiritual enlightenment. The heart-mind is the most spiritual, moral and marvellous functioning. 惟心之謂道。闡道之謂教。... 道也者眾生之大本也。甚乎群生之繆其本也久矣。... 心無有外道無不中。故物無不預道。聖人不私道不棄物。道之所存聖人皆與。是故其為教也。通幽通明通世出世。無不通也。通者統也。統以正之。欲其必與聖人同德。廣大靈明莫至乎道。神德妙用莫至乎心。[47]

This paragraph expresses the Chan non-duality between *dao* and humans' heart-minds, between the sage or the enlightened one and the ordinary human beings, the sage's purest and complete ethico-moral quality and that of the ordinary human beings and so on. In passing, this quotation constitutes an irrefutable proof that the Western dichotomy transcendent/immanent is an ineffective tool for examining the Chinese reality. Importantly, a fundamental difference should be remembered: the difference between 'one' (the *qi* 氣 or *vital breath*-quality emphasized by the Neo-Confucian worldview to be discussed later), 'non-duality' (the Buddhist 'to be one with') and 'duality' (separate entities). The contemporary East Asian Chan teacher Thich Nhat Hanh provides a vivid and straightforward explanation of Chan non-duality: 'Non-duality means "not two," but not two also means "not one." That is why we say "non-dual" instead of "one". Because if there is one, there are two. If you want to avoid two, you have to avoid one also.'[48] Masao Abe also provides a vivid description of Buddhist non-duality:

> It is a well-known story that the Buddha, when asked about the existence of the soul after death, answered with silence. Buddhism teaches neither the imperishability of the soul nor the extinction of the soul. Buddhism originally did not recognize the existence of the soul distinguished from the body, and the problem of death was not understood to be solved merely in terms of immortality or non-extinction, and of eternal life. In Buddhism, resolution of the problem of death is sought in terms of no-birth and no-extinction, or unbornness and undying, that is in terms of transcending 'birth and extinction' or 'birth and death' itself.[49]

Let's resume our discussion of Qisong's paragraph above from the perspective of non-duality. The latter in this context performs the role of a culturally other and has an inspiring task: it suggests to us something that is very much other than a 'separated and consecrated sacred'. The Chan scholar-monk states, 'When interconnected, the beings become corrected and his wish is that all the ethico-moral qualities of all the heart-minds are the same as (*tong* 同) the sage's moral quality.' This 'sameness' of the moral qualities of ordinary heart-minds with the perfect, complete and pure moral quality of the sage is an illustration of their non-duality, explained by Qisong as the interconnectedness of all beings at the profound, spiritual level of the Buddha-nature, that is, the original nature or the original heart-mind. Can one envisage this interconnectedness as a sort of (Chan) Buddhist community, as a subtle level of society? If yes, what would its specificity and difference be in comparison with the Western (Christian, Durkheimian, etc.) understanding of community and society? It seems to me that Masao Abe throws light on the different cultural presuppositions of the non-dual Christian interconnectedness and community in a remark about Paul Tillich's perception of Buddhist community from a Western perspective, which proves to be obtuse with respect to the difference between culturally rooted assumptions:

> In his talk with a Buddhist priest, Tillich said '*Only* if each person has a substance of his own is community possible, for community presupposes separation. You, Buddhist friends, have identity, but no community.' In this connection I am compelled to raise the following questions: are not both community and separation in Christian understanding incomplete insofar as the self as well as God are understood as substantial? Is not the dialectical nature of the Christian understanding of community and separation really not dialectical, thus not reaching the core of ultimate Reality? Buddhist community takes place precisely when there is the *communion* of the 'realizer of Nirvana' with everything and everyone in the topos of absolute Mu in which everything and everyone are *absolute in their particularity* and thus *absolutely relative*.[50] (italics in original)

Let us take a closer look at Qisong's usage of the Confucian *guwen* style in the paragraph translated above. As pointed out earlier, he presented his interpretation of (Chan) Buddhism not in Buddhist style but in the Confucian *guwen* style. Clearly, this essential detail as well as the tone of his essays is his subtle way of conveying several matters: the importance of Confucian tradition for Buddhism; the atmosphere of a culturally rich and coherent Song dynasty culture within which both traditions, Confucian and Buddhist, were living together under the aegis of the former; the complementarity between the two teachings and the potential contribution of Buddhism as an efficacious assistant to the scholar-officials in their efforts to cultivate and preserve peace and harmony in the people's daily living in the society. As an aside, in his article 'Zhuzi dui fojiao de lijie ji qi xiangzhi' 朱子對佛教的理解及其限制 ('Zhu Xi's Understanding of Buddhism, and Its Limitations'),[51] Tsai Chen-feng notes:

> According to Chen Shunyu's *Records of Qisong's Professions* (*Qi Song Hangye Ji* 契嵩行業記), initially anti-Buddhist sentiment was widespread among scholars of the Song dynasty, because all of them 'studied and practiced the *guwen* style of the old texts, and admired Tuizhi's [Han Yu 韓愈 (768–824)] rejection of Buddhism (學為古文，慕退之之排佛)'. However, after Qisong (1007–1072) published the *Inquiry into the Teachings* (*Yuanjiao* 原教) and *On Filial Devotion* (*Xiaolun* 孝論), which devoted more than ten articles to elucidating how the teachings of Confucian *dao* are consistent with Buddhism, those who had rejected Buddhism often read his work 'and not only loved its language but feared defeat by its well-reasoned arguments – not a single one could escape, and all switched allegiances'.[52] Even though the words of Chen Shunyu may be slightly exaggerated, they still offer a glimpse into two very real aspects of the situation at the time: first, the anti-Buddhist discourse was rather unconvincing because it lacked systematicity; second, Buddhists did very well in refuting anti-Buddhist arguments with discourse that persuasively told of areas where Confucian and Buddhist doctrines were in agreement.[53]

Returning to Qisong's quote given above, we observe how he translates into *guwen* Confucian language not only the just discussed Buddhist non-duality but also other Buddhist ideas: the soteriological objective of the Mahayana sage or bodhisattva is presented as an effort to accompany, that is, not to abandon, the other sentient beings, and he does not stop his efforts after attaining his own enlightenment. Qisong draws his Confucian contemporaries' attention to the Buddhist ideas of salvation and liberation in the following *guwen* terms: 'The sage does not consider *dao* as something personal and does not abandon the beings.' Equally, he portrays in ethical Confucian terms the bodhisattva's vow (wish) to help other human beings to achieve enlightenment, thus the soteriological dimension of his teaching. When becoming aware of the Buddha-nature or original nature at the deep level of oneself, one *non-dually* interconnects with others and all sentient beings at this spiritual depth. Qisong explains this interconnection in terms of being able to correct one's behaviour, that is, naturally behave in a perfect ethical way as the sage: 'When interconnected, the beings correct themselves (統以正之) and his wish is that all the moral quality of all the heart-minds is the same as the sage's moral quality.' It bears repeating that Qisong describes his Chan Buddhist teaching in what might be called Confucianized terms as having the objective to interconnect (*tong* 統) individuals at a subtle non-dual level, thus enabling them to correct themselves (正之) by virtue of this interconnection. Clearly, his spiritual *dao* or heart-mind and the practice of correcting sentient beings by non-dually interconnecting them are totally different than the Durkheimian construction of the sacred as aimed at preserving social solidarity.

In the following, Zhu's metaphysical perspective on Neo-Confucian teaching will be addressed. A comment from *Lunyu jizhu* 2: 4, in which Zhu quotes master Hu Anguo 胡安國 (1074–1138) illustrates the religious dimension of his practice: to not lose one's original heart-mind (人不失其本心) or the original goodness bestowed by heaven (see the paragraph translated below). His use of terms is quite similar to that of Qisong. While the Chan scholar-monk refers to spiritual practice that reaches a non-dual level, the Neo-Confucian practice is dedicated to attaining a metaphysical unity – that of the original heart-mind (本心) and the principle of coherence of heaven (天理) from which emerge all particular principles of coherence of the ten thousand specific events and relationships (萬理). The sharp focus on the ethical dimension is their common denominator. Again, this differs greatly from Durkheim's sacred added onto the tangible conception. The Song dynasty social cohesion is cut from a wholly different cloth – spiritual, metaphysical as well as concrete – than the Durkheimian functional notion of commitment to community based on 'fundamental representations' or beliefs that have their origins in society and 'ritual attitudes' having 'objective significations' and performing 'specific functions'.[54] In the following quote, Zhu introduces his perspective on the two-levelled ethical, that is, the unity between metaphysical corporeality (*ti* 體) and its tangible function (*yong* 用):

> Mister Hu says: 'The teaching of the sage proposes many methods. In effect, all he wants is to enable individuals to not lose their original heart-minds. The individual who wants to realize the original state of his heart-mind, should follow with determination the particular teaching that the sage explains to him. By means of going through the ordered sequence of steps of the teaching, one will surely make progress. Having attained the level of "without the slightest flaw", and after achieving complete lucidity into the principles of coherence of ten thousand concrete things, one's original heart-mind resembles the translucent, polished jade when functioning in daily affairs. Among the desires generated by this heart-mind, not one departs from its (root) principle of coherence. Because one's heart-mind is the metaphysical corporeality, one's desires are its functioning. The metaphysical corporeality is the individual's *dao*, and the functioning is the individual's appropriate behaviour. His voice is consistent with his tone, and his physical presence, with the rules.' 胡氏曰:「聖人之教亦多術，然其要使人不失其本心而已。欲得此心者，惟志乎聖人所示之學，循其序而進焉。至於一疵不存，萬理明盡之後，則其日用之間，本心瑩然，隨所意欲，莫非至理。蓋心即體，欲即用，體即道，用即義，聲為律而身為度矣。」[55]

The preceding analysis of the two Song dynasty traditions was based on a comparative, intercultural perspective on Durkheim's theory. What stands out from the analysis are the two following common cultural presuppositions of Chinese philosophico-religious thought: the emphasis on ethical relationships, that is, tangible social life, and on the metaphysico-spiritual source of the everyday ethical interrelationships. In the Neo-Confucian quotation above, the latter are symbolically presented as sincere appropriate behaviour, voice consistent with the tone and physical presence with the rules. There is nothing remotely similar either to Durkheim's idea of sacred, sacred things or objects (see Paden's following quote) nor with the separation sacred/profane.

As stressed above, Durkheim's theory of religion is founded on completely different presuppositions wedded to his dichotomy between sacred and profane. The religion scholar William Paden, too, describes this Durkheimian paradigm of the functional sacred with no content of its own in line with Jonathan Smith's vision mentioned earlier – 'not as a religious object but as a category of world classification and ritual behavior'.[56] In the next quotation, he highlights the metaphysical neutrality of Durkheim's term, the meaning of which results from a social convention, as well as its relational character – that which is acknowledged as sacred is what is not to be profaned. We note how different this conception is from the Song dynasty metaphysico-spiritual corporeality which nourishes and grows humans' tangible ethical actions:

> The *nature* of the objects that are sacred is completely incidental to the fact *that* they are sacred *to* some group. That certain things are sacred to a culture is an accessible, visible observation of behavior; the *content* of what is sacred is a different matter and is 'infinitely varied in relation to different periods of time and different societies …' (Durkheim). … The mark of what is sacred is the inviolability that surrounds it and protects its profanization, and it could easily be shown that Durkheim built his concept of sacredness largely out of the notion of taboo. Here sacredness has no content of its own. It is purely relational. It is what is not to be profaned. As such, the term is metaphysically neutral. There is no ontological referent, nor are there dismissive rationalist insinuations or inflative romantic agendas. The sacred is whatever is *deemed* sacred by any group. Now if sacredness is a value placed on objects rather than a power that shines *through* objects because of their intrinsic, extraordinary qualities, then the difference between this aspect of the Durkheimian approach and the theological model could not be greater.[57] (italics in original)

In addition to sacredness' relational nature as stressed in the this excerpt by Paden, I might also add Durkheim's conception of the religious phenomenon as fundamentally and universally dichotomous: 'What is typical of the religious phenomenon is the fact that it always implies a bipartite division of the known and knowable universe in two genres which include everything that exists, but are radically exclusive. The sacred things are those that prohibitions protect and isolate; the profane things, those to which these prohibitions apply and which should keep away of the former.'[58] His intellectually descriptive theory of religion focuses on answering the question 'what is religion?' To sum up, Durkheim's analysis from a Chinese perspective helps us realize that he builds his explanation based on the polarity sacred-profane as found not within texts but within 'religious phenomena'. The latter embodies another Western presupposition of the meaning of the religious: its perception as concretized within observable and repeatable 'phenomena', within things of which one can take account through one's own experience. This gives them an objective, universal value. The sacred things, for Durkheim, concern religious beliefs and rites: the religious beliefs express the nature of sacred things and their relationships with each other or the profane things; the rites are rules of conduct which prescribe how the human must behave with the sacred things.[59]

This incursion into the Durkheimian space lets us see more clearly the reasons why his theory is not applicable to the Chinese context. Unlike Durkheim's religious beliefs that address the nature of what he calls 'sacred things', the Song dynasty notions of *dao* 道, original heart-mind *xin* 心, principle of coherence *li* 理 discussed above are not to be understood as definable things but as the metaphysico-spiritual corporeality source of tangible reality, of which an individual gradually becomes aware of through practice of the teaching. The latter consists simultaneously in internal ethical efforts to correct one's emotions and improve one's ethico-moral quality and in external ethical efforts to develop and maintain sincere everyday social relationships and decisions without any self-interest involved.

Equally, the Song dynasty Chan and Neo-Confucian rites are something other than merely rules of conduct which prescribe how the humans must behave with things invested as sacred, as on Durkheim's account. I suggest that in the context of Song dynasty culture that focuses on the ethical dimension of life at all levels (spiritual, metaphysical and social), the rites broadly designate the ethical, ritualized interactions in society.[60] In Qisong's Chan thought this notion refers to the precepts *jie* 戒. In his *Encomium of the Platform Sutra*, the scholar-monk depicts the 'accomplished' precepts as no-form precepts (無相戒，戒之最也), prescribing the performance of good deeds, free of attachments to personal interests, expectations and opinions: 'In order to cultivate good deeds and abandon evil ones, the best way is to focus on the no-form precepts [free of all forms of influences and self-serving concerns]' (生善滅惡，莫至乎無相戒).[61] In *Encomium* (*Tanjing zan*), Qisong suggests an original interpretation of no-form (mark or distinctive sign, *wu xiang* 無相). The latter strongly embeds the idea of formlessness in everyday life and practice. In other words, his connotation emphasizes the non-duality of perception: nothingness is tangible daily reality (i.e. the world of dharmas (*fa* 法), physical and mental forms, affairs and phenomena), and, conversely, tangible daily reality is nothingness (i.e. one's inner, spiritual depth at which one is able to experience one's interrelatedness with all sentient beings). 'The essential aspect of no-form,' Qisong emphasizes, 'is what is called the embodiment of the [Buddhist] law' (無相之體，法身之謂也).[62] That is to say, the experience of nothingness serves, in his view, precisely to accomplish the concrete Mahayana ideal of Bodhisattva practice within the community (he focuses on the dimension of everyday ethical interaction), as well as the Confucian ideal of maintaining a stable, harmonious society. This is his particular understanding of nothingness: focusing on no-form precepts, which means cultivating good deeds and abandoning evil ones within the framework of no-form, namely, releasing attachments to personal interests and expectations that arise from the concrete forms (domain of interest) of particular precepts. Again, the emphasis on ethics and morality is obvious.

Zhu remains faithful to the ancient Confucian idea that politics is above all a normative activity that accepts a specific worldview grounded in ordered human relationships and governing rituals (*li* 禮) as their major ordering instrument. Unlike this ancient ritual as external model, and external moral source, Zhu Xi's new perception of the ritual as instrument for the use of political leaders is much more than a normative tool. It is no longer just the set of Zhou dynasty norms but instead 'the coherence principle of heaven'. Ritual is considered the inner master of the individual, 'the concretization of the coherence principle of heaven (*li zhe, tian li zhi jie wen ye* 禮者，天理之節文也)',[63] namely, a metaphysical background to the heart-mind, a transcendent presence of heaven within every individual. Zhu's Neo-Confucian ritual is a moral standard existing simultaneously outwardly and inwardly: outwardly, not in the historical memory as in ancient Confucianism, but in nature as a higher order present within it, an intrinsic good as ethico-moral nourishing source of the universe; and inwardly, equally as a nourishing root of every individual's behaviour. Neo-Confucian ritual as ethico-moral source embodies the above-mentioned vision of order in the universe. This intrinsic good comes from heaven and is imperceptible within us. We have lost contact with it. It is through a process of cultivation that one becomes freshly aware of it in oneself and, in other things, restores contact with it and engages with it; this commitment empowers one to adopt good governance practices and re-establish human interconnections at a deep level.

For Durkheim, religion originates in collective states of mind ('états de l'âme collective') and concerns the formation of communities bound together by a common attitude towards certain sacred objects, places and persons.[64] Unlike the Song dynasty philosophico-religious practice which fully embraces the individual and collective in both dimensions, that is, metaphysico-spiritual corporeality and everyday ethical relations, Durkheim focuses on only one, the collective aspect of religion and completely disregards its inner development within the individual mind. As Jan Platvoet and Olive Freiberger highlight, Durkheim belongs to the group of scholars who hold a critical perspective on religion. Platvoet notes that they 'take a positivist-reductionist view of religion. They contend that all religions are collective delusions. The beings worshipped, or venerated, or manipulated in them do not exist, but are the symbols of causalities and relationships in the empirical realm. They hold that scientific investigation into empirical realities can rationally prove that religion is an illusion.'[65]

John Hick characterizes Durkheim's theory as a naturalistic interpretation of religion, centred on 'the power of society to mold for good or ill the minds of its members', to exercise control over the thought and behaviour of the individual, through fabricating gods or imaginary beings whom men worship:

> The theory claims that when men have the religious feeling of standing before a higher power which transcends their personal lives and impresses its will upon them as a moral imperative, they are indeed in the presence of a greater environing reality. This reality is not, however, a supernatural Being; it is the natural fact of society. The encompassing human group exercises the attributes of deity in relation

to its members, and gives rise in their minds to the idea of God, which, in effect, is thus a symbol for society.[66]

Actually, both interpretations, Platvoet's and Hick's, highlight that major Durkheimian presupposition introduced above: 'what defines the sacred, is the fact that it is added on the tangible.' In other words, unlike the Song dynasty perspective, the core and focus of the theory of religion as Western worldview are indeed the tangible.

The last important comparative examination to be made in the context of Durkheim's theory is related to the concept that lies at the very heart of his development – the sacred – but we have not seen anything comparable with Durkheim's sacred in the Song dynasty sphere. Still, is there anything to be found in the Chinese context that corresponds to or is comparable with the Western notion of sacred? In order to answer this question, let us proceed from the translation in Chinese of the term 'sacred'. The Chinese render it with the terms *shen* or *sheng* 神聖 – sacred or saint. Both terms convey the ambiance and connotations of the translation of the Western sacred in Chinese.

The second character *sheng* 聖 indicates the sage, the ethically, metaphysically and spiritually perfect one who teaches humans. The figure of the sage has been discussed above. Let us look to the first character, *shen* 神. Initially, it designates supernatural forces, the ancestors, the spirits of heaven in relation to the spirits of the earth *qi* 祇, or the spirits as different from the ghosts. Qisong imparts to it a special meaning. The notion of spirit (*lingshen* 靈神) embodies the religio-spiritual viewpoint of his thought. Elsewhere, in his essay *Yuanjiao*, he stresses the clear distinction between his Buddhist meaning of spirit as the quintessential spirit (*jingshen* 精神) of sentient beings and the ancient Confucian meaning of spirit as imperceptible spirits and ghosts (*guishen* 鬼神) (see the next quotation). This distinction also points to the focus of Buddhist teaching which, according to the Chan scholar-monk, is the cultivation of 'quintessential spirit':

> The spirit (神) means the quintessential spirit (人之 精神) of humans; this is not something concerning the spirits and ghosts, who lead people astray. That is, [Buddhism says] if the individual cultivates his quintessential spirit, then he will exhibit good behavior (謂人修其精神, 善其履行). During one's life, one receives rewards (福應); at one's death, one's spirit rises up in purity (其神清昇). When the humans do not cultivate their quintessential spirit, but practice evil and aberrant things (履行邪妄), their life is not a time to celebrate (非慶); and after death, their spirit is punished (其神受誅). When ordinary people hear this teaching, their heart is touched (其心感動); they cease doing evil things and follow good practices. Thus, the humans silently transform themselves. This type of transformation takes place over generations.[67]

In Zhu's Neo-Confucian view, *shen* 神 are the spirits. They are part of the natural movement and constitute a subtle form of the vital breath *qi* 氣: 'The ghosts and spirits are the footprints of the natural movement that generates and transforms all the realities' (鬼神者，造化之跡也).[68] Notably, para. 16 of the ancient text *Zhongyong* addresses the ghosts and spirits. In his commentary on this paragraph, Zhu explains them as a subtle, mysterious (*ling* 靈) dimension of the vital breath *qi* 氣, without form or sound. Like the metaphysical corporeality *ti* 體 of the things, they are the result of the movement of vital breath which circulates and fills in the space. This is the argument for Zhu that, exactly as in the case of metaphysical corporeality, the spirits and ghosts are everywhere as different, subtle qualities of vital breath and influence the feelings of the humans, which themselves are vital breaths of specific qualities. People are to respect them, the ghosts and spirits, and remain vigilant. The spirits are perceptible only through the humans' emotions, especially at the moment of conducting the rituals devoted to them. However, Zhu's interest is not in the spirits as such but in the people's emotions of reverence and vigilance emerging during these rituals. The Neo-Confucian thinker advocates the cultivation of such profound feelings of reverence and vigilance beyond the sphere of spirits – and of ancestors –that is the context of worship celebrations, and extend them into the sphere of everyday relations. Needless to say, these profound feelings advance harmony, order and interrelatedness.

In conclusion, we can observe that the Chinese notions of spirit(s) and sage which approximate the Western concept of sacred include the following meanings: ancestors and spirits of the heaven-nature as subtle, Neo-Confucian metaphysical or supernatural forms of the vital breath; Chan spiritual quintessence of the human which subsists from one life to another and is the substrate of the human's future karmic retributions; the pure sage endowed with the most complete moral capacity and ability to discern the fundamental causes and results, who teaches people how to practise ethical interdependence, correct themselves and, through practice, become like the sage. In addition, these significations are particular to the Chinese 'religiousness' and absent from the Durkheimian definition, which aspires to universality, of the sacred as the quality of an object of being separated, inviolable and intangible. Still, the above examination reveals that, to a certain extent, the Durkheimian sacred and its Chinese translation share a common characteristic: the reverence or profound respect that spirits and sages generate in individuals.

The most important difference is the nature of the 'theory' and its apprehension of religiousness. In the Chinese perspective, theory is focused on following a way, continuous concrete practice, in every moment of daily life. It suggests a holistic teaching aimed to strengthen the ethical human interactions emerging from the awareness of the metaphysico-spiritual interrelatedness of individuals, dispensed by enlightened teachers. Like any Western theory, the Durkheimian theory focuses on describing and explaining the notion of religion. It has intellectual interest and value but no practical, ethical guidance or transformational objectives. Paden concisely outlines the descriptive character of Durkheim's method: he first characterizes religious beliefs and practices and then shows their origin; first depicts sacredness as a phenomenon and then accounts for it in terms of collective consciousness; first points to the nature of religious experience and then to 'the reality at the bottom of the experience'.[69]

Max Weber's work of Chinese religions is the second classical Western theory addressed in this chapter. It is examined in the next section, also from a Chinese perspective. This second comparative analysis will further advance our intercultural understanding in the field of cultural assumptions that surround the term of 'religion', as well as our sensitivity towards Chinese assumptions.

3.2 Max Weber's comparative theory of religion and its presuppositions: Western Puritan ethics and Confucian ethics

The theory of religion of sociologist Max Weber merits attention in this comparative context, all the more so since, without being a sinologist, he was interested in China and published a well-known study about its religious traditions – *The Religion of China: Confucianism and Taoism*. While the main issue in Durkheim's development is social solidarity, Weber focuses on the socio-economic order. To that end, he begins with an analysis of the related communal concepts of social action and of social relationship. Given that Song dynasty thought also stresses these two dimensions of the community, Weber's interpretation deserves deeper reflection. In the following I offer the argument that even if both cultural spheres (Weber and Song dynasty thought) concentrate on these issues, their cultural presuppositions remain very different. As P. Ricoeur notes, Weber constructs a comprehensive sociology; in other words, he focuses on the acting individual and the subjective signification that the individual attaches to their actions. Two Western presuppositions that relate to the Enlightenment heritage, discussed in the introduction, can be discerned in his approach: first, the focus on the person, their actions, decisions, deliberations and significations of the world that they build for themselves; second, on the human's logical, analytical thinking and comprehension.

The latter reminds us of the Western presumption of the complete separation between culture and nature. Equally, it reflects the reluctance of Western thought to learn from nature, that is, from something whose meaning is not provided by the human. Recall, in this regard, Merleau-Ponty's clear distinction mentioned earlier: 'It is nature that has a meaning, without that meaning having been laid by the thought.'[70] Similarly, Weber is attached to the individual's meaning and comprehension, as well, and gravitates away from the organicist metaphor. As Ricoeur explains, 'For him [Weber] these organicist images have at the most a heuristic value: they allow one to identify and delineate the realities to be described; the danger is to take the description of an organic totality for an explication susceptible to substitute the interpretive comprehension: "because we do not comprehend in that way [i.e., comprehensively] the behaviour of the cells of an organism." '[71] This explanation presupposes the same Western assumption of the perception of the organic discussed earlier (see above Pascal, Merleau-Ponty, etc.): the nature/organism is an assembly of cells, it does not think, and thinking is the most important feature of the human. How is this issue addressed in the Chinese sphere? Here is how Zhu Xi and Qisong consider this question.

In the Song dynasty context, organic life is not envisaged as a (non)reasoning dimension of the reality but as the lot or destiny/direction (*ming* 命) that everyone receives from the heaven-nature. It includes one's life for which the individual is responsible and expected to care for, ethically, together with an ethico-metaphysical authentic nature or principle of coherence. The organic metaphor has a specific Chinese meaning, different than its Western counterpart. Its synonymous significations, some unusual for the Western space, are life flourishing, ethico-moral quality, high position, good fortune, reputation and longevity (see the next quotation). There is an intrinsic parallel between organic growth and ethical growth in that the model of the latter is the former (the heaven-nature). The law of organic growth is envisaged on an ethical model that one is to become aware of and to follow. Clearly, this ethico-organic interdependence does not dwell on logical reasoning (comprehension) as is the case in the Western context of the dissociation nature/culture but on the order of organic life. Most importantly, the latter is recognized as a paradigm or model of any kind of growth: not only as a model of thriving and proper biological growth but equally as a model of ethical growth. What is the source of this ethico-organic growing, and why is Western thought so resistant to this way of thinking spawned on assumptions unlike its own? This idea of interdependent growing emerges early in ancient Chinese thought (the classic *Zhongyong* and the *Book of Rites*) and is employed in Chan and Neo-Confucian perspectives by both Qisong and Zhu. It is vividly illustrated in the following quotation from the ancient *Zhongyong* 17:

> Those who possess a great ethico-moral quality are able to naturally accede to a status corresponding to their quality, emolument, reputation, and long life. Thus the heaven-nature gives birth to all things, and according to their different capacities, it takes care of each one of them in a different manner. As to the sprouts, those which can take root in the earth: the heaven-earth supports their growing. Those which bend: it lets them wither. 故大德必得其位，必得其祿，必得其名，必得其壽。故天之生物，必因其材而篤焉。故栽者培之，傾者覆之。[72]

Zhu Xi's Song dynasty commentary on this paragraph reveals the cultural assumptions from which stems the above-mentioned ethico-organic interdependent growing. He explains that 'taking care of each one' means acting in an efficient and sustainable way; 'supporting their growing' refers to the situation where the vital breath is reaching the saturation point and moistens the plant and spurs its growth (氣至而滋息為培); and 'letting them wither', when the vital breath is dispersing out of control, it wanders and disperses (氣反而游散則覆).[73] Zhu's masterful clarification provides deeper insight into the presupposition working through the interdependency between the organic and the ethical. Its cornerstone is the conception of things not as static, fixed objects to investigate objectively and analytically but as dynamic, particular instances of vital breath (*qi* 氣). One now understands why, in this vision of reality built on vital breath, the focus is first and foremost on practice – one's continuous endeavour not only to gather, concentrate and nurture sustainably one's vital breath but also to avoid its dispersing, dissolving, depleting and withering. As discussed above, the other major premise of this world vision is the ethical character of practice: the need to act ethically, to avoid harming others and to multiply good actions on their behalf, thus contributing to the harmony and growth of the entire reality – emulating the heaven-nature's nourishing and sustaining the living things formed of vital breath.

The intrinsic connection between ethical action and organic life is built on another concept – the idea of one's life, that is, destiny or lot, lifetime, as well as life mission or mandate (*ming* 命), highlighted in the same paragraph 17 of the *Zhongyong*, drawing a quote from the *Classic of Songs*:

The *Classic of Songs* reads: 'The exemplary individual is kind and joyful. His moral quality is so manifest! He governs well the people and his action is convenable for the others; his emolument, he receives it from the heaven-nature which preserves his life and protects him. Because he receives from the heaven-nature his important mission!' That is the reason why there are individuals with a great ethico-moral quality. They have received their mandate from heaven-nature. 詩曰:『嘉樂君子，憲憲令德!宜民宜人;受祿於天;保佑命之，自天申之!』故大德者必受命。[74]

Drawing on the Chan perspective of karmic causes and effects, Qisong offers a similar view of the profound interrelatedness between one's destiny, the protection of one's life (organic dimension) and one's ethical everyday action and interrelationships:

All beings have a specific nature and a specific destiny. They love life and detest death. All different categories of living beings made of blood and vital breath are like this. It is for this reason that the sage wishes to encourage life and does not wish the destruction of life. Preserving and destroying life have causes and effects. The good and bad actions produce reactions (*ganying* 感應): pursuing a good cause leads to a good effect; pursuing a bad cause leads to a bad effect. The heart-mind of the one who loves preserving life is good [the good cause of further good actions]. The heart-mind of the one who loves destroying life is bad [the bad cause of further bad actions]. How can one not be cautious about the reactions produced by good and bad actions? 物有性物有命。物好生物惡死。有血氣之屬皆然也。聖人所以欲生而不欲殺。夫生殺有因果。善惡有感應。其因善其果善。其因惡其果惡。夫好生之心善。好殺之心惡。善惡之感可不慎乎。[75]

Here the ethical interrelatedness is presented in the context of the karmic resonance between causes and effect as the spontaneous result of this resonance – the reaction (effect) which is the natural result of an action (cause). As a consequence, because all humans love life by nature, they can preserve and protect their life and others' life through performing good actions. The Chan and Neo-Confucian perspectives complement one another and underscore a specific Song dynasty presupposition: the profound ethical source of organic growth.

On the same subject, one will recall the Chinese presupposition of the identity between nature and culture, of the human as one part among the myriad other parts of nature, as endowed with the same Neo-Confucian authentic nature or original heart-mind, ethico-metaphysical principle of coherence and with the Chan Buddha-nature or original nature and heart-mind. The individual is supposed to become aware within themselves of their deep ethico-metaphysico-spiritual interrelatedness with all humans and manifest it in everyday actions. As discussed above, for this reason, the organic metaphor is profoundly present in Song dynasty Chan as well as Neo-Confucian thought. In conclusion, the Chinese organic perspective embodies the continuity between nature and culture, the prevalence of nature, that is, of life and the law of life as simultaneously ethical, metaphysical and spiritual. In other words, growth is perceived as *dao* organic as well as ethical, metaphysical and spiritual.

These remarks introduce the particular presuppositions that define the Chinese meaning of the notions developed by Weber in his comprehensive sociology. They constitute the first part (Chinese) of the intercultural interpretation developed in this section. It will serve as Chinese backdrop for highlighting the Western specificity of the Weberian theory, that is, of the cultural presuppositions on which his comprehensive sociology and theory of religion are built.

Weber's first Western assumption – the focus on the individual – is therefore very much different than the Song dynasty emphasis on interdependence, on the continuity between human beings, their inner worlds and outer environment. Ricoeur interprets his perception of the acting individual: 'By action we mean all human behaviour to which the acting individual ("l'individu agissant") attaches a subjective meaning. The action thus understood can be either exteriorized, or purely interior and subjective; it can consist in either positively intervening in a situation, or deliberately refraining to intervene, or passively acquiescing to the situation.'[76] In a word, Ricoeur interprets Weber's comprehensive sociology[77] as a methodological individualism that starts from the premise that 'the individual is charged with meaning ("porteur de sens")'.[78] One observes that, for Weber, meaningful action is ethically neutral. Clearly there is no ethical precondition to analyse one's motivations before taking action, even if they include what Weber considers as 'beliefs'. I advance that unlike this Western individualist motivation that both triggers the action and assigns 'subjective' signification to it, in Song dynasty practical thought, the motivation for taking action is not understood as forged by the individual or self in general, that is, the untrained self. The latter's motivations are usually considered to be tainted, as noted out above, by 'subjective', selfish desires, interests and emotions (Qisong and Zhu). Instead, the error-free motivations stem from the deep interdependent self, the one that constantly learns and practises correcting one's specific *dao*, inwardly and outwardly, which is attuned to one's metaphysico-spiritual corporeality, the same in everyone, and nurtures interdependence through ethical motivation and action. In this context, social action is never ethically neutral. Finally, in the case of accomplished or realized Chan or Neo-Confucian practice, that of the sage or of those whose moral quality is complete, their action is spontaneously ethical and not guided by any motivation. This reminds us of Qisong's notion of Buddhist no-form precepts examined above and announces Zhu's interpretation of the sage as comprehending everything clearly (see later: 'A scholar-official whose moral quality is complete is like the metaphysical corporeality and not like a tool: 體無不具').

If the Weberian action in general is perceived as ethically neutral and individualist, what does 'social' action mean for the German sociologist? His answer is – an action that is not only meaningful for the individual but also other-oriented ('orientée vers l'autre'): 'The action is social action insofar as, pursuant to its meaning attached by the acting individual (or acting individuals), it takes account of the behaviour of other individuals ("tient compte du comportement d'autres individus") and by this means is influenced in its unfolding.'[79] Ricoeur translates this Weberian social action as a modality of plural action ('modalité d'action plurielle').[80] On Weber's account, this modality of plural action or the agent's other-oriented action does not mean an ethical action but one which takes into account the behaviour of other agents. Its main feature is the fact that it is 'differentiated', that is, it recognizes and gives expression to differences. This other-orientation, Ricoeur clarifies, covers all kinds of coordination between social roles, the routine, the prestige, the cooperation and competition, the struggle and violence.[81] One could perceive this differentiation or other-orientation (i.e. acknowledging others roles) as a variation of the dichotomic tendency: the Western concern for categorization and classification.

Weber understands the notion of social action in the context of socio-economic order, but he is also interested in the origin of religion and the connection between the latter and the Western capitalism. If Durkheim bases his explanation of the origin of religion on what he sees as a universal need for social cohesion, Weber, in *Sociology of Religion*, starts from the premise that the origin of religion is to be found in the socio-economic order. As discussed above, to that end, he develops an interpretation of action based on the motivations and interests of the agent and of the social action rooted in differentiation. In the preceding demonstration, we comparatively examined the specificity of such Western assumptions in relation to the assumptions of Song dynasty thought. The sociologist Talcott Parsons (1902–1979) provides specific comments on the scope of Weber's broad comparative study of the relations between religious orientation and social structure:

> Weber raised a set of theoretical problems in the field of human social action of the very first order of importance. The central problem was whether men's conceptions of the cosmic universe, including those of Divinity and men's religious interest within such a conceptual framework could influence or shape their concrete actions and social relationships, particularly in the very mundane field of economic action.[82]

Even if Weber embraces the evolutionary perspective like his contemporary Durkheim, he introduces for the first time in the comparative study of religions a significant innovation, which is particularly relevant in the context of this book: he does not work on a universal theory of religion but is interested in cultural specificity, in the religious studies scholar Eric J. Sharpe's terms, treating 'each culture as an autonomous entity shaped by its own deepest traditions'.[83] Weber is interested in the world religions: Chinese religious traditions (Confucianism and Taoism), Hindu and Jewish. However, he also introduces a universalist dimension into his work – the belief in the supernatural is universal. This is something with which the Chinese sphere would probably agree in principle. With a small adjustment: 'belief', that is, faith is very much a Western notion, complementary to the faith or spiritual apprehension, assured belief that something is true, that it is a gift of God. Its major presupposition is the fact that is rooted in an epistemological attitude: knowing without doubt, therefore believing.

Unlike the Western belief, at the core of the classical Chinese philosophico-religious tradition lies not the conviction based on such an attitude but rather the ethical reverence, deep respect in a specific supernatural embedded within the natural, within oneself, which has a strong ethical functioning: *dao*, the path to follow, Chan's original heart-mind or nature, Neo-Confucian's principle of coherence or authentic nature. It can be said that this conviction does not involve an epistemological assumption but an innate responsibility that needs to be activated. This metaphysico-spiritual presence was lost because it was forgotten; without everyday practice it is usually inaccessible to humans. Accordingly, the ethical reverence is founded in an intrinsic obligation to practise, become aware of the path and follow it. Unlike the non-duality (Chan) or metaphysical fusion (Neo-Confucian) between metaphysico-spiritual corporeality and its ethical functioning which are the wellsprings of the above-mentioned reverence as responsibility, Weber regards the belief in a supernatural order as devoid of any 'transcendental goals or focus of interest for man'. Parsons's reflection clearly explains this when he specifies the major distinction between Weber and Durkheim: 'Weber's primary interest is in religion as a source of the dynamics of social change, not religion as a reinforcement of the stability of societies.'[84]

In his influential book *The Protestant Ethic and the Spirit of Capitalism*, the German social theorist demonstrates that the development of the rational bourgeois capitalism in Europe was triggered by the ascetic Protestant ethic. I agree with the sociologist of Chinese religion C. K. Yang 楊慶堃 (1911–1999) when he suggests that Weber wrote *The Religion of China; Confucianism and Taoism* to demonstrate that China failed to develop rational bourgeois capitalism owing to the absence of a particular kind of religious ethic as the needed motivating force.[85] Indeed, the German sociologist's reflections on Chinese society and religion appear to resonate with the theoretical foundations (Western) he built in the volume *Protestant Ethic*. Even if, on the one hand, Weber acknowledges cultural differences, the research objective that he pursues is again universalist: he adopts as standard of reference the religious and cultural specificity from which Western capitalism emerged; he then compares the ascetic Protestant ethic with the Confucian perspective, to illustrate the absence of specific Western features in the Chinese culture and justify its failure to follow the same economic development as the West. To that end, he focuses on the Chinese central bureaucracy and its functioning and the literati's Confucian value system based on the familial emphasis of the Chinese society. In this context, Weber also briefly examined Daoist thought. As the focus of this book is on Song dynasty thought (Chan and Neo-Confucian) and ethical interdependency as one of their major common features, it sets aside the Daoist tradition which has its own interest and is less concerned with social interrelationships.

Starting from Weber's comparative explanatory strategy, the next part addresses the Protestant and Confucian traditions and their cultural premises. I suggest that the cultural assumptions are very different in these two cultural universes and orient them in distinct directions. One could say that modernity does not show a single face, the Western capitalism of Western Europe and America, as the evolutionist perspective prevalent at the time of Weber.[86] There is now a better understanding that, quite the contrary, modernity presents itself in many culturally sensitive ways. Moreover, the sociologist's insistence at the beginning of the twentieth century on what he sees as the Western economic model – rooted in asceticism (which was supposed to curb consumption) that Weber sees as the ethos and ethical spirit of capitalism, in contrast to the inability of the Chinese culture to follow it (he wrote the *Protestant Ethic* in

1904–5, and the *Religion of China* in 1915) – is a hallmark of the Enlightenment heritage. Here again, one could recall how Gadamer deplores, at the end of the same twentieth century, the magnitude and destructiveness of the religion of global economy while urging his contemporaries to learn to think on a large scale, to learn from other cultures. As a far-reaching legacy of the Enlightenment, the religion of global economy grew out of globalized Western capitalism and was fuelled by consumerism.

As Yang highlights in his Introduction to Weber's *Religion of China*, the Confucian worldview is the German sociologist's major argument in explaining the failure of China to follow the same path towards 'modern' capitalism as the West. In the following I will explore Weber's comparative contrast between what he identifies as two dissimilar 'visions on life,' from a Western perspective: the expression of modern times – the 'ethos' or spirit of modern capitalism, which is the 'spirit of Christian ascetism'[87] and characterizes in his view 'the rational and systematic pursuit of profit through the exercise of a profession (vocation, *Beruf*),'[88] and the Chinese ethos of 'official duty and of the public weal', which handicapped the development of the rational entrepreneurial capitalism in China.[89] Thereafter, this contrast is better able to assist us not only in becoming aware of the particularity of the Chinese cultural presuppositions but also to further identify the details of the Western premises.

According to Weber, each of these two visions on life is rooted in a particular ethics. In the following, I argue that while Weber discerns the cultural presuppositions which enable the operation of the Western ethics, his understanding of the Chinese ethical foundations is less discerning. One of the major reasons for this state of affairs is the fact that his sociological work depends essentially – as he himself acknowledges[90] – on the literature of missionaries. Even so, however, his comparative work is extremely complex and erudite. His parallels built from the very core of Western culture provide extremely valuable material for the intercultural study of cultural premises.

In defining the particular Western ethics which underpins modern capitalism, Weber starts from highlighting that this ethics has been stripped of its eudaimonist or hedonist character; it is not about the pursuit of happiness but is devoted to God who alone reveals to the individual the highest virtues to cultivate (honesty, punctuality, hard work, frugality). It may be noted that this ethics is focused on the relationship between the individual and God. It is not concerned about one's behaviour in interpersonal relations when relating with others, as in the case of the Chinese ethics:

> Its *summum bonum* might be expressed this way: earn money, more and more money, while strictly refraining from the spontaneous enjoyments of daily life. To this point, money is considered as an end in itself that appears completely transcendent and absolutely irrational in relation to the individual's 'happiness' or to the 'advantage' that he might feel when possessing them. Gain became the goal that he has set to achieve; it is no more subordinate to the human as a means to satisfy their material needs.[91]

Weber highlights the transcendental source of these virtues which shape the Puritan ethics – God's commandment. Weberian Puritanism refers to the morally rigoristic and Christian ascetic lay communities. A closer look reveals several cultural presuppositions embedded in his perspective. The first one, illustrated in the paragraph above, is a leitmotif of Western thought and has been discussed above in other contexts: the separation between the perceptible reality and the transcendent God. From this stem several corollaries on which Weber focuses: the (Western) Christian ideas of religious duty, of redemption and of belief which justify and infuse into believers the certainty in redemption; the faith in a hidden and supramundane God who assigns these values as religious duties. Suffice to say that these corollaries are not related to the ethics of interpersonal relationships nor with fostering social bonding, care or compassion. In Weber's terms, 'This Puritan ethics demands this self-control' in order methodically to 'concentrate man's attitudes on God's will'.[92] Also, 'In the name of a supra-mundane God the imperatives of asceticism were issued to the monk and, in variant and softened form, to the world.'

This foundation of Western (Puritan) ethics of modern capitalism in a transcendent located beyond, apart from the mundane, which bestows on the human the religious duties of ascetism, is contrasted by Weber with what he sees as the 'organic' character of Chinese ethics. The 'organic' is equivalent for him with the absence of a higher ethical demand that transcends one's obligations and social position. This definition of the concept of organic in relation with the Western assumption of comprehension was discussed above. Equally, one finds, in Weber's contrastive articulation transcendent/organic, a variation of the Western presupposition of the disconnect between nature and culture, an illustration of the Western suspicion with regard to the organic and its perception discussed above (Pascal, Merleau-Ponty) as missing thinking, and therefore, missing ethical dimension. In this case, for Weber, the absence of the ethical dimension is concretized in what he sees as 'organically given, personal relations'. 'The religious duty toward the hidden and supra-mundane God' – Weber stresses in an effort to compare Puritan and Chinese ethics starting from the above-mentioned dichotomy transcendent/organic – 'caused the Puritan to appraise all human relations – including those naturally nearest in life – as mere means and expressions of a mentality that properly reaches beyond the organic relations of life. The religious duty of the pious Chinese, in contrast, enjoined him to develop himself within the organically given, personal relations.'[93] Weber makes reference to the five generic relationships as rooted in blood relationships, organic, therefore lacking metaphysico-spirituality: 'The Confucian ethic intentionally left people in their personal relations as naturally grown or given by relations of social super- and subordination.'[94] A different view, which includes a metaphysical perception of these five generic relationships (*lun* 倫), was given above in the context of the interpretation of the graphic etymology of the term theory *lun* 論, in Section 2.2. From this, it follows that in the Chinese perspective, any particular social relationship can be integrated into one of these interdependence-focused five relationships. As discussed in Section 2.2, this new perception of brotherhood is no longer just a familial or merely organic perspective but a Neo-Confucian ethical project, quite different than Weber's depiction as 'personal relations as naturally grown'. The Chinese organic metaphor stands here for the ethical and for uprightness. As an aside, this Song dynasty ethical transformation of the 'natural' fraternity resembles a similar transformation recorded in early Western culture, embodied in the famous biblical story of Cain and Abel (Genesis 4:9). When God asked Cain, 'Where is your brother Abel?' he replied, 'I don't know. Am I my brother's keeper?' As Levinas stresses, this time in an ethico-ontological perspective, Cain's answer is sincere; it only lacks ethics. There is only ontology in his response, because, Levinas explains, 'I am myself, he is himself, we are ontologically separate beings.'[95]

As a result, from the perspective of classical Chinese thought, society itself and its profound level at which interrelatedness occurs embodies the metaphysico-spiritual dimension. The latter is thus to be found in sincere ethical interrelations between humans, as its nourishing soil. In Weber's view, there is no metaphysico-spiritual aside from the other-worldly Creator, the one who gives orders to his creatures borne through his creative love. In the following quotation, Weber uses Western presuppositions to explain why, in his view, unlike Puritan ethics, the Confucian tradition lacks a God-controlled ethics – because it focuses on merely human, that is, 'creatural' relationships:

> Confucianism hallowed alone these human obligations of piety created by inter-human relations, such as prince and servant, higher and lower official, father and son, brother and brother, teacher and pupil, friend and friend. Puritan ethic, however, rather suspected these purely personal relationships as pertaining to the creatural; but Puritanism, of course, did allow for their existence and ethically controlled them so far as they were not against God. The relation to God had precedence in all circumstances.[96]

Note that their asceticism is another major Weberian notion that embodies the Western cultural presupposition of the separation between nature and culture. This practice constitutes a method of rational behaviour of the human detached from the state of nature: 'Aiming to overcome the *status naturae*, to lead the human out of the power of instincts, to liberate the individual of his dependency on the world and on nature, in order to subordinate him to the supremacy of premeditated willingness and to subject his actions to a permanent control and to a careful consideration of their ethical scope.'[97]

It is evident that Weber's transcultural comparison is anchored in the Western Christian presuppositions and illustrates the very type of appreciation that the New Contemporary Confucians denounce, according to which, let us repeat, 'Chinese people only attach importance to everyday-life ethics and morality and lack a religious transcendent feeling. Chinese ethical and moral ideals were considered merely to be concerned with regulating people's external behavior while neglecting the internal dimension of spiritual life. This misunderstanding can be traced back to Hegel's *Lectures on the History of Philosophy*.'[98] This section offers arguments that such misconceptions arise from the Western disassociations nature/culture and tangible/transcendent (mundane/supramundane), organic/thinking and so on, when applied in the attempt to appreciate a culturally different way of thinking.

The analysis given above of the graphic etymology of the two graphs of *lun* – as theory (written 論) and as human relationships (written 倫) – is founded on the Chinese perception of the continuity and inseparability between nature and culture and elicits the presence and functioning of a metaphysico-spiritual corporeality within the real as metaphysico-spiritual source and nourishment of both organic life and social ethics. It appears to us that this kind of non-Western unity or non-duality is something that Western thinking would do well to 'learn from' the Chinese culture (consistent with the meaning of that term in Gadamer's thought, discussed in the introduction).

Another complementary comparison that flows from this first one is Weber's perception of the Puritan ethic as 'rejecting or fleeing this world' to become virtuous (rationally ascetic) in relation to the Chinese ethics he describes as promoting 'adjustment to the world'.[99] If the Chinese adjustment means, in his view, a naïve, 'optimistic conception of cosmic harmony that has gradually evolved from the primitive belief in spirits',[100] the rejection of the world seen as 'a vessel of sin' by ascetic Christianism is nothing less than 'the truly endless task of ethically and rationally subduing and mastering the given world, i.e., rational, objective "progress".[101] Unlike the Confucian – Weber states while adopting that positive and forward-looking tone the Western culture has kept since Enlightenment times about 'rationally transforming and mastering the world' – 'the true Christian, the other-worldly asceticist, wished to be nothing more than a tool of his God; in this he sought his dignity. Since this is what he wished to be he was a useful instrument for rationally transforming and mastering the world'.[102] I note as an aside that today, almost a century after the publication of Weber's work, we know the actual result of this unbridled pursuit of Western domination of nature highlighted by Gadamer, as well as his view on how we as humanity could correct this heritage.

Weber commends the transcendent power of the 'hero-God' and 'lord creator', 'Yahwe who was and remained first of all a God of the extraordinary, that is, of the destiny of his people in war.' He speaks to humans, calls them for obedience with his wrath ('the most important attribute of Yahwe') and they listen to his word.[103] These depictions illustrate the presence of other Western presuppositions which are implicitly present in his text: emphasis on the thought (human or divine), on the power of the spoken word, on the transcendence manifested as the living logos, divine thought; dislike of written communication and appreciation of spoken conversation as the most effective means to ensure effective bridging of the gap between the mundane and the supramundane.

Let us return to the idea that was suggested in the introduction – the different functioning (written and spoken) of the languages (alphabetical language and Chinese language) and the way in which this specificity plays a key role in structuring specific thinking as well as cultural assumptions. These Western assumptions concerning the difference and separation between nature and culture, mundane and supramundane, spoken and written word, all emerge from the Western interest in separation, distinction and connection, in analysing through separation of elements and contrast. In his interpretation of Plato's philosophical explanations using the letters of the alphabet, of the meaning of writing in the Platonic dialogues and of the living spoken world as a psychic graph, Derrida identifies the origin of this Western interest and predisposition for separation and connection of elements and their difference in the nature of the alphabetical language: 'If the voice names, it is through the difference and relationship which insert themselves between *stoikheia*, the elements or the letters ('les éléments ou les lettres') (grammata). The same word (*stoikheia*) designates the elements and the letters.'[104]

The Chinese graphs emanate from the special type of Chinese divination as focusing on following the spontaneously ethical course of nature. Their perspective is completely different: no letters, no separation between elements, but cohesive and unbreakable graphs which are dynamic and incorporated in the written image, as discussed above, the footprints of the naturally ethical order, that is, the so-called metaphysico-spiritual corporeality and its concrete functioning – the presence within it of the early signs, imperceptible harbingers (*ji* 幾, see Section 2.2) of the unfolding of events. These signs incorporated within the graphs are of two types: those indicating a flourishing unfolding of the events, as natural outgrowth of ethical actions which follow the natural order, and those implying a declining unfolding of the situations as natural outgrowth of unethical actions which work against the natural order.

As for the metaphysico-spiritual corporeality of the naturally ethical order, this is the profound source from which emerge all tangible actions and relationships of the reality: a subtle level that nourishes everything, a metaphysico-spiritual omnipresent environment, which embraces everything. It embodies the transcendent level, background or condition that vivifies the ordinary, visible reality. Under its influence, the natural order or course of events is spontaneously ethical. Because humans are affected by their exchanges with their external reality, they develop egocentric, self-interested emotions, impulses and inclinations; lose contact with their metaphysico-spiritual background; and thus are deprived of their natural ability to act or react in a spontaneously ethical way. The Song dynasty teachings train individuals to re-establish contact with their metaphysico-spiritual corporeality. The latter is only an approximate description of a sense of transcendent/perceptible continuity, something that Weber did not envision, as he built his analysis starting from a positive appreciation of such Western presuppositions as the supramundane, personal creator who speaks to man; the God of the extraordinary. It bears repeating that, as Derrida demonstrates in his *La pharmacie de Platon*,[105] such distinctive marks of the coherence of Western thought arise from the structure and the functioning of the alphabetical language.

It is hoped that these preliminaries will enable the reader to better grasp Weber's comparative parallel between the Western ethos (ethics) of rejecting and dominating the world and the Chinese ethos (ethics) of what he calls 'adjusting to the world'. The above investigation of the their cultural premises taught us that the meanings of the word 'ethics' are different in the two contexts. While for Weber ethical analysis is possible only when it is objective, that is, detached from the state of nature and juxtaposed with a transcendent God, the ethical in Song dynasty thought is to be found within the original state of nature, that is, when re-establishing contact with the deepest level of oneself, the omnipresent ocean/environment of metaphysico-spiritual corporeality within which one, others and the whole of nature are profoundly interconnected.

Interconnectedness means, of course, focusing on peace, harmony, order and not war. Starting from the Western perspective, Weber explains this Chinese preference for peace and impersonal order as a direct result of the absence of spiritual and of a 'salvation religion': 'Tranquility and internal order could best be guaranteed by a power which, impersonal in nature, was specifically above mundane affairs. Such a power had to steer clear of passion, above all, "wrath" – the most important attribute of Yahwe.'[106] And also: 'Confucian reason was essentially pacifist in nature. ... But the ethic remained pacifist, inner-worldly, and solely oriented to the fear of the spirits.'[107]

The Weberian appreciation of the Chinese written language is also established according to the above-mentioned Platonic criteria – priority given to the spoken word; high value assigned to the rationality of the alphabetical form. Weber also shares something that represents the common Western view of his epoch (the sinologist Marcel Granet, his contemporary, takes a similar look; see the introduction): the perception of the Chinese script as pictographic and lacking rational form:

> The literary character [of the Chinese higher education], that is, its written character, was pushed to extremes. In part, this appears to have been a result of the peculiarity of the Chinese script and of the literary art which grew out of it. ... As the script retained its pictorial character and was not rationalized into an alphabetical form, such as the trading peoples of the Mediterranean created, the literary product was addressed at once to both the eyes and the ears, and essentially more to the former. Any 'reading aloud' of the classic books was in itself a translation from the pictorial script into the (unwritten) word.[108]

In this quotation, Weber argues, using one of the Western criteria highlighted above, that the Chinese language is devoid of the analytic spirit. It is understandable that his analysis is founded on the presumption of the disconnection nature/culture and regards reasoning as the process of first separating an issue into parts so as to allow for their reassembly later in the undertaking of defining. One realizes why the Chinese non-alphabetical written language – when evaluated using only this standard of reasoning and disregarding its divinatory roots and the assumption of the deep continuity nature/culture – appears to Weber to be 'stuck in the pictorial and descriptive'.[109] In that post-Enlightenment era, like his contemporaries, Weber builds a Western-centred comparison. This leads him to infer that Chinese thought lacks logical structure: 'The very concept of logic remained absolutely alien to Chinese philosophy, which was bound to script, was not dialectical, and remained oriented to purely practical problems as well as to the status interests of the patrimonial bureaucracy.'[110]

As seen from this comparative study of cultural assumptions, the logical structure of Chinese thought is not a logic of analytical separation but one of organic continuity which preserves the fusion tangible/intangible, ethical/metaphysico-spiritual and so on. This logic follows directly from the specific nature and functioning of Chinese graphs. Weber's clear perception of Chinese philosophy's emphasis on practice is worthy of mention. Needless to say, back then, the time was not yet ripe for an observation of China's own cultural premises, for understanding its own metaphysico-spiritual and coherence of thought. It is worth reiterating that, as will be further detailed in the next part, the latter is non-dialectal. Unlike the Western logic, the hallmark of which is abstract reasoning, Chinese logic is focused on everyday ethical interconnectedness as stemming organically from the all-encompassing metaphysico-spiritual corporeality. On the flip side, all these particularities appear to be paradoxical in the eyes of the dichotomous Western thought.

Additionally, precisely as Weber notes, Confucianism embodies an 'inner-worldly morality of laymen'.¹¹¹ Nonetheless, this inner-worldly morality is rooted in a metaphysical nourishing substrate or environment. As argued above, the profound level of the world is metaphysical in Neo-Confucianism – Mou Zongsan calls it a moral metaphysics: the organic and ethical growths are interdependent and rooted in a metaphysical and omnipresent source, intrinsically ethico-organic, the same for all humans and their activities. As discussed above, its multiple features are the principle of coherence bestowed by the heaven-nature, the original heart-mind and the complete moral quality of the heart-mind. Therefore, ideally, the real Song dynasty 'inner-worldly morality', in Weber's terms, is complete and effectively functional only when the individuals become aware of their metaphysical nourishing substrate and practically, constantly cultivate it within themselves as well as through their actions. Accordingly, as Weber notes in the same paragraph above, 'Confucianism meant adjustment to the world, to its orders and conventions.' However, let us not forget that in mature Confucianism (Song dynasty), the core training that makes possible this 'adjustment' is gaining awareness of the metaphysical ethico-organic source/environment. In Zhu's words, it means becoming aware that the ritual (*li* 禮) (what Weber defines as 'orders and conventions') is nothing less than 'the concretization of the coherence principle of heaven' (禮者, 天理之節文也),¹¹² namely, a metaphysical background to the heart-mind, a transcendent and nourishing presence of heaven within every individual and transcendent environment within which dwells the world of everyday social affairs.¹¹³

The German theorist concludes that in Confucianism, 'the central force of a salvation religion conducive to a methodical way of life was non-existent.'¹¹⁴ After the previous exploration of the various differences between Chinese and Western cultural assumptions, I suggest that, even if a 'salvation' dimension understood in Western terms as deliverance from sin and its harmful consequences – something arising out of the dissociation between this world and another – is absent in mature Confucianism, such a feature is not the only one able to provide the 'central force' necessary to pursue a 'methodical way of life', as Weber suggests. The Song dynasty constantly spoke to the duty of the exemplary individual to inwardly disclose the metaphysical coherence principle of heaven by permanently and vigilantly identifying and removing self-centred desires and emotions. In this way he is not drawn into partiality and is not short-sighted; personal desires do not divert him from the natural order, the interdependent *dao* (故無人欲之私).¹¹⁵ The practice enables him to become a sage, that is, one who is able to assist, to support the regulatory movement of the heaven-earth, and form with it a three-layered unit (謂與天地並立為 三也).¹¹⁶

I offer that this Neo-Confucian ideal of the sage who has the capacity to effectively assist the regulatory ethical movement of heaven-nature could be considered as analogous with the Western salvation ideal. In this single three-layered unit (heaven, earth, sage), the role of the perfected individual is to outwardly cultivate the 'concretization of the coherence principle of heaven' through ordered, harmonious, interdependent, that is, ritual relationships in everyday sociopolitical actions and affairs. If ethically flawless, the latter follow the natural order. Thus, the sage ruler constantly makes society grow and flourish as the heaven-earth permanently makes natural, organic reality grow and flourish. I argue that this constant practice – aiming to assist the natural order of harmonizing – provides the exemplary individual with the metaphysico-religious strength to carry out this task as a way of life not controlled by a supramundane God, one that is not 'according to God's commandment and proceeding from a God-fearing attitude'[117] but inwardly and outwardly sourced by the metaphysico-spiritual habitat. Again, this task entails neither confronting the world nor adjusting to the tangible reality but rather the practice of inwardly becoming aware of this metaphysical source and habitat of the entire nature and following its harmonizing and self-regulating ethical dynamic. Weber's next affirmations are also rooted in the Western presupposition of the separation mundane/transcendent and help us to see even more clearly the particularity of the Chinese cultural premises that this study uncovers and comparatively interprets. Without any doubt, extensive works like Weber's make this development possible. The sociologist observes: 'Not reaching beyond this world, the [Chinese] individual necessarily lacked an autonomous counterweight in confronting this world. … The contrast between this socio-ethical position and the whole religious ethic of the Occident was unbridgeable.'[118] And equally:

> The relentlessly and religiously systematized utilitarianism peculiar to rational asceticism, to live 'in' the world and yet not be 'of' it, has helped to produce superior rational aptitudes and therewith the spirit of the vocational man which, in the last analysis, was denied to Confucianism. That is to say, the Confucian way of life was rational but was determined, unlike Puritanism, from without rather than from within.[119]

Last but not least, of note is the fact that the last quotation introduces the idea of 'vocational man' and another major Weberian comparative dichotomy that deserves our attention: the contrast between what the German sociologist describes as 'the vocational concept of ascetic Protestantism' and 'the Confucian ideal of universality or self-perfection.'[120] Concerning the first, he stresses that 'the capitalist system needs the dedication to the vocation [*Beruf*] to earn money.'[121] His notion of vocation, profession or occupation has a special religious dimension, as well as a supramundane orientation, the one given by Luther and ascetic Protestantism. Obviously, this understanding is built into Weber's theory of the spirit of modern capitalism as rational and systematic pursuit of profit through the exercise of a profession: 'For Luther, as we have seen, the integration of individuals in social classes and professions arising from the historical, objective order have become the direct emanation of the divine will. *Persevering* in one's situation, and within the limits assigned by God, was therefore one's religious duty.'[122] (italic in original).

Accordingly, that one's occupation was perceived as a direct emanation of the divine justified why, Weber explicates, 'the typical Puritan earned plenty, spent little and reinvested his income as capital in rational capitalist enterprise out of an ascetic compulsion to save.'[123] I again note, the imperative of asceticism is understood as the commandment of a supramundane God. By comparison, in Weber's view, China didn't develop a rational, modern capitalism because, unlike the Western ascetic ethics based on other-worldly, divine commands, the ethics of what he calls Confucian rationalism was concerned with rational adjustment to the world and cultivated not specialization but the ideal of universality. To support this claim, he offers the following argument:

> The decisive factor was that the 'cultured man' (gentleman [*junzi* 君子]) was 'not a tool'; that is, in his adjustment to the world and in his self-perfection he was an end unto himself, not a means for any functional end. This core of Confucian ethics rejected professional specialization, modern expert bureaucracy, and special training; above all, it rejected training in economics for the pursuit of profit.[124]

Let us compare Weber's Western interpretation of this famous elliptical and compact ancient Confucian phrase with its classical Song dynasty exegesis by Zhu Xi. In what follows, we take a closer look at his commentary of this idea first given in Confucius' *Analects* 2:12 – 'The exemplary man is not a utensil (君子不器).' Zhu interprets this paragraph:

> Each utensil corresponds to its particular use; therefore, it cannot be equivalent to another. A scholar-official whose ethico-moral quality is complete is like the metaphysical corporeality and not like a tool. Its role (functioning) is suitable for all usages, it does not have only one particular ability, only one particular skill. 器者，各適其用而不能相通。成德之士，體無不具，故用無不周，非特為一才一藝而已。[125]

This paragraph makes reference to the two concepts examined above, which identify two levels of the reality, of all things: the ethico-metaphysical corporeality (*ti* 體), the deep level of the principle of coherence of heaven, the same in everything and to be found everywhere, which nourishes the specific functioning or the utility (*ju* 具) of that reality. This principle of coherence of heaven is one, metaphysical, and ensures every particular ethical functioning, that is, every distinct sociopolitical action or relationship. In this passage, Zhu compares the exemplary man who manages to make his moral quality complete through constant practice – in other words, the sage – with this ethico-metaphysical corporeality from which emerge all individual *dao*s, all specific ethical unfoldings of each and every event. Again, in this way the Neo-Confucian scholar emphasizes the ethical dimension present in each aspect of reality, metaphysical or tangible: only the ideal exemplary individual whose ethico-moral quality is complete or completely fulfilled, and flawless, can be viewed as the metaphysical principle of coherence of society, as the *dao* of heaven, that which holds everything together at a deeper level. The ethical, relational dimension is already embedded in this metaphor.

Each individual or reality embodies two aspects – the unique deeper level or principle of coherence (*li* 理) or *dao* 道 and a specific perceptible level, the mode of functioning of the principle, that is, vital breath (*qi* 氣) or tool (*qi* 器). This reminds us of Weber's earlier argument – the cultured man is not a tool – which suggests propensity for a universalist education, the very reason why he lacks professional specialization. In the translated explication above, Zhu highlights a completely different interpretation of this metaphor. 'The tool' suggests the level of the vital breath, of tangible functioning.

The so-called ethico-metaphysical corporeality, that is, *dao*, is not a tool, but another level present in things and in reality – the metaphysical. In Zhu's view, the metaphor interpreted by Weber as refusal of professional specialization does not emphasize a universalist education lacking professional vocations but the existence in everything and everywhere of the metaphysical presence, accessible to anyone (community leader, scholar-official) through education. And he highlights the holistic unity of these two levels of one reality, their hierarchical interdependency:

> Within the heaven-earth, there is the principle of coherence and the vital breath. The principle of coherence is the *dao* from beyond perceptible appearance, i.e., the root that gives birth to things. Vital breath is the tool from within perceptible appearance, i.e., the utility that gives birth to things. Therefore, the birth of humans and things necessarily relies on the principle of coherence; then, authentic nature occurs. The latter necessarily relies on vital breath; and then, perceptible appearance occurs. Even though the authentic nature and the perceptible appearance of a thing are not 'outside' one another but form a single unity, the distinction between its *dao* and its tool quality is very clear. One cannot confuse them. 天地之間，有理有氣。理也者，形而上之道也，生物之本也;氣也者，形而下之器也，生物之具也。是以人物之生，必稟此理，然後有性; 必稟此氣，然後有形。其性其形，雖不外乎一身，然其道器之間分際甚明，不可亂也。[126]

Weber does not elaborate on the meaning of the notion of universality that for him describes the distinctive character of the Confucian education. On the one hand, from the next paragraph, it is patently clear that he does not refer to the profound ethico-metaphysical level of all realities and of the environment highlighted by Zhu. On the other hand, the Song dynasty interpretation of 'the exemplary individual is not a utensil' clearly does not refer to the 'universalist' meaning proposed by Weber, 'he was a means in himself' (see the following paragraph). In addition, as discussed earlier in this chapter, the Neo-Confucian practice encapsulated in the phrase 'the exemplary individual is not a utensil' is not inquiry aimed at reaching an ideal status but rather a concrete education aimed at discovering the profoundly ethico-metaphysical present inside (emotions/feelings) and outside (daily relationships) and making use of it in every situation. Another difficulty in this Weberian parallel is the difference between two figures. Zhu outlines a Neo-Confucian ethical ideal – the sage, an ethical model the exemplary individuals aim to realize. Like any ideal, this model is difficult to realize in the real world; it is certainly as difficult to achieve as the ascetic Protestant disposition. Weber refers rather to an economic, professional ideal onto which he inserts a supramundane ethical calling. One might equate the figure of the Confucian sage with the subtle interrelatedness of everything, a deep stage of reality, the inherent ethical thread that subtly connects one to another. Unlike this sage, as a transcendent, the Western personal god is an external presence that comes and goes. The deep stage of reality is something that is always there, a corporeality, a nourishing soil inside, a nourishing environment outside. Starting from the West's Platonic presuppositions as standard reference, Weber explains the Confucian education:

> The cultured man, however, strives for that universality which in the Confucian sense education alone provides and which the office precisely requires. This view characterizes the absence of rational specialization in the official functions of the patrimonial state.
>
> The fundamental assertion, 'a cultured man is not a tool' meant that he was an end in himself and not just a means for a specified useful purpose. The all-round educated Confucian 'gentleman' ... supported a status ideal of cultivation that was directly opposed to the socially oriented Platonic ideal. ... The Platonic ideal was established on the soil of the polis and proceeded from the conviction that man can attain fulfillment by being good at only one task. There was even stronger tension between the Confucian ideal and the vocational concept of ascetic Protestantism.[127]

In elaborating on this stronger tension, and distinguishing even more clearly the Protestant idea of vocation, that is, of being an instrument for 'rationally transforming and mastering the world' from what he sees as a Confucian 'rational adjustment to the world', as Confucian 'gentility', Weber further characterizes the exemplary man as having an 'aesthetic value': 'Nothing conflicted more with the Confucian ideal of gentility than the idea of a "vocation". The "princely" man was an aesthetic value; he was not a tool of a god.'[128]

Note in the above citation that Weber proposes as a comparative tool for understanding and defining the nature of the Confucian order in contrast with the Western transcendent order: an aesthetic perspective. To this day, this aesthetic approach continues to be a Western analytic tool for comparatively assessing the specificity of Confucian thought. A similar aesthetical perspective can be found in the 1987 study of the authors Hall and Ames: 'The realization of interpersonal and social harmony is the effect of yielding to appropriate models of aesthetic orderedness as constituted by rituals, language, and music. These communicative media provide the primary tools of the sage in his role as master of communication. The functions of rituals, language, and music are all of a kind. Each serves to promote aesthetic order.'[129] It is by now abundantly clear that the intention of this study is to demonstrate, using the tools of philosophical translation, graphic etymology and intercultural interpretation of cultural presumptions, that the major concern of the Chinese philosophico-religious thought lies in ethical practice: its metaphysico-spiritual source and social functioning.

To conclude this section dedicated to Weber's comparative analysis, I draw the reader's attention to a fundamental tension present in his theory of the religious ethic of the Occident and to the limitations of his explanatory connection between asceticism and material means: the existence of an irreconcilable conflict between the individual interests on which are built the rational capitalist work ethic and its professional standards and the communal well-being concerned with interpersonal relations and based on ethical values as kindness, sharing and caring. The latter does not give priority to economic pursuits but cultivate, as the Song dynasty Chan monk Qisong stresses (see Section 1.2), the capacity to become good, to do good actions rooted in a spiritual substratum. Let us reflect further on the nature and source of this tension.

'The Puritan ethic', Weber points out, 'amounts to an objectification of man's duties as a creature of God.'[130] It emphasizes the individual ethical code and professional standards. In addition, one of the indispensable ethical qualities of the modern capitalist entrepreneur is the 'radical concentration on God-ordained purposes'.[131] Weber affirms that the virtues instilled by God through this religious relation are honesty, punctuality, hard work and frugality; hence, the Protestant asceticism 'opposes with great effectiveness to spontaneous enjoyment of riches and dampens consumption, notably of luxury goods.'[132] Understandably, these attributes have to do with the value of work and the work ethic, much less with human exchanges. Moreover, as mentioned above, the central mission of modern entrepreneurial capitalism, perceived as attitude towards life, is 'the rational and systematic pursuit of profit through the exercise of a profession'.[133]

As Gadamer acknowledges (see the introduction), the capitalism inspired by Puritanism transformed itself into the actual 'religion of the global economy'.[134] Without doubt, this is due to the emphasis on economic 'profit' as the spirit of modern capitalism, which progressively surpassed and replaced the initial religiously valuable conduct, religious duty and ascetic ideal. Inevitably, the salvation religion as central force of the Western capitalist way of life has long been overshadowed by merely economic values and priorities engendered by the specific laws of competition and profit, supply and demand, which determine the market mechanism of all capitalist operations. This inescapable conflict between each individual and their neighbour introduced by the functioning of the market, that is, the source of the implicit tension one detects in Weberian theory, is explained by Max Weber's contemporary, the economist Karl Polanyi (1886–1964) using the notion of 'market price':

> If you refuse yourself to spend your money on luxury goods, you will cause a certain number of persons to lose their jobs; if you refuse yourself to save money, you will cause the same effect on others. As long as you are following market rules, by purchasing at the lowest market price and by reselling your merchandise, whatever this may be, for as much as possible, you are relatively sheltered. The harm done to your fellow men in order to support your own interest are therefore inevitable. Consequently, the more an individual rejects the idea to be of useful to others, the more he will be able to reduce effectively his own share of responsibility for the harm made to the others.[135]

In other words, the market mechanism effectively delimits the moral and ethical development of the individual. The next reflection of Polanyi strongly resonates with main theme of the Chan scholar-monk Qisong's vision of the Song dynasty teachings as aiming to transform individuals, to develop their moral quality to be kind to others: 'In such a system', Polanyi warns, 'human beings are not permitted to be good, regardless of their desire to be.'[136]

Both, the comparison that Weber builds in order to present evidence as to why the Chinese didn't develop a modern capitalism like the West and Polanyi's considerations, give us an opportunity to ask the converse question: why did the Western world fail to profoundly address the importance of the interrelatedness among humans or consistently develop a communitarian perspective on reality? The answer to this quest is to be revealed by comparative examination of the differences between the cultural presuppositions of Protestant and Confucian ethics. It is noteworthy that Weber's and Durkheim's elaborate explanations constitute a salient foundational work that has made subsequent studies, like the present one, which relies on it, possible.

As mentioned, Gadamer suggests learning from other cultures to think on a large scale in order to correct some side effect of the legacy inherited from the Enlightenment. In the following paragraph, Polanyi mentions another precise dimension of this heritage – the preference to disarticulate in order to examine and further understand, that we now need to rectify; remember also the above-mentioned Derrida's similar perspective about the nature and functioning of the letters – reintegrating the various dimensions of society, that is, economic, political, religious and so on:

> In capitalist society, the economic system has been developed separately from the rest of society. The reabsorption of this system within society is the next step towards the completion of community within society. The liberalism disintegrated society, by separating the economic, political, 'religious,' etc. spheres: to integrate them afresh into a whole is the task facing people of our times. This puts pressure on us to accomplish the successive task: changing the economic system.[137]

Learning from other cultures and philosophico-religious ways of thinking could be precisely the trigger which enables our community to realize the necessity of this rectification. After discussing from a Chinese perspective the Western foundations of Durkheim's and Weber's classical theories of religion, Chapter 2 focuses on several contemporary theories of Western discipline of religious studies: John Hick's, Ninian Smart's and Jonathan Z. Smith's.

2

Contemporary theories of Western religious studies and philosophy of religion (John Hick, Ninian Smart, Jonathan Z. Smith): An analysis of their presuppositions from a Chinese perspective

1 Introduction

This book tackles the notion of religion gradually and interculturally in several connected domains: Western philosophy of religion and religious studies, sinology and Chinese philosophy. Part 1 examines classical and contemporary Western theories of philosophy of religion and religious studies. Parts 2 and 3 address the specific assumptions of the Song dynasty philosophico-religious traditions. Based on the analyses developed in the previous parts, Part 3 offers a new interpretive theory tailored according to these Chinese presuppositions. Part 4 of this book is dedicated to the theories of religion belonging to the Western domain of sinology and Chinese philosophy. In this way, it is 'testing' in this Chinese culture–focused context the new interpretive theory formulated in Part 3. Needless to say, 'religion' is one of the many subjects considered in the academic sphere of sinology which, roughly speaking, focuses primarily on Chinese studies, in particular, on language. But before getting into that, let us first approach the concept of religion on its home ground: the field of religious studies, classically called *Religionswissenschaft*, dedicated to the scientific study of religions.

This section addresses several Western contemporary theories: John Hick's, Ninian Smart's and Jonathan Z. Smith's. It uncovers their cultural presuppositions from a Chinese point of view. After the previous consideration of the classical theories of Durkheim and Weber continues the analysis of the Western theories of religion. Its objective is to argue a number of issues: the attempt to deliver a cross-culturally unified (universal) theory of religion is a Western ideal, directly inherited from the Age of Enlightenment, impossible to realize in practice because such a construction inevitably would be indifferent to other cultures' specificities. Instead of looking for such a universalizing theory which, in a sense, would amount to organizing this whole academic area around the biblical myth of the Tower of Babel (see later), a short-term task for the scholars in religious studies to deal with would be to bring to light the Western presuppositions systematically embedded in the research already completed in this field. This task would be an exercise in decentring and challenging these assumptions, an effort of opening the discipline to different cultures to make room for cultural diversity in the initially Western academic sphere of religious studies and philosophy. This step would amount to recognizing the cultural diversity of humankind not as a deficiency resulting from the loss of an initial primal unity but as an original richness we are called upon to embrace. As a result, the construction of not all-encompassing theories but rather culturally perceptive theories would be an effective way to understand why it is valuable to learn from other cultures, from their different perceptions of the religious, as Gadamer recommended.

It is in this same perspective that the Chapter 1 addressed Émile Durkheim's and Max Weber's classical interpretations. Contemporary research works in the field emerge from prior theories like these two and further explore the issues identified by the earlier works. Undeniably, they comprise the same Western assumptions as the earlier studies; however, as will be shown below, this time they are expressed in new forms and from different points of view within the academic field of religious studies.

The objective of this comparative approach is not to offer a new comprehensive synthesis of all that has been written recently about religion but to present a sample of currently used modes of the Western premises, now within the framework of several contemporary theories. In this chapter I will mainly concentrate on John Hick's (1922–2012), Ninian Smart's (1927–2001) and Jonathan Z. Smith's (1938–2017) contributions to this area. Another goal is by connecting Chapter 1 with this one, to help raise awareness of some difficulties that occur when applying Western general theories to Chinese philosophico-religious thought. I emphasize that all the earlier work done in the sphere of religious studies has been helpful because it provides a basis for the emergence of new interpretive and comparative studies on specific topics, like this one: 'religions and their cultural presuppositions'. Needless to say, these previous works and the analysis of their embedded premises and values make it possible to carry out further inquiries that develop interculturally comparative tools and promote as well as advance interculturalism in multiple ways: philosophico-religiously, sociopolitically and so on. It is with this goal in mind that the present part explores these theories of religious studies by attempting to uncover their cultural assertions and differences vis-à-vis the presuppositions of the Chinese thought investigated earlier, in the previous chapters and also in the next part. To repeat, for the reasons set out in the introduction, I adopt Song dynasty philosophico-religious thought as the main reference for the Chinese area. This pattern of thought embodies the subtle mutual enrichment and alchemy between Chan Buddhist and Neo-Confucian traditions that characterized that period. Such implicit and explicit exchanges have become a hallmark of the particular nature and cultural assumptions of the so-called classical Chinese 'religions' and remain so today.

2 The discipline of religious studies and its cultural presuppositions

The religious studies scholar Joseph Kitagawa (1915–1992) recalls that the label *Religionswissenschaft* was first used in 1867 by Max Müller (1823–1900), one of the founders of religious studies and Indian studies, and today it refers to the discipline of the history of religions. The Japanese American scholar stresses especially its indefinite character: 'The apparent ambiguity of the nature of the discipline of the history of religions is reflected in the diversity of names by which it has come to be known, such as comparative religion, phenomenology of religion, science of religions, and history of religions. All these terms, with minor differences, refer to a general body of knowledge known originally as *Allgemeine Religionswissenschaft*.'[1]

I would suggest that this difficulty in defining the field emerges from the concept of religion/religions itself and its Western presuppositions combined with the attempt to apply it to other cultural realities, that is, to weave culturally different meanings of this notion together. What that means from the point of view of this academic field is to scientifically integrate them into a Western theory, that is a 'family', worthy of its Enlightenment essential legacy. I am here echoing Kitagawa's perception of the initial approach of this endeavour by one of the prominent founders of this discipline:

> Like the Enlightenment thinkers, he [Max Müller] was concerned with *religio naturalis*, or the original natural religion of reason, and assumed that 'truth' was to be found in the most universal essence of religion and not in its particular manifestations. The process of differentiation of the original truth into diverse religions was seen in much the same way as the Old testament described the origin of different languages in the legend of the Tower of Babel.[2]

One may observe that, when transposed by the philologist M. Müller in the context of religion/religions, the Babel myth in Genesis 11:1–9, which illustrates the Western/Christian presupposition of the common origin of languages, implicitly puts forward the possibility of retrieving, through a universal theory, something akin to a 'pure religion', encompassing all religions (see Kitagawa's following quotation, note 8), as well as to a common essence of religions. The Babel myth is rooted first and foremost in this ontological assumption, from which also emerges the epistemological approach.

Note, too, that this view advocating their 'familiarity' inevitably sets aside the richness of the plurality and diversity of what might be called religions and of their cultural assumptions. As mentioned, this study advocates that the next step necessary to broaden this discipline would be to go beyond this view of the familiarity of religions celebrated in the Babel myth, which flows, first, from the monotheist Western assumption and, second, from the Enlightenment heritage of a universalizing orientation. Changing this viewpoint would involve, inter alia, not only accepting the original otherness of religious views and practices in various cultures but also learning to grasp the advantages and benefits that arise from welcoming their non-familiarity and to positively analyse them.

As usual, the chapter first introduces the Chinese perspective within which the analysis of the three above-mentioned theories unfolds. In what follows I argue that, first and foremost, the Chinese graphic language and its origins are the dimension which provides a genuine meaning to the idea of religion in this cultural space. As discussed in the previous chapters, an example of such complete alterity is the subtle relation of otherness between the Chinese philosophico-religious and its Western equivalent, due to their different types and functions of languages: the alphabetical language and the Chinese classic (*wenyan* 文言) or 'graphic language serving as writing'[3] – to use the French sinologist Vandermeersch's characterization – which generated the Chinese classic literature. The latter nourishes a specific type of thought: one rooted in the operations of oracle bone divination involving pyromancy[4] and concerned with detecting the incipient, invisible traces of changes, that is, transformations (*yi* 易), their specific ordered sequence as result of ethical or unethical actions. Such is the rationale of the ethical interrelatedness set forth in the *Classic of Changes* (*Yijing* 易經).

The sinologist is precise in asserting that the classic graphic language emerges not only from 'the diviners' need to conserve and recapitulate on a regular basis the results of the previous divinations, but even more, to enrich a "speculation" which led to a quasi-divinatory science, known in the Chinese tradition as the science [learning] of changes (of the *Yijing*): *yixue* 易學'.[5] What is significant about the graphic language? It is the Chinese classic language, written not spoken, which is the authentic root of its traditional philosophico-religious thought. As the French sinologist makes clear, this graphic language disappeared in the wake of the May Fourth Movement (1919), which replaced it gradually with the written expression of spoken language to promote the modernization of China; debates ensued between the defenders of Chineseness and the Westernizers, between Chinese and Western values (democracy and science included).[6] To that one must add the simplification of the graphs which began in 1956 in mainland China. In this context, as Vandermeersch notes, the fundamental issue concerns 'what is the vitality of the ties that the contemporary Chinese culture continues to maintain with its traditional sources, by means of the graphs'.[7] As a positive answer, he remarks the popularity of the practice of calligraphy. Therefore, of particular relevance to the context of this book, which focuses on uncovering specific cultural presuppositions, is the distinction between classic graphic language and modern Chinese language.

It may be observed once again, but in a different light, that the practice of divination provided a foundation for the assumption of the identity between the functioning of nature and culture (human society) and for the mutual interrelatedness of the natural and social changes. From this divinatory presupposition of the continuity between nature and culture results the perception of natural dynamism as having an ethical underlying basis. The divination or learning of changes can be defined as the procedure of anticipatory insight into the continuous unfolding of transformations, prior to their perceptible manifestation. Its goal is to validate or adjust the human inquirer's course of action so that it does not conflict with the spontaneously ethical dynamism of nature, and thereby produce beneficial outcomes.

The Western language generates a conceptual system assisted by the connections between words established through the process of inflexion, that is, their modification expressing different grammatical categories. Such inflexion is possible due to the specific form of words as combinations of letters. Consequently, this conceptual thought focuses on classification, on the ontological division of various objects in genera and species according to their attributes or qualities. Aristotle's *Categories* is the first system of classification which studies the qualities attributed to objects. The generic model of such a division is the inflexion of words in the phonetic alphabetic context. This type of abstract thought rooted in classification took flight during the

Enlightenment era in the form of a universalizing tendency, which was the final result of the classification, that is, finding taxonomic ranks which subsume a number of less general categories. A significant comparison of the functioning and natures of these two language types would involve challenging cultural presuppositions and determine specific ways of thinking.

As mentioned above, this amounts to moving beyond the quest for a common ground of religions and reaching another stage, one which seeks to uncover and interculturally interpret their distinctness embedded in underlying cultural assumptions. This would be a concrete and practical way to answer what we refer to as Gadamer's call: to learn from the culturally other, to think on a large scale in order to be able to correct some unintended aspects of the Enlightenment legacy. Moreover, given that at the core of the Chinese philosophico-religious thought one finds neither an ontological nor an epistemological interest, but rather clear ethical concern, I suggest that learning from this cultural sphere means, first and foremost, to learn to adopt such an ethical view as complementary to the Western ontologico-epistemological approach. The intercultural stage in the study of world's religions that this book proposes acknowledges and treasures their non-familiarity and situates their 'exchanges' at the cultural level of the language.

Returning to the body of studies initially known as *Religionswissenschaft*, as mentioned above, they are centred on two Western assumptions: first, the fact that each religion is a particular expression of a universally human religious dimension; second, the existence of a universal transcendental reality as a common basis of all religions. In Kitagawa's words, 'a religion is thus understood as the particular expression of a universal mode of human reaction to Ultimate Reality. Even today, in the Western tradition of *Religionswissenschaft*, there is an undertone of a search for "universals in religion" or "pure religion" underlying all the empirical manifestations in various religions of the world.'[8] One could identify this predominant angle in the field of religious studies as the Babel myth perspective or family-resemblances view. The next section uncovers and interprets different attempts to reshape this view (Hick's, Smart's and Smith's) and the invisible cultural assumptions that constitute their foundations.

3 The Babel myth perspective and the concept of family-resemblance

3.1 The need for religious pluralism

The major Western premise to be discussed within the context of contemporary theories is what could be regarded as an amended version of the Babel myth perspective: religion as a 'family-resemblances' concept. In his 1989 study, *An Interpretation of Religion: Human Responses to the Transcendent*, the philosopher of religion and theologian John Hick takes up Wittgenstein's analogy of family-resemblances and adapts it to the context of religious studies as a 'pluralistic hypothesis that the great world traditions constitute different conceptions and perceptions of, and responses to, the Real from within the different cultural ways of being human'.[9] He uses this analogy with a view to overcome the explicit universalist tendency of the Babel myth perspective – more specifically, its idea of the existence of a common essence. Hick intends to build in this way a theory that better supports religious pluralism, by replacing the common essence idea with the perspective of a 'continuum of resemblances and differences': 'Using this analogy it is, I think, illuminating to see the different traditions, movements and ideologies whose religious character is either generally agreed or responsibly debated, not as exemplifying a common essence, but as forming a complex continuum of resemblances and differences analogous to those found within a family.'[10] Of course, his use of the concept of continuum, as well as his focus on the idea of family-resemblances, clearly indicates the preference of the British philosopher and theologian for the features religions have in common, for their commonality as a result of sharing of a family spirit, of participating in a continuum. Nevertheless, one must greet as extremely precious, especially in the actual context, Hick's idea of the importance of effectively building religious pluralism.

As an aside, in a beautiful and striking phrase – 'the pluralism of religions keeps them honest'[11] – Smart also emphasizes the same need in our world today to practise and adopt a pluralistic perspective. He mentions several examples of oppressive tendencies of the Western monotheistic Christianity: Saint John Chrysostom and Luther's antisemitism, Cromwell's treatment of the Irish, Papal suppression of Catholic modernism and various Christian links with Fascism. Interestingly, he finds here, in this pluralistic view, a powerful lesson that the Western culture could learn from China, from its so-called Three Teachings (Confucianism, Buddhism and Daoism).[12] Smart refers to the post-Song, late-imperial joint worship of the three traditions. I would add that this process started with the mutual philosophical exchanges between Confucianism and Chan Buddhism during the Song dynasty[13] on which this study focuses. In this same spirit of supporting religious pluralism, Smart's next paragraph explicates another reason – other than Gadamer's reason discussed earlier but fully complementary to it – why it is important for the West to learn from Chinese culture,[14] from the peaceful coexistence and interaction between the Three Teachings from the Yuan dynasty (1271–1368) forward: 'It is because, in part, many traditional Christian views have treated other faiths and cultural traditions as inferior that we have to make special efforts above all in the West to foster an equal dialogue between major religious and ideologically based groups. Perhaps there is a lesson to be learned in China.'[15]

Returning to Hick's idea, one discovers the relative nature of his concept of religious diversity in his advocacy of religious pluralism: in this context, the family-resemblances view still embodies group characteristics like, for instance, sharing a family of languages and similar ways of living religious views and practices. Hence it remains an offshoot of the environment engendered by the universalizing Enlightenment.

Regarding the source of religious differences, he recognizes it in the existence of cultural forces that influenced each religious tradition and defines them as 'a complex of geographical, climatic, economic and political factors'.[16] As seen in the Chapter 1, in his study on modern capitalism, Protestantism and Confucianism, Weber also identifies and interprets such factors. I would also add another one, mentioned above, that is related to those brought out by Hick: obviously, the different natures and functioning of Chinese classic graphic language (embodying 'graphic configurations,' to use Vandermeersch's term[17]) and Western alphabetical language (incorporating spoken configurations).

3.2 Hick's epistemology of belief

The next Western cultural presupposition discussed in this section – the epistemological regard – is complementary to the universalizing view. As one might note from Hick's paragraph above, in spite of his corrective assertion, the construction he proposes remains closely related to the Babel myth because it preserves its Western universalist presumption, albeit in a different way from previous theories (e.g. Max Müller's): he does recognize a common feature of religions, although not as an essence but as an universal truth – a common belief in the transcendent. The latter is a metaphor for faith – this major Western source of religion – and has the epistemic nature (already discussed in the context of Weber's theory, Chapter 1, Section 3.2):

> The feature upon which I shall primarily focus in this book is belief in the transcendent. Although this is not of the essence of religion – for, as I have just suggested, there is no such essence – nevertheless most forms of religion have affirmed a salvific reality that transcends (whilst also usually being thought of as immanent within) human beings and the world, this reality being variously conceived as a personal God or non-personal Absolute, or as the cosmic structure or process or ground of the universe.[18]

In other words, in his comparative theory, Hick maintains the universalist tendency and the quest for resemblances between religions but shifts its focus away from the ontological perspective (the common essence in the Babel myth) and towards an epistemology of religion grounded in what he sees as 'religious awareness' or the existence in human nature of an aspect which acknowledges and reacts to the transcendent: 'The interpretation of religion as our varied human response to a transcendent reality or realities.'[19] This is a cognitive response[20] that he defines as a 'critical realism'.[21] It is noteworthy, however, that this transcendent or Absolute that he identifies, even if it is also immanent, first and foremost, lies beyond the tangible world, other than the phenomenal: a major reference implicit in this idea is the Western religion. As Smart stresses, 'The Western god does not abide in his creation, and it is a heresy to locate him in it.'[22]

The Chinese culture, on the other hand, is aware of *dao* as an ethico-spiritual corporeality or environment which organically and ethically nourishes the tangible reality. 'The way (*dao*)', explains the scholar-monk Qisong in his commentary to the classic *Zhongyong*, 'is that which flows in and out of the ten thousand things' (道也者，出萬物也入萬物也).[23] And the Neo-Confucian Zhu Xi, in the first paragraph of his commentary to the *Zhongyong*, writes: 'Dao is the principle of coherence that all everyday things and affairs must follow. It is the moral quality of every nature. Every heart-mind is provided with this principle of coherence' (道者，日用事物當行之理，皆性之德而具於心).[24]

Furthermore, Hick points out that his construction is inspired by Kant's epistemological model and by Thomas Aquinas's application of the epistemological principle to faith considered as propositional belief.[25] Where exactly does the epistemological dimension lie in his theoretical construction? Interesting enough, in a notion complementary to that of religious awareness: the religious beliefs that he considers as rational and propositional. According to him, the religious beliefs, that is, as a form of epistemological states of mind, exist implicitly within religious experience – a domain which, for him, 'is not *in toto* human projection and illusion but constitutes a range of cognitive responses, varying from culture to culture, to the presence of a transcendent reality or realities'.[26] In other words, as the Hellenist semiologist Claude Calame[27] suggests, the initially ontological universal character of religion takes a new form: religion understood as the cognitivist approach.

In conclusion, even if the unifying dimension of Hick's theory is no longer based on an ontological view (the study of the common essence of religions), the latter is replaced by an epistemological assumption and the idea of belief (i.e. a notion focusing on mental processes) in the transcendent as a dimension of a common religious sensibility. Moreover, one also finds in his approach another Western assumption: the categorical, taxonomic viewpoint. Indeed, the philosopher's notion of transcendent can be seen as a genus which comprises several species that he enumerates: 'the gods, or God, or Brahman, or the Dharmakaya, or the Tao, and so on',[28] 'personal God or non-personal Absolute, or as the cosmic structure or process or ground of the universe'.[29]

Why doesn't the Chinese philosophico-religious really fit within the framework of such a conceptual structure? Incidentally, Hick himself frankly admits that 'there are indeed whole regions, such as the religious life of China that I have had largely (though not entirely) to leave aside'.[30] Nevertheless, the philosopher and theologian systematically includes a general notion of Tao (*dao*)[31] (without specification of further details) within the class of a category of transcendent that he defines as non-personal Absolute. In reply to the above question, one reason is the epistemological nature of Hick's notion of what he calls a transcendent reality (in his view, this would be a non-personal Absolute in the Chinese case), or inspired by Kant, a postulated Real *an sich* as ultimate mystery. As discussed in the previous chapters and in the next one, the Song dynasty philosophico-religious thought does not focus on the epistemology of *dao* but on a special ethical practice – how to follow the *dao* inwardly and outwardly – which has two dimensions: becoming aware of its metaphysico-spiritual corporeality or subtle interrelatedness between individuals, nurturing it and of its tangible functioning in the form of ethical, social interrelatedness of everyday relationships. In other words, one becomes able to follow *dao* not as the result of an epistemological action but through a vigilant effort to apprehend one's self-centred emotions/feelings which block one's awareness of the metaphysical interrelatedness and to strive to eliminate them by constantly preserving ethical interrelationships. Paragraph 7 of the ancient classic *Daxue* 大學 (*Great Learning*) specifies the types of emotions which make one biased: anger (*fenzhi* 忿懥), fear (*kongju* 恐懼), pleasure (*haole* 好樂) and suffering (*youhuan* 憂患). And Qisong in the essay *Guang yuanjiao* (*Extensive Inquiry into the Teachings*) included in his anthology *Fujiao bian* (*Essays on Assisting the Teaching*) offers the following account of the effect of more and less adequate uses or expressions of the sentiments:

> The emotions can produce mistaken perceptions as well as clear discernment (*shi* 識). When people have emotions, then they are able to love (*ai* 愛) others and benefit others; to cherish the loved ones and be distant with the distant relations; they may sometimes do good deeds, and sometimes evil deeds (則為愛, 為惠, 為親親, 為疎疎, 為或善, 為或惡). When people no longer have feelings, they resort to deception; use cunning; act with ferocity, impertinence and greed; they are submerged in desires: and they lose their heart-mind and destroy their inherent nature (則為欺, 為狡, 為兇, 為不遜, 為貪, 為溺嗜欲, 為喪心, 為滅性).[32]

For Zhu Xi, humans are able to reach the depth of the ethico-metaphysical capacity or corporeality present within everyone as authentic nature or principle of coherence and consisting of five natural dispositions: humaneness, sense of duty, spirit of ritual, moral knowledge and fidelity to one's pledged word. One could call this effort ethico-religious practice. It requires two simultaneous steps: becoming clearly aware of one's emotions/feelings and constantly discarding those which set in movement disturbances of this authentic nature, making it cloudy and turbid, therefore impossible to realize and to reach one's authentic nature:

> Master Cheng said: The accumulation of the vital essence of heaven and earth, the accomplishment of the best in the five phases, this is the human being (天地儲精, 得五行之秀者為人). His own nature is authentic and untroubled (真而靜). When this nature is not yet in movement, the five natural dispositions, humaneness, sense of duty, spirit of ritual, moral knowledge and fidelity to one's pledged word, already exist within it (其未發也五性具焉, 曰仁, 義, 禮, 智, 信).[33]

This practice is not an epistemological effort directed to understanding a 'postulated Real' through the use of cognitive beliefs but ethical training at both the metaphysico-spiritual and the tangible (i.e. social interrelationships) levels. Its objective is to restore and preserve the deep identity between nature and society, between *dao* of the heaven-earth and that of the society. This Song dynasty philosophico-religious commitment focuses on ethical effort rooted in one's awareness of one's own emotions/feelings, of both their distinctive and interrelated qualities, therefore of one's independent (self-sufficient) self, interrelated self (Neo-Confucian) or no-self (Chan). In contrast, Hick's philosophical development concentrates on the individual's mind, its cognitive structures and personal relation with the transcendent, on an epistemological pattern of an inner religious awareness. According to him, the mind's awareness is universal and operates in the following form: it naturally responds to the transcendent, knows it and interprets it. And the contents of these generic operations are 'cultural variations': 'The epistemology of religion advocated in this book arises within this contemporary awareness. It understands that the postulated Real is thought and experienced by us in the ways made possible by the structures of our own minds, which in turn reflect cultural variations within the basic human form.'[34]

Moreover, and it bears repeating, *dao* and its subtle references – that is, Qisong's original nature or heart-mind, and Zhu's principle of coherence, or authentic nature initially untroubled by biased emotions – are not regarded as separated and as realities 'postulated' by the human mind, thought and experienced by it but rather as the subtle, metaphysico-spiritual nourishing soil of the tangible things, whose operation is embodied in the form of everyday ethical relations and needs to be maintained through constant ethical action. What is, epistemologically speaking, *dao*, the practicable path? This is not an issue: the question is unnecessary because it lacks any practicability. Its viability finds expression and meaning in the functioning of *dao* not only as ethical (harmonious) relationship of the natural phenomena between sky and earth but also as human's everyday good behaviour. If the ethical action is accomplished at all its levels (metaphysico-spiritual and social) – that is, inside and outside, harmonious individuals and harmonious society through the Chan practice of the cultivation of the quintessential spirit (*jing shen* 精神) and the Neo-Confucian practice of purifying the vital breath (*qi* 氣) – then the *dao*-path (Chan or Neo-Confucian) is followed (see Part 2).

Ninian Smart, the scholar of religious studies, also questions the unifying view of Hick's theory. He raises the example of early Buddhism in querying Hick's theory because this teaching does not postulate an ultimate Substance or Absolute (Smart, *Buddhism and Christianity*, 3). Clearly, his statement would apply equally to Chan Buddhism and Neo-Confucianism. As highlighted above, neither Qisong's original heart-mind and nature nor Zhu's authentic nature and principle of coherence are ontologically envisaged as Substance or Absolute but as a so-called metaphysico-spiritual corporeality which is within everything and sustains as well as nourishes every tangible reality. The 'within' is to be taken literally. In addition, Smart's critical observation below about applying Kant's idea of noumenal world or transcendent, the separated world of 'things in themselves' to non-Western religions, is also legitimate. Again, its validity could also be extended to the context of Chinese Buddhism and Neo-Confucianism. Furthermore, Smart's approach continues Hick's taxonomic effort to define (describe) the transcendent, that is, to classify it into a precise category. He proposes the term 'process' for designating the 'noumenal world':

> It seems to me that this transcendent lies in the region of the cosmos, but on its hidden side: whether it stretches back to the transcendence of the Creator of the Cosmos is a question. But as noumenal it has something to say to Kant. Kant was wrong in two ways, or at least unjustified, in calling the noumenal world that of 'things in themselves'. The *ding an sich* is a *ding*. But things are merely our projections, our wishing to cut the continuum up into things that can be handed both perceptually and through our hands and bulldozers. Behind phenomena it seems much better to think of process or events. Second, Kant wanted the plural, totally unjustified by the rest of his theory. Maybe one should use *process* as a mass

word – neither singular nor plural: in that case the noumenal world is process.[35] (italics in original)

The term 'process' designates an ethically neutral notion that etymologically means 'progression, course' (from the Latin verb *procedere*, *pro-* 'forward' and *cedere* 'go'), that is, a forward or onward movement towards a destination. The latter embodies the Western and Christian presupposition of a linear space-time, of motion understood as towards a point or advent lying ahead in space or time (e.g. the second coming of Christ), development towards an improved or more advanced condition. Earlier, the practice of divination was described as the original source of the identity between nature and culture, between natural process and social process, in the Chinese space, as well as of insight into the functioning of the classic graphic language. Is the divinatory practice, which focuses on the imperceptible and incipient signs of the unfolding of the ordered events, ethically determined, a process? That is, is there a series of actions towards achieving a specific goal? How can one adjust this concept taking into consideration the specificity of the Chinese cultural presuppositions? This issue will be further discussed in Part 3. In this paragraph, Smart also criticizes the misguided view that the following Western presupposition is culturally universal, that is, that the world is an association of things, of immobile, 'non-processual' substances, and therefore bears stable qualities that may be distinguished, analysed and classified. This theme – the effort of categorizing and classifying – is discussed below as emerging from the system of inflection of the Western alphabetical language.

Turning to Hick's above quotation, one discerns that the focus on the individual, as separated from, and master of nature, on human knowledge and reflection – a Western assumption considered earlier, too – is also implicitly present, as the philosopher tacitly emphasizes the experiential dimension of religion as distinguished from other human experiences ('the postulated Real is thought and experienced by us'). Again, this book illustrates and explores the Song dynasty's focus, not on experience which emerges from the experiencer's perception and observation and generates cognition but on social practice and ethical interrelatedness. As Smart rightly observes, the idea of religious experience is rooted in several Western presumptions: it tends towards individualism and was emphasized by Schleiermacher and Rudolf Otto as an essential ingredient in establishing faith.[36] This stress on individualism follows from their focus on the independent individual mentioned above, and the notion of faith implies an epistemological perspective. I contend that if the Chinese tradition does not focus on a special religious experience, it is precisely because the metaphysico-spiritual corporeality of the ethical is not something separated but is present within every reality and everyday relationships and actions. It is for this reason that the so-called religious experience, to use the Western term, is not distinct or different from one's ordinary relationships and constant self-cultivation. One could interpret this fact in relation with the Chinese presumption of the identity between nature and culture: the latter takes the form of an interest in interrelatedness and the ethics of care, to use the ethicist Carol Gilligan's term, while their clear separation in the Western world introduces the focus on a self-sufficient individual and on an epistemological attitude.

In addition, Hick's theory is situated within the tradition of reflexive thinking. The latter focuses on religious experience not as ethical practice but as reflexive experience – that is, the experience of reflexive consciousness, with respect to the reflexive competence of the subject – in this case, of the 'knower' of the transcendent, the one looking to understand it:

> The basic principle that I am adapting from Kant's philosophy – Hick sets forth – had in fact already been succinctly stated long before by St Thomas Aquinas, although without any thought of the kind of application being proposed here, when he wrote that 'Things known are in the knower according to the mode of the knower.' He applied this basic epistemological principle to faith considered as propositional belief, concluding that although God *a se* is simple and undifferentiated, God can only be known by human beings through complex propositions. I want to apply the same principle to faith understood in a very different way, as the interpretive element within all awareness of our environment; and to argue that in relation to the divine the 'mode of the knower' differs within different religio-cultural systems so that the Real is thought-and-experienced in a wide variety of ways.[37]

The historian of religions Jonathan Z. Smith also shares Hick's view – as well as the Western presupposition at its core – the fact that what is called religion is fundamentally connected with thinking: 'Religion is the relentlessly human activity of thinking through a "situation", an understanding that requires assenting to Lévi-Strauss's dictum "man has always been thinking equally well."'[38] Broadly speaking, through these clarifications, both scholars of religious studies, Hick and Smith, identify themselves as belonging to the Western tradition of thought evolving out from the Cartesian cogito through Kant and post-Kantian philosophy. In Hick's case, its major topic is religious awareness, or how the individual responds to the transcendent. This perspective implies that one's knowledge begins with her perfect understanding of herself. Hick's epistemological view presupposes the notion of reflection as a return to oneself seen as a subject, as well as the subject's intellectual clarity and moral responsibility. In Ricoeur's terms, the idea of reflection implies 'a wish for an absolute transparency, for a perfect coincidence of one's self with oneself ("le voeu d'une transparence absolue, une parfaite coincidence de soi avec soi-même"), which would make self-consciousness an indubitable knowledge and as such, more fundamental than all positive knowledge.'[39] It is noteworthy that, in Hick's words, this absolute human transparency of reflection translates into a presupposed 'cognitive freedom' (see next quotation). In addition, he sees the religious reflection, interpretation and meaning as patterned after the physical and ethical reflection and yet constituting the highest level of this cognitive freedom. His vision of the three separated levels of cognitive freedom (physical, ethical and religious) is rich and significant. It also illustrates the Western classificatory propensity:

> Three levels of interpretation or meaning have long been recognised: physical, ethical and religious. In terms of its physical meaning we experience the world as an environment in which we learn to survive and flourish as animal organisms;

and in doing so we exercise a minimum degree of cognitive freedom. Ethical meaning presupposes physical interpretation but involves a much greater degree of cognitive freedom. At this level we are aware of other human beings as persons whose co-presence with us creates mutual claims and obligations. The further religious mode of experiencing involves a yet greater exercise of cognitive freedom, in virtue of which it can take many different forms. As religious beings we continue to live in the world in terms of its physical and ethical meanings, but do so in new ways required by its religious meaning.[40]

Clearly, Hick's perception of the religious fits within this Western idealist conception of reflexive philosophy (succinctly defined above and further developed in the next section dedicated to Ninian Smart) because it presupposes what he calls cognitive freedom: in other words, the subject's revendication, in Ricoeur's above-mentioned terms, of an absolute transparency, which produces – from the self-consciousness itself – an indubitable knowledge.

Notably, this position is unlike Qisong's Chan and Zhu's Neo-Confucian perspectives. As discussed above, they both attribute the formation of a special type of self-seeking and self-serving emotions/feelings to the interactions between inner self and outer environment. Such emotions taint the inner good nature of the individual, that is, they obstruct access to their metaphysico-spiritual corporeality, inhibit the development of the emotions and feelings supportive of a deep sense of interrelatedness and produce biased perceptions and judgements and unethical behaviours. Only through the constant everyday practice of self-cultivation, that is, the alertness to the presence of these emotions/feelings, is one able to 'detect bias', to use Smart's term (see the following quotation), and purify their authentic or original nature. In this Chinese context, the reflection of the individual who is not engaged in such continuous ethical practice is never transparent, never 'dispassionate'. Philosophers like Ricoeur and Gadamer who belong to the phenomenology, hermeneutics and hermeneutical traditions of phenomenology would certainly agree with the following reflection of Smart. It could also be extended to the Chinese cultural area:

> Can we really be dispassionate? Are we not always bringing our cultural biases to bear in cross-cultural analysis? Naturally we are heavily determined by our cultural background. But the question has no meaning unless we can detect bias. If we can detect it, we can correct it. We may not be able to be completely objective, but we can improve, getting a bit nearer the goal.[41]

In contrast, one perceives the Enlightenment legacy at the very core of Hick's perception of the religious – full confidence in human cognition, in the noumenal as epistemologically experienced and thought. In other words, complete reliance in the answer to the question 'how do we know the transcendent'. Obviously, epistemology and ontology are intrinsically connected: his development could also be defined as an ontology of the comprehension of the transcendent.

In contrast with his view, as emphasized several times in various settings, the Chinese philosophico-religious vision does not prioritize the epistemological or the answer to the question 'what is the transcendent', but, to reiterate, prioritizes the ethical view. One must recall that, in contrast with the Western ethical which is limited to the tangible functioning of human relations and rules of behaviour, the Song dynasty ethical has two organically intertwined aspects: the metaphysico-spiritual corporeality which nourishes its social, tangible functioning. As demonstrated in the previous chapter (see Section 1.3), the meaning of the term 'organic' in this Chinese context is completely different from its Western signification. The Chinese ethical is authentic and spontaneous – 'impersonal,' to use Hick's term – an ethical and moral order present at the core of each reality, of which one must gain inner awareness, maintain this awareness firmly and constantly and assist its growth through continuous ethical practice in everyday actions and relations.

If in the Chinese space, the ethico-moral has a metaphysico-spiritual root, in Hick's theory, *dao* (Tao) or the *impersonae* does not have ethical qualities (reserved for persons, in his viewpoint). His notion of ethico-moral is the usual Western notion tied to moral principles and to the knowledge about them: 'The *impersonae* – Brahman, the Tao, the Dharmakaya, Sunyata – do not have ethical qualities and cannot therefore be said to be morally good or bad. Any moral assessment must focus instead upon their effects within human behavior.'[42] When reading this passage, one must keep in mind that the Song dynasty ethical view, unlike the view that Hick specifies here, includes a broad, simultaneously metaphysico-spiritual as well as social sphere. Therefore, it embraces a subtle and natural, complete good (*zhi shan* 至善), beyond the distinction of ordinary good and evil, which does not emerge from concrete human behaviour but is their very metaphysico-spiritual nourishing and natural source. The ethical meaning of the latter not only surpasses the good/bad dichotomy limited to the sphere of social relations but also embraces it.

3.3 Ninian Smart's concept of religion as worldview

Another author who highlights the concept of family-resemblances between religions in a new light is Ninian Smart. This section focuses on his theory of religion as worldview and its Western assumptions, of course, in connection with Hick's and J. Smith's viewpoints and again. He agrees: 'The definition of religion relies on family resemblances.'[43] His starting point is forceful and ambitious: the scholar of religious studies is searching for an efficient approach to 'understanding religions in a deep way, that is by entering into the standpoint and feelings of those who believe them.'[44] For the Scottish scholar of religious studies N. Smart as well, comparative, cross-cultural research means looking for similarities, thus enabling the scholar 'to see that often similar factors enter into differing religions.'[45] His comparative perspective, based on the same universalizing presupposition or research of resemblances, is multifaceted and includes seven dimensions: ritual or practical; experiential or emotional; doctrinal or philosophical; ethical dimension, also understood as in Hick's case as the moral values of the system; the narrative or mythic; social or institutionalization; and material artistic.[46] For this reason, Smart also includes non-religious ideologies within his comparative study of religions.

The broad concept that includes both as a genus of which religious and non-religious systems are species is expressed by the term 'worldview'.[47] The latter literally means the way we see the world; it is rooted in observation, with an ontologico-epistemological assumption. Philosophically speaking, the term has a strong Western connotation: it also reminds one of the etymological source of Western 'theory' – the observer who left on a trip to see the world, of Plato's analogy of vision to cognition/knowledge in the *Republic* VI, 508d.

Like Hick's epistemology of religion, Smart's theory of religions and ideologies, with its analysis of worldviews, also places emphasis on understanding and therefore includes a major epistemological orientation. In his own words, it is an analysis of 'the history and nature of the symbols and beliefs that have helped form the structure of human consciousness and society' and 'conveys a sense of attempted objectivity'.[48] Again, one may contrast this Western interest in the analysis of symbols and beliefs in the context of religion, with the Chinese concern for multi-layered ethical practice. Smart's idea of objectivity indicates again the presence of the analytical assumption, the same confidence in reflexivity – a particular form of it that he defines as 'informed empathy' – in the absolute transparency of human reflection, that is, in one's capacity to suspend one's own beliefs and dispassionately study other religions and secular systems:

> We should use the methods involving informed empathy, and neglecting our own beliefs in judging the worldview of the other. Sometimes this suspension of our own beliefs is called *epoche* from a Greek word pronounced in English epoch. We should understand, through *epoche*, the beliefs and feelings of foreign beliefs and values, not imposing our own beliefs and judgments on the other.[49]

In his work, the idea of the transparency of reflection appears again, not only as the empathy but also as the 'imagination' of the researcher; hence, it remains rooted in their thinking and mental creativity. It is evident that this method is a perfect illustration of the etymological definition of Western theory: 'To understand religious and secular worldviews and their practical meaning we have to use imagination. We have to enter into the lives of those for whom such ideas and actions are important.'[50]

Again, from the perspective of hermeneutical phenomenology, such a high degree of objectivity remains aspirational to say the least. Like Smart, the American historian of religions J. Smith is also adept at utilizing imagination in the context of elaborating a theory of religion. In his case, its use is radical, for in his view, religion is nothing other than an abstract idea, the result of the 'scholarly imagination'.[51] He does not consider religion either a force or an experience but rather 'an artificial taxon applied by scholars'.[52]

Still, Smart also pays attention to the cultural presuppositions. He clearly identifies and highlights the danger of introducing 'the assumptions and slant of the investigator' when studying other religions. As a remedy, he suggests adopting Husserlian phenomenology as a method to study religion in an 'objective' way, that is, 'of describing religions and secular worldviews as they actually are', 'without the distortions created by prior beliefs and assumptions'.[53] According to Ricoeur, Husserl's phenomenology does not have this capacity because it stands in the idealist tradition of Descartes and Kant and remains a reflexive philosophy, that is, in the French philosopher's terms, a tradition that starts from the premise that 'all apprehension of a transcendent is dubious, only the self-immanence is indubitable'. As an aside, this definition of Ricoeur brings into sharp focus the Western perception of immanence – indubitable knowledge of the presence of the immanent self (or communion with God), as state of being existing natural and permanent within and the absolute reliance on its capacity to understand. It is obvious that the immanence as defined in the Western context is absent in the Chinese sphere, which considers the self as dynamic, impure and unable to impartially see the reality as it is and needs constant ethical practice.

Coming back to Husserl, his phenomenology inherits, in part, the Cartesian and Fichtean ideal of the self-transparency of the subject.[54] It is hermeneutics – notably the works of Heidegger, Gadamer and Ricoeur – that effectively transforms this ideal goal of phenomenology into something workable, through building the new mediating conceptual tools of belonging and distancing. The first concerns 'the relation of inclusion that englobes the allegedly autonomous subject and the allegedly adverse object',[55] while the last is based on the idea that 'our way of belonging to a tradition is contingent upon a distance relationship which oscillates between the remoteness and the proximity'.[56] The comparative analysis of cultural presuppositions that this book proposes is inspired by his two devices – belonging and distancing. Its intercultural dimension also broadens their meaning, as Ricoeur's construction belongs within the Western culture and moves historically from one tradition to another, across time periods.

As a matter of fact, Smart himself amends his assertion, preferring to name his method 'structured empathy' rather than phenomenology:

> For various reasons I think it is best not to use the word 'phenomenology', but rather the phrase 'structured empathy'. ... Empathy literally means 'feeling in': it is getting at the feel of what is inside another person or group of persons. It is not quite the same as sympathy, 'feeling with', for sympathy means I *agree* with the other. ... This is why, too, the empathy needs to be structured. We have to comprehend the structure of another's world: in general, we have to try to understand the structures of belief inside the head of the believer.[57] (italic in original)

Although the author does not further develop what would concretely constitute, such a 'structured empathy', I suggest that comparatively addressing cultural presumptions could be a step towards developing an authentic affinity and interest in cultivating togetherness. One understands that Smart's position is still an idealist position as his concept of structured empathy obviously presupposes that the mind of the observer is self-transparent. Nevertheless, Smart equally recognizes that 'we need to be helped to be empathetic'. And he recommends in this sense 'to learn something of the vocabulary of other systems'. Therefore, the scholar of religious studies also assumes that understanding the other calls for the concrete language-mediation: 'By learning something of the general structure and vocabulary of a language we come to understand something of its force. We also learn more about languages in general, and our own in particular.'[58] Needless to add, the present study emerges from a similar perspective: it uncovers and interprets the invisible difference between the specific coherence of a way of thinking that emerges from a graphic language and that of the Western thought rooted in the phonetic alphabetic language.

It is equally clear that Smart's search for objectivity and empathy, besides being a trend of modernity that he wants to introduce in the sphere of the study of religions, also constitutes his specific way of identifying and rectifying the biased perception of non-Western religions viewed as inferior. As generally recognized, this attitude is ingrained in the classical discipline of religious studies: 'For we must remember that, in the past, most of the Western study of religion has been thought of as Christian theology – the study of texts, history, and doctrines of the faith on the assumption that Christian faith, being true, was superior to others. When other religions were studied, they were usually compared unfavorably to Christianity.'[59]

The hermeneutical tradition already raised particular doubts as to one's capacity to understand directly, without the help of mediation, the thought of the historically other. I advocate the possibility of an intercultural comprehension of the other's philosophico-religious thought as mediated by texts. This is consistent with Smart's view that it is useful to learn about the other's language. Examining texts is a choice that reaffirms the fact that, originally, the condition of all human experience and interaction involves language. I therefore consider such intercultural mediation to be possible through philosophical translation. The latter is conducted in awareness of one's own and the other's cultural presuppositions as embedded in language and, in Ricoeur's terms, manifests a form of 'language hospitality' (hospitalité langagière), which builds a 'correspondence without adequacy'[60] as a bridge between the two cultures, religious visions.

In conclusion, it may be remarked that the above reflection on the weaknesses and limitations of the universalist view – both that of the family-resemblances and the Babel myth tools for examining religions – highlights a major concern, also identified by Smart: the actual 'danger' that needs further correction is the homogeneity and domination by one culture (Western culture at the moment). Because, 'with homogeneity there will be a severe lack of criticism, and of the dialectic of argument.'[61] In this perspective, learning from the Chinese philosophico-religious thought would also be a way to develop constructive criticism of Western culture.

But not only that. Because this Chinese philosophico-religious thought is embedded in the Chinese classic graphic language (wenyan 文言), which no longer exists, its study could also benefit the contemporary Chinese culture itself, in its ongoing efforts to recover the richness of its own lapsed philosophico-religious traditions. In the next reflection, the Swiss sinologist Jean François Billeter strikingly raises this issue:

> Over the past century, China constantly defined itself in relation to the West, in terms of ideas, for or against. This continues. As evidenced by the extraordinary vogue of comparative studies, which in all domains, oppose term to term Chinese conceptions and Western conceptions. Over the last hundred years, the Chinese intellectuals did more. They reinterpreted all the Chinese past according to Western

categories in order to 'homologate' it, so to speak. They did so using a vocabulary borrowed from Europe. The majority of the terms used today in the economic, social, political fields, in philosophy, and human sciences are neologisms modelled on European terms. Whether they like it or not, nowadays the Chinese think on their history and civilization by means of notions from elsewhere. Because these neologisms are perfectly Chinese in their form and are now part of the everyday language, they constitute an invisible obstacle to the intelligence of the past. The result is a curious mix of familiarity and incomprehension. The past seems to be on hand, but it does not respond.[62]

3.4 Smith's intellectual resemblances: The issues of difference and classification

Another work that needs to be discussed as attached to the Western assumption of the Babel myth and family-resemblances of religions, yet in a different way, is that of Jonathan Z. Smith. The next remark from his book *Imagining Religion: From Babylon to Jonestown* is another perfect illustration of the Western etymology of the concept of theory discussed in the introduction – as a result of the observer-traveller's journey who left to see the world:

> While there is a staggering amount of data, phenomena, of human experiences and expressions that might be characterized in one culture or another, by one criterion or another, as religious – there is no data for religion. Religion is solely the creation of the scholar's study. It is created for the scholar's analytical purposes by his imaginative act of comparison and generalization. Religion has no independent existence apart from academy.[63]

Smith is right to highlight that the concept of religion refers to an abstract theory – one could add, a Western theory – , in Smith terms, 'a category imposed from the outside on some aspect of native culture'. This is consistent with the view expressed by Calame that 'there is no religious essence of mankind and no ontology of religion'.[64] In this work, *Imagining Religion*, as Hugh Urban argues, the reader discovers that Smith is 'very much rooted in a kind of neo-Enlightenment, highly intellectual and rationalist view of human beings as essentially pragmatic, utilitarian, rational agents who cannot tolerate cognitive incongruities and who constantly search for order and coherence in their worlds'.[65] It might be said that the same applies to Calame's suggestion that religion is still a category, so 'we must give the concept of religion a definition, however much of a working definition it may need to be'.[66] The source of this approach is the Aristotelian presumption mentioned earlier: the concern for categorization, for division of the categories in order to synthesize knowledge and further human cognition.

Through his conceptual approach to religion, which includes four stages of the comparative enterprise (description, comparison, redescription and rectification), Smith focuses on the theory imagined by the theorist, on adjusting or rectifying it, and recommends the following methodological steps:

Description is a double process which comprises the historical or ethnographic dimensions of the work. A first requirement is that we locate a given example within the rich texture of its social, historical, and cultural environments that invest it with its local significance. The second task of description is that of reception-history, a careful account of how our second-order scholarly tradition has intersected with the exemplum, how the datum has come to be accepted as significant for the purpose of argument. Only when such a double contextualization is completed can one move on to the description of a second example undertaken in the same double fashion. With at least two examples in view, one is prepared to undertake their comparison both in terms of aspects and relations held to be significant, expressed in the tropes of similarities and differences, and with respect to some category question, theory or model of interest to the study of religion. The aim of such a comparison is the redescription of the exempla (at the very least, each in terms of the other) and a rectification of the academic categories in relation to which they have been imagined.[67]

Some preliminary thoughts concerning Smith's methodological prescription: First, when used to examine Chinese philosophico-religious thought, rooted in a very different language, this theoretical process based on historical and ethnographic data does not uncover the deepest cultural specificities, the otherness which is embedded in the language and remains not apparent in historical and ethnographic dimensions of a culture. Second, in this approach, the foreign tradition turns out to be not the focus of the theory which concentrates on itself but only its pretext. When the students limit themselves to these dimensions and their scholarly context, one inevitable result is that in doing so, all questions of deep cultural specificity embedded in language and classical texts are nullified. In other words, this theory looks for certain apparent similarities and differences but remains unconcerned about the implicit cultural assumptions that shape other's thinking. Actually, this conclusion is consistent with Smith's own appreciation of the contrast between 'otherness' and 'difference' illustrated in the following paragraph:

> 'Otherness' blocks language and conceptualization; 'difference' invites negotiation and intellection. For 'difference' is an active term – ultimately a verbal form, *differre*, 'to carry apart' – suggesting the separating out of what, from another vantage point, might be seen as the 'same'. By contrast, 'other' has no verbal form, except, perhaps, 'alienate,' which, tellingly, most often appears in the passive voice.[68]

In this quotation, Smith highlights his interest in epistemology, knowledge and theoretical problems and focuses on the scholar-observer's intellective skills and mental operations that result, for him, in cognitively establishing 'similarity' and 'difference'.[69] And he prioritizes seeking difference. The latter represents another major Western cultural presupposition discussed in detail by Plato and embedded in the functioning of alphabetical Western language which reinforces the law of difference as basic to the coherence of Western thought.

One knows, as Derrida highlights,[70] that Plato builds his arguments using the letters of the alphabet: this is how he makes the law of difference visible. In *Phaedrus* and *Philebus*, Thot, the inventor of the alphabetical writing, is presented as the author of difference. And he presents his invention not as graphics but as grammatical science, that is, science of differences. Derrida interprets the way in which, in these dialogues as well as in the *Sophist*, Plato follows the example of grammatical science, of the relationships between the letters in order to explain the system of differences (solidarity-exclusion) of genera or of forms, the interlacing of being and non-being.[71] It is pertinent to consider the system of differences as the very matrix of Western thought. Furthermore, one might also point out that this notion of difference does not refer to otherness but to the differentiation within the same Western language and its categories. At the end of the day, this relative difference also implies a certain categorical similarity within classes, resulting from applying the same conceptual framework: the scholar's. That being the case, the theoretical construction of their comparative theory inevitably remains within the same cultural borders. In these circumstances, Smith's methodological architecture could be envisaged as another offshoot of the Babel myth perspective. This because it is structured by an articulation similarity/difference which evolves at the same level, without interest in a different dimension, that of otherness.

It might be said that intercultural dialogue necessarily entails the 'otherness' of the other culture (leaving aside the Babel myth motif), embodied in what this study calls cultural presuppositions. The result is that the other's (non-Western) exteriority is not merely historical, geographical, spatial or ethnographical. Rather, its distinction lies beyond the similarity/difference articulation and therefore beyond the student's theoretical categories inevitably embedded in their own cultural presuppositions. In the same vein, Timothy D. Knepper highlights that the categories of the philosophy of religion are still of Western forms of religious reason-giving; therefore, 'if actually applied in acts of cross-cultural comparison, would most likely result in the ethnocentric distortion and over-simplification of the non-Western other'.[72] This occurs in cases where what comes first is not improving one's theory but opening oneself up, wanting to learn from the genuineness of the other. I agree with the religious studies scholar Marsha A. Hewitt for whom 'the comparative study of religion is at heart a theory of the other'. She warns about the existence of a colonizing force[73] included in the theory of the scholar/observer who uses the cultural material to test and rectify their own conceptual tools. In fact, one recognizes in her argument, again, that Western presupposition etymologically embedded in the ancient notion of 'theory' – of the traveller who (metaphorically) left to see the world and came back with a rectified theoretical tool:

> If we approach the other as an object out-there whose 'secrets' can be revealed with the correct methodology, we inevitably enact knowledge as colonizing force, making the object fit within our preconceptions. In such cases the primacy of our theory becomes the real concern at the expense of the other. While it is important that our epistemological frameworks are clear and as transparent to ourselves as possible, this does not preclude our entering into an intersubjective relationship with the other that does not conceptually colonize, but lets the other reveal itself, although never fully.[74]

As already noted, this work suggests that one way to enter into such an intercultural and intersubjective relationship would be through the mediation of texts and their translations and through comparatively bringing to light the presuppositions incorporated in those texts by different languages. A parallel reading of the last two quotations brings to light the fact that Smith's scholar looks much more like a solitary researcher who wants to avoid the danger of becoming estranged or alienated.

I offer that the analysis of cultural presuppositions implies a relation of alterity which is neither conceptual nor epistemological. It would seem to me that Gadamer's idea of learning from the other points towards the necessity of establishing a relationship of alterity which acknowledges, respects and values the other's otherness; in other words, entering into an intercultural relationship which does not belong to the epistemological sphere, ethically neutral and non-reciprocal, but to the ethical domain of the give and take. Establishing such an ethical relation of alterity goes beyond the mere decentring implicit in the cognitive approach in which understanding difference allows the researcher – in Calame's terms, 'to cast a critical eye on our own cultural paradigm'[75] but to effectively change. The exchange therefore means an opportunity to accomplish something very difficult for the scholar, the one who controls the theory and its application, that is, to learn to change.[76] Kimberley C. Patton and Benjamin C. Ray rightly acknowledge: 'As scholars, we do not have to be the "other" to speak to or even for the "other", but we must ourselves first change.'[77] I would add that this is not the result of an anthropological pursuit of cross-cultural translation[78] which envisages the difference as conceptual difference. Religious studies could adopt as next methodological step the examination of intercultural difference as ethical difference, that is, to use a Levinasian term, non-indifference to alterity. The non-indifference means that the theorists are being touched by the culturally other they are studying; this experience changes them. Besides, the following reflection of Levinas from *Totalité et infini: essai sur l'extériorité* that introduces the notion of 'absolute difference' could be a powerful response to Smith's advocacy of the pertinence of taxonomy and conceptual difference when approaching a culturally different religious sensibility:

> But the spoken word ('la parole') proceeds from the absolute difference. Or, more exactly, an absolute difference does not occur in a process of specification in which, the order of logical relations, descending from genus to species, runs up against the given which does not reduce itself in relations; ... the absolute difference, inconceivable in terms of formal logic, can be brought about only through the language. The language accomplishes a relationship between terms which break the unity of a genus.[79]

Note that, in the specific context of his thought – an ethical critique of Western philosophy from within – Levinas regards the spoken word ('la parole') as the dimension of language fundamental for the absolute difference. Yet, if one considers the relationship of otherness between Western and Chinese cultures, then, for the reasons set out above, the latter proceeds not from the spoken word but from the written language.

According to Smith, religion means theory, that is, an artificial taxon applied by scholars.[80] Consequently, in his view, the latter are very much akin to the taxonomists: they build a theory of religion by developing a system of classification. It is by borrowing this technique from the natural sciences, where the taxonomic method of the naturalist Carolus Linnaeus (1707–1778), a major figure of the European Enlightenment, is a matter of academic concern, that the American historian of religions understands to distance himself from the contemporary studies built around comparison as research of family-resemblances.

From reading his 1982 book *Imagining Religion: From Babylon to Jonestown*, one realizes that in choosing this approach, Smith wants to fulfil two special missions. He describes the first as 'to free students of religion from the usual preoccupations with political and literary history and the temptation to reduce phenomena to "essences"'.[81] The second is to distance himself from previous scholarship which practised comparison as an affair of recollection of similarity[82] and built theories 'on contagion' while completely forgetting the issue of difference.[83]

In his biographical essay 'When the Chips Are Down', Smith reflects on his deep interest in taxonomy and the biological field.[84] Stimulated by these lifelong naturalist interests, he chooses an approach inspired by the science of botanists who observe different and common traits of plants in order to establish classes and categorize them. From this point of view, he is also a perfect heir of the Enlightenment, who wants to convert a 'natural history' of religion into a 'science', using an adequate taxonomy, able to bring order to a variety of species.[85] It is the taxonomic analysis itself that in the end reintroduces the 'sameness' in his process of religions' classification. As explained earlier, the latter functions by calling upon divisions and subdivisions, compartmentalizations and categories in the same way that the Western alphabetic writing systems proceed. One might observe that, if Hick and Smart are looking for factual family resemblances between religions, Smith focuses on the concept of 'religion' within the study of religion as a theoretical abstract notion, forged by the scholar, and on the classificatory sameness not as existent family resemblances but as intellectual resemblances.

Indeed, the author of *Relating Religion* asserts that, unlike the previous scholarship which deals with 'family resemblances' (see Hick and Smart), in his particular interpretation, the taxonomy is a comparative enterprise which deals with 'asserting significant difference even in the face of apparent resemblance'. However, because in his method, the necessary prerequisite of his explanatory enterprise is the classification of religions and religious traits ('I always viewed comparison and classification as inseparable'[86] – he emphasizes), it becomes clear that in this way, Smith reintroduces into his approach the idea of 'family resemblances', the very view from which he wants to distance himself. There is an implicit tension, which cannot be solved, between his axiomatic presupposition of comparison as 'acceptance of difference' and as intrinsically connected with classification:

> It is axiomatic that comparison is never a matter of identity. Comparison requires the acceptance of difference as the grounds of its being interesting, and

a methodical manipulation of that difference to achieve some stated cognitive end. The questions of comparison are questions of judgment with respect to difference: What differences are to be maintained in the interests of comparative inquiry?[87]

In his book about comparison as a major method for religious studies, Oliver Freiberger pinpoints a recurring intractable difficulty in this academic sphere, resulting in a lack of cultural diversity of approaches and anchored in the Western universalizing presupposition reinforced by its Enlightenment roots: 'Nor is it quite clear how Western scholars (a group to which many postmodern/postcolonialist critics belong as well) could possibly escape at all, in their interests, the diagnosed dominance of Western academia in the "present era of neo-colonialism, cultural imperialism and global capitalism."'[88]

This book suggests that genuine intercultural dialogue of cultural presuppositions could be a possible way to overcome this difficulty. It would build up the relationship between the theorist and a culturally other religious thought, not based on the usual epistemological rapport between the theorist and an object of knowledge but on an ethical rapport which is also a learning exchange: it would connect the theorist as student and the culturally other as their instructor. The hermeneutical translation of philosophico-religious texts focuses on unveiling cultural presuppositions based on the functioning of the language. As Timothy D. Knepper points out, the hermeneutical method would be a thoughtful choice because 'it is attentive to the contexts of both the inquirer and inquired in a manner that is both "affirmative" and "suspicious"'.[89] This is also a medium that allows the establishment of a mediated relationship between the theorist and the culturally other. Such encounters mediated through the specific functioning of written languages as the main bearers of cultural presuppositions would result not in a generic theory but in a specific one, corresponding to the specific culturally other. Part 3 provides an example of such a tool. This could be one way of leaving behind the Western presumption of human innate universals, free of any specific cultural context, that prevents the theorist from learning from the culturally other.

The analysis of the Babel myth perspective and the idea of religion as a family-resemblances concept helps us uncover the Western cultural presuppositions that operate as their basis: a universalizing disposition that assumes multiple forms, an epistemological interest, a system of differences which introduce differentiation and a comparative view based on differences and similarities flowing from categorization. As demonstrated earlier, they all arise from the specific nature and functioning of the phonetic language. This section provides evidence that such assumptions delimit the theory and prevent it from including the Chinese religious perspective, which is based on very different presumptions. If this unit is about uncovering limitations which impede real communication between Western and Chinese religious ways of thinking, the next part illustrates that, despite divergences in cultural premises, they still share some common dimensions. It thus discovers and addresses a neglected feature that connects some Western theories with the Song dynasty traditions: the idea of (self) transformation. The next section further addresses it.

4 Salvific human transformation and self-transformation

This part continues the analysis opened in Section 3.4 and examines the religious concern with human transformation. Hick is a scholar who identifies human transformation as a significant dimension of religion[90] and discusses it at length. Inspired by the Hindu and Buddhist ways of life, he also examines this notion in the Christian context. I suggest that 'transformation' represents a veritable link between the Western and non-Western (Chinese) religious visions. Of course, it should be pointed out that this concept lies at the heart of Frederick J. Streng's (1933–1993) life work. The well-known historian of religions and Indianist defines religion as 'a means to ultimate transformation', explaining that 'the process of transformation may be activated by symbols, social relationships, feelings, and states of consciousness'.[91] Bruce D. Lawrence also discusses it as a critical term for religious studies while highlighting its following traits: largely individual, markedly voluntary and avowedly positive.[92]

As seen above, there are several differences between Western and Chinese cultural presuppositions that render the Chinese philosophico-religious thought incompatible with the all-encompassing definition of religion that Hick suggests. However, the just-mentioned feature – human transformation – does represent a major aspect of the Song dynasty traditions and thus can be viewed as a viable intercultural connection between these perspectives. It is therefore pertinent to examine it in the present comparative context.

When discussing human transformation as salvation or liberation, Hick makes a distinction between the pre-axial religion and the post-axial religion. Only post-axial religions (i.e. the Hindu, Buddhist, Christian, Jewish and Muslim traditions) are in his view concerned with the quest for salvation or liberation that he defines as transformation; the first type focuses on the preservation of cosmic and social order.[93] As noted above, the Chan and Neo-Confucian *dao* of these 'post-axial' Song dynasty religions (to use Hicks' term) involves both human transformation and the cosmic and social order viewed as a metaphysico-spiritual interrelatedness, which is at the same time naturally ethical and organic. Such transformation is based on gaining awareness of this interrelatedness and on cultivating it at multiple levels. This absence of separation between the two dimensions in the Song dynasty philosophico-religious thought would be, in this specific context, the first difference between Hick's project of transformation and its Chinese counterpart.

In order to discern the specificity of the Chinese counterpart in relation to Hick's notion of salvific transformation, the following unveils the salient features of this notion in the Chinese context. The Chan monk-scholar Qisong perceives the heart-mind as engaged in continuous processes of change, eventually reaching its highest level (state) or utmost (*zhi* 至) – at which the human becomes aware of the spiritual dimension of their heart-mind, that is, the Buddhist true reality (*ru* 如), the root of the marvellous (*miao zhi ben* 妙之本) in each thing (being). When this highest or complete state is achieved, the heart-mind does not transform further. Let's note that his view concerning the end of the transformation reveals a connection with a Confucian idea: the highest, complete or utmost level of the individual's cultivation – the utmost or complete good – depicted for instance in the *Daxue*; see *Daxue jing* (至善), and *zhang* 5 (知之至).[94] It is arguable that this Confucian ethical perspective is fused by Qisong into the Chan Buddhist process of transformation (of the heart-mind). Using the correlation between the emotions and the authentic nature, he gives the following explanation of the requirements and outcomes of this ultimate transformation of the heart-mind:

> The heart-mind can certainly attain its highest state (心必至). When attaining its highest state, certainly it transforms itself (至必變). Transformation means the process of consciousness (變者, 識也). Attaining its highest state means reaching the state of ultimate reality (至者, 如也). The state of ultimate reality is a marvellous potentiality that all beings have (如者, 妙萬物者也). Perceiving entails making beings diversified [recognizing distinct individual beings] and considering them as different (紛萬物, 異萬物者也). Transformation is the set of imperceptible signs of movement (動之幾). The highest state is the root of the marvellous. In the world, there is no being without root, there is no being that does not move. It is for this reason that all beings emerge from the process of transformation and enter into the process of transformation. The beings rise from ultimate reality and return into ultimate reality. The transformation of beings is apparent in the human emotions (情); the ultimate reality of the world dwells in authentic nature (性). Through the emotions, one can discern the transformation of beings (辨萬物之變化). Through authentic nature, the human can have sight of the great marvellousness of the world (觀天下之大妙). When the individual excels in both the sphere of the emotions and that of authentic nature, then he becomes able to discuss the way and the teaching of the sage.[95]

One also discerns in Qisong's vision a connection with the divinatory source of Chinese philosophico-religious thought: transformation as the ordered set of the imperceptible signs of changes. The process of continuous transformation continues until the individual attains that state of ultimate reality: they become aware of their original nature. At this level, the human not only perceives the apparent differences between things but equally grasps their subtle interrelatedness pursuant to their belonging to this root of the marvellous. As it is deeply rooted in the Confucian culture, Qisong's work does not highlight the salvific or liberating dimension of his practice à la Hick, but he focuses on the harmonious order of the society in which individuals are transformed through their good deeds. The latter is the perceptible transformation, or the functioning of the imperceptible transformation – the non-dual ethical interrelatedness:

> By understanding good deeds, individuals come to admire them and are encouraged to perform them (人慕而自勸). This transformation lies within the individuals and is not palpable (化之, 故在人而不顯); other people are unable to see it directly to verify the meritorious actions of these individuals; other people are

unable to see it in order to evaluate its results. At the same time, how do we know that a decrease of bad actions in the world is not caused by this transformation? (然天下鮮惡, 孰知非因是而損之?) How do we know that an increase of good actions in the world is not its result? (天下多善, 孰知非因是而益之?) Those who say that Buddhist teaching does not give assistance to the sovereign in his endeavor to govern the world, make that assertion because they do not understand this matter [that the inner transformation is not directly perceptible but has efficient perceptible effects].[96]

Moreover, Qisong defines the goal of this Chan transformative practice as acquiring an imperceptible efficacy: the capacity to 'do good without leaving any footprints' (從善無迹之謂化),[97] that is, to be free of any (considerations of) gain or interest.

In his commentary to the paragraph 1 of the ancient *Zhongyong*, *Zhongyong zhangju* 1 (see the next quotation, note 99), the Neo-Confucian Zhu Xi's view entails the same notions – inner transformation, ethics, good deeds, good nature, in a Neo-Confucian perspective: he understands transformation as one's constant effort towards becoming a sage, that is, through continuous efforts one can purify oneself of the selfish and partial tendencies and emotions/feelings which obscure one's inner, original goodness or authentic nature, or principle of coherence bestowed by heaven and become intuitively aware of it. Through this transformation the Neo-Confucian exemplary individual is able to govern well his community or country and maintain social harmony. As for Qisong, the way *dao* is not a separate reality but an inner and outer depth of every individual and of the natural and social reality:

> Zi Si [the author of the *Zhongyong* who later came to be identified as Confucius's grandson[98]] considers the perfect accomplishment of these efforts: the transformation of an ordinary individual into a sage. He wishes that devoted students attain the *dao* by seeking it within themselves in order to eliminate selfish temptations coming from the outside and realize the original perfection of their good nature (言聖神功化之極。蓋欲學者於此反求諸身而自得之，以 去夫外誘之私，而充其本然之善).[99]

From these parallel paragraphs, one observes that transformation is not only 'liberation from the powerful illusion of "me" or "self"', as Hick envisages it,[100] but a concomitantly inner and outer process which is initiated within the human being and resonates outside by rendering perceptible the permanent subtle interrelatedness – the subtle root of reality – in the form of everyday ethical relationships and interactions. Neo-Confucian transformation concerns one's transition from a small self, dedicated to self-gain and self-interest to a complete, broad self, which includes understanding the specific situation of all others and active service for them as a good leader; Chan training aims at changing a small self into a no-self, who perceives others as oneself and renders them service without leaving any footprints, that is, by virtue only of their subtle interrelatedness through sharing the same original nature and without the slightest consideration of personal interest, the objective to govern them well included.

Hick refers to the transformation sought within the Christian tradition as 'a result of salvation rather than as itself constituting salvation'.[101] This illustrates another major difference between the Song dynasty understanding of transformation as the continuous, everyday ethico-organic process of perfectibility of human being, in accordance with the *dao*, and Hick's theory. Consequently, another important distinction concerns the nature of this transformation. The philosopher of religion stresses what he sees as a major mystical dimension of salvation and envisages it as 'the transformation of human existence from self-centredness to Reality-centredness'.[102] Mystical because from his viewpoint, this transformation in a universal context is the product of the gods and the absolutes (samadhi or satori, he explains), where the latter are different modes of presence of the same ultimate transcendent, therefore separate Reality.[103] Again, in the Song dynasty context, the *dao* is not a separate reality but, as demonstrated earlier, a subtle, metaphysico-spiritual and ethical order and movement of things. The final transformation focuses on following the *dao*, that is, active ethical practice in community. Only if the human being is able to remove by their own efforts the self-centred emotions/feelings which obstruct the presence of *dao* in everything will they be able to spontaneously follow it. In Chan and Neo-Confucianism, this process of transformation as self-cultivation depends not on an absolute (gods, samadhi, satori, etc.) but on the individual's own efforts to cultivate themselves and gain access to their marvellous, profound depth. This constant endeavour includes ethical practice, concentration, metaphysical reverence, non-dual practice of precepts, Confucian consideration for others (*shu* 恕), Chan wisdom of non-duality and so on.

In other words, in these two traditions, there is no personal or impersonal 'saviour' as Hick's theory universally would suggest, because the Chan *dao* or the Neo-Confucian *dao* is not a reality separated from the individual but an inner subtle root concealed by the individual's self-absorbed actions and feelings that need to be brought into one's awareness through their own efforts. The whole process of transformation is thus triggered by the individual's efforts, and the power to continually move forward down this road is entirely that of the individual. This is because the human being is within *dao*, and *dao* is within the human being as its organically, ethically and also spiritually nourishing soil.

The Christian particularity of the sole saviour Christ from whence comes the support for Christian salvific transformation and its difference from the non-Western (non-personal) transformation is contemplated by Hick in the following terms:

> The doctrine entails that Christ is the sole saviour: 'there is no other name under heaven given among men by which we must be saved than the name of Jesus Christ' (Acts 4:12). This in turn entails either, as was generally believed by Christians in the past, that the other great religions of the world are non-salvific or, as is held by many theologians today, that they are salvific as realms to which the redemption won by Christ is somehow extended. The effect of this, particularly in the older and stronger version, has been to make Christians feel uniquely privileged in contrast to the non-Christian majority of the human race and accordingly free to patronize them religiously, exploit them economically and dominate them politically.[104]

I would suggest that in the Chinese (Song dynasty) philosophico-religious thought, the salvific dimension, even if is present, takes a specific form – in Chan Buddhism through influencing one's future life through actual good deeds and in Neo-Confucianism as purification of self-centred sentiments. Still, this does not represent its major concern, and it would be a misrepresentation to transform it as most significant to this sphere. However, as illustrated in Qisong's and Zhu's quotations examined above, there is a fruitful connection between Western and Chinese religious traditions: the possibility of human transformation and its ethical perspective. Note that in the Chinese sphere, the notion of an individual salvation/liberation goal is absent; the objective there is to realize interrelatedness. That is to say, the following soteriological basic criterion elaborated by Hick as the standard for judging what he calls religious phenomena in general is not relevant for the two Song dynasty classical Chinese traditions:

> The basic criterion, then, for judging religious phenomena is soteriological. The salvation/liberation which it is the function of religion to facilitate is a human transformation which we see most conspicuously in the saints of all traditions. It consists, as one of its aspects, in moral goodness, a goodness which is latent in the solitary contemplative and active in the saint who lives in society, serving his or her fellows either in works of mercy, or more characteristically in our modern sociologically-conscious age, in political activity as well, seeking to change the structures within which human life is lived. This stems in each case from a basic ethical requirement; and it is this that provides the criterion for the moral assessment of religious phenomena.[105]

Only its function, human transformation consisting in moral and ethical goodness as the outcome of 'religious' practice, is a representative feature of the Song dynasty Chinese philosophico-religious thought. Therefore, it would be inappropriate to refer to the transformation envisaged by the classical traditions as a 'salvific transformation'. In order to highlight its ethical specificity, I propose referring to it as an 'ethical transformation'. Obviously, as already mentioned, the notion of 'ethical' has multiple levels. Additionally, in the Song dynasty philosophico-religious thought, the concept of religion is not a strictly delimited concept which designates a specific dimension of human activity or of the phenomenal reality as Hick's formula 'religious phenomena' would imply. It is a diffuse concept, an adjective that expresses a certain profound and omnipresent dimension of everyday human action and interaction.

In other words, the Western notion of grace – the divine, salvific influence which operates in human beings through the transformation described earlier by Hick – is completely alien to the two Chinese traditions. Smart's following insightful and critical remark can be directly associated with these ideas, since it is perfectly relevant to the Chinese cultural context. In discussing original (Indian) Buddhism, Smart sees in its absence of grace an active focus on individual effort, the source of the efficacy of its practice and, more importantly, a lesson to teach Christianity. As part of this reflection, he also brings to light some inevitable shortcomings in its practical dimension, caused by the Christian doctrines of faith and of grace:

Buddhism, because of its abstractions like Suchness and Emptiness, the Tathagata, interdependence and so forth, appeals to the scientific and metaphysical mood of the contemporary world. Also, its yogic kind of practicality – especially in a growingly individualistic and eclectic milieu – is alluring. In this it has its lessons to teach Christianity. The latter is much concerned to promote the need of grace and to phase out thoughts of gaining salvation by good works. This is in part an expression of the lone holiness of God. The divine has the power and the sublimity: the faith tries to express this as purely and vividly as possible. Perhaps this has led to some neglect of practical measures for self-improvement. ... The chief lesson of Jesus' (and Paul's) teachings is that salvation comes from God alone. But this belief is entirely consistent with the cultivation of calm and peace, benevolence and compassion, self-understanding and so on. The desire to improve oneself could be motivated by recognition of God's love and goodness toward us.[106]

As an addendum to this paragraph, I would add that unlike the Song dynasty Confucian and Buddhist traditions for which ethical interrelatedness is the result of one's social, metaphysical and spiritual practice with others and within oneself, the Western Christian ethical interrelatedness is a gift of grace, which flows from one's authentic relationship with God. As proof, consider this profound and transformative biblical image, Matthew 25:34–40, which illustrates one's concrete concern of being present to the most vulnerable and disadvantaged others as one's living relationship with God:

> 'For I was hungry,' says the King to those on his right, 'and you gave me something to eat, I was thirsty and you gave me something to drink, I was a stranger and you invited me in, I needed clothes and you clothed me, I was sick and you looked after me, I was in prison and you came to visit me.' Then the righteous will answer him, 'Lord, when did we see you hungry and feed you, or thirsty and give you something to drink? When did we see you a stranger and invite you in, or needing clothes and clothe you? When did we see you sick or in prison and go to visit you?' The King will reply, 'Truly I tell you, whatever you did for one of the least of these brothers and sisters of mine, you did for me.'

One may reply that Qisong's Chan ethical interrelatedness springs to life from the practicing Buddhist's non-dual perception of themselves in the most vulnerable and disadvantaged others (see also Chapter 3), while Zhu's Neo-Confucian ethical interrelatedness arises from the capacity of the exemplary individual to put themselves in their shoes, that is, to become aware of the good within themselves as their connection with others (see Chapter 4); and the Christian, from their perception as, in Levinas's terms, the lieu where 'God is really present' (en autrui il y a presence réelle de Dieu).[107] In the same paragraph, Levinas explains: 'This is not a mediation: it is the way in which the Word of God resounds' (ce n'est pas la mediation – c'est le mode selon lequel la Parole de Dieu retentit).

Note that, at this point, a new idea insinuates itself into the analysis and requires further development: the religious experience. Dichotomy is a major structure of the methods developed by Western scholars. They distinguish the religious experience[108] from other experiences, the religious consciousness[109] as different from its other dimensions, a religious mind (faith and a transcendent order of being) separate from a scientific mind,[110] the religious emotion (*mysterium tremendum*) distinct from the non-religious 'profane' of everyday experience,[111] the religious phenomena[112] from non-religious and so on. Some adopt an affirmative view – religion as sui generis (Max Müller, R. Otto, F. Heiler, Mircea Eliade, etc., and recently Flood, Kripal, Bynum) – while others are critical of religion (Auguste Comte, Émile Durkheim, etc., and recently Russell McCutcheon, Timothy Fitzgerald).[113] One source of these dichotomies is the Western emphasis on classification. No distinctive, separate religious experience or religious consciousness is highlighted in the Song dynasty texts but the existence of a subtle level of imperceptible interrelatedness present in one's day-to-day activities, even if one is aware of it or not. *Dao* is therefore interrelatedness. Following *dao* in everyday life activities and experiences means practising interrelatedness at a subtle level while preserving differences between individualities at the concrete level.

If the Western and Chinese traditions have different presuppositions and put their full attention and efforts into different issues, how could the student of religious studies build a meaningful comparative situation between them, sensitive and responsive to each one's cultural presuppositions? And why would they construct such a connection? The next section proposes a specific response to these questions.

5 Comparison: From a cognitive relationship towards an ethical relationship

The ideas I am developing in this section are inspired by Levinas's work on the radical alterity or otherness of one's neighbour, on proximity, and ethics as first philosophy. Western comparison in the area of religious studies involves various realities. The scholars in the field of religious studies strongly advocate the use of 'different scales of comparison for different purposes' in order to create 'a broader vision of religion'.[114] Patton and Ray suggest that 'comparison is the scholar's own *inventio*-the "magic" of creative insight and mutual understanding.'[115] But what do we compare? Smith explains that comparing is about relations and aspects and not things.[116] Wendy Doniger recommends a postmodern, postcolonial and post-structural comparative study of texts.[117] Timothy Knepper suggests focusing on 'localized human acts of religious reason-giving'[118] in comparative perspective. For Russell T. McCutcheon, comparative designates the cross-cultural nature of the discipline itself,[119] and he endorses Smith's view that comparison is an intermediate step in developing 'maps', that is, 'classificatory schemes, grammars, and taxonomies that scholars devise in their effort to compare and explain human behavior'.[120]

William Paden, for example, looks for 'points of comparability at the level of human behaviors – verbs, as it were, instead of nouns – rather than at the level of cultural meaning'.[121] He advocates the existence of 'a realm of panhuman behavior – behaviors to which religious cultures add their differences of content.'[122] Because, in his view, 'exclusive attention to cultural specificity tends to overlook the salient fact that behind cultural variance we are all bio-human creatures who "do" universes.' It should be added that the scholar of religion uses a Western understanding of the notion of cultural as 'learned', discussed in the introduction and implicitly based on the cultural presupposition of the separation between nature and culture: 'Without trying to adjudicate exactly what is cultural (or "learned") and what is biological (or stimulated by innate genetic wiring) – Paden notes – I do think that there are ways of construing patterns of religious worldmaking such that they can be shown to correlate generally with evolved biological or cognitive tendencies – that is, with our common organic ancestry.'[123]

The preceding section uncovered several Western assumptions which lie at the very core of some theories and inevitably limit their relevance to the Western sphere. For instance, as argued at the beginning of this work, starting from the graphic etymology of the Chinese *wen* 文 (culture) character, the Western meaning of culture as learned, therefore separated from nature, does not correspond to the Chinese perception of human life as partaking of nature and part of nature and of the continuity between its cultural and biological dimensions. 'The act of forming a world or classifying its structures is not culture-specific,' the scholar (Paden) adds, 'even though the content of a specific world is.'[124] It should be added, as already explained and as the following part further argues, that classifying is a Western activity rooted in the alphabetical structure of the Western language. One might say that, according to the specific functioning of language, the act of classifying the structures of a 'world' is not culture-specific but rather belongs to the Aristotelian heritage. Hewitt brings to light Paden's concern 'with achieving general knowledge about different religions' and his 'greater preoccupation with establishing a universal interpretive framework that sacrifices particularity rather than preserves it'.[125]

Paden's concept of 'world' has a profound resonance and carries richness of meanings. As he explains, it includes and goes beyond previously introduced concepts such as 'worldview' and 'system of beliefs'. Significantly, it also embraces language. If this is the case, then the 'act of forming a world' is at least language specific, therefore cultural and not universal:

> The concept of 'world' provides a tool for understanding and analyzing the plurality, contextuality, and self-positing nature of religious cultures. Thus, rather than viewing religions in terms of a given standard – whether religious or nonreligious – of what 'the' world is and then seeing how they, the religions, represent 'it', here the assumption is that religious systems themselves create their own versions of world. Religions are one of culture's primary systems of world definition, constructing universes of language, behavior, and identity with their own particular organizing categories. … The concept 'world' in some ways overlaps with the notions of belief system and worldview but has more textured, contextualistic, and behavioral reference. World encompasses all forms of habitation, action, and language, and not just viewpoints, ideas, or self-conscious doctrines and philosophies.[126]

With the comparison between Western alphabetical language and Chinese graphic language (see Section 2) in mind, I would suggest that the notion of 'world' defined in the above paragraph could be further specified as 'cultural world'.

Coming back to the comparison, as discussed earlier, Smith's work focuses specifically on this method – an approach that he sees, as noted above, as intrinsically connected with classification. In other words, comparison for the purpose of classification plays out in between difference and similarity. The latter are understood in this context as relative concepts, not as notions radically different from each other. This because Smith's classification implies working on difference, based on dividing species as mutually exclusive groups. However, as noted earlier, this exclusiveness is only relative and is also comparative, because different species participate collaboratively in the community of genus. The difference and similarity presuppose only a relative alterity: they deal with distinctions between analogous qualities. Only the latter make classification possible. Building on Smith's theory, Oliver Freiberger's work *Considering Comparison: A Method for Religious Studies* portrays the comparative approach as having two goals: description and classification. If descriptive comparative studies have for him the role of 'defamiliarizing the familiar', the comparative research works having classification as their objective participate at the formation, application, critical evaluation and rectification of metalinguistic terminology.[127]

Obviously, there is no real alterity in the framework of such a cross-cultural comparison. Because it presupposes a pre-existing relationship between those qualitative differences which are relative, in other words, as explained above, engaged in classification and participating in the community of a genus. The scholar's work is a theoretical reflection on the terms of the articulations of similarity and difference. Thus, they resort to a comparison of comparable species within the framework of the genus of religion. By doing so, the student's cross-cultural effort accesses the culturally other religious through their own reflective deliberation, not through communicating with it in an intercultural relation. As noted above, the classification implies a cognitive relation: knowledge produced by the scholar for themselves, which implies a pre-reflexive comprehension of the self of the scholar, a self-awareness, the Cartesian self-conscious thinking (*Cogito, ergo sum*). Understanding is what defines the relationship between the theorist and the culturally other religious that they study using cross-cultural comparison. In this case the other culture is, as Levinas would say, 'culture as knowledge', which reduces the difference to relative difference. In his *Entre nous: Essais sur le penser-à-autre*, he describes the idea of 'culture as knowledge' by referring to the all too famous Platonic doctrine of recollection (see *Meno*, *Phaedro* and *Phaedrus*): 'Since the dawn of the Western philosophy, one learns just what one already knows but had only forgotten within one's interiority.'[128] That is, he notes in *Humanisme de l'autre homme*, 'the philosophy is committed to resorb all Other with the Same and to neutralize alterity.'[129] It may be thought that the classification methodology within the sphere of religious studies, analysed in this chapter, would be such a recollection of 'forgotten' knowledge, the neutralization of alterity.

Besides the relative alterity between difference and similarity in cross-cultural comparison, one can also identify a radical alterity: the otherness. Levinas teaches us to realize that while the (relative) difference is entirely conceptual and therefore ethically neutral, the otherness is ethical awareness of other's alterity. Otherness lies beyond the classification of species. Going beyond the Western perspective of comparison/classification would be to perceive the culturally other religious not as relative and classifiable but as radical alterity; equally, to view the culture, not merely as knowledge but as ethics.

In other words, this implies transforming the relationship with the religious other from a cognitive relationship – based on knowledge, a relationship between the scholar as subject and the religiously other as object – to an ethical relationship; that is, if one accepts that all meaning is to be found in ethics, which is a fundamental presupposition of all culture, of all knowledge. This book advocates the construction of an ethical relationship between theorists and the other's religiousness envisaged as beyond the theorists' knowledge and embraces this relationship not as cross-cultural and therefore cognitive but as intercultural and transformative relationship, from culture to culture, from the assumptions of Western religiousness to those of the non-Western (Chinese, in this context). It also suggests that, in this specific context, such ethical relationship involves uncovering and comparatively examining the particular cultural presuppositions of the religious other – not as relative but as radically different.

What would be the nature of such an interculturally ethical relationship? It could be a relationship in which the theorist takes account of the radical alterity of the culturally other religious they study, or, translated in Levinasian terms, of its irreducibility to the same (i.e. the Western culture). How could this kind of ethical relationship be possible if there is a consensus that human mind is not self-transparent? This is to suggest that the researcher could be very well unaware that their Western cultural presuppositions, cognitive choices and cognitive categories influence their analysis of the culturally other religious. Again, in the context of the comparisons of the functioning of languages, the necessary condition to avoid such deformations would be to redirect one's analysis to consideration of cultural presuppositions. What could give the theorist access to that level? According to this work, the answer is, again, learning from the other's language. Or, as Smart advocates, in a paragraph quoted above, 'learning something of the general structure and vocabulary of a language'.[130]

By means of such an exercise, the researcher can become more aware of their own presuppositions and of their functioning within their analysis. If, first and foremost, the Western scholar were to focus on the functioning of their own language, they would be able to relate their analytical choices to this specific functioning (categorical, classificatory) of their own alphabetical language. In this way, the student would be able to become aware of the presence of Western presuppositions within their analytical framework. This would be the first step of building such an ethical intercultural relationship. Part 1 of this book (Chapters 1 and 2) provides an example of such a first step. The second necessary step would be to learn something about (from) the other language. Part 2 (Chapters 3 and 4) represents this second step in our Chinese context. This stage of the foreign language effectively opens access to the other, that is, to the other's presuppositions. One argument I put forward in favour of this position is the following reflection of Levinas from his 1971 essay *Totalité et infini: essai sur l'extériorité*. And I invite the reader to interpret it in the present context, which is not exactly the Levinasian circumstance of the spoken word but a complementary one – that of the classic written language (text) which incorporates cultural presuppositions and of the classic Chinese-Western language translation, sensitive to these. His reflection also reminds us of Babel myth:

> The language establishes a relationship irreducible to the relationship subject/object: the *revelation* of the Other. It is only in this revelation that the language, as system of signs, can constitute itself. The interpellated other is not a represented, it is not a given, it is not a particular, by one side already offered to generalization. The language, far from presupposing universality and generality, only makes them possible. The language presupposes interlocutors, a plurality. Their commerce is not the representation of one by the other, not a participation to the universality, to a common plan of the language. Their commerce, we will say it, is ethics.[131] (italic in original)

In this ethical relationship rooted in language, the culturally other religious is the alterity or the radical difference that teaches the scholar. Because, one must recall, the essential function of the language is to teach. The teaching of this educator – the culturally other religious – can provide to the learner – the scholar – something that the latter does not know and never knew. This ethical teaching is other than the Socratic maieutic method; it is not an exercise of self-knowledge, a recollection of something already known but yet forgotten by the learner. It opens the latter to the idea of radical alterity, to something completely new. In our specific case, the educator is the classic Chinese philosophico-religious text, its translation. Part 4 of this book is one practical example of the type of ethical relationship to be promoted. The latter focuses on a comparative, intercultural analysis of cultural presuppositions.

In his book dedicated to comparison, Freiberger refers to the focus on difference, plurality, diversity and uniqueness which characterizes the postmodernist and postcolonialist critiques of comparison: Jean-François Lyotard, Theodor Adorno, Michel Foucault, Jacques Derrida and later Edward Said, Talal Asad, Gayatri Spivak and Homi Bhabha. 'It questions', he notes, 'scholarship's claim of objectivity and champions self-referentiality, which, in the final analysis, might be interpreted as cultural, epistemological and moral relativism.'[132] About the cross-cultural comparison, he reiterates the arguments of this type of research:

> If the postmodernist and postcolonialist premises are taken seriously and consequently pursued, they argue, comparison, and especially cross-cultural comparison, has to be abandoned entirely, either because proposing any kind of cross-cultural sameness distorts the uniqueness of cultural (including religious) expressions or because comparison imposes a (Western) categorical framework on them, a framework that reinforces the power and control of Western neo-imperialist dominance.

So, is this an impasse? Probably not. Let us consider the link between the successive stages of the comparative encounter between the scholar and the religiously other. Objectively speaking, cross-cultural comparison is a first, necessary stage in our actual global cultural interaction, as well as within the multicultural societies. In cross-cultural comparison, Freiberger explains, 'The researcher identifies analogies of religious concepts, practices, objects, etc. in separate contexts by observing that the items have similar forms or functions.'[133] One can also add that these analogies may prove to be only apparent or distorted when they do not take into account the differences at the deep level of cultural presumptions. Because, as Freiberger like Smith notes, such reasoning by analogy is heavily dependent on the researcher's context (background, interests, training and individual decisions), that is, the comparativist's situatedness.[134] It goes without saying that, in order to reach the following level of the cultural assumptions and of the interculturality, one can start with the cross-cultural analogies.

Coming back to Freiberger's earlier assertion about the difficulties of the cross-cultural comparison: it appears that the next-stage, the postmodernist and postcolonialist perspectives convey a strong message. They reveal the shortcomings of these previous studies and suggest that the time is ripe to set aside the focus on cross-cultural comparison and to build another level of comparison. This is possible starting from the analysis of their (Western) categorical framework (as in Chapters 1 and 2), with the intent to correct such shortcomings mentioned by Freiberger in the quotation above.

The present study first acknowledges the importance of all these previous levels in broadening the method of comparison. Next, it suggests another subsequent level of comparison: intercultural, which is based on identifying and considering the particular cultural presuppositions of each one of the elements of the comparison (here Chinese religious thought and their Western counterpart). Part 4 provides an example of such interpretation. Its meaning has been set forth in the introduction. This is inspired by the philosophical translation of classic texts, by Gadamer's and Ricoeur's hermeneutical developments, as well as by Levinas's ethics as first philosophy, and his major distinction between difference and otherness discussed earlier. Levinas teaches us to realize that the difference is entirely conceptual and therefore ethically neutral, while otherness is ethical awareness of other's alterity. Moreover, the present context which unfolds in between the otherness/difference of the Chinese classic graphic language and Western alphabetical language allows us to discern first that the (relative) difference is also indifferent to cultural presuppositions, because it unfolds at the Western conceptual level; second, that acknowledging otherness allows for becoming aware of cultural presuppositions and sensitive to them, because it evolves not within the Western conceptualization but in the sphere of the comparative analysis of the different coherences of graphic and alphabetical languages. The latter is possible through mediated intercultural translation and interpretation. Becoming sensitive in the sense mentioned above leads to self-transformation.

Nevertheless, approaching intercultural comparison not as a cognitive process but as the construction of a parallelism which serves to make the reader aware of the differences between ways of thinking and spiritualities emerging from the Western phonetic and Chinese graphic languages, as this appears through the translation of philosophico-religious Song dynasty texts, has an additional advantage: the possibility of distancing from that self-transparency of the scholar examined earlier, which is inevitable in the epistemological approach. This because such a comparative endeavour strives to build an ethical relationship between the theorist and the culturally other religious, beyond knowledge, occurring within the process of hermeneutical translation and interpretation. In other words, it raises awareness about the different functioning of the two languages. This sort of thing cannot be exposed in a relation developed on epistemological analogy or on a classification-based analogy, but in one of complete alterity, in the absence of any analogy. In his own philosophical context, Levinas understands the beyond knowledge as the non-knowledge which characterizes the ethical relation.[135] In the present context, the non-knowledge as dimension of this ethical relation between theorist and culturally other religious can be understood as the motivation not to assess but to learn from the other.

Another major dimension of this ethical relationship, complementary with cultivating the motivation for learning, is the responsibility to deal with the culturally other religious in the most honest way, that is, to avoid introducing in the translation-interpretation distortive Western cultural assumptions. Such accountability arises from the researcher's duty to possess prior knowledge of the Western cultural presuppositions embedded in the theoretical tools (like those discussed in Part 1). I am not referring here only to a Western theorist. This accountability is a two-way street. Because the situation is the same – that is, a non-ethical relationship – when the researcher is non-Western, let us say, a Chinese scholar in the process of manipulating the Western theories they master, who is applying them to their own cultural content, without a prior understanding of the presuppositions embedded in those theories. They eventually end up giving a misleading account of the content they manoeuvre.

The next part attempts first to construct two such translation-interpretations of the notion of interrelatedness in the writings of the Northern Song Chan scholar-monk Qisong and in those of the Southern Song Neo-Confucian thinker Zhu Xi. Second, endeavours to build an interpretive theory of the theme of interrelatedness as core of the Song dynasty philosophico-religious thought mediated through the analysis of the texts previously introduced. This interpretive tool adapted to the Song dynasty traditions constitutes the effective result of the intercultural philosophico-religious communication which is the process of translation. It is possible to define this operation as the transfer of the coherence of thought rooted in the classic Chinese graphic language to the environment of the Western alphabetic language.

Part 2

Chinese Cultural Presuppositions: Ethical Interrelatedness in Song Dynasty Philosophico-Religious Traditions

3

Ethico-spiritual interrelatedness: The meaning of ethico-religious practice in the Chan scholar-monk Qisong's writings

1 Introduction: Context and approach

This chapter[1] tackles the peculiar cultural assumptions of the philosophico-religious writings of the Song dynasty Chan scholar-monk Qisong 契嵩 (1007–1072). Together with Chapter 4, dedicated to the Neo-Confucian scholar Zhu Xi 朱熹 (1130–1200), it forms the basis for the development in Part 3, of a theory of religion specifically designed for the Chinese space and its distinct cultural premises.

Concretely, it explores in depth one aspect of a topic that looms large in Song dynasty (960–1279) thought – the mutual interaction between Confucianism and Chan Buddhism and their common cultural presuppositions – as envisioned in the work of the Northern Song Chan scholar-monk Qisong. This is a time when a significant philosophical and cultural confluence of these two main teachings takes place in China. Under their reciprocal influences, both experience meaningful and definitive changes. This Song philosophico-religious legacy became emblematic, and has remained so until now, of the classical Chinese way of thinking. It therefore represents a pivotal period for Chinese thought, and the interconnection between these two main paths of reflection and practice (Confucian and Buddhist) requires further detailed study. This is why in this study, the two major Song dynasty spiritualities – (Confucianized) Chan Buddhism and Neo-Confucianism – are considered as representative of the 'Chinese religion' and its distinctive cultural presupposition, the interrelatedness.

Specifically, Chapter 3 deals with a less examined issue and aims to fill this gap: the influence of Confucian thought on Northern Song dynasty Chan Buddhism. The hermeneutical framework that I propose for this analysis is the notion of interrelatedness. This chapter identifies interrelatedness as one of the main Song dynasty issues of concern to both teachings and explores the interpretation of interrelatedness by one of the prominent thinkers of the time: a Buddhist highly proficient in Confucian classics, the scholar-monk Qisong. It examines his collection of essays written in Confucian *guwen* 古文 style, *Essays on Assisting the Teaching* (*Fujiao bian* 輔教編). This work was composed during the 1050s and approved in 1062 by Emperor Renzong (r. 1022–63) to be incorporated in the Song Buddhist Canon.[2] It includes the essays examined below: *Inquiry into the Teachings* (*Yuanjiao* 原教), *Extensive Inquiry into the Teachings* (*Guangyuan jiao* 廣原教), *Letter of Advice* (*Quanshu* 勸書), and *Encomium of the Platform Sutra* (*Tan jing zan* 壇經贊).³ The scholar-official Chen Shunyu 陳舜俞 (1026–1076), in his book *Duguanji* 都官集 (*Collected Works of a Town Official*), records that Qisong's explanation of Buddhism in the *Essays* was compatible and complementary with Confucianism and was very well received by his Confucian contemporaries.⁴ Qisong's use of the Confucian style, known as *guwen*, enables one to clearly perceive Chan Buddhism's interaction with Confucianism and its transformation starting from the common issue of practising ethical interrelatedness. This is the major dimension of his strategy of explaining Buddhist doctrines in Confucian terms. Moreover, it highlights the strength and vitality of Song Confucian culture and its core focus, namely, the importance of building social harmony, ethical interrelationships and peace through teachings (not only Confucian but also Buddhist).

My starting point is therefore Qisong's usage of Confucian *guwen*. As he himself stresses,⁵ the Chan scholar-monk adopts it in order to explain Buddhism to his Confucian contemporaries. This constitutes for me the most powerful and original innovation of Qisong – his utilization of Confucian terms and references from Confucian classics, in order to persuasively interpret a special form of socially engaged Chan Buddhism and highlight its connections with Confucianism. His usage of this Confucian *guwen* device, how he implements it in order to explain in Confucian terms and within Confucian contexts the distinctive features of his 'cohesive' Chan Buddhism, was my guiding line when clarifying textual issues and Qisong's interpretations of Confucian concepts.

2 Transformation for the purpose of experiencing interrelatedness: Chan Buddhism and Confucianism

2.1 Interrelatedness as 'making people good'

As will become apparent later, for Qisong, Buddhism means Chan Buddhism. However, his is a holistic, non-sectarian perspective. Qisong does not want to separate and distinguish between Buddhist schools, as was the tendency during the pre-Song period, and after his time, but rather to integrate various Buddhist practices and doctrines (*Huayan*, for instance – see *Guang yuanjiao*, 0654b07) in an all-encompassing idea of Buddhism, organized around the central Chan notions of heart-mind and original nature. This study preserves this widely inclusive meaning that Qisong confers to his teaching.⁶ As will become clear, he also includes Confucian teaching within the Chan Buddhist training.

His writings intend to defuse the feeling of animosity largely shared by the Northern Song Confucian scholars who considered themselves as the guardians of the Confucian culture.⁷ In order to redefine his own school of thought in terms comprehensible for them, Qisong strategically starts from a new global definition of the teachings. The latter are in his view the tools the sages use to explain the way (*dao* 道), which they adapt according to the individual circumstances and needs of the people they teach.⁸ His aim is to demonstrate that, contrary to the always critical view against Buddhists taken by Confucians (see Han Yu's 韓愈 (768–824) article *Inquiry into the Dao* (*Yuan dao*)),⁹ the two teachings are not only compatible but also complementary and interrelated. This is because, he emphasizes, they have a common goal, which Qisong defines with much originality as 'making people good [willing to perform good actions] (*wei shan* 為善)': 'The teachings [Confucianism and Buddhism] provided by the sages are different (不同); however, they are identical in that they make people good [stimulate their good actions] (而同於為善也).'¹⁰

In other words, in Qisong's view, both teachings have a common goal pursuant to which they can be seen as identical: seeking to engage people and society in an ethical transformation – simultaneously at the social and spiritual levels – which means fostering a proactive, 'enlightened' impulse to perform good actions. It is recalled that the term 'ethical' implies multiple meanings, even if he highlights in this context its social dimension. One may recognize in his ideas a little nod to Mencius, who taught that all human nature is good,¹¹ and a continuation of his thought. Through this appraisal, the monk-scholar not only introduces a new interpretation of the essential Confucian goal of active ethical leadership and engagement, in which good action is taken as imperative, but he also elaborates on the different natures of Buddhist and Confucian transformation. It is in this context that he expresses the ideas of the necessary complementarity between Confucianism and Buddhism. Qisong notes the incompleteness, inefficiency, even failure of the Confucian ethical transformation throughout history and suggests that the transformation of individuals enabled by his teaching has the potential to assist the Confucians to ensure good governance:

> From the Three Dynasties, the country's governance has deteriorated, and the bad behaviours of ordinary people have increasingly worsened. The [Confucian] ritual and behavioural rectitude (禮義)¹² were no longer sufficient to govern the people (不暇獨治). It is for this reason that Buddhist teaching spread throughout China. Together, Buddhism and Confucianism advise the people, and due to them, the people harmoniously undergo transformation (遂與儒並勸, 而世亦翕然化之). Through practicing Buddhism, there are individuals who have achieved positive change, and people who have moved away from bad behaviour; and there are those who have been able to discover by themselves their own original nature and thus correct it (自得以正乎性命者). Therefore, until today, people have depended on Buddhism. It is for this reason that I think that Buddhist teaching provides a complementary support to Confucianism and makes society better. (乃相資而善世也)¹³

Note then, when discussing his sub-school of Chan Buddhism as an efficient transformative teaching, Qisong does not highlight the practice of individual meditation, for which Chan is probably best known in the West, as the main source of transformation. Instead, Qisong emphasizes the socially oriented application of the *Five Precepts and Ten Good Deeds* (五戒十善) – that is, eliminating the desires to kill, to steal, to engage in illicit sex, to lie, to drink intoxicating drinks, and 'speaking clearly, without unnecessary embellishments (不綺語), 'not having two tongues (i.e. not talking behind another person's back) (不兩舌), 'avoiding verbal abuse, as well as things that do not correspond to the sense of duty (不惡口), 'not being envious (jealous) (不嫉), 'not reacting with anger (不恚), 'not being stupid (not failing to distinguish good from evil) (不癡).[14] He considers them to be the Buddhist counterpart of the Confucian practice of the *Five Permanencies* (五常) from which stems Confucian ethical interrelatedness – kindness (*ren* 仁), appropriate behaviour (*yi* 義), spirit of ritual (*li* 禮), moral knowledge (discerning what is right and what is wrong) (*zhi* 智) and fidelity to one's pledged word (*xin* 信); these correspond to the *Five Relationships* (人倫)– father and son, ruler and subject, husband and wife, seniors and youths, friends (see *Mencius* 3.A.4, included in *Teng Wen gong zhangju shang* 滕文公章句上, in *Zhuzi quan shu* 朱子全書 (*The Collected Works of Master Zhu*), vol. 6 (ZZQS 6: 316)). In his view, this Buddhist practice enforces the appropriate norms which structure the hierarchical relationships of interrelatedness of the Confucian society. Elsewhere I discussed this topic.[15] Qisong's comparative approach allows us to develop a more accurate view of the diversity of the Chan practices within Song Confucian culture and their inclusive character. In his view, the *Five Precepts and Ten Good Deeds*, which are everyday social actions and interactions widespread in the lay community, form an integral part of his inclusive Chan sub-school. The scholar-monk stresses that Song Chan's focus is on large-scale social transformation starting from individual transformation, within the context of Confucian social relationships. In other words, this community transformation through Buddhist undertakings makes it possible for Confucian interdependence to function effectively:

> When there are people guided by means of the *Five Precepts and Ten Good Deeds*, how can those from their neighbourhoods help but transform themselves (相化) by following their lead? From the villages to the towns, from the towns to the whole province, from the province to the whole country, the scholars from the imperial court and everybody from the imperial palace, all feel this influence. ... If one can follow only one of these [*Five Precepts and Ten Good Deeds*], this is enough for them to become sincere to themselves and help other people.[16]

Let us observe the specific terms in which Qisong suggests the communitarian and hierarchical nature of the Confucian transformation and interdependence (villages, towns, provinces, imperial court and palace) in comparison with the individual character of their Buddhist equivalents ('becoming sincere to oneself and helping (benefiting) other people (誠於身而加於人)'). In this way he focuses on the fact that, in the end, the Buddhist transformative actions performed by individuals can assist and support the Confucian communitarian transformation.

Through stimulating the reader to view Confucianism in a new way, namely as transformational and life-changing, the scholar-monk spotlights the metamorphic efficiency of Buddhism while introducing a differentiation between the two different transformative qualities. Moreover, he justifies this contrast in Buddhist terms: when strategically adopting a historical perspective (an inevitable decline in the quality of the governance and of people's behaviour), he presents Confucianism as a provisional, temporary teaching (i.e. limited to the ethical sphere of everyday transient relationships of the present life) and Buddhism as a definitive one (i.e. a teaching that embraces Confucian ethics but also goes beyond it, because it roots one's good or bad actions in the connection between one's previous, present and future lives, resulting from the indestructibility of the spirit (*shen* 神)). Notwithstanding his clear interest in bringing out the difference in their ethical natures (Confucian social and Chan spiritual), Qisong ultimately focuses on the ethical goals of the two life-changing teachings as being the most important dimension of both: 'giving up doing wrong actions, and applying oneself to doing good actions (舍惡從善)'.[17]

2.2 Experiencing interrelatedness, sameness and peace

In the background of this definition of the common transformative purpose of the different teachings, one perceives an overall concern of the Song culture – the Chinese native concept of social, ethical interrelatedness, as the moral agent's good actions are performed for the benefit of others and presuppose interaction with others, closeness to and concern for them. The role of the teachings, Qisong stresses in Confucian language (see the following citation from Qisong's essay *Yuanjiao*), is to restore the proximity or interrelatedness between people, that is, first and foremost, the social peace, 'living peacefully' (*an* 安). Social peace is set in place durably only when the interrelatedness between individuals is achieved and upheld through the practice of teachings, which instil awareness among the people of the profound sameness (*tong* 同) between individuals, by virtue of the fact that they all share the same original nature. Here one discovers embedded in the notion of sameness another major Chinese cultural presupposition. 'Sameness' is in this case positively valued as the wellspring of communitarian harmony, while 'difference' (*yi* 異) – that is, excessive focus on the visible diversity – is to be avoided because it triggers conflict. Qisong explains in the following terms the socially pacifying effect of the search for sameness –an awareness of the common nature within individuals that defines his Buddhist teaching:

> The nature of individuals is the same, their emotions are different (性相同也, 情相異也). When seeking difference, among the people, rarely is there no rivalry (天下鮮不競). When seeking sameness, among the people few are those who do not live peacefully (天下鮮不安). The sage [Buddha] wants to guide them towards living peacefully together, therefore he promotes the fact that the nature is the same in all individuals (推性而同群生); the sage wishes to bring rivalry to an end, therefore includes everyone into his bosom, and he is in all living beings (推懷而在萬物) [as Buddha-nature, or heart-mind].[18]

One should note in passing that in the period after Qisong, the Neo-Confucians of Zhu Xi's School of Principle significantly develop this idea of sameness through the introduction of the Neo-Confucian concept of principle[19] (see Chapter 4).

The source of the quest for peace – that is, the harmonious social interaction embodying the highest Chinese cultural ideal of interrelatedness – can be found in ancient Confucianism (the well-known *Daxue, jing* formula: 'all under heaven' (*tianxia* 天下)),²⁰ as well as in Neo-Confucianism (see later).

Qisong provides evidence of the presence of this cultural ideal in Northern Song Buddhism. In his view expressed in the previous quotation, peace arises therefore from effective interrelatedness (as individual awareness of being endowed with the same nature, or heart-mind, as all other people), and he implicitly highlights the fact that achieving this social ideal requires every individual to effectively experience one's profound sameness with others. As will be seen below, the Buddhist sameness means acquiring access, through religious training and social practice, to suchness, the real reality. The interrelatedness that results from Chan awareness and cultivation of the sameness is emptiness, in other words, absence of an individual self (i.e. egocentric). Buddhist sameness goes beyond and encompasses Confucian interrelatedness and sameness rooted in the mandate of heaven (*tianming* 天命),²¹ which in the scholar in Buddhist-Christian studies Frederick J. Streng's (1933–1993) terms, might be called the natural law of an ethical religion.²² This Confucian external natural law of organic and ethical growth, which applies throughout heaven and earth, is reflected in the next paragraph. In contrast, the Buddhist source of this ideal of peace is inwardly situated within each individual.

By preserving its well-known hierarchical perspective – the distinction between governing elites (exemplary men 君子) and the people (the multitude, the hundred family surnames 百姓 or the depersonalized community) – these Neo-Confucians, a generation younger than Qisong, situate the source of this ideal of interrelatedness and universal peace outside of the individual people, within the ruler-scholars who serve as role models for the people and their behaviour. This vision clearly emerges in Zhu Xi's following note to the *Analects* 14:45, where he quotes Master Cheng:

> Master Cheng says: 'The exemplary man cultivates inwardly, in order to enable people to live peaceful lives (安百姓). He keeps watch over himself constantly and for this reason he makes all under heaven stand together (天下平). When all the people from top to bottom are one through their watchful and respectful behaviour, heaven and earth are naturally in their right places, ten thousand things are spontaneously growing and developing, the vital breaths are in harmony, and the four efficiencies (*ling* 靈) [heaven, earth, man, ten thousand things] are fully accomplished'. 程子曰：「君子脩己以安百姓，篤恭而天下平。帷上下一於恭敬，則天地自位，萬物自育，氣無不和，而四靈畢至矣。」²³

The source of the Confucian transformative teaching is clearly perceptible, observes the scholar-monk, because it is located within the scholar-official's exemplary behaviour, that is, in his Confucian relationships (*Five Permanencies*) with all others of different status and role. In contrast, the Chan source of the *Five Precepts and Ten Good Deeds* belongs to the inner ultimate reality, imperceptible at an ordinary level. This is why, Qisong concludes, the contemporaries (*shi* 世) have difficulty in identifying it, perceiving its effects, and therefore trusting it: 'What emerges [individual transformation] from it [the Buddhist way of the *Five Precepts and Ten*

Good Deeds] does not come from the scholar-official, and the transformation it talks about is hidden, difficult to see, therefore people fail to understand it and to completely trust it' (但其所出不自吏而張之。亦其化之理隱而難見。故世不得而盡信。).[24]

The scholar-monk highlights not only the social engagement of his teaching, a dimension of Buddhism not recognized by Confucians and a major source of their criticism against Buddhists, whom they characterize as selfish (*zisi* 自私, see *Jinsilu* 13: 6),[25] but also the non-duality of the Chan way, which is simultaneously socially and also individually transformative because its source is the inner thusness. It not only supports the Confucian *Five Permanencies*, here identified in well-known Confucian terms as 'social relationships related to sovereign, official, father and son 君臣父子', but also assists individuals in their efforts 'to nourish their present life and take care of their future one (生養之道)':

> How could the Buddha limit himself to his personal issues? Thus, how would the way of the Buddha be concerned only with one's personal affairs? It concerns all the people and the whole country. Even if the way of the Buddha exists in the social relationships related to sovereign, official, father and son, how could this prevent individuals from nourishing their life [present and future] with this way? 佛豈苟癖於人焉。如此者佛之道豈一人之私為乎。抑亦有意於天下國家矣。何嘗不存其君臣父子邪。豈妨人所生養之道邪。[26]

Both teachings stress realizing interrelatedness through experiencing the sameness of all individuals. The next section examines Qisong's interpretation of sameness in Buddhism and Confucianism through the articulation of 'heart-mind' and 'names'.

3 Experiencing interrelatedness as sameness (*tong* 同)

In pre-Song Confucianism, the interrelatedness is mostly understood as cultural sameness, that is, belonging to the Confucian culture of the *Five Permanencies* (rule-ordered relationships). This is embodied in the ideal of the *Great Sameness* (community) (大同) originated by the *Gongyang Commentary to the Spring and Autumn Annals* (*Gongyang Zhuan* 公羊傳). The Chinese historian Kung-chuan Hsiao 蕭公權 (1897–1981) sees the latter as the source of China's conception of a unitary world and of the thought of the authoritarian, bureaucratic empire.[27] Qisong infuses new meaning into this notion of sameness.

Let's recall first his original definition of the common goal of both teachings: to make people good. From this stems his innovative rendering of interrelatedness between individuals as their sameness, where the latter has the meaning of being good, kind: 'The good people are not close relatives, yet see themselves as being the same [close] (故善人非親而善人同之).'[28] In other words, Qisong explains interrelatedness between individuals as flowing not from their cultural identity but from their sameness-kindness. Clearly, for him, sameness is the common result of following the teachings

(Buddhist or Confucian). The monk-scholar perceives sameness as the shared identity of all who are committed to performing good actions. Note that this is a completely new interpretation of Confucian tradition, which is generally explained as a political and ethical philosophy.

Sameness in the scholar-monk's view is participative and inclusive of all teachings, whether Buddhist or Confucian, yet he focuses first on its socio-ethical connotation. Using the metaphors of the natural forces that form oceans and mountains, the author highlights the power of sameness – an awareness of which is acquired due to transformative teaching – to bring about a large-scale, synergetic, cooperative and durable ethical change (*daode* 道德) in the community, through the common participation of all sages, that is, of all teachings:

> Many watercourses accumulate their sameness, which becomes a deep current, thus forming the river-sea water; many clumps of soil accumulate together their sameness, which becomes a pile, thus forming the highest peak of the mountains. Many great men [sages] accumulate together their sameness, which becomes wide, thus promoting the moral norms. 水多得其同則深為河海。土多得其同則積為山嶽。大人多得其同則廣為道德。[29]

In his essay *Guang yuanjiao*, Qisong explains this sameness of the teachings at the ethico-moral level (其德同),[30] beyond their different methods, as the result of the fact that all sages, Confucian, Buddhist or belonging to the various philosophical schools, have the same heart-mind (心則一).[31] On one side, he highlights that both teachings and sages (Confucian and Buddhist) share the same quest for interrelatedness through cultivating sameness and that only together they can morally transform society. But on the other hand, as already mentioned, he also stresses that the two types of sameness sought by Confucians and Buddhists differ with respect to their depth. In his Chan view, Confucian sameness is the hallmark of a teaching which is temporary, expedient (*quan* 權), gradual (*jian* 漸), partial (*pian* 偏) and conditioned by circumstances, while the Chan Buddhist sameness can be achieved only through the permanent, real (*shi* 實), sudden (immediate) (*dun* 頓) and complete (*yuan* 圓) practice of the heart-mind.[32] In the same passage, he is careful to also point out their interrelatedness, the fact that beyond their different natures, the real method relies on the expedient one, and that the sages use the latter with a view to moving towards the first.

In order to illustrate the dissimilarity in their natures, he suggestively introduces the distinction between 'heart-mind (*xin* 心)' and 'names (social status, reputation) (*ming* 名).' It is important to note that this articulation is particularly relevant when drawing a comparison between Chan Buddhism and Confucianism: the heart-mind is the core notion around which Chan Buddhism is configured; the name is clearly an allusion to the Confucian doctrine of names (*ming jiao* 名教) or doctrine of ritual (*li jiao* 禮教). All of these latter terms refer to Confucian ritualism, the set of norms and standards of behaviour modelled on hierarchical interrelationships and statuses. The next two sections explore Qisong's interpretation of Chan Buddhist sameness as rooted in the heart-mind and of Confucian sameness as rooted in the hierarchy of names. They further unfold the multiple meanings of the notion of 'interrelatedness/sameness' as Chinese cultural presupposition.

3.1 Chan Buddhist sameness as rooted in the heart-mind

Qisong suggests that the heart-mind is the Chan vehicle for interrelatedness as emptiness, the driving force that triggers an individual's transformation. He explains the latter as first understanding the differences between various things and affairs and then materializing transformation at the level of human feelings/emotions.[33] Thus, human interrelatedness becomes effective in ethical interaction with others in everyday life. It was this less explored dimension of Chan Buddhism that Qisong emphasized during the Song times.

Even if human transformation and the functioning of interrelatedness/sameness manifestly occur at the level of perceptible reality, their source in Qisong's view is the heart-mind, which belongs to the Buddhist ultimate reality, the so-called thusness (*ru* 如) or suchness (*shi* 實). It is ultimate or permanent because at this level, no change or transformation is needed anymore. He identifies this reality using the Chinese native term 'the great marvellous (*damiao* 大妙)' (see, e.g. Zhuangzi, chapter *Yu Yan* 寓言, and Laozi, par. 27[34]). However, Qisong's concept of marvellous is non-dual. In other words, at the level of everyday affairs and impermanent changes, it manifests itself as ordinary (little) marvellous (*miao* 妙), at the level of suchness (of the connection between past, present and future lives) as great marvellous.[35] In the above-mentioned paragraph, he describes it as completeness (*zhi* 至), or the root of all beings and of the marvellous. Elsewhere,[36] he identifies the marvellous with the spirit (*shen* 神, another Chinese native notion whose meaning has been redefined by Chinese Buddhism) of the individual that subsists from one life to another. Moreover, the monk-scholar equates the latter with the universal, original nature (*xing* 性), that is, Buddha-nature. Through establishing a relationship of synonymy between all of these Buddhist and traditional Chinese (Confucian) notions, Qisong enriches the original meaning of the Confucian ancient terms with Chan resonances. He operates an effective comparison between the two teachings and operatively connects them through introducing both in a common context: interrelatedness-sameness.

The Chan heart-mind, as embodiment of sameness, lies beyond the socio-ethical dimension and is transtemporal and transpatial (emptiness (*wu* 無): everyone's heart-mind is Buddha's heart-mind), a spiritual connection, a common spiritual feature (*ling* 靈) that profoundly interrelates individuals at the level of suchness, of emptiness perceived as interrelatedness: 'The spiritual feature of each of the ten thousand living beings is the same; it is the so-called heart-mind (萬物同靈之謂心).'[37] The heart-mind is emptiness because it restores the non-duality of heart-mind and no-heart-mind (see the Song dynasty, mature version of the *Platform Sutra* 六祖大師法寶壇經, T48n2008, 0357c19). And also, Qisong says, 'There is an ancient sage, his name is Buddha. First, he completely rectified his heart-mind. Then he wanted to extend (*tui* 推) his heart-mind to all the people in the world, so that everyone would be the same. (古之聖人有曰佛者。先得乎人心之至正者。乃欲推此與天下同之。)'[38]

One observes in the tone and terms of this paragraph that describes the Buddha's mission, certain similarities with the Confucian expression of the exemplary person (*junzi* 君子). The Buddha described here resembles a Confucian role model who goes beyond himself in order to reach out to those he governs. In his commentary *Zhongyong zhangju* 13,[39] Zhu Xi quotes Master Zhang Zai 张载 (1020–1077), a Confucian contemporary of Qisong, who defines the Confucian consideration for others (*shu* 恕), in terms similar with Qisong's, as 'extending oneself to others [putting oneself in someone else's position] (推己及人為恕)'. The Confucian consideration for others is an illustration of the Confucian ethics of interrelatedness structured by the *Five Permanencies*. However, while the terms at first glance may appear similar, the realities behind them are different. The Confucian extension of the exemplary man's self is temporal and limited to the ethical level. The members of the Confucian society ethically transform themselves, that is, become aware and cultivate the interrelatedness between them, under the external influence of the leaders acting as role models for their communities. In Zhu's Neo-Confucian view, this ethical interrelatedness is social as well as metaphysical. Through social practice, the individuals realize the presence of the principle of coherence of heaven in everyone. In order for this to happen, the rulers as role models have to cultivate their own self and make it complete. Only the Neo-Confucian whose self is complete acquires the ability to put themselves in the place of those they govern (understand everyone's feelings), maintain and cultivate the society as a whole, as well as the inner and outer ethical harmony of the interrelated individuals within communities.

The Chan idea of extension puts forward a spiritual, transtemporal extension of the Buddha heart-mind, which makes it possible to experience interrelatedness not only at the level of everyday ethics but also at the level of ultimate reality. When the individual is able to crack the wall that limits their self-consciousness and thus experience their own 'nature-emptiness' and 'no-self' – that is, the self connected with everything or the interrelated self – a profound transformation occurs: one's emotions become non-contaminated and non-distorted, and the human is spontaneously pure not only at the social level of everyday ethical interactions but also at the spiritual/religious level of the interconnection between their past, present and future lives, of the karmic causes and fruits.

Qisong constantly highlights the non-duality or absence of separation between the two levels of reality, which in people's everyday life he considers to be one – that is, emotions (ethical everyday relationships) and their Chan root (a rectified heart-mind, suchness, spirit, no-self or interrelated self). He opens his *Encomium of the Platform Sutra* (*Tanjing zan* 壇經贊) with an explanation of the heart-mind as root of sameness at both levels, of tangible, temporal transformations and of marvellous, transtemporal, pure reality:

> The *Platform Sutra* is that by which the Complete Man [Huineng 惠能 (638–713), the Sixth Patriarch, presumed author of the *Platform Sutra*] disseminates the influence of his heart-mind. What heart-mind? The marvellous heart-mind transmitted by the Buddha. The great heart-mind! It provides support for the

beginning of the transformations (changes), yet it remains permanently pure. Whether ordinary individual or sage, whether hidden or perceptible, there is no place that this heart-mind cannot reach. It is said that the sage is enlightened and the ordinary individual, ignorant. The ignorant evolves at the level of the changes. The enlightened returns [to thusness]. Even if changes and returning are different, the marvellous heart-mind is one. 壇經者，至人之所以宣其心也。何心邪？佛所傳之妙心也。大哉心乎！資始變化，而清淨常若，凡然聖然幽然顯然，無所處而不自得之，聖言乎明，凡言乎昧，昧也者變也。明也者復也。變復雖殊而妙心一也。[40]

Note in this paragraph that unlike the stereotypical perception of Chan as a teaching without words, beyond the text, a direct transmission from the master's heart-mind to the disciple's heart-mind, Qisong highlights the importance of the written traces of the sage's heart-mind (here, the *Platform Sutra*), just as Confucians hold high regard for the classics. One also observes how this quotation unfolds a non-dual description of the heart-mind: as simultaneously temporal and transtemporal, heart-mind and no-heart-mind – it is not only one's present heart-mind but also the heart-mind of the Buddha and other sages, such as Huineng; as both transspatial and spatial – pure, therefore beyond transformation, and yet the originator of spatially perceptible transformations; as the same heart-mind of the enlightened and of the ignorant – beyond distinctions and yet embracing them; as concurrently including the unfolding of changes – at the spatio-temporal level of everyday interactions, affairs, emotions/feelings, in ordinary, ignorant people – and the folding backup of change – the return to the suchness level (the completeness, the great marvellous) in enlightened people. It thus embodies the simultaneous transtemporal, transindividual interrelatedness as well as societal.

In the following paragraph (*Guang yuanjiao* 0655a19), Qisong depicts the same idea of the non-duality of the Chan sameness rooted in the heart-mind, a sameness that concurrently functions at different levels of reality (of discursive understanding, emotions/feelings and the heart-mind and its universal nature):

> The consciousness [of mind] makes the ten thousand sentient beings many and various, considers them as different. The transformation (變) means the first indicator of movement. The state of completeness [ultimate reality] (至) is the root of the marvellous. In the world, there is no thing without root, that is, no thing that does not move. It is for this reason that the ten thousand things move out of the process of transformation and move into it (萬物出于變入于變); the ten thousand things leave the state of completeness and return to it (萬物起于至，復于至). The transformation of the ten thousand things is apparent in the emotions/feelings. The world's state of completeness lies in the universal nature. Through the emotions/feelings one can differentiate between the transformations of the things (以情可以辨萬物之變化). Through the universal nature one can be aware of the great marvellous of the world. When one excels in both the realm of the emotions/feelings and universal nature, then one is able to discuss the way and the teachings of the sages.[41]

In this quotation, alongside his description of the non-duality of the heart-mind, Qisong clearly stresses that the Chan sameness or interrelatedness rooted in the heart-mind does not exclude the emotions/feelings, the sphere of human interactions and social relationships. Elsewhere,[42] he also urges people to experience their heart-minds and thereby widen their understanding to not only include one specific and limited teaching but also to become aware of the sameness of the multiplicity of teachings (ways) of the sages[43] – the way of the spirit (*shen dao* 神道, which he defines as the effort to become aware of authentic nature), the way of humans (*ren dao* 人道, defined as the effort to cultivate good actions) and the extreme moral quality (*ji de* 奇德, another ethical training). He refers to their sameness from the perspective of the ultimate reality which is their common root – the heart-mind – rather than only from the perspective of their common aim – social cohesion. In order to have access to this deep sameness rooted in the heart-mind, Qisong warns above, one has to 'excel' (to be good at, *shan* 善) in both realms, that of the names (society and its hierarchy) and that of the ultimate reality. An oversimplified image of Chan emphasizes individual meditation as the method which enables practitioners to get access to ultimate reality. In his Northern Song view, quite differently from this popular unidimensional perspective, getting access to ultimate reality is intended not to help individuals distance themselves from society but to enable them to re-enter in a new way, transformed and purified, into the everyday reality of the differences between names/appellations, that is, the ethical realm of Confucian social relationships.

3.2 Articulation of the heart-mind and names

Qisong highlights the social dimension (names/appellations) of the deep sameness rooted in the ultimate reality or heart-mind. This is his particular interpretation of Chan Buddhism as the spiritual root of social regeneration. This idea illustrates his Chan sub-school as organically integrated in the soil of the Song dynasty Confucian culture. In the next quotation, the scholar-monk starts by considering various teaching traditions as equivalent because of their common goal of making the people good through rectifying (*zheng* 正) their heart-minds. He then distinguishes them according to their source or nature, differentiating between teachings emphasizing sameness and ultimate reality (Chan Buddhism) and those that emphasize names, by which he means concrete differences, and social realities (Confucianism). The scholar-monk thus introduces a new articulation – names/ultimate reality – which builds another efficient connection between Chan and Confucianism. And he encourages people to 'leave behind (*yi* 遺)' the names. Clearly, this does not mean to abandon them but to consider them not as primary but as secondary reality, from the perspective of the ultimate, true reality (*shi* 實). This is because attachment to them (*zhi ming* 執名) encourages people to forget their true reality and their essential sameness, and thus uprooted from ultimate reality, people remain caught within the net of their superficial differences and apparent sameness (i.e. cultural sameness, sense of belonging to one, Confucian-ordered culture of names). One should first leave behind the names (hierarchical relationships), and only after they become aware of their deep sameness with others from the perspective of the ultimate reality should they correctly come back to the names:

The teachings are the means by which people correct their heart-minds. In order to distinguish between the different ten thousand sentient beings, nothing is better than the names (appellations). In order to make them the same, nothing is better than [awareness of] the ultimate reality. The [Buddhist] sage teaches people using the ultimate reality because he wants them to form a great sameness [great unity]. The [Buddhist] sage encourages the people to leave behind the name, so they guard themselves against the great difference. When looking at the method by means of which the sage teaches, one sees clearly that he aims for people to completely leave behind the name and to completely realize the ultimate reality. 教也者，為其正之之資也。別萬物莫盛乎名，同萬物莫盛乎實。聖人以實教人，欲人之大同也。聖人以遣名勸人，防人之大異也。觀夫聖人之所以教，則名實之至，斷可見矣。[44]

Note that, in Qisong's view, Chan sameness indicates the experience of emptiness, while pre-Song Confucian sameness points to the sense of belonging to the same culture of names. In a renewed effort to describe the non-duality of the individuals' sameness starting from the articulation of the correlatives' name/ultimate reality, the scholar-monk yet again convincingly connects Confucian and Buddhist perspectives in his eleventh-century collection *Essays on Assisting the Teaching* written in Confucian *guwen* style. Thus, he first borrows the well-known Confucian notion of rectified heart-mind (*zheng xin* 正心) from the ancient classic *Daxue*, *jing* (*Great Learning*, canonical section *jing*). Then, in a surprisingly creative articulation, he equates it with the Buddha. This constitutes in his view the highest level of sameness of the individuals – where individuals experience the Buddha and all humans as one:

What is the Buddha? It is the individual's rectified heart-mind. What is the human? It is the individual who turns to this rectified heart-mind and commits to making efforts towards it. The Buddha and the human are one. The so-called ten thousand things are the names. The so-called complete universal principle is the ultimate reality. If people attach to names and ignore the ultimate reality, how can they understand the state of completeness? 佛者，何謂也？正乎一者也。人者，何謂也？預乎一者也。佛與人，一而已矣。萬物之謂者，名也。至理之謂者實也。執名而昧實。天下其知至乎。[45]

Note the quasi-Confucian terms in which he presents the Chan ideal of experiencing the level of ultimate reality, attainable through effort by each individual, as meaning, instead, experiencing that everyone is the Buddha, interrelatedness is the Buddha. In ethical terms this means to respect others as you would the Buddha. The transtemporal rectified heart-mind is the Buddha, and everyone is able to gain access to one's rectified heart-mind, provided one makes the effort to go beyond names while incorporating them. Moreover, Qisong highlights that enlightenment emerges in the daily life of all people, most of the time while they are not even aware of it.[46] In terms of Confucian and Buddhist resonance, he defines enlightenment, not only as the state in which one transcends beyond the cycle of life-death but also as achieving exactly the same moral quality as that of the sage (聖人同德).⁴⁷ The above-mentioned complete universal principle makes reference to Huayan Buddhism's conception of 'principle' and its philosophical belief in the interpenetration and inseparability between principle (transtemporal reality, connection between past, present and future) and things (temporal realities) (see, e.g. the *Essay on the Arousal of the Bodhi-Heart-Mind in the Huayan* of the third patriarch of the Huayan school, Fazang, T45n1878, 0652c29, 0653a03). It is interesting that during the next generation after Qisong, the Neo-Confucians would establish the School of Principle – one might argue, precisely in order to introduce and justify in Confucianism, too, a metaphysical idea of sameness, beyond the differentiation provided by names.

This Chan ethico-moral quality that he discusses does not arise exclusively out of the socio-ethical domain of putting oneself in another's place but from experiencing the sameness of all sentient beings emerging from the no-self – the other is me, I am the other. This Chan experience is for him the ultimate reality, the non-dual heart-mind. In other words, according to the Northern Song monk, the nature of the Confucian moral source is socio-ethical, belonging to the way of humans (*ren dao* 人道, which means cultivating good action and practising ethical interrelatedness in ongoing daily interaction⁴⁸) and emerging from the presupposition of the difference between oneself and the other – one is not the other, as one's name, social status, interests and wishes are different from those of the other. It is through Confucian teaching that one learns to make the effort to leave behind one's own concerns and go beyond oneself, beyond one's name, project oneself outside the boundaries of one's immediate self, and voluntarily and mentally overcome this presupposed duality, in order to be able to put oneself in the place of others, and morally govern them. The nature of the Chan moral source in Qisong's view belongs to the way of the spirit (*shen dao* 神道, which also embraces the way of humans and means becoming aware of the inner, original nature, cultivating ethical interrelatedness rooted not in exceptional, external role models but in experiencing the sameness of all heart-minds). While cultivating the names ensures, merely, the control of people on the outside (制其外), of their outward behaviour and appearance, Qisong points out,⁴⁹ the exemplary men who govern starting from experiencing their heart-mind and universal nature have the ability to rightly govern the people through touching them inwardly (感其內), by resonating with their heart-minds. This resonance is effective when individuals inwardly experience their own heart-mind, which is also the heart-mind of others. This is precisely what is meant by interrelatedness, 'a heart-mind interconnected with everything (心通)'.⁵⁰

Whilst in his view, Confucian sameness springs from the will, and the mental process of connection across difference, Chan sameness is a lived experience, not only mental but within the body. How is it possible for one to gain access within oneself of this Chan sameness? Qisong answers concretely that it is through trusting one's heart-mind (信其心): 'I encourage the exemplary persons [rulers] to trust their heart-mind – and then, to deal with the affairs which correspond to their name according to their own heart-mind (曰勸夫君子者自信其心。然後事其名為然也。)."⁵¹ In other words, according to the scholar-monk, experiencing the heart-mind is trusting it. And experiencing the Chan heart-mind is experiencing one heart-mind, the same one shared by all. He thus suggests a model of good governance and peace where moral administration originates not in the difference of names but in the experience, by officials, exemplary men and by ordinary people, of the sameness of all heart-minds, that is, emptiness of the individual self. Only after this experience do the expedient (Confucian) names become efficient:

> The heart-mind is the root of the sage's morality [sense of duty]. The name is only an expedient used by the sage in order to encourage people [officials] to perform good actions. When one devotes one's efforts to the expedient without being aware of its root, are one's good actions really good? When put into action, is one's morality really moral? 夫心也者,聖人道義之本也;名也者,聖人勸善之權也。務其權而其本不審,其為善果善乎?其為道義果義乎?[52]

Using such hybrid language, which adopts simultaneously Confucian and Chan Buddhist ideas and expresses them in Confucian *guwen*, a style that praises the Confucian values and makes ample references, both implicit and explicit, to the Confucian classics, Qisong aims to create a close, cooperative relationship between the two teachings despite their different natures and as a means of soothing the cultural animosity of Confucian rulers. Remember that the Confucians officially interpreted the two teachings as opposite and Buddhism as a body of 'heterodoxies (*yiduan* 異端)', that is, of deviations from the accepted or orthodox Confucian norms of Chinese Confucian culture (see *Jinsilu* 13, *Bian yiduan* 辨異端, *Distinguishing Heterodoxies*[53]).

4 Conclusion

This chapter presents and interprets multiple dimensions of the interrelatedness/sameness as a major cultural presupposition of the Northern Song Chan Buddhism, as it emerges from the works of the Chan scholar-monk Qisong. It argues that, according to him, experiencing the interrelatedness of human beings is a common primary purpose of both Song Buddhist and Neo-Confucian teachings. It focuses on his interpretation of interrelatedness as unfolded in the context of his comparative appraisal of Buddhism and Confucianism. In his special understanding of Chan Buddhism that I identify, for the reasons given above, as including a strong 'Confucianized' dimension, Qisong revisits and reinterprets Confucian terms (like rectified heart-mind, names, hierarchical social relationships, moral quality) in order not only to explain Buddhism to his contemporary Confucian readers and auditors 'who do not know Buddhism'[54] but also to advocate its compatibility and interrelatedness with Confucian teaching and its usefulness for the Confucian rulers.

The chapter builds an interpretative intercultural experience between Qisong's Song dynasty classical text written in Confucian *guwen* style and the Western philosophical translations put forward as arguments. Together with the proposed philosophical interpretation, these translations constitute the body of this intercultural exercise on the theme of interrelatedness and its multiple meanings. Through proposing this specific methodology rooted in hermeneutical translation and interpretation mediated by classical texts, the essay strives to bring out cultural presuppositions of Qisong's thought, without changing their cultural meaning, and also to illustrate how he adopted and instilled new meaning into Chinese native terms. It also points out the peculiarity of the scholar-monk's thought within the Song philosophical landscape – his pursuit of non-duality (Buddhism and Confucianism) through forging a new meaning of the notion of interrelatedness.

Another intended contribution of this chapter is to suggest and explore a less often addressed feature of Song dynasty Chan Buddhism (Qisong's Northern Song Chan sub-school *Yunmen* 雲門): its social involvement and engagement and its in-depth focus on contributing to social wellness. The scholar-monk is interested in explaining his teaching as the practice of interrelatedness in everyday life and affairs. This dimension of his work has not been addressed before. Its examination is important not only for advancing our knowledge of the creative exchange between Buddhism and Confucianism during the Song dynasty but also because it contributes to our rigorous understanding of the specificity and richness of Chinese Chan Buddhism, beyond labels and stereotypes.

Qisong's interpretation of Chan Buddhism and the strategic selection of topics he identifies as representative of his teaching (i.e. ethical interrelatedness, sameness, heart-mind and names) aim to highlight the complementarity between the two teachings in Northern Song dynasty Confucian culture and the usefulness of his teaching for promoting Confucian good governance. Clearly, these themes presented in Confucian *guwen* style are somewhat different from the usual, medieval image (Tang dynasty (618–907)) of Chinese Chan Buddhism. The study offers arguments for why one should not dismiss Qisong's 'Confucianized' perspective and interpretation of Chan Buddhism as non-orthodox. Quite the opposite, it can be said that his comparison calls for a more complex understanding of the multiple dimensions of Song dynasty Chan Buddhism, which was developed within Song Confucian culture itself, and is not an alien, acclimated element.

The monk's perspective challenges and stimulates a broadening of our perception of Chan Buddhism and a rethinking of the boundaries between Chinese Confucianism and Buddhism, which goes beyond their officially construed perception by Confucians as conflictual, recognizing them, instead, as open and interconnected. It also allows us to gradually perceive the major common assumptions which give shape to what this book refers to as 'Chinese religion': here in the context of the Northern Song Chan Buddhist texts; in Chapter 4, within the framework of the Southern Song Neo-Confucian commentaries.

Therefore, this chapter is directly connected with the next one, which examines the perspective on interrelatedness of Zhu Xi's Neo-Confucian School of Principle. Qisong's comparative philosophical analysis of the different natures of interrelatedness in pre-Song Confucian and Chan Buddhist traditions – socio-ethical and socio-spiritual – provides persuasive arguments with respect to the societal effectiveness of the Chan ethical practice. This chapter also suggests that the monk's philosophico-religious demonstration probably influenced the Neo-Confucian masters who founded the School of Principle,[55] a generation younger than Qisong. Because, as Chapter 4 argues, they introduce a metaphysical dimension – a Neo-Confucian 'interrelatedness/sameness' – in their own ethical tradition, non-existent in the pre-Song Confucianism.

4

Ethico-organic interrelatedness: The meaning of ethico-religious practice in the Neo-Confucian scholar Zhu Xi's writings

1 Introduction: Context, approach and methodology

This hermeneutical chapter[1] explores the theme of interrelatedness in Zhu Xi's thought, starting from his meaning of the good (*shan* 善) and its practice,[2] as exemplified in his commentaries on the *Four Books*. I suggest that this topic is the cultural presupposition at the core of his understanding of what might be called ethico-religious practice. Chapter 3 analysed the Chan scholar-monk Qisong's perception of the good and ethico-religious practice in his comparative presentation of the complementarity of the two Song dynasty traditions – Chan Buddhist and Confucian – in the *Essays on Assisting the Teaching*. The approach used in Chapter 3 and this chapter is based on the old hermeneutical principle that one can understand a detail only in terms of the whole 'text' and the whole only in terms of the details.[3] Its aim is to uncover and investigate the cultural premises of classical Chinese religion as ethico-organic focus, heart-mind, spiritual and metaphysical interrelatedness and so on as well as how those evolved from the ancient classics. The 'text' in this case is the Southern Song Neo-Confucian Zhu's set of commentaries on the *Four Books* (*Collected Works*, hereafter ZZQS, vol. 6). This body constitutes his twelfth-century interpretive understanding of the Confucian tradition and epitomizes the spirit of Neo-Confucianism.[4] The details are the various facets of the good and its practice that he explores in these works.

The chapter suggests that in his school of thought, the purpose of the good for exemplary individuals (*junzi* 君子) – that is, members of the ruling elite – is twofold: first, to realize the existence of an ethico-organic interrelatedness between oneself and those governed; second, to make this interrelatedness concrete and permanent through ensuring that their heart-minds are continuously present and nourished.[5] It is this well-cared-for heart-mind that enables individuals to put into practice interrelatedness through performing good actions. And it is in this specific context that, inspired by the ancient Mencian perspective – he asserts explicitly – Zhu also builds a theory of the heart-mind. His development is probably and latently stimulated by Chan Buddhist philosophical analyses of the Confucian tradition like those of the Northern Song Chan scholar-monk Qisong written in *guwen* style. The topic of the good including its key element, the heart-mind, emerges from a new set of Neo-Confucian philosophical interests, which can be directly tied to Chan Buddhist influence: heart-mind analysis, experience of the self and introspection.[6] Charles Wei-hsun Fu also highlights the connection between Mahayana theory of Buddha-nature, the primordial goodness and absolute purity of man's heart-mind and nature and the Mencian ideas reinterpreted by Zhu Xi.[7]

This chapter demonstrates that the Neo-Confucians brought a whole new meaning to the notions of interrelatedness and sameness in Confucian thought – the good(ness). It will be remembered that Chapter 3 focuses on this idea as developed by the Chan scholar-monk Qisong, in his Chan Confucianized texts, a hundred years before Zhu Xi. Chapters 3 and 4 are therefore complementary and connected. They illustrate mutual influences and exchanges between Confucianism and Chan Buddhism during the period of Song dynasty.

In the feudal world, including the Spring and Autumn and Warring States Periods, interrelatedness and sameness were embodied in the concept of 'all under heaven, one embracing world (天下)' and the emphasis of cultural identity; in addition, the doctrine of the 'great community/sameness (大同)' was developed after the establishment of the authoritarian imperial system.[8] In ancient Confucianism, interrelatedness is developed at the social level and expressed in the context of the interpersonal, hierarchical relationships (see the classic *Daxue* 大學). The new Song dynasty Neo-Confucian signification of interrelatedness indicates a change in the conceptualization of the interrelatedness. Is part of the new meaning a deeper understanding of one's psychology, oneself and emphasis on self-control?[9] Interrelatedness signifies now not merely cultural and political unity but also ethico-metaphysical sameness and unity. It might be said that the major driver of this change in meaning was the interaction between Confucianism and Buddhism.

The term 'metaphysical' that I choose to use in this context has a particular signification: it means transphenomenal, that is, transphysical, subtle dimension or 'environment' present in all realities, which is both beyond physical and within it. We shall call this minimized, interdependent duality physical/transphysical correlativity. It does not mean separated reality as in the Western thought. Obviously, this particular perception of 'metaphysical' implies that in Chinese culture, phenomena are not merely tangible, perceptible realities but complex, multidimensional and interrelated, both sensible and metaphysico-spiritual, organic and ethical things. This particular perception flows from the fact that they are not considered as static and form-determined substances but as subtle, living therefore dynamic vital breaths (*qi* 氣). Sections 1.1 and 3.1 of Chapter 1 offer a detailed perspective of Zhu's understanding of this notion.

The first part of this hermeneutics examines the various dimensions of the meaning of the Neo-Confucian notion of good and its connection with the idea of interrelatedness. The second part provides an overview of the fertile Chinese philosophical ground from which emerges Zhu Xi's Neo-Confucian idea of the good; in other words, its cosmological and ethico-metaphysical presuppositions: ethical interrelatedness and interrelated self, as discussed in the *Book of Changes* (*Yijing* 易經), the *Zhongyong* 中庸 and the *Mencius* 孟子. This ground provides the Song dynasty standard and justification of the good, including good conduct. It also represents the organic and moral demand for doing good deeds. For that reason, its examination is a precondition for exploring Zhu's perspective on the inner practice of the good. In the next section of the hermeneutics, this inner practice is considered to be the motive power behind the practice of the good in everyday affairs. It focuses on the notions of the heart-mind (*xin* 心), authentic nature (*xing* 性) and the process of keeping an individual's heart-mind present (存其心) in order to subsequently correct it (正其心)[10] and nourish the individual's nature (養其性).[11] The conclusion provides some critical reflections on this Neo-Confucian moral perception of the good as interrelatedness and its presuppositions.

2 Zhu Xi's Neo-Confucian interpretation of the good as interrelatedness

2.1 Knowledge and the good: The identity among homogeneous good (均善), authentic nature (性) and principle of coherence (理)

In his commentary to paragraph 20 of the classic *Zhongyong*,[12] Zhu Xi brings forward the concept of 'homogeneous good (*jun shan* 均善)', which is a whole, complete and coherent good and not some mixture of different components potentially containing infinitesimal constituents that are evil (*e* 惡). In this context, he cites Lü Zuqian (呂祖謙, 1137–1181), who equates this homogeneous good with the authentic nature (*xing*性) of human beings while emphasizing that this good dimension or authentic nature is something all humans share: 'The homogeneous good in which there is no evil – this is the authentic nature by which humans are all the same. (均善而無惡者, 性也, 人所同).'[13] In this way, he implicitly stresses that the intact (homogenous) good is nothing other than interrelatedness, that is, the experienced affinity or natural connection between people, governors and governed, an inner dimension that makes all alike (人所同) despite their social and hierarchical differences. It is the subtle thread that connects all – in other words, the basis of a unified, harmonious and well-governed Confucian society. It is interesting to view his twelfth-century perception of the inner good as interrelatedness in parallel with Qisong's eleventh-century idea of interrelatedness as 'making people good', discussed in Chapter 3, Section 2.1. This parallelism reflects what could be called the deep ethico-moral holism of the Song dynasty philosophico-religious Chan and Confucian traditions.[14]

Furthermore, Zhu equates authentic nature (*xing* 性) with the principle of coherence (*li* 理)[15] received from heaven-nature (*tian* 天) and highlights again that the good within – authentic nature or the principle of coherence – is the same for all, both legendary sage emperors and common people: 'Master Cheng said: "Authentic nature is the principle of coherence, and this principle of coherence is the same, from Yao and Shun to ordinary people (程子曰:「性即理也, 理則堯, 舜至於塗人一也.」)."'[16] Through these equivalent concepts, the good, the Neo-Confucian metaphysical notions of principle of coherence and authentic nature, the scholar conveys in different ways the interrelatedness between people, their everyday affairs and various relationships. In his view, the common good is primarily an experiential state but also a mode of action and knowledge: first, it refers to experiencing in oneself what effectively connects one with others, what brings together their everyday affairs. As the principle of coherence bestowed by heaven-nature, the good embodies a simultaneously organic and ethico-metaphysical interrelatedness; as authentic nature (the original metaphysical state of each human's emotions/feelings, present but not having been developed, see Zhu Xi, *Zhongyong zhangju* 1), it embraces socio-affective interrelatedness: 'The authentic nature of humans and of everyday interrelationships is also the exemplary individual's (我)[17] authentic nature (人物之性，亦我之性).'[18]

This paragraph clearly introduces the metaphysical source of the ethical behaviour in his thought. In Zhu's view the good means many things. By inference from these related quotations, it is clear that for him, the good is to be understood, first, in terms of a human dimension of socio-affective interrelatedness with which individuals have been endowed by heaven-nature; second, as a metaphysical or 'transmoral'[19] dimension of the conceptual/physical reality – the principle of coherence given by heaven that connects (the meaning of the Latin prefix 'trans') realities at a subtle, unapparent level. However, this unique principle or complete good is perceptible, therefore knowable, not in its essence (i.e. as the principle of coherence of heaven (*tian li* 天理)) but only in its particular manifestations in every individual human, action and relationship (i.e. the specific principles of coherence of each individual, everyday affair and relationship (*shi li* 事理)).[20] The principle of coherence is therefore one and many. While it is one, is assumed to denote metaphysical (or transmoral) potential, heaven's moral endowment; it becomes many (or moral) when set in motion so that it can be present in all distinct human affairs, thus ordering them. It becomes clear that heaven endows morality as it endows life. According to Zhu, this moral endowment can be known when people have acquired complete comprehension of the whole set of these individual principles of coherence, which represent the morally good or right course for every action or relationship. This is so, because it is from this common or complete good (*zhi shan* 至善) or one and only principle of coherence of heaven that arise all these individual moral principles of coherence. Consequently, he equates homogeneous good (*jun shan* 均善) with complete good (i.e. including absolutely every particular good and its specific principle). In his commentary to the *Daxue*, Zhu notes, 'The complete good is the indubitable utmost extent (*ji* 極) of the coherence principles of affairs (至善，則事理當然之極也).'[21]

This assertion is illustrative of Zhu's rational-intellectualist perception of the good.[22] What is, in fact, the utmost extent of a principle of coherence of a thing, human or affair? It goes without saying that these principles are to be understood in the context of Confucian leadership and governance. Through this idea of utmost extent (*ji* 極), Zhu indicates the progressive process of understanding the principles of coherence, the necessity to completely understand (*zhi* 知致, see *Daxue zhangju, jing*), that is, to grasp principles of affairs to the utmost extent. In other words, lesser understanding that is limited, conditional, incomplete and partial is not enough to achieve the knowledge of the complete good and of the principles of coherence. This pursuit implies an ongoing need for meticulous reasoning in conjunction with close interaction between consciousness and things. Accordingly, Zhu Xi values rational, intellectual thinking in the conventional sense, based on intelligence and reason.

The next citation illustrates his conviction that, through one's adequate willingness, one can understand the principles of coherence of the governance of affairs completely, to their utmost extent. This implies that the unique principle understood to mean highest good is comprehensible through the complete understanding of the specific principles of coherence of affairs and things (窮至事物之理). The unique principle as complete good and the multitude of principles of affairs are thus objectified: being objects, their complete comprehension is possible by the knowing subject. Moreover, this perspective also indicates that the knowledge of the principles is gradual and accumulating:

> Complete: this means to the utmost. Understanding: in other words, knowledge. Expending to the utmost one's knowledge, refers to one's willingness to make one's knowledge complete. ... Getting to the bottom of the principle of coherence of affairs and things, refers to one's willingness to ensure that his knowledge is brought to the utmost and reaches everywhere. 致，推極也。知，猶識也。推極吾之知識，欲其所知無不盡也。… 窮至事物之理，欲其極處無不到也。[23]

Hence, there clearly appears to be a tension, more precisely still, a duality or correlative relationship (conceptual thought and direct experience), in Zhu's perception and ethical knowledge of the good simultaneously understood to mean the principle of coherence and authentic nature: he considers the nature of the good as both experiential (authentic nature concerns the direct, non-mediated experience of emotions/feelings as they unfold in everyday interaction) and conceptual (the individual principles of coherence can be conceptually understood). However, in his view these dimensions are very much complementary, and they both illustrate the above-mentioned interrelated character of the good. Through direct experience, introspection and experience of one's self and one's emotions/feelings, the individual becomes aware of the good within themselves as their metaphysical connection with others. This means that the individual really has the feeling that they are close to others. Knowledge of the good through utmost knowledge of the principles of coherence also connotes interrelatedness: through continuous engagement in acquiring knowledge, the activity of the self becomes more profound and broader. The image of one's 'utmost knowledge that reaches everywhere' (其極處無不到) is an illustration of the widening of the self and of its activity and suggests gradual inclusion of new things, previously unknown by the self, in its sphere. This progressive inclusion of new knowledge effectively conveys a vision of interrelatedness.

Note that, through his conceptualization of the moral principle of coherence of affairs (*shi li* 事理) presented above, which was a new Neo-Confucian concept inspired by the universal principle of the Huayan Buddhist tradition (see, e.g. the *Essay on the Arousal of the Bodhi-Heart-Mind in the Huayan* of the third patriarch of the Huayan school, Fazang, T45n1878, 0652c29, 0653a03), Zhu reinterprets an ancient idea, already present in the *Classic of Poetry* (*Shijing* 詩經), one that Mencius also mentions – the existence in each thing (*wu* 物) of its norm (*ze* 則): 'The *Classic of Poetry* says: "Heaven gave birth to the people. Every being and thing has its own norm" (詩曰:「天生蒸民, 有物有則.」).'[24]

Zhu Xi's introduction of the Neo-Confucian principle of coherence into his explanation of the goodness of human nature constitutes a major development in comparison with Mencius's thought. The latter defines innately good human nature as being primarily feelings or emotions (*qing* 情) (see *Mengzi*, *Gaozi shang* 6), while Zhu Xi sees it as a metaphysical principle of coherence bestowed by heaven.

In his explanation about this section (*Gaozi zhangju shang* 6), Zhu Xi notes that while interconnected and related through the common initial goodness of human nature, humans are also unrelated and unconnected, because they have different innate abilities (*cai* 才) that come from distinct vital breaths (*qi* 氣)[25] also provided by heaven-nature. These make individuals unalike, namely, relatively intelligent or unintelligent, strong or weak and so on. They also disconnect people and deteriorate their initial goodness or principle of coherence bestowed by heaven-nature. In this commentary to the *Mencius*, Zhu makes clear his view on the articulation between innate abilities and vital breath. Again, he highlights his intellectual perspective, namely, that these natural differences can be overcome through study, in other words, through understanding, reason and practice (see next citation).

Nevertheless, sameness understood as initial complete goodness or interrelatedness is what prevails in his thought, while individual differences, namely, distinct mixtures of the principle of coherence and vital breath, are held to be only secondary, impermanent and meant to be overcome through learning and understanding. Again, one may describe his position as correlative (the interdependent good, authentic nature, moral principle of coherence – disconnectedness, self-interest, particular differences, innate ability, vital breath) and intellectualist (focused on studying, apprehending, *xue zhi* 學知). From this perception springs his conviction that 'everyone can reach in themselves their initial goodness and return to the root of their authentic nature'. Yet, this original and intact resource, existing prior to vital breath and deep inside it, can easily deteriorate when in contact with the latter:

> Innate ability is provided by the vital breath [at birth]. This vital breath can be clear or muddy. Those who have received a clear breath become eminent individuals. Those who have received a muddy one, become unintelligent. The vital breath of those who study and therefore understand is no longer clear or muddy; all of them can reach their initial goodness and return to the root of their authentic nature. 才稟於氣, 氣有清濁, 稟其清者為賢, 稟其濁者為愚. 學而知之, 則氣無清濁, 皆可至於善而復性之本.[26]

Consequently, in Zhu's conceptual context of the good as interdependence, these natural differences can be construed as hallmarks of the independence and autonomy of individuals because their role is to separate, divide and disconnect them. Obviously, this distinction between humans, their otherness, is easily and clearly perceived, while the sameness embodied in the common initial authentic nature or good is something one cannot discern without effort, without intellectual and ethical learning and (also explained later) heart-mind investigation and social practice. In the early period, Mencius optimistically postulated a certain spontaneity of the inner good: 'In human nature, the good manifests just like water, which immediately flows downwards (人性之善猶水之就下也).'[27] It is worth noting that Mencius's image represents a Confucian, socially oriented adaptation to the human context of Laozi's holistic and vitalistic perspective. Equally, note that Daoist thought places the same emphasis on sameness as accord and conformity concretized in the image of the all-nourishing water while also disapproving opposition, in other words, competition: 'The higher good is like water,' explains the paragraph 8 of the Laozi, 'water does good to all ten thousand things, and does not compete with them (上善若水, 水善利萬物, 而不爭).'

In the next section, I illustrate how Zhu Xi philosophically develops further this incipient, ancient idea of the inner good as natural spontaneity. I suggest that, for him, this means 'sameness'. A century earlier, Qisong also discussed about experiencing the profound sameness between individuals (see Chapter 3, Section 2.2).

2.2 The good as sameness (*tong* 同)

According to Zhu, the above-mentioned ancient Confucian and Daoist images both emphasize the good as harmony and unity emerging from sameness, and they both discourage competition and conflict, which they see as originated in separateness. This initial quality of resemblance or sameness (同), which is latent in humans, exists in the form of their original goodness and needs to be activated through learning. One may concur with Zhu that sameness is what makes individuals agree with each other and not compete with each other, holds community together and ensures a high level of social harmony, peace and stability: 'Authentic nature', Zhu states, 'is that by which humans are all the same' (性也，人所同也。).[28] Obviously, not at a visible level but at a metaphysical level (see also Section 3.4). This constitutes a new meaning of sameness – namely, innate ethical nature, goodness. Note that the Neo-Confucian sameness is also related to the Buddhist notion of original nature and is different from the ancient sameness. The latter is understood rather as cultural and political unity, as belonging to the same Confucian culture (see Section 1, Hsiao, *A History of Chinese Political Thought*, and the doctrine of the great community/sameness 大同). These inferences drawn from Zhu Xi's Neo-Confucian meaning of good as the attribute of sameness of original human nature leads the individual to clearly discern that, in his view, the good is what relates individuals to one another, their profound interrelatedness, of which they are able to become aware through ethical experience and study.

One also finds that, when further developing the initial Mencian view through conceiving the good as that by which humans are interrelated, Zhu Xi introduces another new original interpretation: he identifies the nature of human interrelationships not as merely natural or organic but as from the outset ethical. What relates humans is the sameness of their goodness. Sameness in his view has an ethical connotation. My goodness is the same as the other's goodness and is what enables us to come together not in an unemotional, intellectual, indifferent or merely organic way but in an ethical way.

In the next note to paragraph 10 of the *Great Learning* (*Daxue* 大學), Zhu Xi provides further clarity about how human nature is perceived as the same good dwelling in every human being. Here he concretely describes the interrelatedness that naturally results from being endowed with this inner good equivalent to the fact that, when aware of it, people like and dislike the same things, and they all see the same things as good and as bad. In other words, the good perceived as interrelatedness means therefore that people spontaneously 'like what is good and dislike what is evil' (好善而惡惡，人之性也).[29] This good does not have a substantial nature but designates a universal state of mind shared by individuals who are aware of the unique goodness of their authentic nature and a unifying force that interconnects individuals and drives them to care for one another. It obviously follows that, if they are not able to see the same things as good or likable and evil or unlikable, this is because they are not aware of the good within themselves – their same common, original nature – and they are driven by selfish desires that prevail over the search of the common good. In this case, the good (best) for each one takes different forms depending on each one's particular interest.

3 The ancient philosophical background of the good as ethical interrelatedness: The 'organic' and 'ethical' ancient cosmology

This section provides an overview of the ancient Chinese theories that explain the standard of the good and its justification. It is noted that Zhu Xi develops this perception of interrelatedness as ethical (i.e. the good is the connecting link) starting from an original element of ancient Chinese thought (the *Book of Changes* (*Yijing* 易經, *Zhouyi* 周易), the *Zhongyong*, the *Mencius*): a simultaneously organic and ethical cosmology. It is noteworthy that the *Book of Changes* is the core of the learning of changes mentioned in Chapter 2, Section 2, as study and interpretation of the processes of divination. As discussed at length, from the latter and their subtle law of changes emerge the Chinese graphic language and the specific power of the graphs.

This perception of the cosmos or heaven-earth (天地), the texture of which is composed of relationships, is both organic and ethico-moral – in other words, it is governed by a universal law or order that is simultaneously metaphysico-organic and ethical. The relationships between the realities which together constitute the texture of the cosmos take the form of an intrinsic and multivalent continuity, interrelatedness: between physical and human worlds (*tiandi-ren* 天地-人); between individuals' inner world (thoughts, emotions that inwardly initiate one's interaction with others) and their outer world (behaviour, effective interaction within society) (*nei-wai* 內-外). However, even if continuity is the element emphasized by Zhu Xi, this is the result of starting from dichotomies. He stresses the organic unity of these correlative, moral relations – organic unity of the heaven-earth-men, organic unity of individuals within society – a unity into which unfold all different elements of life. One could say that, in this way, he minimizes the initial duality but does not completely transcend it (in the non-dualist Buddhist sense). Let's consider the difference between 'one' (Neo-Confucian organic unity) and 'non-duality' (the Buddhist 'to be one with'), as embodied in a vivid and straightforward explanation by the contemporary Chan teacher Thich Nhat Hanh: 'Non-duality means "not two", but not two also means "not one". That is why we say "non-dual" instead of "one". Because if there is one, there are two. If you want to avoid two, you have to avoid one also.'[30]

The next section suggests that it is from this ancient perception of the presence of an all-pervading universal law simultaneously organic and moral that stems Zhu Xi's perception of the good as interrelatedness.

3.1 Ethical interrelatedness in the *Zhouyi*

From this idea of the identity between organic and ethico-moral originates another directly related presupposition, mentioned earlier, on which Zhu's theory of the good is based: the implied continuity between humans' inner world, or their emotions/feelings, which is the root and essence of their moral efficacy; and humans' outer world, or their behaviour, which is the concrete functioning of their moral efficacy in daily affairs and interaction with others.[31] This implied continuity takes the form of an ethical interrelatedness. In the *Zhouyi*, the commentary (*wen* 文) of the second hexagram (*kun* 坤) describes it as a continuity between the straight line and the square:

> Inwardly, the exemplary individual cultivates reverence (*jing* 敬)[32] in order to render his inside a straight line. And outwardly he cultivates his behavioural rectitude (*yi* 義) in order to render his outside a square. As soon as reverence and behavioural rectitude are present, the moral efficacy of the individual is no longer completely isolated within. 君子敬以直內, 義以方外, 敬義立而德不孤.[33]

Inner moral efficacy is one's inner 'complete good'; the motivation for one's good works has two facets (i.e. inner intent and outer action). Ethico-moral efficacy is 'isolated' (*gu* 孤) within one's self, when its presence is only intent, devoid of any action. This means that the individual is not aware of its presence and does not make it function. When they experience it and put it into practice, inner ethico-moral efficacy is no longer completely isolated within – that is, it takes concrete form inwardly and outwardly: it is respect in its substance and behavioural rectitude in its action. This image describes what I call the ethical interrelatedness between one's self and one's external context.

It is obvious that the notions of straight line (which represents the inner space governed by respect) and square (which represents the outer space consisting of ordered relationships) no longer belong to the basic geometry responsible for ordering organic space but rather target the higher level of ethical development. The square centred on the eminent person gives us a well-balanced, harmonious image of community perceived not as a collectivity of individuals but as a network of relationships. This figure, which would seem limited to physical space and cosmology, perfectly incarnates the key presuppositions of the Confucian thought that natural order is inextricably linked to moral order, as the inner space (the straight line, respect) is tied together with the outer space (the square assembled from straight lines, behavioural rectitude).

3.2 Ethical and organic interrelatedness in the *Zhongyong*

The identity, inherent in ancient thought, between the law of organic life (birth and growth in living beings) and ethico-moral law (standards of goodness and of good action, of righteousness, of responsibility for others), between unimpeded organic growth (*yu* 育, see next quotation) and ethico-moral efficacy (*de* 德), is the very source of inspiration of the well-respected Song Neo-Confucian thinker. This ancient perception of organic and moral interrelatedness is well illustrated in paragraph 30 of the *Zhongyong*:[34]

> The ten thousand beings grow together without harming each other. They follow together their individual paths without obstructing each other. The little ethico-moral efficacies (小德) are as rivers that carve out their bed and flow in it. The great ethico-moral efficacy (大德) is what urges the transformations of beings. It is what makes heaven-earth big [all-encompassing]. 萬物並育而不相害，道並行而不相悖，小德川流，大德敦化，此天地之所以為大也。[35]

The connotation of the good(ness)/interrelatedness as sameness was examined previously. To that, it should be added, this paragraph also includes a new simultaneously organic and ethico-moral meaning of the good(ness), complementary to that of sameness: no mutual harm (不相害), no mutual obstruction (不相悖). These terms interpret the good(ness)/sameness as an absence of conflict between individuals or a oneness of the social landscape similar to the organic unity of the natural landscape.

Therefore, both above-mentioned ancient presumptions, the identity between organic and ethico-moral and the continuity between the sage's inner world and his outer world, can be defined as archetypes of the notion of interrelatedness. They are illustrated in the next image from the *Zhongyong* 31. Obviously, the most complete eminent person and perfect embodiment of these presumptions – the Confucian sage – is a ruler, a community leader, and the good deeds that result from his perfect inner efficacy are to be perceived in the context of good governance:

> The sage's moral qualities are vast and wide, profound as the source of groundwater, and therefore they manifest themselves at all times. Vast and wide: that means like

heaven. Profound as groundwater's source: that means like deep water. The people who observe him respect him – all, without exception. The people who listen to him all trust him, without exception. What he does raises absolutely no criticism from the people. 溥博淵泉，而時出之。溥博 如天，淵泉如淵。見而民莫不敬，言而民莫不信，行而民莫不說。[36]

In his commentary to this section 31 of the ancient *Zhongyong*, *Zhongyong zhangju* 31, Zhu Xi further clarifies and develops the sociopolitical scope of this paragraph and of the two above-mentioned premises, namely, the interrelatedness ('the inner accumulation reaches its height and becomes manifest outside', see later) between organic and ethico-moral, between inner life and outer life:

> This means that those five moral qualities accumulate within the inner self of the sage [the most accomplished sage in the world 天下至聖] and appear outside. This paragraph shows how the inner accumulation reaches its height and becomes manifest outside, at the right time. 言五者之德，充積於中，而以時發見於外也。言其充積極其盛，而發見當其可也。[37]

What are those five specific attributes that embody the continuity between organic and ethico-moral, inner and outer and therefore the inner source of the good and good action? The ancient *Zhongyong* 31 describes them: 'bright and farsighted understanding (聰明睿知)', 'wide and ample tenderness (寬裕溫柔)', 'manifest strength and resolve (發強剛毅)', 'serious posture consistent with the rules, impartial and upright attitude (齊莊中正)' and 'relevant and judicious reasoning, free of confusion (文理密察)'. Note that all those inner five qualities are understood as generating good works directly related to the harmonious relationships between rulers and ruled, and each one illustrates a different facet of this relationship. The first quality, the *Zhongyong* 31 explains, allows the sage ruler to look after his people (*you lin* 有臨); the second – to embrace all (*you rong* 有容); the third – to take charge of affairs (*you zhi* 有執); the next – to gain the respect of his people (*you jing* 有敬); and the last – to distinguish between good and evil (*you bie* 有別).

In the twelfth century, Zhu Xi highlights the first capacity – being able to look after the people – and identifies the last four ancient descriptions with the ethico-moral qualities of kindness (*ren* 仁), sense of behavioural rectitude (*yi* 義), sense of ritual (*li* 禮) and sense of moral knowledge (*zhi* 智). This interpretation also bears witness to the efforts he made to build an ethico-moral theory, starting from these aforesaid presuppositions of the ancient thinking, implicitly put forward by the 31st section of the *Zhongyong*: the correlation between the inner and the outer, between the natural macrocosm and the human microcosm, between organic phenomena and sociopolitical moral phenomena.

Interestingly, Julia Ching explains the Neo-Confucian emphasis on the organic cosmology as a reaction against Buddhism, 'meant to counteract the Buddhist view of an illusory world based on the causative action of karma'.[38] Zhu's ethico-moral theory can be characterized as 'organic morality', and the present study suggests that the core of it is the notion of the good which is equated with ethical interrelatedness. The previous subsections explored its ancient source from the *Zhouyi* to the *Zhongyong*, and the next, from the *Mencius*.

3.3 The interrelated self in the *Mencius*

In the early period of Confucianism, Mencius understands human nature essentially as feelings. He expresses the following view: because human nature is initially good (性善, *Teng Wen gong shang* 1, 滕文公上 1, in *ZZQS* 6: 306), humans' feelings can become good (乃若其情, 則可以為善矣, 乃所為善也).[39] He thus brings to light the notion of the heart-mind – what might be called the interrelated self, as the place where human nature dwells. In this specific context of the good, Mencius expands the well-known training project described in the *Great Learning*.[40] The latter requires that one start with correcting one's heart-mind (*zheng qi xin* 正其心) in order to be able to cultivate oneself (*xiu qi shen* 修其身) and to govern well (*zhi qi guo* 治其國). By focusing on the heart-mind and recommending such self-analysis, Mencius fundamentally changed the nature of the standard of the good and of the norms of conduct.

In former times, Confucius advocated a standard external to the heart-mind and self, one embodied in Zhou ritual whose authority he wanted to revive. For him, Zhou ritual was the expression of the highest good, the way of the legendary emperors Yao 堯 and Shun 舜, of the ancient kings Wen 文 and Wu 武, whose good deeds Confucius revered (see *Zhongyong* 30). The standard for good conduct was for Confucius embodied in those who behaved according to Zhou ritual, and he advocated following (*cong* 從) this external standard. His theory of the good is also intellectual as Confucius presupposed that practice of the good spontaneously follows from an understanding of the good: 'I listen a lot,' he reveals in the *Lunyu* 7: 27, 'so I can distinguish what good behaviour is and follow it. I watch a lot so I can differentiate it [from bad behaviour]. The knowledge of what is good follows from this (多聞擇其善者而從之，多見而識之，知之次也).'[41]

Through his perception of human nature or emotions as initially good, Mencius leaves aside Confucius's viewpoint of the good equated with an outside standard that has an external underlying justification. Instead, he situates the inherent natural source of the good within the human heart-mind. The latter, Mencius points out, organically generates the following feelings that might be called the natural sprouts of good within individuals' heart-minds, of which they do not think (*fu si* 弗思, see next quotation), in other words, of which they are not aware because they have yet to examine their heart-minds: empathy (*ceyin* 惻隱), shame (*xiuwu* 羞惡), respect/reverence (*gongjing* 恭敬), the ability to distinguish between right and wrong (*shifei* 是非). And Mencius identifies in these four feelings the source of the four dimensions of the good and of the Confucian ethics referred to above, namely, the sense of kindness (仁), the sense of behavioural rectitude (義), the sense of ritual (禮) and the sense of moral knowledge (智):

Every individual possesses a facet of the heart-mind which is the feeling of empathy, a facet of the heart-mind which is the feeling of shame, as well as the feeling of respect and the ability to distinguish between right and wrong. The empathy facet of the heart-mind – this is kindness. The shame facet of the heart-mind – this is behavioural rectitude. The respect facet of the heart-mind – this is the sense of ritual. The facet of the heart-mind that concerns the ability to distinguish between right and wrong – this is moral knowledge. Kindness, behavioural rectitude, the sense of ritual and moral knowledge do not come from the outside, so one need not internalize them. They are naturally within one's self, but one does not [naturally] think of them. 惻隱之心, 人皆有之; 羞惡之心, 人皆有之; 恭敬之心, 人皆有之; 是非之心, 人皆有之. 惻隱之心, 仁也; 羞惡之心, 義也; 恭敬之心, 禮也; 是非之心, 智也. 仁, 義, 禮, 智, 非由外鑠我也, 我固有之也, 弗思耳矣.[42]

In Mencius, justification of the good no longer comes from an external source (a law or a model) but instead results from choices of one's will, provided that the latter does not ignore one's heart-mind but rather thinks about it, that is, investigates it. Mencius's focus on thinking (*si* 思) in this context suggests an interest in cultivating introspection or self-analysis as a means of becoming aware of the existence of these sprouts-feelings within the inner self. Therefore, the standard of the good is for him in the will (*zhi* 志),[43] an inner standard which emerges from emotional self-regulation.

However, it is by drawing inspiration from the organic dimension of ancient thought that Mencius introduces ethico-moral law but again locates it within human nature, synonymous with an innate dimension, and not an external model of good behaviour inherited from the legendary sage emperors. It can be said that in his view, the justification of doing good is inherent to the heart-mind, exactly as life is inherent in the nature of the cosmos. Moreover, it is important to note that, in the context of organic thought, the heart-mind or the self (*wo* 我) that Mencius envisages is an interdependent heart-mind, an interdependent self. This because each one of these dispositions that germinates inside of the individual is a relational concept, an other-oriented emotion, and hence is intended to develop interrelatedness and human communication. Consequently, feeling empathy is an individual's capacity to respond to another's feelings – known as kindness; feeling shame for one's bad deeds is humans' capacity to become aware when they hurt others, and this is what drives them to repair bad deeds and rectify their actions – named behavioural rectitude; feeling respect for others is one's capacity to valorize them and avoid behaviour that could offend them – so-called solemn (ritual) behaviour or a sense of ritual; and the feeling of understanding the difference between right and wrong regarding an individual's relations with others is their capacity to consider others when acting instead of prioritizing self-oriented motivations.

I suggest that this perspective is what might be called the ethico-religious vision of ancient Confucianism. The Mencian theory of the inner justification of the good discussed above lies at the base of Zhu Xi's philosophical interpretation of the inner practice of the good. This topic is addressed next.

4 The inner ethico-religious practice of the good and interrelatedness in Zhu Xi's thought: The middle path of emotions

4.1 Interrelatedness as removing one's self-centred emotions and making whole one's original goodness or principle of coherence

Zhu Xi further elaborates this Mencian viewpoint about the justification of the good and the interdependent self as the foundation of good action. In what follows, it is argued that the sphere of the emotions is the major subject that lies at the heart of Zhu's approach. By citing Master Cheng, he develops the above-mentioned five inner moral qualities as elements of human authentic nature bestowed by heaven-nature. In his view, they are the five dimensions of authentic nature or natural dispositions (*wuxing* 五性).[44] For Zhu, they form authentic nature, or the interrelated self, which he describes as real (i.e. naturally present within one's self) and calm. This authentic nature or interdependent self can be easily damaged by the eruption of self-interested emotions (joy, anger, sadness, fear, fondness, hatred and desire). He regards them as never tempered but continuously expanding, overflowing and flooding. They damage the interrelated self and transform it into an egocentric self, focused on an individual's own interests, which inevitably enters into conflict with others. The restoration of the real and calm interrelated self or authentic nature – which might be called an inner ethico-religious practice – totally depends on what Zhu calls the middle path of emotions (合於中), which is the application related to restraining and removing self-centred emotions, those blocking interrelatedness and stimulating disputes. Zhu defines this process in the well-known ancient terms of 'rectifying one's heart-mind' (正其心) and 'nourishing one's nature' (養其性):

> The human being is the result of the accumulation of the vital essences of heaven-earth, the one who received the best of the five elements. His original nature is real and calm. When his original nature is not yet manifest, it is already endowed with the five natural dispositions, namely, kindness, behavioural rectitude, sense of ritual, moral knowledge and fidelity to one's pledged word. When the perceptible appearance [i.e. feelings/emotions] of his authentic nature emerges, external things strike it and set the inside of the human being in motion. Once the inside is set in motion, the seven emotions/feelings come out, that is, joy, anger, sadness, fear, fondness, hatred, and desire. The emotions are sparked, catch fire, and burn uncontrolled, and the authentic nature of the human being is damaged. For this reason, those who study reduce their emotions so that the latter correspond to the middle. In this way they rectify their heart-mind and nourish their authentic nature. 天地儲精，得五行之秀者為人。其本也真而靜。其未發也五性具焉，曰仁，義，禮，智，信。形既生矣，外物觸其形而動於中矣。其中動而七情出焉，曰喜，怒，哀，懼，愛，惡，欲。情既熾而益蕩，其性鑿矣。故學者約其情使合於中，正其心，養其性而已。[45]

Interdependent feelings, which, according to Mencius, are natural, represent the source of the good in an individual's heart-mind and the driving force behind their good works. Zhu Xi further develops in a new direction the Mencian interest in the heart-mind and his theory of these inner sprouts as interdependent feelings while also integrating it with the previously mentioned ancient perspective of the existence of a natural, all-pervading, universal law.

Zhu's Neo-Confucian school is also inspired by the Buddhist notion of universal principle (理) that reached its pinnacle in the non-dualist identity between universal principle and phenomena (事). His tradition of thought transposes these non-dualist concepts into the sphere of the organic unity discussed above. Thus, it forges the Neo-Confucian interpretation of *li* 理 not only as natural but also as metaphysical universal law, as *dao* 道 or way of life (see the following quotation) and metaphysical root (*ben* 本), and also as natural endowment in humans and daily affairs. The Neo-Confucian *li* 理 is a dynamic law which is both an ethico-moral and organic coherence and a metaphysical source of the good in human hearts, too. One can say that in a sense, Zhu's principle of coherence not only is inspired by Buddhism but also constitutes a Neo-Confucian development of the ancient idea of norm (*ze* 則) present in each thing (see the previously discussed notion of the norm of things that appears in the *Classic of Poetry*; Mencius cites it in *Gaozi shang* 6, see Section 2.1). Unlike the non-dualist Buddhist principle, Zhu's principle of coherence is perceived in the perspective of a metaphysico-organic unity that could be called 'minimized or diminished duality' – transorganic or transphysical and organic – and stands in a correlative relationship with the vital breath (氣). And he explains that the latter is the functioning or activity (*yong* 用), the instrument (*qi* 器) or the utility (*ju* 具) of the principle of coherence understood as metaphysical corporeality (*ti* 體). Again, he minimizes the dualist perspective, because in his view, the principle is not only temporally but also ontologically prior to the perceptible appearance of humans and their affairs (see later). In other words, the principle of (organic and moral) coherence pertains to the quasi-vertical, transmoral/metaphysical, *dao* 道 dimension, while its functioning (perceptible appearance, instrument quality *qi* 器) belongs to the horizontal, temporal dimension. Chapter 1, Section 1.3, in order to avoid the Western idea of separate realities traditionally incorporated in the terms 'metaphysics' and 'verticality', privileged the translation 'metaphysical corporeality' for the Neo-Confucian principle of coherence and demonstrated its pertinence in this context. This rendering relies on what might be described as an etymological semiotic of the Chinese character *ti* 體 – here translated as metaphysical corporeality. The good as the principle of coherence has a metaphysical/transmoral dimension for Zhu (it is prior to and beyond the emergence of perceptible appearance 形而上), and it is weakened by the vital breath manifested in the form of emotions:

> In heaven-earth there is the principle of coherence, and there is the vital breath. This principle is the *dao* prior to the emergence of the perceptible appearance, it is the root that gives birth to things. Vital breath is the instrument subsequent to the emergence of perceptible appearance, it is the different utilities that give birth to things. The birth of humans and things necessarily relies upon the principle of coherence; after that authentic nature comes into existence. The latter necessarily

relies upon the vital breath, and then, the perceptible appearance comes into existence. Even if the authentic nature and perceptible appearance of a thing are not external to one another and form a single entity, the distinction between its *dao* quality and its instrument quality is very clear. One cannot confound them. 天地之間，有理有氣。理也者，形而上之道也，生物之本也; 氣也者，形而下之器也，生物之具也。是以人物之生，必稟此理，然後有性; 必稟此氣，然後有形。其性其形，雖不外乎一身，然其道器之間分際甚明，不可亂也。⁴⁶

As is evident from this commentary, Zhu's theory of the good further develops the ancient Mencian view by adding a super sensible (metaphysical or transphysical) reality consisting of the principle of coherence or authentic nature. Within the individual, this is living unity, not only a metaphysical feature but also an organic and ethico-moral initial root inside the individual's heart-mind. Initially pure and clear at the moment when heaven-nature bestows it at one's birth, the principle is obscured thereafter by the permanent activity (functioning) of the vital breath embodied in egocentric (personal (*si* 私), see next citation) feelings, emotions and desires. It is worth noting that Zhu sees the latter not as real (*shi* 實, see later) – that is, an inner presence – but as coming from the outside, from contact with external things. They are blocking out the inner presence of principle of coherence or original goodness. In the paragraph below, he equates them with humans' specific, private objectives, shaped by the quality of their vital breaths, which obscure their original goodness (本然之善). In his commentary to the first paragraph of the *Zhongyong*, Zhu Xi explains that the individual's highest goal of learning consists of becoming aware of the original inner goodness (i.e. the aforesaid *dao* or principle of coherence), keeping it present and nourish it,⁴⁷ and just as the Buddhists, he equates the result of this effort not with following an external moral norm but with individual inner effort, through an inward transformation. Again, in this context, the difference between the two traditions is embodied in the contrast between metaphysico-organic unity (i.e. 'making whole' the original goodness, in the next paragraph) and spiritual non-duality: 'Zisi 子思 [(481–402 BCE), the presumed author of the *Zhongyong*] wishes that disciples return to seek the *dao* within themselves and achieve this transformation from within. Thus, they eliminate the private [selfish] external temptations and make whole their original goodness (蓋欲學者於此反求諸身而自得之，以 去夫外誘之私，而充其本然之善).'⁴⁸

Zhu Xi also quotes Master Lü who explains that this transformation (*bianhua* 變化) is about purifying the unclear vital breath, which makes individuals different. A purified vital breath allows individuals to experience their innate goodness, namely, their 'ethico-moral capacity'. Unlike the unclear vital breath that establishes differences, this 'homogeneous good' (均善) is what unites and interrelates people and their metaphysical sameness (人所同, see also Section 2.1):

Master Lü says: The exemplary individual learns so he can transform his vital breath quality (氣質). When one's ethico-moral quality (德) outweighs one's breath quality, even the unintelligent become capable of intelligent reasoning, and the weak, of power. When it is not possible for one's moral quality to outweigh one's breath quality, even if one has the willingness to learn, the unintelligent cannot be enlightened, nor can the weak stand up straight. The homogeneous good in which there is no evil – this is the authentic nature by which humans are all the same. 呂氏曰:「君子所以學者，為能變化氣質而已。德勝氣質，則愚者可進於明，柔者可進於強。不能勝之，則雖有志於學，亦愚不能明，柔不能立而已矣。蓋均善而無惡者，性也，人所同也。」[49]

Therefore, using the correlative concepts of emotions/feelings and the principle of coherence, Zhu describes the inner practice of the good, which might be defined as ethico-religious, as a transformation involving two inextricable facets: the practice of 'removing people's self-centred emotions' and the practice of 'making whole their original goodness'. It is worth repeating that the latter, that is, the complete original goodness, is synonymous with the metaphysical principle of coherence or ethico-moral capacity. One recalls in this context Streng's definition of religion as 'a means to ultimate transformation', as well as Hick's theory of the mystical dimension of religion as 'transformation of human existence from self-centredness to Reality-centredness' (see Chapter 2, Section 4).

It is to be noted that, seen from this correlative, unitary perspective (principle of coherence/ethico-moral capacity – vital breath/emotions), the good as interrelatedness, is also equated with an organic twofold reality. The following analysis details the two sides of the practice of the good: an inner nature or metaphysical corporeality and an outer functioning. The first dimension concerns the experience and self-analysis of the interrelated self, which is the acting self or the heart-mind where dwells one's authentic nature. It might be said that, in a sense, this so-called metaphysical or transphysical constituent is not only a result of the Buddhist influence on the Confucian renewal during the Song dynasty but also the Confucian counterpart of the Chan Buddhist meditation or concentration (*ding* 定).[50] As indicated earlier, the other constituent of the practice of the good is the practice of socially and politically good actions, good governance and social solidarity.[51] It goes without saying that the inner practice, that is, the absolute precondition for the outer, is the most complex element of this correlation, its bedrock. In the next section, it is addressed starting from the incipient theory outlined by Mencius (in *Jinxin shang* 盡心上, par.1) about the original good nature of humans. He advised that, in order to fully develop this original good nature, people should practise inwardly 'keeping their heart-minds present (存其心)' and 'nourishing their authentic nature (養性)'. This section also examines how Zhu Xi further developed this Mencian exhortation into a theory of the good as interrelatedness.

4.2 Interrelatedness as keeping one's heart-mind present

In Zhu's view, this process of returning to the original, inner homogeneous good implies the necessity to control one's vital breath quality, which is to say, one's self-centred emotions. This practice involves 'the requirement of keeping present and nourishing this root (homogeneous good) within the heart-mind through controlling oneself (存

養省察之要)'.⁵² Obviously, he makes implicit reference to Mencius's twofold process of becoming aware of the inner good and nourishing it, found in the first paragraph of the chapter *Jinxin shang* 1 (in *ZZQS* 6: 425): keeping the heart-mind present (存其心) and nourishing the authentic nature (養其性).

Also, of note is the peculiarity of Zhu's description of the tendencies that damage the inner good: the inclination to fulfil private or selfish desires emerging from 'external temptations' (外誘之私, see earlier). He describes these desires as being not 'real' (*shi* 實) from the inner point of view, because they come from the outside. The *dao*, the authentic nature, the principle of coherence or the homogeneous good, for Zhu Xi are synonyms of the 'real essence' (*shi ti* 實體), from which the individual cannot be separated because all are endowed with it by heaven-nature: 'Having been provided with it [the root of the *dao* 道之本原], one cannot be apart from it (其實體備於己而不可離)'.⁵³ It is understood that Zhu's viewpoint is based on the premise that the original goodness-interrelatedness (本然之善), namely, the principle of coherence or authentic nature, is a real and permanent dimension of people's heart-minds, while he considers the self-centred emotions to be devoid of reality, impermanent and illusory. As a side note, the Buddhist influence on his thought is also evident in this context.

In order to put into practice the inner good, which is equivalent to ethico-moral efficacy (*de* 德), humans need to keep the heart-mind present (*cun* 存), through examining and controlling their private desires: 'Harbouring in one's heart-mind moral efficacy: this is what is called keeping present the good with which one is naturally endowed (懷德，謂存其固有之善)'.⁵⁴ Unlike the Buddhist view, Zhu Xi's Neo-Confucian perspective considers an individual's capacity to examine and control their heart-mind to be self-evident and unquestionable. He views the latter as the 'master of the individual' (身之所主).⁵⁵ As mentioned earlier, the classic *Daxue* expresses the view that the exemplary individual must correct their heart-mind (正其心). Mencius develops this perception: in order to be able to examine oneself (correct one's heart-mind), an essential precondition should be fulfilled: the heart-mind must be kept present (*cun qi xin* 存其心). And Zhu further expands this approach. According to the *Daxue* 7, when present, the heart-mind can be corrected through the process of examination, because it is not driven away by its movements – desires and egocentric emotions, such as anger (忿懥), fear (恐懼), joy (好樂) and worry (憂患). Consequently, a present heart-mind is a heart-mind which feels the sensation of interconnectedness. There is no interconnectedness when the heart-mind is missing. Its presence is therefore a prerequisite for being able to practise the Neo-Confucian good associated with interconnectedness.

In his commentary to this paragraph of *Daxue* 7, Zhu Xi defines these self-centred emotions as 'movements of the heart-mind, inherent in every individual (皆心之用，而人所不能無者)'.⁵⁶ And he offers a new, Song dynasty explanation of how they carry the heart-mind far away, making it impossible to correct it, because it is absent and unable to perform good actions:

When one of these [egocentric] emotions emerges within oneself and, as a result, one cannot examine himself, desire is set in motion, the emotion seizes oneself, the heart-mind moves and follows it. Thus, his heart-mind cannot be corrected. When his heart-mind is not completely present, the individual is incapable of examining himself. … Once their heart-minds are permanently present, people [an exemplary person, a community leader or official] are able to fully cultivate themselves. 然一有之而不能察，則欲動情勝，而其用之所行，或不能不失其正矣。心有不，則無以檢其身. … 心常而身無不修也.[57]

4.3 Interrelatedness as being sincere and being real

The ancient *Daxue* specifies 'making one's thoughts sincere' (誠其意) as the preliminary condition for being able to correct one's heart-mind and, therefore, effectively keeping it present, but it does so without any concrete explanation about the practical content of this process. In his commentary (see next citation), Zhu Xi elaborates on this issue. He equates 'being sincere' (*cheng* 誠) with 'being real or authentic' (*shi* 實).[58] The Neo-Confucian meaning of this notion was examined above; 'the real' is the inner metaphysical (transphysical depth) dimension bestowed by heaven-nature: the *dao*, the principle of coherence, homogeneous good, authentic nature. Zhu adds to this 'real' dimension – one can become aware of and cultivate through ethico-religious practice – another equivalent: the quality of being sincere.

Note, equally present in this context of the meaning of 'being real' is the Neo-Confucian interpretation of the above-mentioned ancient presupposition of the identity between laws of organic growth and those of ethics. It can be understood that reality (i.e. what has the particular attribute of 'being real', actually existing and not supposed) is the ethico-moral quality. Consequently, in Zhu's view, the thoughts devoid of a metaphysico-real or authentic dimension are thoughts inconsistent with morality, that is, corrupt, dishonest and unprincipled. Thus, it is understood that he implies the existence of the natural organic and ethico-moral law at work within reality and human individuals and suggests that everything in accordance with this law, for example, perfectly sincere thoughts and good actions, has indeed reality – in other words, is real and not simulated even in its imperceptible aspects – while everything which is only invisibly incompatible and indiscernibly in conflict with this law, with the growth of life and the growth of ethico-moral capacity, for instance, merely imperceptibly insincere thoughts and evil actions, is still devoid of reality, that is, false and meant to deceive. To correct one's heart-mind means not only cultivating but fully cultivating the initial, real (i.e. complete) goodness with which the heart-mind was endowed. Furthermore, this practice that one could define as embodying the Song dynasty ethico-religious vision implies making sincere absolutely everything that emerges from the heart-mind, in order to avoid damaging it.

As a side note, 'being sincere' is a major Confucian idea developed in the ancient *Zhongyong* (see the examination of this notion in Chapter 6, Section 4.2). It is relevant to say that, when connecting this Confucian notion with 'being real', Zhu draws inspiration from the Buddhist 'true reality', which is different from the illusory phenomena. However, he adapts it to the Confucian context and gives it new meaning, when introducing this idea in the context of the organic and ethico-moral law. This might be a concrete example that supports Julia Ching's above-mentioned viewpoint

(2.2) about the Neo-Confucian emphasis on the organic cosmology as a reaction against Buddhism.

Thus, Zhu's perception of the good within one's heart-mind is standing for the sincerity of one's own self, which continues to be real even if obscured, while the actions of one's self when the latter is swept away by one's inclinations, even when directly observable, are considered to not be real, devoid of reality (*weishi* 未實) and evil because they drive away the heart-mind, hence depriving the self of its rightful master. The Neo-Confucian scholar provides a concrete description of the effort to make one's thoughts sincere, eliminating through self-examination everything else that is insincere, to ensure in this way that the master heart-mind is present. Hence, in his view, cultivating interrelatedness as ethico-religious day-to-day attitude has another special meaning: the practice of being sincere. The latter has a distinctive Neo-Confucian connotation, totally different from the signification of the Western sincerity:

> When individual's thoughts become sincere, the evil aspects actually exist no longer, and therefore the good within themselves is real. Only then does it become possible to make the heart-mind present, so that one can examine oneself. However, when one only has knowledge about how the human can make their thoughts sincere, but without being able to perfectly examine if their heart-minds are present or not: In this case, too, the individual is neither able to correct themselves, nor to cultivate themselves. 蓋意誠則真無惡而實有善矣，所以能是心以檢其身。然或但知誠意，而不能密察此心之 否，則又無以直內而修身也。[59]

According to Zhu, knowing how to make one's thoughts sincere and practise good deeds, yet still developing movements inside oneself devoid of reality, that is, guided by personal desires and self-interest, means the individual is still lacking sincerity. He also calls this self-deceit (*ziqi* 自欺) or failing to admit to oneself that something is true: developing heart-mind movements devoid of reality (*wei shi* 未實). The latter could include, for instance, seeking an official position while not devoting oneself to good governance or the well-being of the community despite declaring to do so in a loud voice but actually trying to reap the personal benefits of holding office: 'It is said that a person deceives himself when he knows how to practice the good and to distance himself from the evil, yet he still develops within his heart-mind movements devoid of reality (自欺云者，知為善以去惡，而心之所發有未實也。).'[60]

By appealing to the meaning of 'real' in order to define the last-mentioned connotation of 'keeping the heart-mind present' as being sincere, it is apparent that an attending heart-mind or self is real and not false; it is a good, sincere heart-mind, when it is able to examine itself and recognize when emotions/feelings disturb it and is also able to guard itself against private and selfish personal desires. Zhu thus warns that when such desires emerge and develop within people's heart-minds because of their inattention, their heart-minds are swept away, and they end up deceiving themselves. He explains this internal process through focusing on the idea of the good and highlights the importance of choosing to perform good deeds (i.e. 'become one with the good (其一於善),' in an organic unity) in order to keep the heart-mind present, that is, real or fully effective, in this way ensuring that the emotions/feelings which develop within are kept sincere. Again, it may further be noted that, in Zhu's view, this is an intentional, rational process, based on the full commitment of the will: 'To make sincere what emerges within one's heart-mind means to be willing to become one with the good and to not deceive oneself (實其心之 所發,欲其一於善而無自欺也。).'[61]

It is relevant to perceive the training of keeping the heart-mind present – that is, of experiencing the inner original goodness of the heart-mind and putting it into practice – as equivalent to constantly cultivating an interdependent heart-mind and interdependent-self. This is the specific content of what might be called the Neo-Confucian ethico-religious practice. By contrast, a heart-mind that is not sincere because it is taken away by self-centred feelings is fundamentally separated from others. As discussed earlier, in Zhu's viewpoint, the constant exercise of good as interrelatedness is also synonymous with the effort of being sincere.

4.4 Interrelatedness as nourishing the innately good heart-mind (*liang xin* 良心), preserving and protecting its breathing

This section explores another dimension of the Neo-Confucian ethico-religious: the practice of the vital breath (*qi* 氣), of respiring (*xi* 息) – for an analysis of respiration in the context of Chinese 'creativity', see Chapter 6, Sections 4.2 and 5.1 – that Zhu Xi recommends in order to keep the heart-mind present and to maintain the functional potential of the inner good. Obviously, the vital breath is the core of the organic and ethico-moral cosmology he develops. It argues that starting from the Mencian idea of the original inner good as organic ethico-morality rooted in the vital breath, Zhu Xi develops a new, Neo-Confucian understanding of the practice of keeping the heart-mind present. Mencius calls this original heart-mind the innately good heart-mind (良心) (Mencius, *Gaozi shang* 8). And he compares the innately good heart-mind, pestered by egocentric emotions/feelings, with the trees of the forest which are chopped, a little bit more every day (to harvest firewood). The selfish feelings and desires that damage the heart-mind are like the lumbermen's axes that every day cut a bit from the living trees. It is inevitable, explains Mencius, that the trees cannot remain beautiful for long. This is because they respire during the day and night (日夜之所息), and the physical harm they suffer (from having living leaves and limbs trimmed) is quicker than their slow but continuous organic growth, so they are suffocating. In this context, the generic practice of keeping present the heart-mind takes the concrete form of restoring the vital breath of the innately good heart-mind.

Zhu Xi describes the originally good heart-mind (本然之善心) as a living organism that breaths during the day and at night. He differentiates between the breath at dawn (平但之氣) of a heart-mind calm and present, which is pure and produces growth after a whole night with no contact with other things, and the breath of the day. During the daytime, the individual interacts in many ways with others, and these interactions provide an opportunity for the heart-mind to be swept away by egotistic emotions. The private, selfish desires, which his heart-mind inevitably develops, damage the night growth:

> One's vital breath of the dawn, when one's heart-mind has no contact with things, is a pure and clear vital breath (清明之氣). In this case, what he likes and dislikes

is close to what others like and dislike (好惡與人相近); which is to say, he achieves what is common to the heart-minds of all individuals (得人心之所同然也). ... Even if the innately good heart-mind (良心) is already let go, during the days and nights this innately good heart-mind necessarily experiences some growth. At dawn, when one's heart-mind has no contact with things, at the moment when one's vital breath is pure and clear, this originally good heart-mind has some perceptible manifestations. But these perceptible manifestations are already minimal, and because what the heart-mind did during the day was not good, these already minimal manifestations disappear, like the already chopped down mountain trees that have sprouts and new shoots growing from cut stumps, which are again eaten by cattle and sheep. What the individual does during the day, damages the growth [resulting from respiration] that occurs during the night; the growth occurring at night cannot override what was done during the day, and thus the originally good heart-mind suffers much damage. As for the growth through the vital breath of the night, this gradually diminishes day after day and it is not enough to keep present the innately good heart-mind of kindness and behavioural rectitude (不足以存其仁義之良心); and the vital breath of the dawn also cannot be purified (平但之氣亦不能清). Then, what one likes and dislikes is very far from what others like and dislike (好惡遂與人遠).[62]

In this new context of organic growth, Zhu Xi highlights again that the innately good heart-mind (良心) is a quality all heart-minds have in common – a common thread that links all of them together (人心之所同然也). In point of fact, Zhu develops it here through using a notion discussed earlier, in the context of the good as sameness (see Section 1.2): the common inner good all humans share is equated with that which makes them spontaneously like and dislike the same things, namely, universally good deeds and evil deeds (好善而惡惡).[63]

When an individual's vital breath is pure, Zhu clarifies, what they like and dislike are close to what others like and dislike (好惡與人相近). Evidently, the closeness explained in this way refers to another concrete manifestation of the interrelatedness/sameness between individuals. When their vital breath is pure and clear, they are aware of the common goodness they share; therefore, they all harmoniously like what is, in reality, good (what has reality as an endowment received from heaven-nature) and dislike what is evil (what does not have reality because it comes from contact with external things).

It is worth highlighting that this idea of people spontaneously liking and disliking the same things (i.e. good things and actions) also represents a Neo-Confucian interpretation of the ideal good governance and a peaceful society. When one's vital breath is contaminated and murky, one's heart-mind is carried away by private, self-centred feelings, and therefore, Zhu explains, what they like and dislike are very far from what others like and dislike (所好惡遂與人遠). Obviously, as previously discussed, this is due to the fact that in this case, what the individual likes and dislikes arises from their self-centred interests, which exclude or disregard the interests of others. Fortune, fame, avarice and other egocentric desires coexist with leadership. In this way, Zhu emphasizes, one (a member of the government or a local community leader) has drifted apart from others, and their original, metaphysical interrelatedness is disrupted. The actions of the rulers or local community leaders thus disconnected from the people, instead of being good deeds, rather reflect poor leadership and bad governance. As a result, the society is conflictual and divided.

In addition, Zhu offers here an original, organically dual interpretation of the individual's vital breath of the night. He distinguishes two specific kinds of vital breath and stresses that the evening breath is different from that of the day because it is free from direct contact with daily affairs. People's vital breath of the night is calm and vigorously engaged in a continuous process of purification, because this activity, perceived by Zhu Xi as organic and permanent, is not obstructed by daily relationships and affairs. In his Neo-Confucian vision, like organic growth, moral growth means a continuous and inevitable purification of humans' vital breath, in the silence of the night, when their daily interactions stop. For this reason, it can be said that night respiration is non-obstructed purification. Like the permanent renewal of organic life symbolized by the emergence of sprouts and new branches on tree stumps, moral growth – in other words, keeping present the heart-mind – is understood by Zhu Xi to be constant accumulation of concrete good deeds. In the previous quotation, the latter are equivalent to 'perceptible manifestations of the originally good heart-mind' (良心必猶有發見者).

Zhu uses his metaphysical concept of the principle of coherence (理) in order to illustrate the organic character of ethico-moral development and its challenges, as well as the identity between the organic functioning of a living organism and the ethico-moral functioning of the human heart-mind: 'The mountain tree and the human heart-mind share the same principle of coherence (山木人心, 其理一也).'[64] With this principle of coherence coming from heaven-nature and being the same for humans and non-humans, Zhu Xi introduces a broader interrelatedness, which is not merely anthropocentric and concerns not only human beings but also all living beings. It is possible to perceive here another certain Buddhist inspiration – the Buddhist universal principle *li* 理 is all-pervading and applies to all sentient beings.

Equally, one could interpret Zhu Xi's perspective (of Mencian inspiration) on the vital breath, which produces growth during the night and regenerates itself in absence of interaction with everyday circumstances and governance matters, to be suggesting through an organic image, a Neo-Confucian method of detaching from the flux of emotions or feelings that result from the busyness of daily interaction, and of purifying the vital breath and the heart-mind: by paying attention to the night respiration of the heart-mind and acting during the day with a view to protect it. To a certain extent (see Section 3.1), this may be a preoccupation of the Neo-Confucians to provide a Confucian practice having a similar result to the Chan Buddhist practice of concentration (meditation) (*ding* 定). Even if Confucians see the effect as similar – pacifying the heart-mind – there is a major difference between the natures of the two trainings. The Neo-Confucian objective of avoiding damaging the vital breath purified during the night has an organic, ethical and metaphysical nature: focuses on the ethical self, its moral will and principle of coherence. Unlike the Neo-Confucian concentration, the Chan practice has a spiritual and non-dual nature: it finally aims to break through the self and heart-mind in order to connect with the no-self and no-heart-mind (無心) and restore their non-duality (see the Song dynasty, mature version of the *Platform Sutra* 六祖大師法寶壇經, T48n2008, 0357c19). Another distinction to be made is that between the non-dual nature of the Buddhist universal principle and phenomena and the unitary nature of the Neo-Confucian metaphysico-organic correlation between the principle of coherence and vital breath.

It is observed that in this context of the vital breath, Zhu articulates a Neo-Confucian theory of the heart-mind. This is best illustrated in the next quotation. In the light of his arguments examined above, it can be concluded that another Neo-Confucian approach to keeping people's heart-minds present (存心) is to focus on avoiding damaging (*hai* 害) the growth of the goodness of the heart-minds that occurs during the 'night'. Obviously, the night is a generic term that designates times when they are free from dealing with governance and everyday affairs.

Master Cheng, whom Zhu Xi cites, also explains that individuals must be careful to avoid stifling growth of their heart-minds (不至梏亡, see next citation). Moreover, in order to avoid injuring this ethico-moral growth, and therefore assist and nourish the heart-mind (*yang xin* 養心), as a grower assists and nourishes plants by preventing them from drying out, in the *Jinxin xia* 35, Mencius suggests restraining one's desires, therefore having few (*gua yu* 寡欲).[65] Zhu retakes and elaborates this ancient idea. If one keeps one's heart-mind present, he emphasizes, then wherever they go, kindness (*ren* 仁) and behavioural rectitude (*yi* 義) are with them (無適而非仁義也, see next citation). In other words, these ethical sprouts are present and growing in the form of concrete good actions. Kindness and behavioural rectitude are the major internal and external components of the innately good heart-mind, and both involve interrelatedness – that is, care for those governed.

For kindness and behavioural rectitude to guide people's behaviour inwardly and outwardly, the growth of the purified vital breath must be protected. In the next paragraph, Zhu Xi suggests a method of preserving its nocturnal growth. He explains this effort as the practice of taking care of the heart-mind (*cao* 操), being vigilant not to abandon it, through inwardly practising restraint and outwardly good works. Such vigilance involves constantly nourishing (*yang* 養) the heart-mind through keeping its quintessence pure (神清) and the vital breath calm (氣定) not only at night but also when carrying out everyday affairs:

> Confucius mentions the heart-mind. When one takes care of it, one's heart-mind is present and remains in place (操之則在此). When one abandons it, one's heart-mind is lost and leaves (舍之則失去). There is no predetermined time and place for its coming and going. Mencius cites this and clarifies that the quintessence (神明) of the heart-mind is not predetermined, it is easy to lose it, it is difficult to keep it. People cannot neglect nourishing it for a single instant. Those who study must strive every moment to permanently keep the quintessence of their heart-mind pure and their vital breath calm (神清氣定), as at the moment of the dawn. In this way, individual's heart-mind is at all times present, and wherever he goes, kindness and behavioural rectitude are with him (則此心常存, 無適而非仁義也). Master Cheng says: 'How does the heart-mind come or go? It is through taking care of it

or abandoning it (亦以操舍而言耳). The method of taking care of it is to cultivate respect in order to render one's inside straight as a line, and that is all (操之之道, 敬以直內而已).' I heard my master saying: 'For humans, their heart-mind of behavioural rectitude and principle of coherence (理義之心) always exists [even if not present for them]. But people have to support it, so their heart-minds can be present (人, 理義之心未嘗無, 維持守之即在爾). If during the day one avoids stifling it, the vital breath of the night becomes pure. If the vital breath of the night is pure, then at dawn, when one has no contact with things, the appearance of this vital breath, which is profound, right, empty and clear, can naturally be seen (湛然虛明氣象自可見).'[66]

In this paragraph Master Cheng suggests a method for taking care of one's heart-mind using the above-mentioned *Zhouyi* formula (Section 2.1), from the commentary (*wen* 文) of the second hexagram (*kun* 坤): 'to cultivate respect in order to render one's inside straight as a line' (敬以直內). This citation illustrates the profound trust Neo-Confucianism places in the individual's will and consciousness, due to its presupposed connection with organic and moral law.

It can be seen that Zhu Xi's commentaries reflect the Neo-Confucian viewpoint that the private, selfish desires (*siyu* 私欲) are not difficult to eliminate from an individual's self. One only has to cultivate respect, and to think about their natural and original goodness and its sprouts, in order to have access to the tools they need to analyse and restrain their personal emotions and desires (約其情, see Section 3.1, Zhu Xi, *Lunyu jizhu* 6.2). Common to all these interpretations of Zhu is the firm trust in the force of one's will as the trigger that, through ongoing effort and determination, enables humans to keep present their original good heart-minds, or in the terms of the *Daxue*, 'to dwell in the complete good (*zhi yu zhi shan* 止於至善)'.[67]

5 Conclusion

This chapter demonstrates that the Cheng-Zhu Neo-Confucian School of principle brought a whole new meaning to the notions of interrelatedness and sameness in Confucian thought – the good(ness). It argues that this new Song dynasty Neo-Confucian signification of interrelatedness indicates a change in the Confucian conceptualization of the interrelatedness. The latter implies now not merely cultural and political unity but also ethical and organically metaphysical sameness and unity. This analysis shows that one major driver of this change in meaning was the interaction between Confucianism and Buddhism.

It investigates the meaning and practice of the good as interrelatedness in Zhu Xi's Neo-Confucian thought, together with the ancient philosophical background that constitutes the source of his theory. Several layers of the meaning of the good-interrelatedness are discussed: homogeneous good, the principle of coherence, authentic nature and sameness and effort of being sincere. The chapter also uncovers multiple dimensions of the practice of the good-interrelatedness: the middle path of emotions, the practice of removing one's self-centred emotions and making whole one's original goodness or principle of coherence, of keeping present one's heart-mind, along with the ongoing effort to be sincere and real, to preserve and protect the night and day breathing of the innately good heart-mind.

The chapter thus demonstrates that in Zhu Xi's commentaries of the *Four Books*, the good understood as interrelatedness is a major topic which has two dimensions: an ethico-moral facet related to the inner self, the ethico-moral agent, the will, and a metaphysico-organic feature embodying a universal law of organic and metaphysical growth. Zhu harmonizes these two approaches, thus developing a perception of the good from a correlatively unifying point of view.

Moreover, the analysis illustrates that, in the context of this new meaning of the good, Zhu develops a theory of the heart-mind. Even though Mencius did pay attention to the heart-mind, he did not elaborate on it. Likely under the influence of Chan Buddhism, Zhu Xi takes up the seed idea sowed by Mencius and grows it into a Neo-Confucian theory of the heart-mind as master of the individual, as an arbitrator that mediates between one's feelings and one's behaviour. Chapter 3 has developed this notion in the Chan perspective of the scholar-monk Qisong.

However, note also Zhu Xi's optimism and confidence in the capacity of the heart-mind to cleanse itself through people's hard work and commitment. In this way, he continues an idea stated by Confucius in the earliest period of Confucianism that 'it is not difficult, day after day, to restrain personal desires, and to eliminate them (日日克之，不以為難，則私欲淨盡)'.[68] This reliance on the will and self is totally alien to Chan Buddhist theory, where pacifying (quieting) the heart-mind (*an xin* 安心) and freeing it of destructive emotions imply a complex practice which involves breaking through the individual self. Pacifying the heart-mind (an *xin*安心) is a major concept of Bodhidharma菩提達磨 (?–535), the founder and first patriarch of Chan, in the *Great Master Bodhidharma's Essential Discourse on Entering the Mahayana Path*菩提達磨大師略辨大乘入道四行觀.[69] In conclusion, it could be said that Zhu offers a metaphysico-rationalistic theory of the heart-mind.

Furthermore, this examination also demonstrates that, whereas ancient Confucianism was focused on restraining (*ke*克, see earlier, *Lunyu jizhu* 12: 1) egotistic emotions/feelings, and in so doing, overcoming them, Zhu Xi's Neo-Confucianism develops a sophisticated practice of self-mastery. This training process focuses on the heart-mind and includes keeping it present, taking care of it through protecting it day and night breathing and nourishing it through performing concrete, everyday good works.

Part 3

Ethical Interrelatedness

5

Ethical interrelatedness: An interpretive theory for Chinese religious traditions

1 Introduction: Chinese ethics and its assumptions

The analysis built in the previous chapters made us more aware of the Western cultural presumptions embodied in classical and contemporary theories of religion and the particularities the Chinese religious traditions are based upon. The latter make the application of those general theories based on Western assumptions inoperable for the Chinese cultural domain. Accordingly, this chapter integrates the key findings from the inquiry carried out in Chapters 1–4 in an interpretive theory specifically tailored for these Chinese traditions: ethical interrelatedness. It represents a pivotal moment in this book's development as it relates to a change in focus: as a matter of fact, the transition from Parts 1 and 2 to Parts 3 and 4 is a change in focus from religion and theory to the distinctive traits of the Chinese philosophico-religious space.

This study's dedication to ethical interrelatedness stems from two sources: my dual training as both a 'professional philosopher' (to borrow Fingarette's term)[1] and a sinologist. It is based on two previous works of translation from classic Chinese and philosophical interpretation. The first work addresses the 'dynamic continuity' in the Southern Song Zhu Xi's ethical thought embodied in his Neo-Confucian commentary on the classic *Zhongyong*.[2] This is a comparative and intercultural work. It attempts to uncover and examine the cultural presuppositions of the Confucian notion of 'continuity' between the individual's inner and outside world, as an ethical leitmotif emerging from Zhu Xi's interpretation of this text, in juxtaposition to the ethical presuppositions of Western (Greek) philosophy. The second book focuses on the Northern Song Chan scholar-monk Qisong's *guwen* essays and analyses his overall goal of building a philosophico-religious 'bridge' between two full-fledged manifestations of the Chinese culture: the Confucian and Buddhist traditions.[3] The present work on ethical interrelatedness as major cultural presupposition of the Chinese philosophico-religious traditions emerges from these previous inquiries.

Starting from the findings of Part 1 – concerning the Western presuppositions of the contemporary theories of religion – and Part 2 – on ethical interrelatedness as it appears from the analysis of the philosophical translations from Qisong's and Zhu Xi's works – the present chapter is intended to build a hermeneutical theory specifically tailored for the Chinese sphere. It involves a reflection upon its distinctiveness as mediated through the above-mentioned Song classical writings.

It is important to emphasize from the outset that these texts treat ethical issues, human nature and emotions/feelings and do not tell 'stories' in the sense of Richard Bevan Braithwaite (1900–1990) who distinguishes religions according to their thinking through various narratives (or allegories, fables, tales, myths, etc.).[4] As illustrated in Chapter 3, Qisong's essays are not stories about Chan masters, dialogues between a Chan master and his student about meditation, personal religious experience of enlightenment and so forth – the typical Buddhist style – but rather philosophico-religious arguments about Chan's inner and outer ethical dimensions transposed in Confucian *guwen* style. As his interlocutors are Confucian scholars, Qisong does not discuss topics related to the monastic followers but the Buddhist way of life of lay followers: a major topic is not Chan meditation, but the Buddhist precepts explained as counterparts of the Confucian Five Permanencies, as embracing and going beyond them in a Chan context. His texts resonate with Zhu Xi's Neo-Confucian commentaries on similar issues. This is a little-known facet of Chan literature, which arguably disappeared gradually after Qisong, when his *Yunmen* Chan sub-school was assimilated into the *Linji* Chan sub-school – the Chan as we know it today, via its Japanese version Zen.

Furthermore, this book proposes a special interpretation of the Song dynasty ethical leitmotif as ethical interrelatedness embracing two facets: a simultaneous metaphysico-spiritual corporeality (體) and its concrete functioning (用). The account of the Chinese notion of ethics presented here is based on its own cultural assumptions, as having a much broader horizon than its Western counterpart, which is limited to social relations and rules of behaviour. Equally, unlike the Western ethics which concerns matters of value and has an axiological perspective – the study of 'goodness' as value, as reasoning that follows the rules of axiology – the Chinese ethics functions in a totally different way: it is not a judgement of value but a constant, simultaneously inward and outward training, on ordering and purifying of one's emotions as well as a cultivating of the individual's capacity to build ethical relationships. Both facets are necessary in order for the individual to gain access to a profound metaphysico-spiritual level – their original goodness – and nurture it through everyday ethical actions and reactions. The humans belong to this deep corporeality; however, the latter is inaccessible without this continuous effort. Defining and examining the Chinese ethics as well as comparatively uncovering its cultural assumptions and providing textual evidence in supporting them represent the present book's special contribution to the areas of religious studies and ethico-philosophical and comparative studies.

In her study about the religious thought of Zhu Xi, Julia Ching (1934–2001), the eminent scholar of religion and East Asian studies, formulates a similar conclusion concerning the difference between the meaning of ethics in Chinese and Western cultures. She also pinpoints the above-mentioned cognitive Western premise:

> The Chinese approach to ethics is quite different from the many schools we find in today's West, which tend to focus on ethical theories, dwelling often on analysis of words like 'be' and 'ought,' 'right' and 'good' with the aim of making cognitive

distinctions without direct bearing on the good and moral life. In this regard, the growing importance of applied ethics is making an impact, even if this subfield tends as well to carve out preferred specific domains of ethical action rather than to discuss the moral person.[5]

In her own words, the preoccupation of Chinese ethics is 'not with what is or is not moral but with *how* to achieve sagehood, granted the presupposition that all have the innate goodness and potential to become sages'.[6] The cultural assumptions rooted in divinatory thinking and graphic language examined in this book are resonant arguments in support of this distinction between axiologically classificatory, theoretical and meta-ethical presuppositions of Western ethics and those of its Chinese counterpart which focus on inner and outer ethical practice. It is worth repeating that the latter does not concentrate on the nature and classification of values but on the way to follow and its particular steps, on how to become sensitive to the imperceptible signs of changes in the course of events due to the ethical quality of human actions involved – that is, in *Zhongyong*'s and Julia Ching's term, to become a sage. As discussed, one major dimension of this training involves becoming aware of one's emotions/feelings and eliminating those that are unidimensional and self-serving. In contrast, in the next quotation, note the way in which the scholar of comparative theology, John H. Berthrong, draws on the above-mentioned Western theoretical assumptions when classifying Confucian thought as an axiological thought:

> Along with form, dynamics and unification, I will often make use of the notion of axiology in defining process theology and Confucian thought. I believe that process thought, Neo-Confucianism and New Confucianism represent religio-philosophic metasystems defined by the values and harmonies generated by the creation of individual entities. In short, they are essential axiologies.[7]

Another special contribution of this study is its focus on the connections between the two Song dynasty traditions (Chan Buddhism and Neo-Confucianism), based on detailed interpretive translation analyses of Qisong's and Zhu's writings. As noted, Qisong belongs to the *Yunmen* Chan sub-school, a renowned Chan sub-school at the beginning of the Northern Song, which was well received by the Confucian scholars during the first part of this dynasty but was assimilated by the *Linji* Chan sub-school during its second part. A special achievement of this book lies in uncovering a different facet of the Song dynasty Chan: focused on ethics, rooted in ethical social relationships and socially engaged. Usually, Song Chan Buddhism is presented as focused on meditation, awakening the Buddha-nature and lacking interest in ethical practice. These are key characteristics of the *Linji* Chan sub-school which became prominent from the last part of the Song dynasty. Therefore, an original result of this study is its demonstration that these thinkers (Qisong and Zhu Xi) were complementary and shared common goals based on a comparative interpretation of their texts, despite the general image of their two traditions as very much opposed to one another. Zhu Xi was a critic and fierce opponent of Chan Buddhism in general (that he understood as having the characteristics of the *Linji*, the popular sub-group during his time, a century after Qisong; see Chapter 6, Section 2.1). This analysis provides evidence that Qisong represented a Confucianized Chan sub-school that endorsed Confucian practice while at the same time going beyond it, and moreover that his vision has much in common with Zhu's Neo-Confucian perspective.

The book works with the notion of ethical interrelatedness in two ways: first, as an interpretive theory, that is, a research tool rooted in uncovering and comparatively examining Chinese assumptions, intended for the scholars working in fields connected with Chinese culture and society; second, in the particular areas of religious studies and philosophy of religion, as providing the meaning of the so-called classical Chinese (Song Chan and Song Neo-Confucian) way of being religious as well as religious practice in an intercultural perspective.

2 The Western phonetic language: A universalizing orientation

The analysis carried out in Part 1 has unveiled and interpreted several cultural premises, which belong to our Enlightenment legacy and lie at the core of the Western theories of religion examined earlier: a universalizing disposition; an interest in organizing a system of differences which introduces differentiation; a focus on classification; and a comparative view based on differences and similarities flowing from categorizations. It has also been demonstrated that these orientations are predetermined by the nature and functioning of the Western alphabetic language. This section further interprets the above-mentioned premises discussed in Chapter 2 from the perspective of the functioning of the Western language. Its purpose is to provide complementary arguments that these postulations are not related to the coherence of the Chinese classic graphic language and its uses. This scrutiny is thus the first component in determining what sorts of reasons we need to set aside when trying to design a philosophical, interpretive theory about the particularity of the two Song dynasty philosophico-religious traditions: Chan and Neo-Confucianism. To this is added, of course, a second component: the interpretive findings of Part 2, the two previous chapters about Qisong's and Zhu's perspectives on interrelatedness as they emerge from the translations of their works.

Let us start with a recall of the predispositions (universalizing and theorizing) one needs to set aside – because they are of Western origins and therefore culturally and linguistically inappropriate constructions – when interpreting the Chinese religious traditions. The first issue to be addressed is the Western universalizing disposition. The following is a demonstration of its unsuitability for the Chinese context based on the dissimilarity between the functioning of graphic (Chinese) and of phonetic (Western) languages. This tendency to universalize should be viewed as an orientation towards a certain type of abstract reasoning. It has generated the quest for a unified theory that could englobe and explain with its categories all the religious views of the human race, or as much as possible. From the multidimensional demonstration based on the classical Song dynasty texts undertaken in Chapters 3 and 4, it has become clear that, owing to the specific cultural presuppositions flowing from its graphic language, the Chinese philosophico-religious thought does not display such a universalizing propensity. To reiterate, unlike the occidental language, the Chinese emerges not from recording spoken communications but from the graphics resulting from divinatory practices. The latter does not focus on universalization but on contextual, invisible details which are already at work within the course of events but not yet apparent. In other words, one might say that, unlike the Western abstract reasoning which moves towards universalizing, the Chinese abstract has another nature: its premise is detecting particular inchoate signs. That is to say, it is the Western language itself that introduces the above-mentioned presuppositions like the universalizing one within the Western way of thinking and, subsequently, within the theories of religion previously discussed.

A further complementary argument which illustrates this difference between the operational efficiencies of the two languages is the very nature of the Western theory itself: it is a theoretical construction, aimed to explain a general concept of 'religion', rooted in universal principles. Namely, the latter are independent of the specific forms of religious views in different cultures, that is, unattached to them. Such a structure is supported by the particular way in which the linguistic signs of the Western language operate. Their functioning is based on a conceptual invention, that is, in Ferdinand de Saussure's (1857–1913) terms, the 'acoustic image' – the word or phonic signifier, which is arbitrary. Moreover, this is abstractly, that is, artificially and not naturally, connected with the concept – the mental object or signified which tends to be generic due to its speculative character and a referent or the real thing designated by the word. He insists on the arbitrary nature of the connection that unifies the signifier and the signified: in other words, the word-signifier is arbitrary in relation with the concept-signified, with which it has no natural attachment in reality.[8] Indeed, this is because, according to the myth mentioned by Plato in his *Phaedrus* 274b–278d, the letters which create words are an invention – of the god of writing, Thoth. It is this convention that generates not only the separation between signifier, signified and the referent, and their abstract connection (Saussure's semiotic triangle), but also the possibility of the creation of a systematic theory, like those discussed in the previous part. I interpret the above-quoted paragraph of the Swiss linguist which emphasizes the arbitrary (i.e. invented) and not natural character of the link between signifier and signified as equally suggesting the possibility of the construction of such an abstract theory, which is unattached to a specific referent. To be sure, this conceptual association is the prerequisite that makes the abstraction possible and efficiently encodes it: 'The idea of "*soeur*" [sister], he illustrates, is not linked by any inner relationship with the series of sounds s-ö-r ['sistə(r)] which acts as signifier for it. It could be just as well represented by any other: as proof, the differences between languages and the very existence of different languages.'[9] Saussure refers here to alphabetical languages – it might be added. This reasoning suggests that it is this arbitrariness (invention) that enables and supports the construction of generic concepts emerging from these encodings and of Western theories based on such notions.

Again, the classic graphic language functions differently: it does not pay particular attention to the theoretical (abstract) approach and result. Rather, it is interested in a practical and active attitude to language and philosophico-religious thought, one that pays close attention to significant details: for example, those which distinguish the progressive sequences of an unfolding undertaking, as well as the multiple layers of meaning of a character. Harbsmeier clearly describes this contrast in the following paragraph: 'Whereas Greek philosophers were very often preoccupied with the notions of factual and evaluative truth for its own sake, their Chinese counterparts looked upon language and thought as much more pragmatically embedded in social life. Their key concept was that of the Way (*dao*) of conducting human affairs, not of objective factual or doctrinal truth.'[10]

One could also explain these distinct attitudes – the Western gives priority to the theoretical, while the Chinese, to socially engaged practice rooted in a metaphysico-spiritual source – starting from the dissimilarity between the functioning of graphic and of phonetic languages. In the quotation above, Saussure highlights the 'arbitrary' link – that is theoretical and abstract – between signifier and signified (and gives the example of the word 'sister'). In the case of the Chinese graphic language, it must be pointed out that another link is important – that between the graph and its referent – which is natural and not arbitrary. This because the script character which emerges from the process of divination is not an invented convention as the letter but illustrates the real mark of the evolving or changing reality that it embodies and also its dynamic context. I offer that the Chinese graph which developed from the oracle bone inscriptions is simultaneously realistic and dynamic. Let us remember the semiotic etymology of the word 'graph' *wen* 文 (see Introduction, Section 3.3) and the Chinese perception of a thing not as a static material substance but as an animating vital breath (*qi*氣), as evolving and as ethical vitality. Incidentally, the semiotic etymology (Dictionary *Shuowen*) of *qi*氣 depicts the ear of the rice, grains in the middle and the successive waves (three) of vapor rising out when boiling rice. This graph thus embodies what nourishes and animates life: food and breath(ing) with its two correlative steps – inspiration and expiration, *yin* and *yang*.

Without going into detail, let us return to Saussure's example: note that the same word 'sister' in Chinese takes practically not one but two (graphic) forms (observe the preference for factual details, here designating the order of human relationships): elder sister (*jie*姐) and younger sister (*mei*妹). It suffices to observe that both include the graph woman *nü*女, which is the realistic (i.e. derived from the naturalistic image) profile picture of an individual assuming a subservient stance, in a kneeling position, her hands crossed before her. Both graphs have as component this same woman radical that concretely connects them as characters embodying related realities: two graphic communications which transmit something about women. Briefly, let us also add that the other graphic components of the characters 姐 (elder sister) and 妹 (younger sister) also factually indicate the ideas of hierarchy and respect: 'elder' *qie*且 (deceased paternal grandfather, ancestor; *Shuowen* dictionary: a straw mat as display for the offerings) and 'younger' *wei*未 (the last, the lowest in the order, secondary, accessory).

This functioning of the graphs embodies the dynamism of the natural realities – their changing place and evolution within their context. It can also be viewed as a further argument supporting the emphasis on the aforementioned identity between nature and culture which characterizes the Chinese world. Given the divinatory origin of the graphs as graphically embodying the changing ethical dynamism working within all realities, I also stress that they do not epistemologically envisage static external realities as referents or things signified, as is the case for the Western language and its abstract connection between words and the concepts they represent. The graphic signs, as well as their primitive forms – the hexagrams of the *Classic of Changes* (*Yijing*易經) – may be said to incarnate the mark of the ethico-organic dynamism of the natural course of events.

I use the term 'ethico-organic' in order to highlight that they do not embody a causal order, a merely mechanistic determinism, but an ethical order which corresponds to the spontaneous perfect ethical quality of the nature and depends on the ethical quality of the participants' actions in a course of events, that is, on how clean their vital breaths (*qi*氣) are. Consequently, this also has an organic dimension, but the latter is different from the Western idea of organismic structure – assemblage of separated but connected organs, coordinated with each other and performing determined functions. A further point to note is that the Chinese idea of organic reflects the activity of the vital breath (see Section 3).

What does this ethical nature really mean in the context of divinatory thinking and of the natural law of changes? To summarize the analysis developed in the previous chapters, it means that the law of natural changes is naturally ethical and that the heaven-earth and the human form a profound unity. In other words, the metaphysico-spiritual nature as sponsoring a continuous course of events is spontaneously good when not influenced by disruptive non-ethical emotions and actions; equally, righteous actions resonate positively with this naturally good dynamism and enhance it. Second, the unfolding course of events of the human world and its social changes all depend on the same active ethical order of natural changes. Equally, this course of interactions relies on the ethical quality of the human's actions. This idea will be further argued in the next section.

3 The Chinese graphic language: Interrelatedness as metaphysico-spiritual corporeality

This comparative examination of the functioning of the two languages built in the previous section teaches that universalizing is not the focus of the Chinese way of thinking. The contrastive study continues in this Part 3 and demonstrates that its coherence is not rooted in an universalizing attitude but emerges from cultivating interrelatedness.

The view that the inflected character of the Western language translates into a tendency towards classification and categorization has been discussed at length. This is not the case for the Chinese graphic language. Harbsmeier suggests that, unlike the Western alphabetic language, the Chinese language may be described as upholding a 'categorial continuum'. I wholeheartedly agree. He also points out that, when compared with the phonetic language, this attribute is usually interpreted negatively as 'grammatical indeterminacy' or vagueness.[11] His next remark is highly pertinent. Like Smart[12] who suggests the method of informed empathy when judging the worldview of the other, and advocates learning something of the general structure and vocabulary of a different language, but in the specific context of an analysis of the classical Chinese, Harbsmeier advocates building empathy with a different culture by expanding one's knowledge of that foreign language: 'The appearance of vagueness in a different language is often simply a symptom of the ethnocentricity of the person who complains about the vagueness. It is the result of insufficient empathy with the strange language, not a feature of that language itself.'[13]

Without doubt, ethnocentricity in this context includes one's absolute cognitive dependence on their own language. I entirely concur with the author when he rejects the idea of the lack of precision of the classical Chinese grammar and advocates its grammatical suppleness and flexibility as richness. The above section explained this as the specific coherence of a particular type of abstract thinking – that is, detecting invisible signs; becoming aware of the metaphysico-spiritual corporeality to which we belong all, human and non-human – quite different from the Western thinking. Equally, it may be added that this malleability which does not attach a graph to a single grammatical category proves highly conducive to the construction of a dynamic connectedness between realities, the continuum between human and natural worlds, between the naturally ethical and inherent organic movement of the physical world and the changes in the human behaviour. Therefore, one should not regard it as a weakness resulting from imprecision because this emphasis on categorial continuum that distinguishes the functioning of the graphs has another function. It is not intended to facilitate clearly organizing things, that is, associating them with more abstract groups in a classificatory process that requires precise divisions – this constitutes one of the main objectives of the alphabetical language but rather results from the nature of the process of recording results – inchoative realities, in the context of divinatory process. Let us take a moment to discuss this specific development.

This Chinese practice from which the graphic language emerged during the ancient Shang 商 (Yin 殷) dynasty (c. 1600–c. 1046 BCE) was not directly inspired by a god as was the case for the Greeks but by the graphic traces of signals of the unfolding of processes of reality, produced through the cracking of turtle shells or scapulae (speal bones) when exposed to fire. The sinologist and historian of the Chinese religions Léon Vandermeersch describes the genesis of the Chinese graphic language as the gradual process of transformation of the rudimentary graphic signs of the primitive scapulimancy, functioning as 'signals of the future', into graphs functioning as linguistic signs.[14] Let us look at how this practice gave rise to not only the classic graphic language and its ethico-metaphysical coherence but also a way of thinking that is attentive to the naturally dynamic, transforming interrelatedness, that is, to a relationship between human and non-human dynamic realities whose mutual changes weave the fabric of the *dao*. Vandermeersch defines the latter as 'the transphenomenal projection of the reason of things'[15] to distinguish it from the ontological separation of levels in Western thought – mundane and transcendent. Chapter 1 takes a similar precaution when describing the Neo-Confucian 'metaphysical' as a transphenomenal subtle interrelatedness. It also discusses the Chan spiritual which embraces the latter and goes beyond it, suggesting a karmic interrelatedness at the level of the individual's empty self.

Due to its divinatory origin, the Song dynasty metaphysico-spiritual idea of *dao* embodies a certain invisible connection between the successive sequences of the unfolding of an event or of an evolving, dynamic thing: as discussed in Chapter 1, Section 1.3., *dao* is both metaphysico-spiritual and organic, that is, a metaphysico-spiritual corporeality and its functioning or growing. Furthermore, it must be pointed out that the meaning of the notion of corporeality is attached to its Chinese etymological sense *ti* 體 and also connected to the idea of vital breath as its functioning *yong* 用 discussed above and not to the concept of static substance which is Western. With its ties to the natural and changing realities of the tangible world, the graph bears within itself this invisible dynamism that structures the continuous change of the visible world. This vision does not relate to the concrete realities perceived as assembly of static substances but, as mentioned, includes them as dynamic things, that is, as fluid structures of interrelated dynamic and changeable or evolving natural phenomena and human actions and as different qualities of vital breath. Their power is that they embody the presence of an abstruse dimension described above in Chapter 1 as the nourishing metaphysico-spiritual corporeality that exists within evolving phenomena and actions (the metaphysical refers to the Neo-Confucian dualist thought, while the spiritual to the non-dual Chan). Both are reintroduced below in an argument justifying the interrelatedness as presupposition of the functioning of the Chinese graphic language, as well as of the way of thinking emerging from it: this metaphysico-spiritual corporeality traverses everything and dwells in everything.

Zhu Xi describes the structure of heaven-earth as the principle of coherence (*li* 理) or *dao* 道, and its mode of functioning, vital breath (*qi* 氣) or utensils (*qi* 器), and he underscores their holistic unity and hierarchical dependency.[16] His explanation provides what could be called a 'diminished' dualist framework (see Chapter 4, Section 3), nevertheless with a certain emphasis on their distinction. One could regard it as the definition of the Neo-Confucian metaphysics:

> Within heaven-earth, there is the principle of coherence and the vital breath (天地之間，有理有氣). The principle of coherence is the *dao* from beyond perceptible appearance (形而上之道也), that is, the root that gives birth to things. Vital breath is the utensil [things for use] within perceptible appearance (形而下之器也), that is, the utility (具) [use, utilization, way in which something can be used] that gives birth to things. Therefore, the birth of humans and things necessarily relies on the principle of coherence; and then, authentic nature occurs. The latter necessarily relies on vital breath; and then, perceptible appearance occurs. Even though the authentic nature and the perceptible appearance of a thing are not 'outside' one another but form a single unity, the distinction between its *dao* and its utility quality is very clear. One cannot confuse them. (雖不外乎一身，然其道器之間分際甚明，不可亂也。)[17]

The duality of the imperceptible (so-called transcendent) and the perceptible illustrated here is a particular duality that I suggest emerges from the specific functioning of the graphic language which incarnates an original divinatory interest for the imperceptible early signs. The latter indistinctly connect the successive changes within the evolving events while also indicating in advance their subtle direction. Yü Ying-shih explains that the meaning of this 'Chinese duality' differs from the significance of the term in other cultures, 'by being not as sharply differentiated'. Earlier it has been defined as minimized or diminished (see Chapter 4, Section 4). 'The typical Chinese description of the relationship between these two words', he notes, 'is "neither identical nor separate" (*buji buli*不即不離). This description may be hard to comprehend for those who are accustomed to dichotomist thinking, but it does constitute a central feature of Chinese transcendence.'[18] In what follows this lessened duality (Zhu Xi's Neo-Confucian) and non-duality (Qisong's Chan, see later) illustrating the participation and presence of the *dao* (transcendence) in things is considered as a form of interrelatedness.

In order to highlight its nature simultaneously perceived as metaphysico-spiritual and organic, this study refers to it as metaphysico-spirituality corporeality. In addition, it bears repeating that, as the texts of the two authors illustrate, the Song dynasty nature of this Chinese transcendence as interrelatedness is profoundly ethical, that is, it has a deep ethico-moral quality (*de*德). In other words, the *dao* is intrinsically a naturally ethical dimension of realities. In his *Zhongyong zhangju* 1, the Neo-Confucian scholar declares: '*Dao* is the principle of coherence that all everyday things and affairs must follow. It is the ethico-moral quality of every nature. Every heart-mind is provided with this principle of coherence (道者，日用事物當行之理，皆性之德而具於心).'[19]

This ethical feature is also deepened in Qisong's Chan works. Indeed, throughout his book, Qisong emphasizes not only the metaphysical or lessened dual perspective (Neo-Confucian) on the *dao* but equally its other, spiritual and non-dual nature (Chan), with reference to his *guwen*. His non-dualist view embraces the Confucian lessened dualist view and goes beyond it. In his *Zhongyong jie* 中庸解 (*Exegesis of the Mean*), a commentary on the Confucian classic *Zhongyong*, he equates one's Buddhist universal principle with one's authentic nature, which he considers as spiritual (*xing ling*性靈). In the following quotation, he outlines this Chan spiritual non-duality:

> What heaven endows (天命) is the dynamic ordering of the vital movements of heaven-earth (天地之數), and the authentic nature is the spiritual authentic nature (性則性靈也). In other words, the human belongs to this dynamic ordering of the vital movements of heaven-earth, and fuses (生合) with the spiritual authentic nature. The authentic nature is therefore the universal principle, which is always with us (性乃素有之理也). The emotions originate from what one experiences and feels (情感而有之也).[20]

The Chan spiritual and non-dual *dao* is the way of the spirit and is to be found everywhere, last but not least, within the human's heart-mind:

> If one wants to convince the people to accept and obey 'the way' with all their hearts and cultivate themselves (人心服而自修), it is best to convince them from the inside (莫若感其內), by touching their heart-minds. If one wants only that the people to say what he wants them to say and appear obedient (人言順而貌從), it is best simply to control their overt behaviour (莫若制其外). Control from the outside must follow the way of humans, otherwise it cannot succeed. What

touches humans inside must follow the way of the spirit, otherwise it cannot transform their heart-minds. Therefore, the Buddhist way must concentrate on the spirits of individuals first, and then on their behaviour; this is what it means to touch the inside first, and only then control the outside (感內而制外).[21]

However, as the conclusion of this paragraph intimates, at the end of the day, what is most important for Qisong when cultivating this non-dual spirituality is an ethical transformation of people's behaviour as well as of the community as a whole. In the following quotation, the scholar-monk emphasizes this ethical dimension as heart of the Chan Buddhist everyday practice and way of living:

> If all people were to cultivate each of the precepts [of (Chan) Buddhist teaching], even though they could not be reborn in a heaven, this would be sufficient for all people to become good individuals (而人人足成善人). As to a world where all people are good and which is not well governed – there is no such thing (人皆善而世不治, 未之有也)![22]

Chan non-dual ethical behaviour is grounded in one's awareness of the non-dual relationship between oneself, others and everything. In the next paragraph, the contemporary Chan scholar in the field of philosophy of religion, Thich Nhat Hanh, suggestively conveys in simple and easy terms the indefinite, broad configuration of this non-dual relationship which evades definition because its meaning cannot be put into words:

> Just as a piece of paper is the fruit, the combination of many elements that can be called non-paper elements, the individual is made of non-individual elements. If you are a poet, you will see clearly that there is a cloud floating in this sheet of paper. Without a cloud there will be no water; without water, the trees cannot grow; and without trees, you cannot make paper. So the cloud is in here. The existence of this page is dependent on the existence of a cloud. Paper and cloud are so close. Let us think of other things, like sunshine. Sunshine is very important because the forest cannot grow without sunshine. So the logger needs sunshine in order to cut the tree, and the tree needs sunshine in order to be a tree. Therefore you can see sunshine in this sheet of paper. And if you look more deeply, with the eyes of a bodhisattva, with the eyes of those who are awake, you see not only the cloud and the sunshine in it, but that everything is here: the wheat that became the bread for the logger to eat, the logger's father – everything is in this sheet of paper.[23]

In the phonetic language based on clear separations emerging from abstract relationships (e.g. those of signifier, signified and referent), such non-dualist or 'neither identical nor separate' constructions make no concrete sense, or rather a poetic, imaginative sense. Here, this book suggests, their meaning grows from the interdependent, divinatory context of the Chinese graphs, as well as from the natural connection between the graphs and the reality it incarnates. For this reason, it is important to reiterate that the word 'metaphysico-spiritual' tries to intimate in this context the subtle and multivalent dimension of the *dao* which is not only inscrutable as such but also concretely functions within the tangible realities, as their nourishing soil.

As demonstrated in Chapters 3 and 4, the *dao* in the Song dynasty texts is not only a metaphysico-spiritual corporeality but it also has a profound ethical resonance. As stated above, this study advocates that the graphs and the presupposition of interrelatedness, which is the keystone of their functioning, originated from the divinatory process. As every chapter of the book demonstrates in various ways, the latter can be defined as a systematic effort to become aware of the interrelatedness between events, actions and behaviours at its initial imperceptible stage. This divinatory practice from which the hexagrams arise, the graphs and the principle of interrelatedness form the profound origin of the classic Chinese language at the root of Confucian culture. Moreover, they remain at the heart of the Neo-Confucian school and weave themselves into the Chinese Buddhist tradition. In order to elicit the profound quality of human beings, that is, the interrelatedness, Chapters 3 and 4 use the terms 'spiritual' and 'metaphysical' and investigate them in the Chan and Neo-Confucian contexts.

This type of deep interrelatedness (of divinatory origin) can be regarded as an attempt to infuse new meaning into the transcendent and the metaphysical. As such, it could constitute another kind of insight that Western culture could learn from the Chinese philosophico-religious thought. As has been mentioned several times in this chapter, both terms – 'transcendent' and 'metaphysical' – are sensitive notions, which have a particular resonance in the Western sphere. For this reason, it is also possible to consider, for instance, their signification as fixed and determined by the Western thought, to which the latter maintains its exclusivity. Vandermeersch is one of those who maintain this second position, to a certain extent. For this reason, he prefers the concept of metacosmological instead of metaphysical and the transphenomenal as an alternative for transcendent, in order to underline the specificity of the Chinese context when compared with the Western, without amputating its subtle level beyond the physical reality: 'Metacosmology rather than metaphysics, because the transcendental aspect specific to the divination is not ontological, but only transphenomenal. As the classic *Yijing* itself qualifies it, it marks the "beyond the sensible forms" (*xingershang*) and not the physical reality.'[24]

Once again, it may be noted that precisely because of its divinatory origin, which concentrates on decoding the presence of imperceptible signs of the deep connections between individuals, social and natural events, this type of transcendent aspect – transphenomenal and transmoral (the etymology of the Latin prefix trans- denotes its nature) – does not have a different ontological status; it is the nonphysical embodied in the physical reality: the *dao* understood as deep interrelatedness incorporated in the order of nature and of society. Besides, ontology is a Greek invention. In this section, as well as in previous chapters, this subtle interrelatedness has been highlighted as ethical quality. Its source is what might be called a 'transcendent of divinatory origin'. This transcendent is different from its Western (Kantian) equivalent because, it bears repeating, unlike the latter which is anchored in a cognitive and ontological perspective as Western cultural presupposition, the Chinese notion is based on an ethical assumption focused on interrelatedness. As noted earlier, many paragraphs quoted from Qisong's and Zhu Xi's works in Chapters 3 and 4 illustrate this point. This book presents this transcendent of divinatory origin as another specific Chinese presumption from which the Western culture can learn several essential things: a different meaning of the notion of ethics, one which is not limited to the moral principles involved in the individuals' behaviour, concrete social action and interaction; a different perception of human relationships; and as already mentioned in Chapter 2, a different way to envisage intercultural relationships, not as merely cognitive but as ethical. These connotations of classical Chinese ethics are examined thoroughly in the next section.

4 Specific Chinese meanings of ethics

4.1 Interrelatedness as transformative ethical practice

Another major meaning of the notion of interrelatedness in this particular theory tailored to study the Chinese traditions is transformative ethical practice. It is elaborate in this section. Throughout the book, the ethical quality is highlighted as the attribute that best defines the profound nature of human interrelatedness: an ethico-religious at the core of the Song dynasty thought (Chapter 1). It has been discussed as having two coexisting and inseparable levels of depth but not as constituted of two separated *dao* elements: 'ethical as metaphysico-spiritual corporeality' (the ethical's subtle body (*ti*體)) and the 'performative ethical' (its social, concrete functioning (*yong*用)). Also, it has been described as being integrated in a fusion between ethical and organic, especially in the Neo-Confucian thought (Chapter 1 and 4). The previous section discusses interrelatedness as the metaphysico-spiritual corporeality of the living beings which interconnects them at a deep level – that is, the dynamic *dao* omnipresent within them and in the surrounding reality. As we know, for the Neo-Confucian Zhu Xi, it is equated to the principle of coherence or authentic nature, and for the Chan scholar-monk Qisong, to the universal principle, original nature or Buddha-nature. In Chapters 3 and 4, it has been amply demonstrated that this ethical dimension constitutes a leitmotif in the Song dynasty texts examined: it is embodied in the form of a concrete emphasis placed on the genuine performance of good deeds (*shan*善) free of any covert personal motives in Qisong's Chan texts, and based on an ethico-moral quality (*de* 德) bestowed upon everyone by the heaven and materialized as one's consideration for others (*shu* 恕) and wholehearted commitment (full involvement) (*zhong*忠) in Zhu Xi's Neo-Confucian works.

Reaching the deep level of ethical interrelatedness with all others is the highest objective of both disciplines. The leading feature of this interrelationship which emerges from Qisong's Chan and Zhu's Neo-Confucian texts examined in Part 2 is its transformative character. The Northern Song monk describes this goal of the two teachings as seeking to engage people and society in an ethical transformation – simultaneously at the social and spiritual levels – which means fostering a proactive, 'enlightened' impulse to perform good actions (see Chapter 3). Becoming aware of humans' profound ethical interrelatedness and cultivating it mean 'making people good'. He stresses that Song Chan's focus is a large-scale social transformation starting from individual change, within the context of Confucian social relationships. In other words, this community metamorphosis through Buddhist undertakings facilitates Confucian familial and social interdependence.

Readers are reminded that Qisong also considers the heart-mind as the Chan vehicle for interrelatedness as emptiness, the driving force that triggers an individual's transformation. When they are able to crack the wall that limits their self-consciousness and thus experience their own 'nature-emptiness' and 'no-self' – that is, the self as connected with everything or the interrelated self – a profound change occurs: one's emotions become not contaminated, that is, non-distorted, the human then is spontaneously pure, not only at the social level of everyday ethical interactions but also at the spiritual/religious level of the interconnection between their past, present and future lives, as well as of the karmic causes and fruits.

Zhu Xi perceives the Neo-Confucian learning as transformative as well (see Chapter 4): he explains that the individual's highest goal of cultivating consists in becoming aware of the original inner good (i.e. the aforesaid *dao* or principle of coherence), keeping it present and nourishing it; like the Buddhists, he equates the result of this effort not with following an external moral norm but with an individual inner effort, through an inner transformation – from a limited self, focused on the pursuit of one's own interests and advantage to a complete self in which the original inner good is fully actualized. Such a whole self acquires the ability to put themselves in the place of others and understand how to act for their benefit. Again, in this context, the difference between the two traditions is embodied in the contrast between metaphysico-organic unity and spiritual non-duality of the interrelatedness. Just as for Qisong, the emotions/feelings also have a central place in Zhu Xi's transformative ethical practice. He describes the inner practice of the good, which might be defined as ethico-religious, as a transformation involving two inextricable facets: the practice of 'removing people's self-centered emotions' and the practice of 'making whole their original goodness'. It may be recalled that the latter, that is, complete original goodness, is synonymous with the metaphysical principle of coherence or ethico-moral capacity. From the works of these two Song thinkers, one understands that this transformation is not only self-transformation but simultaneously manifests itself as a resonance or echo between organically interconnected levels: the human self, the wider society and the environing nature.

The Contemporary New Confucians also identified ethics with the Chineseness of the Chinese culture and discussed it as the driving force of its modernization.[25] In *Zhongguo zhexue de tezhi* 中國哲學的特質 (The Specificity of Chinese Philosophy), the eminent Contemporary New Confucian and philosopher Mou Zongsan stresses, too, that the Chinese philosophy focuses on ethics and that the source of this interest lies in what he calls the notion of 'concerned consciousness' (*youhuan yishi* 憂患意識) (中國哲學之重道德性是根源於憂患的意識).[26] He adds that this concept was conceived by his friend, the distinguished Contemporary New Confucian and historian Xu Fuguan徐復觀 (1904–1982). Also a signatory of *Manifesto for a Reappraisal of Sinology and the Reconstruction of Chinese Culture* like Mou, Xu conducted significant research on the Zhou周 (c. 1046–256 BCE), Qin秦 (221–206 BCE) and Han漢 (202 BCE–220 CE) dynasties. In particular, he examined their sociopolitical structures and intellectual history. Based on his original studies, Xu's above-mentioned term is complex, and its meaning is difficult to render. I justified my translation as 'concerned consciousness'.[27]

Obviously, the analysis of the Song dynasty philosophico-religious texts developed in this book fully supports Mou Zongsan's view concerning the prominence of ethics in the Chinese culture. According to the present study in general and the following section in particular, it can be affirmed that the continuous development of the process of divination, its fine observations of the invisible links between changes in natural and human world, represents the source not only of the classic graphic language but equally of the interest in ethics of the Chinese tradition.

The first part of Section 4.2 assembles in a comprehensive definition all the significant features of the Chinese notion of ethics brought to light and examined in the previous chapters related to the classic texts of the Song dynasty. In the following, a complement to this presentation is offered. It is devoted specifically to the divinatory practice. Starting from the contemporary concept formulated by Xu Fuguan, it addresses the peculiar significance of ethics in the Chinese culture by demonstrating first that this focus grew out of the ancient practice of divination practised at an early stage during the Yin (Shang) dynasty and of its progressive transformation over the next period, Zhou dynasty (c. 1046–256 BCE). In the following, I build up the multiple, specific facets of the classical Chinese 'ethical quality', an interpretation of its meaning as mediated by the translations of the Song dynasty texts – Qisong's and Zhu Xi's – previously analysed. As mentioned, the connotation of ethics and ethical practice which emerges from these writings is significantly distinct from that in its Western analogue. For this reason, it could teach the members of Occidental world, which is dedicated above all to furthering individual development and rights, new ways to build enriching relationships between oneself and others.

4.2 Ethical practice and its divinatory sources

What does it mean 'ethical practice' in the Chinese sphere? Cultivating a particular sense of responsibility, as we shall now see.

Classical Chinese culture, in general, and Song dynasty traditions, in particular, regard ethics as a crucial feature of everyday actions and interactions and as the heart of its philosophico-religious practice. One might say that, in its own context, the classical Chinese world develops ethics not only as 'first philosophy', to use Levinas's term in a different environment, but also as its main cultural presupposition. What does ethics mean in this different environment? Let's start from a broad and familiar definition, like that offered by Frederick J. Streng (1933–1993): roughly, it is an attitude of life and a practice that are focused on one's relations to others. In his book *Understanding Religious Life*, Streng provides an interesting explanation of the religious significance of fulfilling human relationships which, for the most part, illustrates well the Chinese social reality and the importance that it places on ethics. The American historian of religions, a strong proponent of religious pluralism and comparative religion, acknowledges that 'social relationships provide channels for expressing human values, especially those sets of values that we call "morality" and "ethics". … "Moral actions", Streng points out, "reveal the parts of human existence that deal with rights and obligations in relation to others. Modern history suggests that the urge to seek social justice or to establish an ethical society inspires and transforms people whether or not they believe in God." '²⁸ In the same paragraph he makes reference to Confucianism as a tradition envisaging ethics as a reflection of the natural good.

According to their views presented in Part 2, both Qisong and Zhu Xi would probably assent to this description as a global interpretation of the teachings of the Chinese sages while emphasizing the need for individuals to actively strive to become effectively aware of this good and nurture it through dedicated cultivation and conscientious conduct of ethical actions and interactions in everyday life. However, in the Chinese sphere, ethics is not explicitly concerned with 'rights and obligations in relation to others', as Streng affirms – 'rights' is a specifically Western assumption – but rather, as discussed below, with the human being's responsibility for their own behaviour. The next part which is focused specifically on this sense of responsibility examines it as core of the Chinese ethics and its source as a distinct transcendent of divinatory origin.

Mou Zongsan stresses that this feeling of responsibility is expressed in the concept of concerned consciousness defined by his friend Xu Fuguan as embodying the wellspring of Chinese philosophico-religious thought. In *Xu Fuguan in the Context of East Asian Confucianisms*, Huang Chun-chieh thoroughly examines the creative historical work of this prominent member of the so-called group of twentieth-century New Confucians from Hong Kong and Taiwan. Xu Fuguan's next paragraph from his 1969 study *Zhongguo renxing lunshi: Xian Qin pian* 中國人性論史先秦篇 (A Historical Essay on Chinese Human Nature: The Pre-Qing Period) elaborates on his perception of the origin of ethics as feeling of responsibility:

> The Zhou people did change the mandate of the Yin; in the other words, they became the new winners. However, what one understands from reading the texts and documents from the beginning of the Zhou dynasty does not give the impression of the high-and-mighty atmosphere that characterizes most nations after winning a war. The feeling reflected in those texts appears more like what the classic *Yizhuan* [Great Commentary on the Classic of Changes] called a 'concerned' consciousness. ... The formation of a concerned state of mind is precisely the result of the rulers' reflection, at a given moment, on chance or bad luck, on success or failure. While reflecting on the political change they have caused, the Zhou elites have thus discovered the close link existing between, on the one hand, chance or bad luck, success or failure, and on the other hand, the rulers' behaviour. ... In this way they learned how to determine responsibility and identify those responsible.²⁹

Let us take a moment to reflect on this paragraph. At the end of the Yin (Shang) dynasty – the ancient dynasty that witnessed the emergence of the graphic language from the practice of divination – the last king of the Yin is a bloody tyrant. Around 1046 BCE, the first ruler of Zhou, King Wu 武王 (d. 1043 BCE) succeeds in eliminating him – the heaven thus withdraws the mandate to rule previously conferred on the Yin. The conquerors liberate the people and establish their new, Zhou dynasty. In the above quotation, Xu Fuguan remarks that the feelings reflected in the texts of the period are not those of happy winners but of rulers who know that they bear responsibility for their actions: namely, the destruction of the Yin, among others. In other words, even if they have removed a cruel leader, the replacement of the ruling house was still violent – they betrayed and killed him – and not a good and ethical action, like those which arise in nature, the spontaneous sequences of the uninterrupted movement, interdependent growth of life. As a result, a sense of responsibility arises from the depths of their hearts. It makes them conscious that their actions were not 'completely ethical' (see later); therefore, they will naturally incur adverse consequences afterwards. This triggers the emergence of what Xu Fuguan calls a 'concerned consciousness': being motivated by a constant concern to eliminate non-ethical, self-interested motives and adherence to one's own preferences and one's own good.

In order to better understand this idea of 'completely ethical', and therefore the emergence of the concerned consciousness at the beginning of the Zhou dynasty, that is, of a constant concern to ensure that the ethical quality of one's actions is not only partially ethical but entirely complete, let us read the next paragraph in which Zhu Xi gives a twelfth-century Neo-Confucian commentary of the *Lunyu* 3: 25, including his explanation of the difference between King Wu's good action – the founder of the Zhou; Xu Fuguan's quote above makes reference to his action – and those of the legendary sage emperors Yao堯 and Shun舜:

> Shun舜 was Yao's堯 continuator and pursued his way of governing. King Wu武王 attacked the Zhou紂 tyrant [posthumous name given to the last king of the Yin] and took his place in order to assist the people. Their efforts for the benefit of the people were similar, and for this reason their [ritual] musics were both of complete beauty. But the ethico-moral quality of Shun stems from his authentic nature. Yao ceded him the throne, and Shun received the world (有天下) to govern it. The ethico-moral quality of King Wu is the opposite. By leading a military campaign and putting to death the tyrant, he took the world (得天下) to govern it. The true natures of their acts were different. 舜紹堯致治，武王伐紂救民，其功一也，故其樂皆盡美。然舜之德，性之也，又以揖遜而有天下;武王之德，反之也，又以征誅而得天下，故其實有不同者。[30]

The concerned consciousness which emerges from the feeling of responsibility functions as a constant and positive occupation to completely materialize in one's actions, and not only to some degree, the metaphysical authentic nature or complete ethico-moral quality bestowed by heaven, the so-called complete ethico-moral quality of the sage (*shengren zhide* 聖人至德).[31] In Mou's terms:

> Chinese 'concerned consciousness' is in no case born of the sins of human life, but what it stimulates is a positive moral conscience, the concern that one might not sufficiently be following the moral, that one might not be learning what one should learn. This is a feeling of responsibility. Its derivative concepts are respect – the respect for morality, the fact of making the luminous moral power shine brightly, and the mandate of Heaven. ... The preliminary expression of this concern is the serious and responsible attitude of 'undertaking actions in a cautious manner'. The 'respect' emerges from the fear and attention that spring from this serious and responsible attitude.[32]

It could be observed that, in the previous Shang (Yin) period, the anticipated, imperceptible but inchoative signs of the good and bad fortune – resulting from the interaction of the human actions, especially the rulers', with the naturally ethical law or order – was something understood through the process of divination relying on the interrelatedness between the sequence of events and on the naturally ethical course of nature that the human world as part of the nature should also follow. The Zhou winners and their successors were living an awakening that such a precursory perception of the imperceptible signs of change, prior to their realization, can be directly experienced as inner and concrete feeling of responsibility for their actions and not only mediated through deciphering the result of the process of divination.

What is this awareness? The realization that a good action or behaviour spontaneously and naturally generates a good fruit, in other words, good fortune, and vice versa. In the previous period, this interrelatedness between the sequences of the unfolding of an event, in light of its ethical and non-ethical components, was detectable through the resulting graphs on oracle bones. Over the next period, during the Zhou dynasty, this process, in a sense, evolves and becomes more holistic: it integrates the human inner world in the form of a feeling of responsibility that spontaneously translates the ethical or unethical nature of rulers' actions first and then of human actions. This also corresponds with the contents of the *Classic of Changes* and its ethico-political interpretations of the numerical hexagrams which replace the tortoise shell and bone divination. In Xu Fuguan's words, 'This concerned consciousness is the expression of the direct feeling of responsibility that the human mind begins to experience toward all human activities and toward external reality. That is, the human mind becomes self-conscious.'[33]

In order to further illustrate the emergence and development of this concerned consciousness and its feeling of responsibility from the ancient divinatory thinking which seeks to determine the incipient shape of future misfortune or fortune, war or peace, let us first consider, for example, a divinatory note. In her beautifully illustrated book about the Chinese graphs, Cecilia Lindqvist (1932–2021), a student of the Swedish linguist Bernhard Karlgren (1889–1978), describes the result of a Shang dynasty process of divination:

> An inscription from King Wu Ding's rule in about 1300 B.C. contains the king's question, the oracle's answer, and a note on what actually happened: On the day 'gui-si,' the diviner Ques consulted the oracle: 'Will any misfortune occur in the next ten days?' The king read in the cracks and said: 'Misfortune will occur. Perhaps disturbing news will come.' When it came to the fifth day, 'ding-you', disturbing news did indeed come from the west. Guo from Zhi said: 'Tufang is besieging our eastern border and has attacked two villages. Gongfang has also plundered the fields on our Western border.'[34]

At this incipient stage of the practice of divination, the practitioners already show interest in decoding the interrelatedness at work within the course of events, as subtle connection between the gradual unfolding sequences of the changes. The latter take the form of divinatory cracks – intersecting lines and trajectories that gave rise to the

Chinese characters. Over time, from the Shang (Yin) period to the Zhou period, this divinatory tradition becomes more sophisticated and gradually interconnects more aspects of reality, that is, it interconnects the natural and human realities through the *yin* and *yang* features of their vital breath and through the phenomenon of resonance between them. One can view this as a gradual introduction of human actions in resonance (i.e. vibratory response) with the natural phenomena of the heaven-earth. This process embodies a gradual transformation of the nature of this resonance: from a purely organic (based on the *yin* and *yang* action and reaction of vital breath; see Section 1 for the Chinese meaning of organic) to an ethical resonance (i.e. sense of responsibility). This ethico-organic resonance with and response to stimuli is apparent in the next divinatory result, dating from 486 BCE, eight centuries later. It is quoted by Vandermeersch in the translation of the French Jesuit missionary to China Séraphin Couvreur (1835–1919) from the *Chronicle of the regional state of Lu*, the home state of Confucius, that is, *La chronique de la principauté de Lou* (*The Spring and Autumn Annals* and *the Commentary of Zuo*):

> When in 486 B.C. the prince Zhao Yang of Jin hesitated to provide alliance to the principality of Zheng attacked by that of Song, the scapulimancy revealed that the circumstances were those of the water encountering the fire and that the fire will be drowned out by the water. Which meant, according to the diviners, first that a war could break out, because the war, as the water, falls within the dynamics of *yin* which prevailed; and then, that the prince Zhao Yang, if he can go himself to war, because he belonged to a family marked by its surname as *yin*, should not go to war against Song, because the family of the Song princes was also *yin*; however, he could attack the prince of Qi whose lineage descends from an officer of fire, certainly making it a *yang* family. The history reports that consequently, Zhao Yang has been careful not to attack Song to defend Zheng as he had intended, but that shortly after, he took up a military expedition against Qi and effectively, came back victorious.[35]

This gradual evolution of the divinatory operations and of their interpretation clearly shows, on the one hand, the progressive, effective fusion between human and nature as deeply interacting according with the same dynamic, spontaneous order or law and, on the other hand, the progressive understanding of the nature and natural life as identical to human life and accordingly its omnipresent order as an ethical organization. This can be observed in the *Classic of Changes*, which contains interpretations of hexagrams arising from numerical divination. The commentary (*wen* 文) of the second hexagram (*kun* 坤) mentioned earlier makes reference to two geometric figures, the straight line and the square, which present similarities with the inner space or heart-mind and the outer space of acting and behaviour and ethical implications:

> Rendering one's own quality of being righteous as a straight line, rendering one's own sense of duty as a square. Inwardly, the noble individual is respectful in order to make his inside a right line, and outwardly he cultivates his sense of duty in order to make his outside a square. As soon as respect (*jing* 敬) and the sense of

duty (*yi* 義) are present, the moral power of the individual is no longer completely isolated within.³⁶

Clearly, a direct result of this progressive development of the divinatory interpretation is the emergence of the ethical quality as the heart of the Chinese culture and philosophico-religious practice. Xu Fuguan and Mou Zongsan present this as a positive ethical awareness – the concerned consciousness, a constant impulse to fully complete the development of one's ethical quality, that is, to fully put it into practice.

The next feature of the ethical transcendent is discussed in the following section: it is the idea of resonance.

4.3 Ethical practice as process of resonance

It must be noted that according to the logic and specific coherence of the divinatory practice, the factual functioning of the ethical transcendent of divinatory origin arises from a dynamic of resonance at work between all levels of reality, thus intangibly connecting the phenomenal world, social world of behaviours and interactions and the human's inner sphere of emotions revolving around their central sense of responsibility.

In Qisong's words, this law of resonance operates in the form of the interrelatedness of the stimulus (*gan* 感) and response (*ying* 應). He differentiates emotions as good or bad, superficial or deep, and understands them in terms of the type of response they generate in practice, either disaster or happiness (good fortune) (*huo* 禍 or *fu* 福):

> When the heart-mind moves, its movements are either with [the nature] or against [the nature] and thus arise the good and bad emotions. When good and bad emotions (善惡之情) develop, then in response arise disaster and happiness (good fortune) (禍福之應). Among the good and bad emotions, there are superficial ones and deep ones (淺深); therefore, their retribution in disaster and happiness is also either heavy or light (報之有輕重). Light retribution can be discharged, heavy retribution cannot be avoided. There are before and after good and bad emotions, the retribution in the form of disaster and happiness can be slow or fast, the mutual stimuli traverse ten lives, and ten thousand lives and cannot be avoided. They never appear during only one life.³⁷

The Chan scholar-monk suggests a comparison between the Buddhist idea embodied in the previous citation and the Confucian notions of auspicious testimony and ominous testimony sent by heaven in response to the acts of the sovereign and of the people: 'Concerning retribution (*baoying* 報應), Confucians, too, speak about auspicious testimony (*xiu zheng* 休證) and ominous testimony (*jiu zheng* 咎證). When good deeds accumulate, favours from heaven arrive (積善有慶). When evil deeds accumulate, calamities arrive (積惡有殃). This is very clear.'³⁸

As for Confucianism, paragraph 30 of the ancient *Zhongyong* illustrates this ethical resonance using the metaphor of a river flowing – great rivers (great moral qualities which are transformative) and small rivers (small moral qualities, weakened and dried up by selfishness and desires). Ethico-moral law and law of life are thus two inseparable facets of the Confucian reality:

> The myriad things grow together without harming each other. Together, each one continues on its own path without getting in another's way. The small moral qualities are like the rivers digging their riverbeds and flowing into them. The great moral quality is what multiplies the continuous transformations of reality [individual realities]. This is what makes heaven-earth large. 萬物並育而不相害，道並行而不相悖，小德川流，大　德敦化，此天地之所以為大也。[39]

All these quotations reflect the Song dynasty philosophico-religious vision of the imperceptible ethical interrelatedness between humans as induced by natural resonance. As demonstrated in the previous chapters, it functions as a metaphysico-spiritual corporeality. It is important to reiterate that the meaning of the notion of corporeality is attached to the Chinese etymological sense of the graph *ti* 體 and also connected to the idea of vital breath discussed earlier, not to the concept of static substance which is Western: the corporeality is dynamic and resonant. This was the first dimension of the ethical interrelatedness discussed in Section 2.

A second feature, typically Neo-Confucian, follows from the last quotation: the ethical interrelatedness between humans flows from their effort to become good through rectifying their heart-minds (*zheng xin* 正心); it also has an organic quality – it nourishes and regenerates cosmic life. This organic feature of the ethical interrelatedness as nourishing the innately good heart-mind, preserving and protecting its breathing was discussed in Chapter 4, in the context of Zhu Xi's thought.

In his commentary on *Zhongyong*, paragraph 1, Zhu Xi further elaborates on this organic attribute of the ethics by comparing the latter with a root of the cosmic organism which nurtures the vital breath of all realities, preserves the cosmic harmony and ensures the full flowering of all diverse things. In the following quote, the ethical quality is illustrated using several of its aspects highlighted above: the constant vigilance over himself of the exemplary individual who is thus able to rectify his heart-mind, that is, eliminate self-centred feelings and motives; obviously, this practice to rectify one's heart-mind requires self-discipline, that is, one must constantly identify the types of feelings which unfold in one's heart-mind, structure and cultivate those which build an interdependent self, while purging those which separate the individual from others; further, one must develop the capacity to flawlessly respond to things when resonating with them, in other words, to vibrate with them not in just any way, but in an ethical manner, so as to protect and preserve the breathing of his innately good heart-mind:

> Vigilant when alone and with his spirit focused, the individual is able to respond to things, without the slightest error and in every specific circumstance. In this manner, the human achieves the complete harmony and, in this case, all ten thousand things are looked after and fed. This is because, from the beginning, the

heaven-earth, ten thousand things, and myself form one body. When my heart-mind is rectified, this also makes the heaven-earth's heart-mind rectified; when my vital breath is in good order, this also makes the heaven-earth's vital breath in good order. 自謹獨而精之，以至於應物之處，無少差謬，而無適不然，則極其和而萬物育矣。蓋 天地萬物本吾一體，吾之心正，則天地之心亦正矣，吾之 氣順，則天地之氣亦順矣。⁴⁰

4.4 Interrelatedness as sameness

Its third aspect – ethical interrelatedness understood as profound, invisible sameness of individuals, of their originally good heart-mind (in Qisong's Chan and Zhu's Neo-Confucian works) – is the focus of this section. Chapters 3 and 4 have both elaborated on this sameness as the basis for ethical interrelatedness of humans and on its specific signification in the context of the writings of the two Song dynasty thinkers. This topic reconnects our analysis with its Western dimension, with the first section of this chapter dedicated to the particularity of the Western language and its universalizing orientation. At first sight, one might make the following observation: that Song dynasty sameness as ethical interrelatedness (*tong* 同) and the Western universalizing tendency appear to be similar standpoints. Let us take a moment to comparatively discuss them and uncover their different natures and cultural presuppositions.

As seen in Section 2, the Western propensity for generalizing is part of the Enlightenment heritage and provides the foundation for the categorizing and classifying processes which are part of the theoretical endeavour. In this effort, as one may remember from Chapter 2, the theorist is looking for differences and similarities between certain perceptible aspects of culturally specific visions of religion: it combines them into categories. As shown above, in this operation the researcher is unable to take account of the invisible, specific cultural premises like those introduced by the functioning of language in which are rooted particular aspects of religions which may appear identical on the surface. At the end of the day, this allows them to discover a universalizing dimension which makes it possible to bring together various 'relatively different' visions under a single 'theory', without considering their cultural assumptions. Paden formulates this Enlightenment ideal of classification and generalization in a very precise way: 'We are not comparativists simply to repeat what religions say and do, or to recreate their particular worlds,' he notes, 'but more importantly, to find amidst those systems linkages with what we have learned from all of them and to form generalizations.'⁴¹

Chapter 2 explains that this orientation is based on relative difference and not on otherness, as the comparative work is done on the same palpable level. That being the case, the theoretical construction of the researcher's comparative theory inevitably remains within the same cultural borders: the theorist's. Usually, it chooses a specific feature of human existence, considers it as universal and builds around it a universalizing definition or theory of religions built upon interpretive and separated categories, dispositions or issues which revolve around the particular features of human existence selected. The theorist thus considers that the cultures provide different answers for the unique chosen feature, as, for example, those discussed in Chapter 2. One of the most common is the idea of religious belief – the core of Geertz's conception of religion, for example, based on, as Talal Asad notes, the Christian presupposition which emphasizes the priority of belief as state of mind rather as constituting activity in the world (Asad 1993: 47).

Paden's theory and its presumptions are an edifying example in this regard, as well. I consider it in particular because it provides a clear understanding of the Western idea of sameness, which will next be compared with the Song dynasty sameness. The scholar of religion is looking for 'a broadened notion of human behaviors underlying and shared by all cultures' and sees it as 'panhuman behaviors to which religious cultures add their differences of content'. He proposes to focus on biological sameness, on the fact that 'behind cultural variance we are all bio-human creatures who "do" universes', 'with our common organic ancestry'.[42]

As explained in Chapter 2, such generalizing categories often rely implicitly on Western dichotomies, like those of Paden, which connect what Western culture sees as two separated features of the human, that is, her biological (i.e. nature) and social (culture) inheritances: 'As humans', he stresses, 'our roots are in both. We are hominids and we are also Muslims and Pure Land Buddhists; we are organisms, and we are also Ukrainians and Chinese.'[43] Therefore, one Western presupposition, already noted, which lies at the root of this theory, is the separation between nature and culture (see Chapter 2, Section 5). Other examples of dichotomic articulations in Western theories of religion: when considering the universal meaning of religion, Thomas Tweed sees religion as involving both dichotomic terms, that is, considered as different: 'finding a place and moving across the space', 'intensify joy and confront suffering', 'spatial and temporal orientation', 'organic processes and cultural practices', 'boundaries between the embodied self and the natural world'.[44]

Needless to say, in this specific approach (Paden's), the major dimension chosen is the universal biological/hominid inheritance, and its presupposition is full confidence in the total objectivity of the scholar – let us remember the Western ideal of the self-transparency of the subject that lies at the heart of Descartes's, Fichte's and Husserl's philosophies – in the process of determining the universal categories. In this case, if the biological inheritance is the universal trait, according to Paden, it is supposed to be the structure of the selected universal species within which each culture introduces different contents: cultural data assigned to their classificatory boxes. It goes without saying that in this case, the distinct cultural contents are different only with regard to their perceptible characteristics, that is, only relatively different (see Chapter 2) and devoid of their specific, unseen and radically different (other) cultural presumptions. In other words, because culturally different contents can be sorted in the same boxes due to apparent similarities, it means that not all their peculiar qualities are considered – those deeply and specifically cultural remain unnoticed. In this way, only after removing the latter, these different cultural contents can represent variations on a common evolutionary human structure.

In the case of Paden's theory, the sameness that culturally different religious visions share is considered to be biological. I would offer that, at the end of the day, the classificatory boxes of his theory are not only universally biological but also Western-culture inspired. As evidence in this sense, consider, for example, a universal category mentioned by the author: 'That groups invest certain objects with authority and charisma is universal; what the objects are is diverse.'[45] Recall that the logic of Hick's theory analysed in Chapter 2 has the same structure universal/particular: 'In relation to the divine the "mode of the knower" differs within different religio-cultural systems so that the Real is thought-and-experienced in a wide variety of ways.'[46]

As a counterexample, I would offer that the Song dynasty philosophico-religious Chan-Confucian texts reflect a view which is devoid of this type of interest in objects invested with authority and charisma. It is focused instead on ethical interrelatedness, where the ethical, as developed in this chapter, is a wider notion than its Western analogue: it has a metaphysico-spiritual, imperceptible corporeality and a perceptible, social functioning. In the performance of the Confucian ritual at Confucius temple, for instance specific objects are used, but they do not have authority and charisma (see Chapter 4). The same observation applies to Qisong's Chan Buddhism which does not focus on objects but concentrates instead on inner Buddha-nature and social everyday practice (see Chapter 3).

This example demonstrates the fact that carefully choosing the categories in the process of classification is inevitably loaded with the theorist's cultural assumptions. In Smith's terms, discussed in Chapter 2: 'Religion [the Western concept] is solely the creation of the scholar's study. It is created for the scholar's analytical purposes by his imaginative act of comparison and generalization.'[47] This confirms Ricoeur's idea concerning the difficulty for the researcher or interpreter to be fully self-transparent – therefore their difficulty to uncover and comparatively examine different cultural presuppositions. Aside from agreeing with him, this work argues that one privileged access to the culturally other is that mediated through texts, through language. There is no doubt that this access – learning the other's language – has the potential to experience and ameliorate our unavoidable self-opacity. This (experiencing the theorist's self-opacity) could be fruitfully considered as another objective of comparative research. In this case, one could see this goal as an embodiment and another interpretation of Gadamer's suggestion to learn from the other, to learn to think on a large scale.

Undoubtedly, such a perspective could help us understand the diversity that surrounds us. It could also assist Western culture in its effort to use with caution a specific Enlightenment heritage and a specific universalizing presupposition: the generalizing of the critical attitude. When uniquely cultivating this critical attitude, one is interested in preserving their analytical tools and standard of judgement; one is not open to question their own presuppositions nor willing to learn from the culturally other as a student learns but as a master. Because, it is worth recalling, learning as a master from the other means the scholar's interest in scanning the examined other's specific visible features and introducing them into their own classificatory categories. As a result, the content of their boxes-classes is richer in substance. However, learning as a student from the other refers to experiencing the researcher's self-opacity as well as that ethical relationship suggested by Levinas of non-indifference to alterity, which is focused not on intellectually categorizable and perceptible difference but on otherness. Otherness lies beyond the classification of species.

In conclusion, to return to the Western perception of sameness, one could define it as the result of the classification of dimensions of various religions using the Western universalizing tools but without being aware of their invisible cultural assumptions embedded in language and in thinking. This sameness functions at the tangible level, as defined by the Western assumptions. Therefore, as suggested in multiple contexts, one way to enrich this comparative endeavour is to start the analysis by trying to descend to the opaque level of those premises, Western and non-Western.

As discussed in Part 2, ethical sameness in the Song dynasty philosophico-religious texts examined functions differently: first of all, it dwells at a profound, invisible level, the field of the human depth. Second, it is not ethically neutral but belongs to the ethical sphere. In Qisong's Chan texts, sameness is the closeness of all heart-minds, an awareness of the common nature within individuals, a non-dual Buddhist sameness. It requires acquiring access, through religious training and social practice, to suchness, the real reality. The interrelatedness that results from Chan awareness and cultivation of sameness is emptiness; in other words, it involves the absence of an individual self (i.e. egocentric). Buddhist sameness goes beyond and encompasses Confucian interrelatedness and sameness rooted in the mandate of heaven. In order to have access to this deep sameness rooted in the heart-mind, Qisong warns, one has to 'excel' (to be good at, *shan*善) in both realms, that of the names (society and its hierarchy) and that of the ultimate reality.

In the Neo-Confucian thought, sameness is inner goodness. Zhu Xi builds a new interpretation of interrelatedness: not merely cultural and political unity but also ethico-metaphysical sameness and unity. Sameness understood as initial complete goodness or interrelatedness is what prevails in his thought, while individual differences, namely, distinct mixtures of the principle of coherence and vital breath, are held to be only secondary and impermanent and meant to be overcome through learning and understanding. Obviously, this distinction between humans, their outward appearance, is easily and clearly perceived, while the sameness embodied in the common initial authentic nature or good is something one cannot discern without effort, without intellectual learning and heart-mind analysis and social practice. Chapter 4, for instance, is dedicated to Zhu Xi's discussions on several layers of the meaning of the good as interrelatedness: homogeneous, that is, complete good, the principle of coherence, authentic nature, sameness and the effort of being sincere.

In the writings of both Song thinkers, sameness constitutes the metaphysico-spiritual substrate of the interrelatedness and has an ethical nature. This chapter outlines an interpretive theory of interrelatedness as the very heart of the Song texts. Its structure is supported by two beams. The first one consists of the findings of Chapters 3 and 4 which present significant philosophical translations from the two thinkers' works: they help us to define the multiple facets of the ethical interrelatedness. Each one of them is the subject of a separate section of this chapter. The second pillar of this structure is the twofold effort to uncover the Western presuppositions of the theories of religion and the Chinese assumptions of the ethical interrelatedness.

In conclusion, the theory proposed does not focus on an abstract 'universal' resulting from the process of classifying and categorization. Instead, it considers the notion of 'ethically interrelated' as core of the Chinese philosophico-religious traditions and presents multiple layers of meaning and practice of its two components, that is, ethics and interrelatedness: metaphysico-spiritual corporeality, ethical transcendent, transformative ethical practice, concerned consciousness and responsibility rooted in the ancient divinatory thinking and sameness as metaphysico-spiritual substrate of the interrelatedness.

Chapter 6 is the last one and discusses the reliability of this new theory, what is new about it and the new issues it is raising. More precisely, it assesses its innovative potential, performance and effectiveness in a comparative perspective: in other words, in relation to several sinological and philosophical contemporary approaches to Chinese meaning of ethics and transcendent.

Part 4

Contemporary Sinological, Philosophical and Buddhological Approaches to Chinese Religious Traditions

6

A comparative perspective: Similarities and differences

Part 1 of this book discusses the Western presuppositions involved in the core structures of several prominent theories of religion in the area of cross-cultural research. Part 3 sets forth an interpretive theory about ethical interrelatedness built on the Chinese assumptions that were elicited through translating the Song texts presented in Part 2. This philosophical hermeneutics is concerned to avoid using the distortive sorts of Western assumptions uncovered in Part 1. As mentioned earlier, the latter focuses on the articulation of the notions of religion and theory and on their cultural presuppositions, Western and Chinese. Part 2 deals with the Chinese cultural presuppositions of the Song dynasty philosophico-religious traditions. It therefore represents a pivotal moment in this chapter's development as it relates to a change in focus: it prepares the transition from Part 1 to the rest of the book and the change in focus from Western generalizing approaches to religion and theory to their distinctive traits within the Chinese philosophico-religious space.

This Part 4 considers the theory about ethical interrelatedness built in Part 3 – consisting of several dimensions dependent on each other, including transcendent as metaphysico-spiritual corporeality, divinatory sources, transformative and resonant qualities and sameness – in relation to other sinological, philosophical and Buddhological methods specifically designed for the Chinese cultural context and sensitive to various dimensions of ethics and interrelatedness. Chapter 6 thus allows testing the reliability of the proposed theory centred on interrelatedness and highlights the innovative elements it introduces through making it enter into a dialogue with these other approaches. Such a dialogue enables us to discover the contributions of the interrelatedness to several academic fields – namely filling a need to interculturally and comparatively bring the Chinese cultural presuppositions into the picture, thus widening and diversifying the spheres of sinology, philosophy, Buddhology or religious studies.

Some of the authors introduced in this chapter have a special interest in the religious and ethical features of the traditions of this culture, specifically Buddhism and Confucianism. Others focus on the philosophico-religious thought of the Song dynasty. They recognize the existence in the Chinese culture of a genuinely transcendent feature and strive to clarify it. This part addresses their significant contributions to this area of studies, as well as their connection with the rubric of ethical interrelatedness highlighted in the present book. The chapter thus brings to light some affinities and some differences between this study about interrelatedness and previous research works in this domain.

This approach not only opens a dialogue between this new viewpoint and existent studies – as a method of testing it, so to speak – but also facilitates understanding Chinese philosophico-religious thought as a way to learn from a non-Western culture, in order to rectify the side effects of the legacy of Western humanism, remedy deficiencies in the area of religious studies and broaden it. It offers deep insight into the philosophico-religious interactions between Confucian and Buddhist traditions within the Chinese culture and East-Asian cultural sphere, the exchanges between Buddhism and native Chinese traditions as well as into the Confucian transcendence and creativity in an intercultural Chinese/Western perspective. We begin with the first feature examined above in the introduction, out of which the whole story of ethical interrelatedness unfolds: becoming aware of the side effects of the Enlightenment legacy which impede authentic intercultural communication and the imperative to rectify them through learning from the culturally other.

1 Interrelatedness, ethics and the legacy of Western humanism: A dialogue with Kirill Thompson

A strong interest in Chinese interrelatedness, in learning from its distinct way of thinking, emerges from the work of the philosopher and sinologist Kirill Thompson. He perceives and examines early Chinese thought – Confucian and Daoist – as being able to provide 'rich conceptual resources for responding constructively to some problems associated with received Western Humanism'.[1] Concerning the latter, the author identifies two key problems: its individualistic predilection – the atomic individual self[2] – and species centrism. His effort to find efficient remedies in the Chinese thought can also be seen as another way to answer Gadamer's call mentioned in the introduction: the imperative of learning to think on a large scale, from other cultures.

With regard to the first issue, the author calls attention to the harmful effects of the individualist legacy of the Enlightenment:

> During the past 250 years, various socio-economic forces, such as industrialization and urbanization and the resulting mass society, mass culture and mass media – including rising consumer culture, the Internet, and globalization – have denuded the conceit of individual selfhood and hollowed out, if not eradicated, local cultures, languages, *Lebensformen*.[3]

In this context, he introduces the Chinese humanism and its ethics as a potential means of escaping the dangers of individualism that the Western humanism involves. For this purpose, Thompson suggests in particular the Confucian practice of being humane (*ren* 仁) and the Chinese relational humanistic ethics as it emerges from the Neo-Confucian Zhu Xi's work.⁴ Regarding this difficulty that needs correction, he uncovers new insights in Confucius's ethics as a viewpoint which focuses not on the individual self as autonomous subject but on the self as relational being.⁵ Starting from this insight and inspired by Kenneth Gergen's study *Relational Being*, the author examines the Confucian ethics as relational ethics having two dimensions which both stimulate 'responsive interpersonal regard': first-order morality (i.e. 'values inherent in the constitutive patterns of any viable relationship') and second-order morality (i.e. 'involves the general idea of relational responsibility').⁶ Note the connection between the latter and Xu Fuguan's concept of concerned consciousness discussed in Chapter 5. In the following quotation, Thompson clearly brings to light the difference between this relational ethics attached to human flourishing in real life and the traditional Western notion of ethics based on the perception of the individual as autonomous and transcendent normative rules:

> Viewed in the context of relational self/being as opposed to that of autonomous individual subjects, virtues and ethics take on a different complexion; their role changes, from setting transcendent normative rules governing conduct or standards of moral personhood, to immanently *moderating the play* of relationships as confluences. Rather than being justified by abstract criteria, such as the categorical imperative or the utilitarian principle, they are deemed appropriate and applicable to the extent that they support and sustain human flourishing in real situations in the flow of life.⁷ (italic in original)

With respect to the second problem, the Western species centrism, the philosopher and sinologist offers an effective response through examining the ancient Daoism, a significant topic which is not discussed in the present work. One notes that his analysis of the Daoist perspective offers another vivid illustration of a Chinese cultural presupposition which was uncovered and examined throughout this study – the identity between nature and culture. It also expressively suggests what the West could learn from it:

> Regarding Western Humanism's inherent species centrism, Laozi and Zhuangzi made the case that it was self-diminishing and defeating to view the human narrowly through the human, and to fancy ourselves as somehow superior to the myriad other creatures in the world. After all, species evolved by the same natural processes and go through similar processes of formation and dissolution and return indistinguishably to *dao*. Laozi and Zhuangzi thus argued that the human is nested, contextualized in the natural, and that people ought to meditate and cultivate so as to appreciate their identification holistically together.⁸

Becoming aware of human's dwelling in the natural and cultivating it flow from the above-mentioned cultural presupposition of the oneness between nature and culture. I would also add that it is precisely from this assumption, too, that the Chinese culture's focus on practice, on 'human flourishing in real situations in the flow of life', to use Thompson's terms, on answering the question *how* it flows. One may identify the source of this interest in what the present work calls divinatory thinking and its heightened interest in detecting the imperceptible traces of changes and transformations before their occurrence, with the view to ethically redress those which need such attention before they manifestly emerge; because, if the human dwells in nature, it is only through following the way of the nature that the human is able to live well. Such a standpoint embodies the requirement to understand and follow the *dao* of nature, as the ethically and beneficent way for all living beings, human and non-human. It is in this sense that, in his study about Zhu Xi's view on inquiry and learning, Thompson interprets the Neo-Confucian philosopher's famous formula 'attaining knowledge lies in investigating things' (*zhizhi zai gewu*致知在格物) from his 'Supplement to Chapter 5' of the *Great Learning*.[9] The following paragraph expresses beautifully the two Chinese cultural presuppositions – the affinity between nature and culture, that is, in Thompson's words, Zhu Xi's 'seeking a firm grasp of the patterns of change and transformation that constitute the world and human life', and the focus not on theoretical understanding (in the Western sense) but on practice (life *praxis*[10]), that is, on understanding and following the naturally ethical way:

> In my view, Zhu Xi's exuberance about not just learning and reading but inquiry in general traces back to his inveterate hunger to probe to the marrow, and understand deeply and practically the world and human existence. His existential resolve to realize himself as a sensitive, responsible, self-conscious person is not just to fulfil the Confucian ideal, but more broadly to be conversant with the flux of reality in nature as well as himself.[11]

In addition, his interpretation of the idea of reverence (*jing*敬) and its cultivation as religious dimension of Confucian tradition are particularly significant. The author highlights that it also emphasizes one's responsibilities, thus bringing out its simultaneous religious and ethical meaning:

> In support of Confucius' cultivation and practice of humaneness, reverence signifies an awareness of one's overwhelming responsibility to care about others, such as a father and mother's concern for the family and the ruler's concern for the welfare of his people. Reverence encompasses both the fear of failing to carry out one's responsibilities and the single-mindedness with which one carries out one's responsibilities. In Song times, the reverential attitude in the senses of alertness and concentration was broadened to the proper mindset for engaging in cultivation and practice generally.[12]

The way this book intends to achieve this objective – correcting side effects of Western humanism, perceptible in the domain of the religious studies, such as the atomic individual self and species centrism suggested by K. Thompson – is through investigating the philosophico-religious interactions between Confucian and Buddhist traditions and their specific presuppositions. It thus enters into an enriching dialogue with his work. The next section offers reflections on this issue based on the works of Julia Ching (1934–2001) and Charles Muller who dedicate their works to these Confucian and Buddhist interactions.

2 Confucian and Buddhist philosophico-religious interactions: A dialogue with Julia Ching and Charles Muller

Chapters 3 and 4 discuss the notion of ethical interrelatedness in Qisong's and Zhu Xi's writings. Both also argue that the Song dynasty is the moment when for the first time, not simply socio-economic comparative evaluations, but a new, this time, intellectual relationship – philosophico-religious – emerges between Confucian and Buddhist traditions. One major contribution to the sphere of Chinese studies of the present interpretation of ethical interrelatedness is its aim of providing a line of argument that demonstrates that the profound connections between the two traditions developed during that time – ethical practice, commitment to society and life – constitute the emblematic features of the Chinese culture until today; hence, in building a perspective which integrates both, it focuses on their complementarity and common views.

Usually, these academic spheres – Confucian and Buddhist – still remain watertight and don't overlap. Probably, also because on the one hand, the Confucian official discourse (Zhu Xi's writings included) formally criticizes Buddhism as incompatible with Chinese Confucian society and having a destructive effect on it; on the other hand, for the reason that, starting from the second part of the Song dynasty when the Chan *Linji* sub-school became dominant and appropriated the other Chan sub-schools, Qisong's included, the texts of this school of Buddhism do not focus on its connections with the Confucian culture, that is, on interpersonal relationships and life in the society but on distinctive Chan features: the pre-eminence of the personal experience of enlightenment, meditation, non-dual wisdom, creativity and so on. The other Neo-Confucian school, the Lu-Wang school, developed later by Wang Yang-ming 王陽明 (1472–1529) also integrates such specific Chan dimensions. Section 3 examines buddhologist Robert H. Sharf's persuasive account of the clear dividing line that indeed does exist between these two areas of research.

It might be said that the eleventh-century Chan thinker Qisong, who focused on features like commitment to the community in his Buddhist training and other qualities equally valued by the Confucians, influenced Song dynasty culture, stimulated the emergence of Neo-Confucianism and greatly contributed to the emergence of a fruitful philosophico-religious dialogue between the two traditions. It is in this sense that the present book underscores his unique decision to write in the language familiar to the Song Confucians and most representative of the Chinese culture: the *guwen* style, directly related to what is called the classical graphic language in the present study. In a different perspective, Julia Ching also addressed the issue of their interaction through investigating the impact of Buddhism on

Neo-Confucian Zhu Xi's thought. The next section is dedicated to her work and its close ties with this work.

2.1 Zhu Xi and Buddhism

The present book provides arguments to demonstrate the ethical connection between Qisong's Chan and Neo-Confucianism, not only to illustrate their common ethico-religious nature but also as proof of Chan's Chinese deep identity and impactful presence within the landscape of Northern Song culture – not as a foreign but as an entirely native tradition. While developing in a different direction, it also follows the leads provided in the work conducted by Julia Ching (1934–2001), the well-known scholar of the Song religions who was the first to offer a systematic presentation of Zhu's religious thought, including the Buddhist influence on his philosophy and the philosophico-religious interactions between Chan and Neo-Confucianism during the Song dynasty.[13] I heartily agree with her that 'together with Buddhist thought, Taoist philosophy helped to focus Chu Hsi [Zhu Xi] on questions of cosmology and philosophical psychology, supplying him with ideas and concepts, as well as a technical vocabulary that inspired his metaphysical formulations'.[14] Part 2 of this book, which builds a transhistorical dialogue between Qisong and Zhu Xi, focuses on their interactions through the presence in their works of similar issues and notions like the concrete, everyday presence of transcendent *dao* in people's lives, the significance of constantly addressing and analysing one's emotions, human nature, heart-mind and so on.

Starting from an examination of the Neo-Confucian thinker's works, Julia Ching assesses the common thread between the two traditions as follows: 'We see a parallel in the focus on the Confucian striving for sageliness and the Buddhist quest for enlightenment.'[15] However, the scholar of religion is of the opinion that the differences between them outweigh the similarities, because:

> Chu's [Zhu's] philosophy has an architectonic structure, covering cosmology and metaphysics, human nature, ethics, and spiritual cultivations. Buddhist systems may discuss metaphysics, human nature, and spiritual cultivation, but they pay less formal attention to ethics, which is replaced by something quite different: the rules and prescriptions of the sangha.[16]

I would add that Qisong's ideas exposed in the present study are unique owing to the fact that, unlike those of the *Linji* Chan sub-school, they address exactly the issue of ethics highlighted in this quotation and interpret the Five Buddhist precepts as counterparts of the Confucian Five Permanencies. Julia Ching's general perspective on Buddhism expressed in the above quotation follows from her examination of what she calls the Chan Buddhism of Zhu Xi's times – the twelfth-century *Linji* sub-school – especially Dahui Zonggao's 大慧宗杲 (1089–1163) *Recorded Dialogues* (*Dahui Pujue Chanshi yulu* 大慧普覺禪師語錄, T47n1998A, CBETA), which she demonstrates that Zhu Xi had read. Dahui, who was born roughly three generations after Qisong, emphasizes the use of *gongan* 公案 as a central meditation device for achieving enlightenment. A *gongan* refers to a dialogue or an event between a Chan master and his student.[17] It is a Buddhist tool used for something else, especially in the monastic context it is not used for ethical practice or cultivating social interrelationships. In her work, Julia Ching highlights the extensive Buddhist influence on Zhu Xi in the areas of metaphysics, his philosophy of human nature and teaching of self-cultivation (Ching 2000: 184). She also accurately evaluates Zhu Xi's criticism of Buddhism as 'rhetorical exaggeration':

> Chu [Zhu Xi] knew well the Ch'an [Chan] Buddhism of his time, especially the Lin-chi [*Linji*] lineage of transmission, with its emphasis on sudden enlightenment. It would also appear that Chu did not know very much about earlier Buddhist history or doctrinal developments. ... We should briefly evaluate Chu Hsi as a textual critic of Buddhist scriptures. Even if we acknowledge the influence of Taoist ideas and terminology on Buddhist developments, we should regard Chu's views as a gross exaggeration. Perhaps we may characterize it as a *rhetorical exaggeration*, given that Chu Hsi's motive was less to discredit Buddhism as such and more to exalt Confucian teachings. ... But he also tends to identify Ch'an with Buddhism as a whole. His criticisms of Buddhism would therefore be criticisms of the Buddhism of his time, namely, Ch'an Buddhism as he knew it in Sung times.[18] (italic in original)

In this respect, this work on ethical interrelatedness complements her study. It builds a transhistorical analysis – constructed around Qisong's eleventh-century and Zhu Xi's twelfth-century writings – which reveals little known common points between eleventh-century (Neo)Confucianism and Chan thought – that is, Qisong's Yunmen Chan – different from those noted by Julia Ching concerning the Chan of a century later: the ethical dimension. It is clear that Qisong's Chan writings discussed in this study, which emphasize à la the Confucians' 'the moral and social responsibility' of the lay Buddhists are an exception to the Chan *Linji* literature, as results from the following description of its usual themes by Julia Ching:

> The dividing line between Confucians and Buddhists is in their metaphysical perspective of reality and in the importance given to moral and social responsibility. This does not mean that Buddhists were 'immoral', in our understanding of the word. But it does mean that, to the extent that their religion places primary importance on monastic pursuit, including that of mystical enlightenment for its own sake, it is different from Confucianism.[19]

The above account represents the usual, formal comparative evaluation of the differences between Confucian and Buddhist traditions. Yet, Qisong's essays put forward another facet of the Northern Song Chan Buddhism, which allows us to nuance this appreciation and discover less emphasized but equally relevant connections between the two traditions that permeated Song culture and continued to be relevant afterwards. This study on ethical interrelatedness is dedicated to them. The Northern Song monk's special focus on ethical relationships and social engagement as deep ties between Confucian and Buddhist Chinese schools, as well as his deliberate use of the Confucian *guwen* style, are unique in the Chan landscape. However, he is not the only Chan thinker who raises such ideas. In the wake of Qisong, but in his own specific context of the importance of *gongan* meditation, the experience of enlightenment for lay followers, Dahui, the above-mentioned *Linji* Chan monk, also places emphasis on the profound complementarity of the teachings, which all are aimed to train individuals to realize their original nature and rectify their heart-mind. It might be said that his following passage depicts the profound, non-dual sameness between humans and non-humans:

> If one achieves a genuine breakthrough, then [one realizes that] a Confucian is no different from a Buddhist, a monk is no different from a layman, and a layman is no different from a monk; an ordinary man is no different from a sage, and a sage is no different from an ordinary man. [In fact] I am you and you are I; Heaven is earth and earth is Heaven; waves are the same as water, and water is no different from waves.[20]

Ever since the Song dynasty, the debates between Confucian scholars and Chan monks, influenced by the Song dynasty texts like those of Qisong and Zhu Xi, have flourished elsewhere around East Asia, such as in Korea, Vietnam and Japan. The next section addresses the work of a Korean buddhologist: Charles Muller.

2.2 Korean Chan Buddhist and Confucian interactions

A pioneer study in this incipient area of East Asian studies on the connections between Buddhism and Confucianism is the religious studies scholar and Korean buddhologist Charles Muller's book, *Korea's Great Buddhist-Confucian Debate: The Treatises of Chong Tojon (Sambong) and Hamho Tuktong (Kihwa)*. This study is based on his translation of two writings which crystalize the fourteenth-century debate between the Confucian statesman Chŏng Tojŏn (1342–1398) and the eminent Joeson Sŏn (Chan Buddhism) monk Kihwa (1376–1433) and their Chinese foundations.

In his comprehensive introduction to these translations, Muller traces the historical development of the interaction between Buddhist and Confucian traditions and their philosophical conversations. Starting from their initial meeting in China, he highlights the period of Buddhist pre-eminence during the early-to-mid Tang dynasty, the anti-Chan criticism of the Song dynasty Neo-Confucian school of the Cheng brothers (Cheng Hao 程顥 (1032–1085) and Cheng Yi 程頤 (1033–1107)) and Zhu Xi 朱熹 (1130–1200), the development of Korean Neo-Confucian criticism and its Korean Buddhist responses. The author stresses that the Cheng-Zhu school of Neo-Confucianism was accepted as orthodoxy in Korea, and he estimates that the fourteenth-century writings of the Korean Neo-Confucian Chŏng, whose translation he provides, are 80–90 percent based directly on the works of the Cheng-Zhu school.[21]

In his introduction, Muller also presents the situation in China from a philosophical perspective. He traces the contours of a highly interesting and relevant feature of the Buddhist texts composed in East Asia, which he regards as a significant component of the so-called Sinification of Buddhism: his argument – the resonance that occurs between the Confucian notion of humaneness and the Buddhist enlightened mind – also recalls Julia Ching's above-noted observation about the correspondence between the Confucian striving for sageliness and the Buddhist quest for enlightenment. Muller introduces it in a different perspective by means of the articulation *ti/yong*, translated in this book as metaphysico-spiritual corporeality/function:

> A Buddhist view of human consciousness that had been contoured to indigenous Chinese understandings of the human mind as being something intrinsically pure, and that, although existing in a defiled, obscured state, could be perfected through training. The 'humaneness' articulated by Confucius and Mencius was transmuted to the 'originally enlightened mind' spoken of in these texts, and the structural paradigm for this transmutation, whether stated overtly or not, was that of essence and function, with the original pure mind being essence (K. *ch'e*, Ch. *ti* 體) and good, enlightened, pure behavior being function (K., Ch. *yong* 用).[22]

Another idea on which Muller focuses, directly tied with the *ti-yong* 體/用 paradigm, is 'study as practice':

> The most important implications of both essence-function and interpenetration can only be fully apprehended when seen as descriptions of developments in actual practice rather than as abstract metaphysical categories. The concept of 'study as practice' reflects an aspect of the East Asian religious/philosophical attitude that encourages study as manifested in actual practice. Conversely, it refers to the character of 'religious practice' in Confucianism, Daoism, and East Asian Buddhism, which in most cases is deeply informed by textual study.[23]

This perspective which stresses the focus on constant training and actual practice fully resonates with the standpoint of the identity between nature and culture which runs through this entire study on ethical interrelatedness, as well as with Thompson's notion of life *praxis*.

Muller mentions the issue of Sinification or Sinicization of Buddhism in China, a notion that introduces the next section. This process points to the exchanges between original Buddhism and native Chinese traditions and represents a major element of the buddhologist research. Kenneth Ch'en presents it as 'the adaptation of Buddhism to Chinese conditions. While Indian ideas were gaining ground, the Chinese were also fashioning changes in the Indian ideas and practices, so that Buddhism became more and more Chinese and more acceptable to the Chinese.'[24] The next section introduces the work of Robert H. Sharf and examines what he calls a 'hermeneutics of Sinification', his specifically buddhologist approach in relation with the particular philosophico-sinological method employed in the present study. This is an effort not only to elicit the peculiar significance of each one but also to highlight the complementarity of these methods in the area of Chinese studies.

3 Chinese medieval Buddhism, Song Buddhism and the 'sympathetic resonance': A dialogue with Robert H. Sharf

In this section, starting from the medieval understanding of the notion of 'sympathetic resonance', that is, stimulus/answer, discussed by Sharf as inspired by its perception in Han dynasty Confucian commentaries, I demonstrate how this idea evolved in Chinese Chan Buddhism and how it has acquired in Qisong's Song dynasty works a complex sense of spiritual interrelatedness between inner heart-mind and outer reality, between emotions/feelings and behaviour, between one's past, present and future lives.

I have already mentioned the separation of these two areas of studies (Confucian and Buddhist 'camps', to use Robert Sharf's term) and fully agree with his enlightening evaluation of this situation:

> The modern study of medieval Chinese religion has been divided broadly between two camps: the sinologists and the buddhologists. While the former often ignored Buddhism, the latter tended to ignore everything but. Such proclivities are not difficult to fathom. Sinologists were predisposed, by virtue of their historical and philological training, to identify with the literati culture of the 'Confucian' elite, a culture that held Buddhism to be a morally corrupting foreign intrusion. ... Buddhologists, in contrast, were naturally influenced by their training in Buddhist languages, history, and doctrine as well as by the considerable weight of contemporary Japanese Buddhist scholarship. Consequently, when seeking historical and intellectual antecedents for Chinese Buddhist phenomena, they tended to look toward India rather than toward non-Buddhist China.[25]

This section focuses on a specific perspective in sinitic Buddhology, the one presented by Robert H. Sharf in *Coming to Terms with Chinese Buddhism: A Reading of the Treasure Store Treatise*. This perspective is quite different than the usual buddhologist view of the development of Chinese Buddhism 'in terms of an extended encounter between India and China ... of processes of domestication and transformation, which raise the issue of the fidelity of Chinese Buddhism to Indian models'.[26] Instead, the author's new 'point of departure is the pervasive and enduring role played by early Chinese cosmology in sinitic representations of Buddhism'.[27] Obviously, his perspective and the approach of this book have points in common.

The author offers an interesting illustration of the influence of native Chinese cosmology starting from the translation of a medieval Chinese Buddhist text of the Tang dynasty (618–907) but attributed to the fifth-century Buddhist master Sengzhao 僧肇 (374–414), a prominent disciple of Kumarajiva: the *Treasure Store Treatise*. The text was probably composed in the latter part of the eighth century within an early Chan community associated with the Oxhead school.[28] More pertinently, Sharf demonstrates, through an examination of its terms, the Daoist influence on this text, notably Laozi's *Daode jing*, the *Zhuangzi*, and the third-century Neo-Daoist thinker Wang Bi 王弼 (226–249): 'The essays [of Sengzhao] incorporated not only the terminology, but also the dense poetic texture and literary sophistication of the Taoist classics that appealed to generations of Chinese cognoscenti irrespective of their philosophical leanings.'²⁹ Through his study of the key terminology of the text and its textual allusions, the author demonstrates that the Daoist tradition most visible in the background of the *Treatise* is that of the 'Twofold Mystery'.³⁰ In the context of the efforts made by the Tang court to promote Daoism as the legitimizing ideology of the dynasty, the author sees this text as a Buddhist response: 'Rather than arguing the superiority of the Buddhist path or Buddhist doctrine, the *Treasure Store Treatise* integrates elements borrowed from the Taoist classics, notably the *Tao-te ching*, into Chinese Buddhist discourse, declaring all such doctrines to be expressions of a single truth'.³¹ From the very beginning, the Chinese Buddhism incorporates Daoist concepts, and this process continues during medieval times. The reader will also recall, several centuries later, Northern Song Chan scholar-monk Qisong's significant efforts to develop and demonstrate, this time, the non-dual unity of all teachings, and, in particular, the complex and challenging complementarity and mutual influence between Buddhism and Confucianism.

Sharf uncovers the influence on the text of early Chinese cosmological and metaphysical notions of the so-called correlative thought and Five Phases, with a focus on the late Zhou and early Han notion of 'sympathetic resonance' (*ganying* 感應). And he interprets this fact as evidence of the impact of this idea on 'the Chinese understanding of Buddhist cosmology, philosophy and monastic practice'.³² Obviously, this concept embodies a certain meaning of interrelatedness and constitutes another link between Sharf's Buddhological study and the present chapter. Qisong interprets it as karmic resonance, that is, 'the good and bad actions produce reactions (*ganying* 感應)', see Chapter 1, Section 1.2, as touching individuals' heart-minds (感其內), see Chapter 3, Section 3.2, and Chapter 5, Section 3.

When comparing this study's presentation of the eleventh-century Chan scholar-monk Qisong's essays on the philosophico-religious connections between Buddhism and Confucianism and Sharf's account of the *Treasure Store Treatise*'s historical and cosmological background, one sees that these works complement each other and show similarity as well as differences. What they have in common is an interest in bringing to light their anchorage in Chinese culture by examining their terminology: the Daoist influence in the case of the medieval Tang dynasty, early Chan treatise and the Confucian influence in regard with the classical Song dynasty Qisong's essays. Both perceive Chinese Buddhism as an element of the Chinese culture. However, in advancing this similar aim, these investigations display significant differences.

First, the styles and approaches of the translated texts are different: the medieval *Treasure Store Treatise* belongs to the sphere of Chinese Buddhology; it is written in the Buddhist style and develops several themes central to Tang Buddhist thought, like Buddhahood, the Buddha's true nature, ritual veneration of images, the theory of multiple Buddha bodies, invocation rites, particularly in a monastic context; that is, inducing a response in a buddha (i.e. 'affect or touching the buddha' *gan fo* 感佛) 'through the technology of invocation, which turns out to be the crux of Buddhist soteriology and monastic practice'.³³ The author constructs what he calls 'a hermeneutics of Sinification' in which he discusses the 'the ubiquitous and persistent influence of native Chinese cosmology'³⁴ on a probably eighth-century, early Chan, Chinese medieval Buddhist text and its doctrines.

In contrast, the Chan scholar-monk Qisong's eleventh-century *Essays on Assisting the Teaching* are Buddhist texts not written in usual Buddhist style but in Confucian *guwen* style, which make implicit references to sutras as well as to Confucian classics, in order to present persuasive evidence concerning the specificity of Chinese Buddhism and its deep connections with Confucian teaching. This is not a context of Sinification, of an integration of a non-Chinese element, but a dialogue between two fully Chinese dimensions of the Song culture. The essays provide a series of philosophico-religious arguments making the case that the two traditions (Chan Buddhist and Confucian) are complementary, that Chan Buddhist practice and education can positively assist the Confucian tradition and administration to ensure and preserve the harmony and well-being of society, by training people to improve their ethico-moral quality.

The perspective on Chinese Buddhism of this work is thus different from that of Sharf's *Coming to Terms with Chinese Buddhism*. It does not build a hermeneutics of Sinification, which sets out to define the context of the previous, medieval time but rather philosophically explores the way in which, within Chinese culture, Qisong enriched the Confucian *guwen* style and well-known Confucian notions with Chinese Chan Buddhist nuances. This is not a cross-cultural process of Sinification any more but a philosophico-religious intracultural exchange within the Song dynasty Chinese culture.

To that end Qisong demonstrates the interdependency between the Confucian and the (Chan)Buddhist traditions, the compatibility between their principal goals and doctrines and how they could efficiently work together for the benefit of the Song society. The Chan monk's use of the *guwen* style to discuss the Chan Buddhist vision is the strongest proof that his writings do not belong to a situation of Sinification but represent a 'written' (*wen yan* 文言) exchange within the Chinese culture itself, between two Chinese interlocutors (Chan Buddhism and Confucianism) who 'speak' the same language, the graphic written language, that is, the very source of the Chinese culture. Additionally, while Qisong's essays are oriented towards social practice and regard the Chan (Buddhist) ethico-religious practice as socially engaged (for lay followers belonging to the Song dynasty Confucian culture, this means ethico-spiritual transformation, individual and communal), the medieval Buddhist text *Treasure Store Treatise* in contrast refers to Buddhist monastic practice and embraces the 'mystical' tone of dark-learning Neo-Daoist authors like Wang Bi.[35]

The buddhologist vision of Sharf's study is important and reflective of the early stage of the development of Chan. It illustrates a process of 'adaptation and domestication', 'how Buddhism was inexorably, if unintentionally, "sinified", in the very act of rendering it in a Chinese idiom'[36]:

> I would not want to minimize the significance of the intentional repackaging of Buddhism so as to render it palatable to native literati tastes. My immediate interest, however, lies rather in the process that logically precedes the intentional adaptation and domestication of Buddhism by Chinese apologists. I refer to the conceptual transformation that occurs in the initial act of transposing Indian concepts into the semiotic and cultural universe of China.[37]

On this issue, in his work on the eighth-century early Chan text, Sharf focuses on its adoption of 'the late Zhou and early Han notions of sympathetic resonance and the manner in which this enduring metaphysical postulate informed the Chinese understanding of the nature of Buddhahood and the logic of Buddhist practice'.[38] It should be highlighted that the text is concerned with the monastic Buddhist practice not with the lay Buddhist social practice.

Three centuries later, the scholar-monk Qisong writes extensively on the latter topic – active engagement with society – and he refers primarily not to Han interpretations but directly to the ancient Confucian classics. As Qisong himself points out, his Song dynasty Chan interpretation of this notion is completely different from its Han (202 BCE–220 CE) meaning identified by Sharf as present in the medieval Chinese Buddhist writing. We should also add that the Han Confucian thinking is representative of the beginning of the imperial era: an interpretation of ancient Confucianism in the specific context of the political unification of China and creation of the empire.

A direct connection can be highlighted between Qisong's Song interpretation and Sharf's analysis of the Han 'sympathetic resonance' as embraced by the medieval Buddhist treatise. The author refers to it as an example of 'coordinative' and 'correlative thinking' (citing Needham, *Science and Civilisation in China*), as 'categorical thinking' (Bodde, 'Types of Chinese Categorical Thinking') and as an illustration of 'the Chinese penchant for finding repeating patterns and order throughout the cosmos'.[39] The Aristotelian idea of classificatory category previously discussed as Western presupposition continues to come up.

Qisong's eleventh-century perspective is different, and its architecture is more fully articulated. He enriches this initially cosmological broad notion with new meaning and further defines it as a spiritual dimension (*shen* 神). First, he presents it in the context of the 'authentic human nature' (*xing* 性), which he sees as spiritual and not only as (the root of) the emotions (as in ancient classic of Mencius). The Song dynasty monk thus highlights the difference between his Chan understanding of this notion and its famous ancient Confucian, Mencian analogue:

> When Mengzi says that the nature of the dog is the same as the nature of the ox (犬之性猶牛之性), and the nature of the ox is the same as the nature of man (牛之性猶人之性) [see Mencius, *Gaozi shang* 6.A.3], what Mengzi describes is the manifestation of human nature (*xing* 性) in the form of desires (性之所欲也); this is not the same thing [as that which I discuss]. What I am talking about is the authentic nature (*xing* 性); what others are talking about is the emotions (情).[40]

The scholar-monk further stresses that his understanding of the human nature is not only different from that of ancient Confucianism but also from that of Han Confucianism, which focuses on what he calls 'external stimuli' in the context of the notion of resonance, that is, stimulus and response (*gan ying* 感應) – 'sympathetic resonance' in Sharf's terms. In fact, as Qisong explains in the next quotation, this Han concept indicates the ancient meaning of the term that focuses on outside incitements but does so through the new unifying theory of the five elements. He refers to the commentaries of Zheng Xuan 鄭玄 (127–200), the Eastern Han Confucian scholar who annotated the Confucian texts.[41] Clearly, according to the Northern Song Chan scholar-monk, the Han cosmological perspective of the resonance stimulus-response – considered by Sharf as inspiration for the eighth-century *Treasure Store Treatise* – does not correspond to the spiritual dimension of Chan Buddhism. The next quotation constitutes a clear proof in this sense. In his commentary *Zhongyong jie* to the classic *Zhongyong*, written in the form of a dialogue between him and a student, the latter asks the monk the following question:

> Regarding Master Zheng's commentary on the phrase 'what heaven endues with (*tianming* 天命) is what is called authentic nature': He says that this is what heaven assigns to an individual at his birth; it is for this reason that it is called assigned authentic nature (性命). The spirit of wood is humaneness (木神則仁); the spirit of metal is appropriate behavior (金神則義); the spirit of fire is ritual behavior (火神則禮); the spirit of water is capacity of understanding (水神則智); the spirit of earth is fidelity to one's pledged word (土神則信). When examining Mister Zheng's doubtful explanation, it follows that if *tianming* gives birth to the individual, then his authentic nature comes from what one experiences [in other words, a response to an external stimulus *gan* 感]. When the spirit of wood affects him, this produces the nature of humaneness; when the spirits of metal, water, fire and earth affect him, this produces the natures of appropriate behavior, ritual behavior, capacity of understanding and fidelity to one's pledged word. In other words, the individual can acquire them without any practice (似非習而得之也). This is different from what Confucius says, that in order to acquire and perfect the natures of humaneness 仁, appropriate behavior 義, ritual behavior 禮, capacity of understanding 智, and fidelity to one's pledged word 信, one needs the teaching (必教). I respectfully ask: What does this mean?

Qisong answers:

> How can we say that authentic nature comes from what the individual experiences as outside influences (感而得)? When things don't yet have a concrete form (物之未形), then they do not have an authentic nature, nor do they have life; how can they experience an outside influence? When the human is born, why wait until he experiences the outside influence of things and of spirits, in order to have his authentic nature? Metal, wood, water, fire and earth make things without having any knowledge about this process; why repeatedly talk about this? Master Zheng's explanation is flawed, he didn't fully think it through. If what he said were true, why would the sage need to teach (聖人者何用教為)?[42]

The scholar-monk further connects this new spiritual understanding of the human nature with a new nuance of 'resonance' (stimulus-response), understood as having two dimensions: an outside resonance (i.e. the emergence of feelings/emotions under the influence of external stimuli) and an inner resonance (within the heart-mind itself, and connected with the idea of karmic causes and fruits, and in an ethico-spiritual perspective):

> The movements of the heart-mind (心動) are the so-called karmic acts (ye 業) [physical actions, words or thoughts] that will produce a fruit or effect in the future. The accumulation of karmic acts (會業) is the so-called stimulus (gan 感). The stimulus is what connects the inner heart-mind with outer reality (通內外). There are no heart-minds in this world that do not move. There is no karmic act among the myriad things which is not the result of a stimulus. The principle of karmic acts is something obscure (業之為理也幽). The power of this stimulus manifests itself for a long time (遠) [i.e., in future lives], but the people do not see it, and therefore, they are not afraid (民不睹而不懼).[43]

Qisong here develops the meaning of the Buddhist notions of causes and fruits based on a new signification of the ancient concept of stimulus (gan 感). This is the first term of Sharf's 'sympathetic resonance' (gan ying 感應) – in our translation, 'stimulus and response' – mentioned earlier. Note the complexity of the different connotations of this notion in Qisong's interpretation. In the essay Guang Yuanjiao 0655c16, the Northern Song monk describes causes (yin 因) as inner stimuli (nei gan 內感) or triggers (zhao 召) and fruits (guo 果) as external stimuli (wai gan 外感) or responses (ying 應). In this paragraph, he stresses the universality of the relationship between cause and fruit within the phenomenal world: 'All sentient beings that have an appearance participate in causes and fruits (因果, 形象者皆預也).' In other words, traces of acts carried out in previous lives do not disappear but rather subsist from one life to another within the most profound consciousness of the human heart-mind and become the inner stimuli for present acts. The present acts triggered by these accumulated causes, in turn, are external effects; that is, they take shape in elements of concrete conduct (physical actions, words and thoughts). Obviously, the principle of interdependence (stimulus-response or cause-fruit) is intrinsically connected with one's behaviour or acts, specifically with the moral quality of those acts (good or evil). As discussed above, the moral quality of one's actions depends on one's emotions.

Therefore, according to Qisong's theory, becoming aware of the existence of stimuli as causes and of responses as fruits and understanding their functioning amount to paying attention to the quality of the inner stimuli generated by good and evil emotions, which translate into external responses, namely, good or evil deeds: this is what positively impacts the continuity of causes-fruits. Incidentally, K Thompson explains a similar idea reflected in the teachings of the thirteenth-century Japanese Soto Zen master Dogen (1200–1253); the fact that even if cause and effect (causality that is, interdependence) are difficult to discern, binding and always operative, there is a way to positively impact causality through evaluating the fairness of a situation and responding in a manner that is ethically sound:

> Dogen asserts that when the mind of the enlightened person is in a meditative state of emptiness, an inner steelyard weighs the equilibrium of the contents of

experience from within experience. This steelyard weighs situations' fairness and one responds appropriately.[44]

Moreover, Qisong specifies in the next citation that good deeds promote life while evil deeds destroy life. The Neo-Confucian interest in organic life and growth and its association with harmonious social life and morality have been stressed above. The reader will recall Julia Ching's suggestion that this is a reaction against Buddhism and its view of 'an illusory world based on the causative action of karma'.[45] In the following paragraph of the same *Guang yuanjiao* (*Extensive Inquiry into the Teachings*), the Buddhist prohibition against the killing or harming of life is thus introduced by the Northern Song scholar-monk, in a positive way (to love and nurture life) and in a moral context (good and evil deeds and emotions), both familiar to Confucians. His method of presenting Chan in *guwen* and focusing on the ethical dimension of life not only assists building bridges between Buddhism and Confucianism but also substantially enriches the 'classical' substrate of the Song culture with new metaphysico-religious resonances:

> Sentient beings love life and detest death (物好生, 物惡死); all the different categories of living beings are like this. It is for this reason that the sage puts forward life and does not promote destroying life (聖人所以欲生, 而不欲殺). Actions that preserve life as well as actions that destroy life have causes and fruits, the good and evil deeds have stimuli and responses (夫生殺有因果, 善惡有感應). Pursuing a good cause results in a good fruit. Pursuing an evil cause results in an evil fruit. The heart-mind that likes preserving life is good (好生之心善). The heart-mind that likes destroying life is evil (好殺之心惡). Therefore, how can one not pay attention to the stimuli generated by good and evil emotions (善惡之感)?[46]

This brief incursion into Qisong's new mature Chan meaning of the notion of stimulus-response or 'sympathetic resonance' (Sharf's translation) together with the archaeology of its original connotation by Sharf in his *Coming to Terms with Chinese Buddhism: A Reading of the* Treasure Store Treatise, which also demonstrates that the medieval early Chan text endorses it, helps us understand this term's multiple sediments of sense – original Confucian (Zhou and its Han interpretation), (neo)Daoist, early Chan (Tang) and mature Chan (Northern Song), not only that but also the creative and successive work done by generations of Chan masters to establish their Chinese school, which allowed it to take permanent root and flourish in the soil of the Chinese culture, as an authentically local product. In the light of this demonstration, to this new meaning of the 'stimulus-response', one might add the Song dynasty ethico-religious transcendent.

The latter, including its various facets, is the specific notion that this study in philosophy of religion highlights and examines. The next section presents the principal connotations of this term within the Confucian context, with reference to the works of two leading contemporary scholars of this domain: Julia Ching and Tu Weiming. Another link between their works and the present book, besides the perception that the nature of the Chinese transcendent is ethico-religious, is the fact that all three focus philosophically on the Confucian classic *Zhongyong*, originally the 28th chapter of the *Liji* 禮記 (*The Record of Rites*),[47] considered as embodying the metaphysical dimension of this tradition. After elaborating on the resonance between stimulus and response – as ethico-religious particularity of Song classical Chan Buddhism in relation to its Tang medieval predecessor – it is time to comparatively reconsider its Confucian counterpart.

4 Confucian ethico-religious transcendent: A dialogue with Julia Ching and Tu Weiming

4.1 Zhu Xi's Neo-Confucian commentary on the *Zhongyong* and its ethics of self-transcendence

Julia Ching examines the ethico-religious and transcendent features of the Chinese culture in Zhu Xi's thought, and she finds they are best encapsulated in his commentary on the *Zhongyong*.[48] In her view, this commentary conveys Zhu's 'religious 'wisdom'.'[49] Incidentally, the present study shares the same interest in this text and in Zhu's construction of a metaphysical element in the Confucian tradition. Ching sees his commentary as conveying a new metaphysical facet of Confucian thought in bold response to the Buddhist challenges and focused on questions of human nature, the emotions and personal cultivation. In her interpretation, the Southern Song thinker introduces the notion of self-transcendence in connection with the ideal of sagehood:

> In giving these texts pre-eminence, Chu Hsi [Zhu Xi] and the other Neo-Confucian philosophers oriented Confucian scholarship increasingly to metaphysical and spiritual questions, at a time when Buddhism had made great inroads. ... The result is a new synthesis, a *Weltanschauung* that builds on the old moralist answers to questions about life and the world, with a clearer metaphysical framework and spiritual profundity. The basic Neo-Confucian quest, while it has its scholastic roots, is definitely oriented to self-transcendence in the achievement of sagehood, rather than to rising on the bureaucratic ladder simply by passing official examinations.[50]

Furthermore, as noted in this paragraph, a key feature of Ching's hermeneutical study of Zhu's *Zhongyong* is her emphasis on the inner dimension of the notions of ethics and transcendence. She sees the latter as essential traits of the so-called Chinese humanist tradition. Ching considers the ethical aspect of his commentary as an 'ethics of perfectibility' of the human embodied in Zhu's teaching of sagehood: this teaching purports that everyone is able to perfect themselves and become a sage through their own efforts. I would argue that this teaching flows from two related presuppositions of the tradition which are also examined in Chapters 4 and 5, but in a different perspective – that of the divinatory thought and graphic etymology – and which Ching highlights in Zhu's commentary: first 'the goodness of both human nature and the nature of universe' and second the 'correlation between the two – a correlation that is both ontological and moral'.[51] She also draws attention, in her own manner, to what the present study calls the Chinese premise of the identity between nature and culture. In her view, this is interpreted as the ethical (i.e. 'order', 'conscious continuum', see the following quotation) and organic (i.e. 'harmony' and 'animate continuum') continuum between the human being and the universe: 'The union between the two is conceived as a conscious and animate continuum, as a sharing of life and experience that makes for order and harmony.'[52]

A distinctive characteristic of her reading is the apprehension of the ethico-transcendent feature of Zhu's thought as aimed towards the ethical transformation of the individual, that is, the inward dimension of transcendence that she calls 'self-transcendence', the potential of becoming a sage present in everyone, which is the natural source of one's dedication to fully actualize their inner goodness bestowed by the heaven. Julia Ching argues that this practice has a metaphysical or transcendent dimension in the following terms: 'Self-transcendence goes beyond self-fulfillment … For Chu Hsi the goal of human existence is self-fulfillment, but the definition of self-fulfillment is also self-transcendence, that is, transcending one's selfish desires and becoming a sage.'[53]

It will be recalled that, inspired by the graphic etymology of the essence/metaphysical corporeality (*ti* 體) and vital breath (*qi* 氣), the present study also addresses this special idea of transcendence as at once immanent and transcendent and expresses it in terms of metaphysical corporeality and its perceptible operation. Ching sketches their inseparability starting from the Neo-Confucian thinker's explanation of the indivisible articulation between the coherence principle *li* 理 and the vital breath *qi*: 'According to Zhu, human nature transcends mind while being inseparable from it, the way *li* transcends *qi* without being separate from it. … Thus, the transcendent, the absolute, is also immanent not only in the totality of the universe but also in every individual human being – indeed, in every individual being.'[54] This continuity of the transcendent and immanent – another presumption built into the foundation of the Chinese ethico-religious – is particularly resonant to her in terms of the profound dissolution of the apparent subject-object dichotomy: 'What the text [*Zhongyong*] points to is a unitary experience between the human and the cosmic in which the subject-object dichotomy is transcended.'[55] In a complementary perspective, this book starts from uncovering the Western presuppositions of the transcendent and immanent – recalls their dichotomy, the ideal of self-transparency of the knowing subject and the focus on knowledge – and demonstrates that the Chinese assumptions embedded in language are different. For this reason, instead of using the Western concepts of transcendent and immanent, it prefers to build a new idea – rooted in graphic etymology – that captures more fully the specificity of the Chinese context: the metaphysico-spiritual corporeality.

Ching chooses to focus on one important dimension of Zhu's ethical thought – the human's striving towards perfectibility understood as their responsibility to activate the transcendent present within themselves, that is, their original goodness bestowed by heaven. For this reason, she discusses Zhu Xi's inner practice, the practice that takes place within the individual's heart-mind. This refers to his practical teaching of reverence – creatively described by the scholar of Chinese religions as 'the inner disposition necessary in the quest for a good life'[56] and of the extension of knowledge (i.e. investigation of principles of coherence). The latter is also discussed by Thompson (see Section 1). Obviously, this is understood as moral knowledge, 'discovered in life itself, through the practice of reverence … and in Confucian classical texts'.[57] While she emphasizes Zhu's development of the inner practice likely inspired by the Buddhist practice, the present comparative analysis (between Qisong and Zhu Xi) dwells on the inextricable link between inner and outer behaviour, on their inseparability. Each of these works offers complementary insights on the ethical and metaphysical aspect of Zhu Xi's commentaries. Moreover, Ching's analysis is directly related to Tu Weiming's account of the ancient text *Zhongyong* as an exposition of Confucian religiousness. This is dealt with in the following section.

4.2 *Zhongyong*'s Confucian religiousness

The present part endeavours to identify and examine elements of Tu Weiming's understanding of the *Zhongyong* that are directly related to the theme of this section: the ethico-religious and metaphysical facets of the Confucian tradition. The philosopher considers this ancient classic, a text which he regards as personally important as well as embodying what he calls the Confucian religiousness: 'My belief that Chung-yung [*Zhongyong*] is one of the most important texts in the Confucian tradition, it also reflects the fact that this text has been exceedingly meaningful to me personally.'[58] I agree wholeheartedly with this sentiment; for me as well, this text, especially its interpretation by Zhu Xi, has been personally inspiring and a significant source of ethico-metaphysical and intercultural reflection.[59]

Just as for Julia Ching, in Tu's view, Confucian religiousness is to be found in a deliberate practice of self-transformation, of human perfectibility:

> Confucian religiousness begins with the phrase 'ultimate self-transformation', which implies a critical moment in a person's life as well as a continuous process of spiritual transformation. For us to be actively involved in ultimate self-transformation, we must make a conscious decision to do so. Since being religious is tantamount to learning to be fully human, we are not religious by default but by choice.[60]

Tu also underlines the distinctiveness of Confucian tradition as humanism or its so-called human way as the source of a specific religiousness, having a metaphysical, transcendent significance. In other words, the actualization of this human way depends upon human effort; 'to actualize this underlying identity', Tu stresses, 'is not to transcend humanity but to work through it'.[61] Both Tu and Ching highlight a specific form of Chinese humanism that Confucianism embodies, and they bring to light its specificity as ethico-transcendent dimension. The latter is what distinguishes this humanism from its Western counterpart. In the same vein, K. Thompson also takes interest in what he calls 'early Chinese Humanist impulses', and he explores how these 'might offer solutions to some of the problems associated with received Western

Humanism: specifically, its *individualist predilection* and its inherent *species-centrism*' (italics in original; see Section 1).

Tu finds evidence of this transcendent dimension in the opening line of the *Zhongyong* which states that the (authentic) human nature is originated in heaven (about this issue, see also Chapter 1, Section 1.2.; Chapter 2, Section 3.2; Chapter 4, Section 2.1; Chapter 5, Section 2). And he defines this text's line of reasoning as a form of metaphysics, specific to the Confucian religiousness, which includes metaphysico-ethical features following from the peculiar quality of human nature as bestowed by heaven. One can view the next paragraph as Tu's definition of the Confucian understanding of the fusion between ethics and metaphysics – I suggest it has close links with the notion of metaphysical corporeality and its social functioning developed in the present study. It further emphasizes the *Zhongyong*'s uniquely Chinese ethical assumptions, by comparatively speaking of Western presuppositions and concepts as 'moral theology', 'ultimate reality' and 'creation':

> What *Chung-yung* envisions is not merely a moral community, definable in terms of harmonized social relations. Nor is it the approximation of a moral theology, laying claim to clear and certain knowledge of the natural law. Rather, it is a form of metaphysics which advocates that the ultimate reality is perceivable and realizable in the moral life of every person because human nature is potentially a genuine manifestation of that reality. This is predicated on the assertion that human beings, by nature, share the reality of Heaven. They are not in any sense 'created' by a higher order of being that is beyond the comprehension of human rationality. Precisely because their essence is identical with that of Heaven are they said to have partaken their nature from Heaven. In practice, however, there is no guarantee that, with his heavenly endowed nature, each human being can effortlessly form a complete union with Heaven. Moral self-cultivation is required to actualize that ideal.[62]

Like Julia Ching, Tu presents the continuity or what he calls 'mutuality' between transcendent and immanent, between heaven and human, as an essential aspect of this Confucian metaphysics of the human way. Tu's book *Centrality and Commonality: An Essay on Confucian Religiousness* also refers to the issue of reciprocity and continuous interaction in terms of resonance (previously discussed in Chan Buddhist perspective in Section 3). Again, in his attempt to describe the Chinese cultural presumption of the interdependence between transcendence and immanence, heaven and human, Tu spotlights what differentiates it from Western premises like theocentrism and anthropocentrism which are based on the presupposition of their division or separation: 'The human way is neither theocentric nor anthropocentric. Rather it points to the mutuality of Heaven and man. By insisting upon a continuous interaction between them, the human way necessitates a transcendent anchorage for the existence of man and an immanent confirmation for the course of Heaven.'[63] In a different perspective, this study illustrates this mutuality of heaven and man embodied in the Song Neo-Confucian tradition through constructing a two-levelled 'ethico-organic' religiousness: a metaphysical corporeality within oneself and its perceptible socio-organic functionality (see Chapter 1, Section 1.3).

For Tu Weiming, the Chinese meaning of the transcendent, which is obviously different from that of its Western counterpart, does not involve circumscribing a category but highlighting its categorical permeability, so to speak: 'the fruitful ambiguity of the Confucian selfhood'[64]; 'the Confucian advocates a humanism that neither denies nor slights the transcendent'[65]; 'our spirituality is in fact, embedded in our materiality'.[66] Obviously, his interpretation resonates with the idea of ethico-organic religiousness composed in Chapter 1. Similarly, in order to avoid using a Western dichotomist misrepresentation, Chapter 5 discusses the 'lessened' duality (principle and vital breath) of Zhu's thought, also described by Yü Ying-shih as 'neither identical, nor separate'. Tu depicts this position as neither denying nor slighting the transcendent and the humanity as 'a creative tension between immanence and transcendence: we are earthbound but also united with Heaven'.[67] It is obvious that these are clear examples which vividly illustrate what Harbsmeier calls the categorial continuum of the Chinese language that reflects its grammatical suppleness and organic flexibility (see Chapters 1 and 5). I advance that they articulate a specific Chinese way of understanding the transcendent as woven into the fabric of a 'lessened' duality, ethically contextualized. The philosopher and sinologist Kirill O. Thompson addresses this issue in terms of 'co-involvement and co-presence of *li* and *qi* in things'.[68] He also interprets this distinction between *li* (*dao* 道) and the things (*qi* 器 implements, artifacts) using the articulation 'above forms' (*xing' ershang* 形而上) and 'within forms' (*xing' erxia* 形而下):

> To Zhu Xi, 'form' means discernable formation and shape. So, in effect, above forms means imperceptible while within forms means perceptible. For Zhu, the paradigmatic assertion is that the way (*dao*) is above forms (imperceptible) while implements are within forms (perceptible). Although this distinction at first sight appears to provide a marker between *li* and *qi*, unformed *qi* is no more perceptible than is *li*; nor are *yin* and *yang*, which are basic *qi* motions of contraction and expansion. Tangible, perceptible stuff appears with the formation of the five phases. Hence, the distinction between above and within forms does not correspond to the distinction between *li* and *qi*. In fact, *yin* and *yang*, which are purely of *qi*, lie on the border of the porous continuum between above and within perceptible forms.[69]

In terms close to those of the philosopher and theologian Paul Tillich's (1886–1965) theory of religion as 'the state of being grasped by an ultimate concern', Tu Weiming calls attention to the specificity of the Confucian ultimate concern. In his view, the latter is the continuous effort of ethical transformation, where the notion of ethical has a unique meaning that is simultaneously metaphysical and social: 'The ultimate Confucian concern', Tu observes, 'is self-transformation as a communal act and as a faithful dialogical response to the transcendent.'[70] This idea is important for both Qisong and Zhu. Chapters 3 and 4 concretely and comparatively examine its meaning as it emerges in their writings.

This quality of building a categorial continuum is examined earlier from the perspective of the graphic and divinatory source of classical graphic language. As a reminder, the present book on ethical interrelatedness clarifies such categorial continuum by invoking the graphic etymology of what I have translated in an oxymoronic way as the 'metaphysical corporeality' of the Confucian ethics (*ti* 體, usually translated as 'essence'). Hermeneutical evidence was provided to support the continuity between its metaphysical (or self-transcendence in Tu's words), organic and social levels. Notice that Tu also offers a translation that is close to the idea of corporeality: 'embodiment'. In the next paragraph, he suggestively describes the specific functioning of this embodiment that never ends and which incorporates in its movement all the above-mentioned levels:

> The true self, as an open system, is not only a center of relationships but also a dynamic process of spiritual and physical growth. Selfhood in creative transformation is the broadening and deepening 'embodiment' (*t'i* [*ti* 體]) of an ever expanding web of human relationships, which we can conceptualize as a series of concentric circles. As the process of 'embodiment' never ends, we never reach the outer rim of these concentric circles. We continually reach out to 'form one body with Heaven, Earth, and the myriad things'. Nevertheless, when we reach out to form one body with the most generalized commonality, we also come home to reestablish and reconfirm the centrality of our selfhood.[71]

In this vivid formulation, one adjective stands out in particular: the 'creative' transformation of selfhood. It merits closer examination. The following is an analysis of this concept. In the author's view, the Confucian creativity that emerges from the *Zhongyong* is a genuine 'cosmic creativity':

> The ontological assertion that there is a possibility of human participation in the cosmic creativity is itself of great significance. It implies that the meaning of what is normally believed to be a personal quest for self-realization can no longer be restricted to the psychosocial realm; moral self-cultivation necessarily assumes an 'anthropocosmic' dimension.[72]

Presumably, Tu is referring here to paragraph 22 of the *Zhongyong* (see the next quotation). This passage together with paragraphs 24 and 26 are astonishing because they introduce a particular term in connection with what Tu perceives as 'human participation in the cosmic creativity': the Confucian 'sincerity' (*cheng* 誠).

In the subsequent development, this concept is spotlighted for the reason that, as will be seen, it is very closely related with the ethical interrelatedness, which is the core subject of this book. It will be shown that the Confucian sincerity is an ethico-metaphysical root that nourishes the deepest interrelatedness of individuals as well as that between nature and culture (human society). The practice of being sincere in Zhu's thought was thoroughly analysed in Chapter 4, Section 4.3. *Zhongyong* 22 reads, 'The sage, that is, the ethically complete individual, takes part in the activity of the heaven-earth (*yu tiandi can* 與天地參).'[73] As Tu remarks '*Ch'eng* [*cheng*, sincerity] is not merely an ordinary form of creativity; it is that which brings about the transforming and nourishing process of heaven and earth.'[74] Let us consider *Zhongyong* 22 in detail and carry out an archaeology of the Confucian sincerity – a concept that is intrinsically linked with Tu's above-mentioned images of 'cosmic creativity' and 'selfhood in creative transformation'. As in this hermeneutical study the focus has been on cultural presuppositions, I shall attempt to demonstrate that, if the sincerity is characterized as 'creativity', as Tu does, then the 'sincerity' conveys a unique understanding of the notion of 'creativity' as rooted in specific Chinese cultural presuppositions and highly dissimilar from its Western counterpart grounded in the idea of novelty. For the reasons elaborated below, I will depict this creativity rather as an ethical vitality and not as novelty. Here is the original *Zhongyong* 22 text:

> In this world, only the sage has complete sincerity. Through it, he is able to fully carry out all the possibilities of his authentic nature. Because he is able to do this, the sage also has the means for fully carry out all the possibilities of the humans' authentic natures. Since he is able to do so, the sage can also fully carry out all the possibilities of the authentic natures of all realities. For this reason, he has the power to assist the movement of the heaven-earth which transforms and gives birth. By being able to assist the movement of the heaven-earth, the sage takes part in the activity of the heaven-earth [a threefold unity]. 唯天下至誠，為能盡其性; 能盡其性，則能盡人之性; 能盡人之性，則能盡物之性; 能盡物之性，則可以贊天地之化育; 可以贊天地之化育，則可以與天地參矣。[75]

In this paragraph, the figure of the sage is the emblem of everyone – as Julia Ching would say – who dedicates their efforts to ethically transform, that is, to continuously improve and enhance their transformative quality. The passage illustrates the above-mentioned anthropocosmic – to use the words of Tu – dimension of the self-cultivation. As with all other human endeavours, including good actions (see Chapters 3 and 4), the sincerity in the Song dynasty philosophico-religious thought has a highest level, the metaphysical level of 'the complete sincerity' (*zhi cheng* 至誠), which corresponds with the perfectly ethical way of the sage and of the heaven-earth. It should be pointed out that, only when whole, sincerity achieves a profundity which is not merely ethical but also metaphysical. At all its other levels of incompleteness, sincerity has only an ethical meaning. Their co-activity (the sage and the heaven-earth) depicted in paragraph 22 illustrates the most profound, complete and therefore efficient interrelatedness between humans, and between humans and the physical world: it is ethically, metaphysically (Neo-Confucianism) and spiritually (Chan Buddhism) efficient.

Furthermore, in the *Zhongyong*, the sincerity (at its different levels) does not designate a virtue or a static characteristic possessed by someone. As illustrated in the image above that depicts the multiple layers of cosmic interrelatedness, the complete sincerity designates first, the spontaneous and subtle ethically natural activity of the heaven-earth, and second, the co-movement of nature (heaven-earth) and the human who is as ethically complete as nature. I suggest that this is the practical ideal of the divinatory way of thinking: when complete, the ethical capacity becomes capacity to detect and therefore correct if necessary, the earliest signs of change in the course of events. Through constant practice and determined effort, everyone can reach this level and dwell in it for as long as possible. The training to achieve, through everyday action, an increasingly higher degree of sincerity, that is, an increasingly complete moral interrelatedness, constitutes the profound ethical transformation of the human. The latter is synonymous with the efficient functioning of the complete sincerity of heaven-earth within the individual. As a result, until this is achieved, the interrelatedness between nature and culture (human world), and between individuals, is not whole.

The next quotation is from the ancient *Zhongyong* 24; it is a perfect illustration of what this study calls the divinatory thinking as source of the Chinese ethics; of its perception of metaphysical corporeality and social functioning; of its focus on detecting imperceptible beneficial and deleterious signs of the course of events, in the light of ethical or unethical actions of those involved in it. It presents the metaphysical complete sincerity exactly in this perspective. Obviously, detecting these traces means not merely understanding but fully understanding this metaphysical presence of the complete sincerity in the concrete everyday actions and interactions. This training – undertaken with a view to acquiring an ever higher ethical ability to perceive the imperceptible and to rectify it when necessary – can be viewed as metaphysico-religious practice. It is, first of all, a feature of the self-transformation, as well as the major incentive to refine one's sincerity and one's own ethical quality. It also triggers a societal transformation, that is, it lends a concrete and practical form to social interrelatedness:

> The way of the complete sincerity can be understood before it manifests itself. If the country will soon be on its way to becoming prosperous, early favorable warning signs will certainly appear. If the country will soon be in the process of destruction, early adverse warning signs will certainly appear. These signs manifest themselves during the divinatory process using yarrow sticks or tortoise shells, as well as in the behavior or human beings. If calamities or favorable destiny are foreseeable, the good event will be certainly understood before its manifestation; the event which is not good, too. Because the complete sincerity is like the spirits. 至誠之道，可以前知。國家將興，必有禎祥; 國家將亡，必有妖孽; 見乎蓍龜，動乎四體。禍福將至: 善，必先知之; 不善，必先知之。故至誠如神。[76]

As noted in *Zhongyong* 26, the natural (i.e. of the heaven-earth), that is, whole, complete sincerity is a continuous process, without interruption (*zhicheng wu xi* 至誠無息).[77] Tu also notes, as creativity, *ch'eng* [*cheng*, sincerity] is 'ceaseless'[78] (*wu xi* 無息). The graphic etymology of ceaseless *xi* 息 is breathing – inhalation and exhalation, expiration through the nose of the breath coming from the heart-mind. Julia Ching interprets this metaphor for breathing as 'being at one with the universe'.[79] According to this etymology, the process of constantly refining one's sincerity seems to be equivalent with inexhaustible vitality, continuous endurance and unstoppable practice. Breathing seems to privilege less the idea of creativity as producing something new and more the quality of a training characterized by an unbreakable perseverance and resolution, an endlessly renewable vivacity, a continuous persistence, patience and discipline. These are truly qualities of natural life, of natural forces, of the permanent movement of seasons. As mentioned above, Tu equates the sincerity with a special form of 'creativity': 'The profound person, through a long and unceasing process of delving into his own ground of existence, discovers his true subjectivity not as an isolated selfhood but as a great source of creative transformation.'[80]

The Chan monk Qisong enriches this Confucian notion of sincerity expressed as ethico-organic feature of natural and social life with a new, spiritual dimension. After him, the Neo-Confucian Zhu Xi adds a supplementary reading of sincerity as metaphysical corporeality (examined in Chapter 1, Section 1.3). In the next paragraph, the Northern Song scholar-monk suggests that sincere moral practice mainly means heartfelt and effortless action of the no-self, devoid of self-interest. In making this assertion, he elaborates on sincerity and its effects from a Chan perspective. At the same time, Qisong implicitly warns about a very common deficiency of Confucianism: acting falsely, apparently in accordance with the norms of the Five Permanencies (filial devotion, kindness, loyalty, etc.) but for personal gain. Hence, he significantly widens the nature of this old Confucian notion of sincerity and changes its grounding from cosmological to spiritual/religious:

> The heart-mind is the source of intelligence and wisdom (心也者, 聰明叡智之源也). If one cannot find this source, everything emanating from oneself is false. It is for this reason that the sage wishes that individuals trust their own heart-minds (人自信其心); it is through trusting their heart-minds that they rectify (*zheng* 正) themselves. This makes their constancy (*chang* 常) sincere, their good deeds (*shan* 善) sincere, their filial devotion for their parents (*xiao* 孝) sincere, their loyalty (*zhong* 忠) sincere, their kindness (*ren* 仁) sincere, their affection for their children (*ci* 慈) sincere, their spirit of concord (*he* 和) sincere, their conciliatory spirit (*shun* 順) sincere, their understanding (*ming* 明) sincere. When one's understanding is sincere, he has influence on heaven and earth (感天地), moves the ghosts and spirits (振鬼神) [note that the Confucian interpretation of sincerity is limited to these two levels], further comprehends the transformation death-life [the Buddhist interpretation of sincerity includes this level] and finally acquires [the way of the sage] (更死生變化而獨得).[81]

According to this paragraph about Chan and conforming to the Neo-Confucian *Zhongyong* (Zhu Xi), Confucian sincerity belongs to the sphere of ethics, metaphysics, cosmology and life – this present life – and its attendant natural vital and moral changes. In the scholar-monk's vision, sincerity is not only a presupposed source of natural order and vitality as explained in the *Zhongyong* 26 but also a spiritual one which comes from the depths of an individual's heart-mind. It is a state of inner awareness about the presence of the no-self, that is, the intangible continuity between oneself and the others and about the connection of one's present life with the last and the future ones. In other words, the ethico-moral motivations find their spring not only in one's awareness of the naturally ethical and orderly continuity of the spontaneous changes in individuals' lives, which presently go on within nature (heaven-earth), but also in their realization of their profound interdependence with all other sentient beings, of the unbroken continuity of their three lives (past, present and future). In this way, Qisong makes his contribution to the enrichment of the ancient notion of sincerity.

Looking back at Tu Weiming's interpretation of this term, a question comes to mind: Why does the philosopher identify it with 'creativity' and qualify self-transformation as 'creative'? Just as with the notion of 'transcendence', in the Western context, the term 'creativity' is heavily loaded. One possible answer (see Tu, *Confucian Thought: Selfhood as Creative Transformation*, 14) is that in this way he is attempting to offer an appropriate response to the sociologist of religion Robert Bellah (1927–2013). Using the above-mentioned textual and interpretive arguments based on the *Zhongyong*'s sincerity, Tu argues against the latter's view that in Confucian culture, 'creative social innovation as in the Protestant case was precluded by the absence of a point of transcendent loyalty that could provide legitimation for it'.[82] Such a perspective emerges from Weber's position, as it may be recalled from the analysis of his comparative assessment of Western Puritan ethics and Confucian ethics unfolded in Chapter 1, Section 3.2.

One may say that this statement reflects the same misunderstanding against which the New Confucians are fighting, as highlighted by Lee Ming-huei (see the introduction). It is particularly fitting, in this context, to recall the Westerners' erroneous perception that 'the Chinese people only attach importance to everyday-life ethics and morality and lack a religious transcendent feeling'.[83] One might say that through highlighting a Confucian sincerity, its Chinese nature and meaning as something creative, differently innovative than the Western notions of 'creative social innovations' and 'transcendent loyalty', Tu gives a strong answer to the issue raised by Bellah. In the same vein, Thompson highlights the precise scope and purpose of Tu's book *Confucian Thought: Selfhood as Creative Transformation* – to put forward philosophical arguments against this common Western misconception:

> The key to this venture is to liberate Confucian studies from the fetters imposed on the system by most received interpretations. Such accounts commonly reduce Confucianism to a collection of moral truisms, a system of etiquette, a normative scheme of family-social organization, or a philosophy of imitative correct action based on age-old ritual norms. Tu vigorously questions the scope and validity of such reductions and urges that 'self hood as creative transformation' be understood as the animating core of Confucianism round which everything else revolves.[84]

As the notion of 'creativity (creative)' is frequently used in the sphere of sinological studies, the following section deals with its cultural presuppositions. It intends to demonstrate that creativity involves Western assumptions which somehow diverge from the Confucian spirit; therefore, one needs to shape its other meaning in accordance with its Chinese cultural premises.

This reminds us of a tendency in Western sinology to render as 'creativity' the expression ceaseless (*wu xi* 無息), as an attribute of the *Zhongyong*'s sincerity in considering Zhu Xi, as Berthrong notes, as 'an example of an earlier East Asian form of process thought',[85] and Alfred North Whitehead's (1861–1947) process thought and creativity as 'a viable appealing and even suggestive possibility for the merging conversation between Confucianism and Western philosophy and theology'.[86]

The next and last section of this chapter suggests a new direction for this enriching conversation which so far, focuses on similarities between Western creativity and process and their Chinese counterparts: it outlines their different cultural presuppositions. This is also a way to enhance the meaning of creativity with intercultural resonances. Berthrong interprets the above-mentioned notion of ceaseless as the characteristic of 'ceaseless productivity' of the cosmos and highlights that 'Chu [Zhu Xi] needed to show how the mind-heart was able to provide the fulcrum of creativity for human beings within a cosmos itself characterized by ceaseless productivity'. The scholar of comparative theology also claims that both 'Chu's and Whitehead's philosophies are relational, organic, and processive in nature'.[87] The last section of this chapter offers a commentary on these observations from the perspective of ethical interrelatedness as embodied in the Song notion of sincerity and by uncovering the different cultural presuppositions of creativity and process in Whitehead and Song dynasty thinkers. Furthermore, this comparative analysis and interpretation of the distinct cultural presumptions (Chinese and Western) of creativity and process gives an example of how to cultivate pluralism not only within the specific field of philosophy of religion but also within the traditionally Western general area of philosophical reflection.

5 Creativity and process: Interrelatedness in Whitehead and Song dynasty Neo-Confucian tradition

5.1 Creativity: Etymologically explained

Many authors incorporate the concept of 'creativity' in their interpretation of the Confucian thought, in their attempts to develop it comparatively. In the Western context, John Dewey (1859–1952) develops this notion, as does the mathematician and philosopher Alfred North Whitehead (1861–1947). Mou Zongsan (1909–1995) also makes reference to it in his analysis of the specificity of the Confucian tradition. After Tu, let us consider Berthrong's remarkable effort to present creativity as the common denominator between Whitehead and Zhu Xi. Note in the following passage, a certain proximity presupposed between Whitehead's and Zhu Xi's perspectives and the perception of natural growth as creativity:

> There is always a protean power of self-creation or generation as noted by Whitehead and Chu Hsi [Zhu Xi]. Wherever we find dialectic as the generation of interacting forces, we find the dynamic element of the cosmos as growth, newness and creativity. The very matter-energy of the universe is constantly in flux. It is what Whitehead called creativity and what Chu Hsi thematized as *qi* [translated in this book as vital breath, according with its etymology], the most difficult of

Chinese philosophic concepts to approximate in English. *Qi* is the formless power of all creation; it is also the primordial nature of God for Whitehead in its aspect as unceasing eros driven by creativity.[88]

He also establishes an analogy between Whitehead's insistence on creative activity and values and Zhu Xi's notion of principle of coherence (see also, the problem with the Western axiological perspective discussed in Chapter 5, Section 1). In the following paragraph, the scholar of comparative theology discusses the cosmological dimension of Neo-Confucianism in relation with the notion of creativity and with the Whiteheadian novelty:

> The notion of creativity is also a key feature of the Sung Neo-Confucian and New Confucian movements. The creative advance into novelty, so central to process thought, would hardly have seemed novel to Chu Hsi, Mou Tsung-san or Tu Wei-ming. The notion of creativity as *sheng-sheng pu-hsi* (ceaseless creativity) [discussed above in the context of Tu Weiming's interpretation of the *Zhongyong*, see Section 4.2] is key to understanding Neo-Confucian cosmology. The whole Neo-Confucian tradition shares with process thought a commitment to a cosmology grounded in creativity with an outcome of a pluralistic cosmos.[89]

In order to interculturally examine the appropriateness of these assertions by appealing to their specific cultural presuppositions, let us first compare etymologically the two culturally different creativities and then briefly address Whitehead's thought, the Western and Whiteheadian resonances of creativity. This section attempts to further this dialogue in progress on creativity and sincerity, to elaborate the meaning of interrelatedness in this context, and demonstrate that the Western creativity and the *Zhongyong* creativity have different foundations. The first embodies the sense of novelty (see above Berthrong's quotation) and is ethically neutral and abstract, while the second, the Chinese sincerity has a strong ethical dimension which takes shape as interrelatedness, already discussed in the previous sections. It is concerned with the continuity of personal practice and the constant renewal of one's ethical quality.

Let us start with the cultural presuppositions incorporated within the Western notion of creativity and, subsequently, within its Chinese equivalent. It is interesting to note that, as Kirill Thompson and Alan Bullock recall in a different context, the recent, nineteenth-century understanding of the term is related to the Enlightenment and particularly refers to the humanist education movements which have sought to cultivate individuals, both culturally and spiritually, to unleash their creative potential.[90] In this context, creativity amounts to imagination. One already mentioned Western presupposition of the creative sense or imagination is abstraction: the human faculty to depict the immaterial or abstract. 'What I call imagination', notes the early nineteenth-century French moralist Joseph Joubert (1754–1824) in his *Recueil des pensées de M. Joubert*, posthumously published by Chateaubriand in 1838, 'is the faculty to render perceptible everything that is intellectual, to incorporate what is spirit; in a word, to bring to light, without distorting it, what is of itself invisible.'[91]

It also refers to the faculty of inventing new concepts and speculation. This brings us back to the Western meaning of creation as actions resulting in the production of something new ('novelty'), something that didn't exist previously.

What about the 'complete sincerity' (*zhi cheng* 至誠) brought out by the *Zhongyong* as natural, ethico-organic law, which renews itself ceaselessly (*wu xi* 無息)? As discussed, the renewal or regeneration is not simply organic but significantly ethical: it is about the continuous transformation from a lower level of sincerity – incomplete sincerity, to higher and higher stages, increasingly close to the quality of the whole, flawless sincerity of the heaven-earth. The metaphor of this permanent ethico-organic process is breathing (*xi* 息) with its twofold continuous rebalancing of the vital breath: expiration and inspiration. The Western content of creativity focuses on the creation of something new, the result.

The core of the Chinese metaphor of the complete creativity of the heaven-earth as breathing is not novelty, the production of something previously unknown, change as innovation, creative potential unleashed, but rather the continuity and persistence of change, of not interrupting the continuous renewal of one's ethical quality that is sincerity. The point underscored here is the persistence of continuing in a sustainable manner in a context where there is identity between organic breathing and ethical change. Let us recall Xu Fuguan's and Mou Zongsan's concerned consciousness, of being concerned about not doing enough to complete one's sincerity, that is, becoming aware of the original goodness within bestowed by the heaven and ceaselessly putting it into practice. As an aside, Ricoeur notes that 'a human can go on a hunger strike, but not on a breathing strike'.[92] The Chinese creativity as complete sincerity and vitality highlights precisely this 'binding' (in Ricoeur's sense) continuity of breathing as metaphor for an ethical moral change as unrelenting as vital change. This etymological detour reveals the significant cultural assumptions that one needs to take into account when choosing to use the term 'creativity' to illustrate the Confucian notion of sincerity.

5.2 Creativity, ethics, process alive and lifeless process: An intercultural view

In the following, a comparison will be drawn between the sincerity as metaphysico-spiritual corporeality of the reality and things – the interpretation proposed by this book – which reflects the identity between ethical and organic change and growth and its Whiteheadian counterpart. We will see that Whitehead's vision is consistent with the Western assumptions uncovered above by means of the etymological analysis and follows from them.

In this way, I am bringing the theoretical tool of interrelatedness to a specific case the cultural assumptions Western and Chinese present in a comparative reading of the notion of sincerity in Whitehead and the *Zhongyong* – to test its functionality and usefulness. This is the end of the intercultural journey about ethical interrelatedness.

Let's first start by recalling that, while in the *Zhongyong*'s creativity as sincerity, the ethico-moral training is as omnipresent as life and as close to everyone and inseparable as breathing, Whitehead's philosophy conveys the Western perception of ethics and morality as a separate and therefore limited dimension of the human life, not as a continuous concern. This shows in his commentary about an afternoon performance of the opera Carmen: 'The point that I now wish to make is that our enjoyment in the theatre was irrelevant to moral considerations applied to the performance. Of course smugglers are naughty people, and Carmen is carefree as to niceties of behaviour. But while they are singing their parts and dancing on the stage, morals vanishes and beauty remains.'[93]

The classical Chinese world has another perspective in which ethical interaction, like breathing, is an inseparable dimension of one's life. As evidence of its inherent and intimate place in the life of the individual who trains in holistically transforming themselves, the following anecdote is told by the well-known calligrapher Fu Shan 傅山 (1607–1684) and recorded in the magnificently illustrated book of Jean François Billeter, *The Chinese Art of Writing*:

> In my youth I studied the Chin and T'ang masters of the regular script, but I could not contrive to resemble them. Then I got hold of a manuscript by Chao Meng-fu [Zhao Mengfu 趙孟頫 1254–1322] whose easy touch and full-bodied shaping delighted me, I practised my hand at it and succeeded fairly soon in making copies which could have been taken for the original. But I became ashamed of myself: was I not in the position of someone who, having sought to pattern himself on a man of integrity but not being strong enough to rise to his elevation of character, was getting out of hand, consorting with rascals and keeping low company to the point of considering it natural? So I began to study Yen Chen-ch'ing [Yan Zhenqing 顏真卿709–785] and realized that I had been the victim of Chao Meng-fu for thirty years. I have not yet rid myself entirely of the vulgarity that I contracted from him, but if ever I cure myself, the credit will go to Yen Chen-ch'ing's *Altar of the Immortal Lady*.[94]

As Billeter mentions, Fu Shan's confession shows that the formal qualities of the writing are bound up with the human qualities of the calligrapher. Zhao Mengfu was a descendant of the Song dynasty's imperial family. After it was defeated by Kublai Khan who established the Mongol Yuan dynasty (1271–1368) of China, Zhao Mengfu betrayed the Song and became a Yuan scholar-official. The other impressive calligrapher, Yan Zhenqing, journeyed through the history of China as a well-known example of honesty. This parallel equally reminds us of Zhu Xi's commentary on the difference between the complete beauty of the music of the sage emperor Shun and the beautiful but less complete music of King Wu, the founder of the Zhou (Chapter 5, Section 4.2). It also illustrates well Qisong's idea of resonance examined earlier: good deeds, that is, good stimuli naturally give rise to good responses.

While the Song dynasty philosophico-religious thought establishes, as we have seen, an identity between ethical growth and life as organic growth, one of the last works of Whitehead, *Modes of Thought*, introduces the difference between the concept of 'nature lifeless' and that of 'nature alive', as well as the essence of life as production of novelty, therefore embodying this Western presupposition of creativity discussed above in its etymological context. In other words, he perceives life as undoing the previous order and establishing a new one, which has never existed before: 'The essence of life is to be found in the frustrations of established order. The Universe refuses the deadening influence of complete conformity. And yet in its refusal, it passes towards novel order as a primary requisite for important experience.'⁹⁵ Second, he also understands life as 'self-enjoyment': 'Life is the enjoyment of emotion, derived from the past and aimed at the future. It is the enjoyment of emotion which was then, which is now, and which will be then. This vector character is of the essence of such entertainment.'⁹⁶ In the next paragraph, the philosopher connects active enjoyment and self-creation. As we read it, it becomes clear that he sees the latter not as a continuum (breathing) but as a process formed of a combination of initially separated and distinct sequences (past, present, future). If *Zhongyong*'s sincerity as creativity – one could say, the Chinese counterpart of the Whiteheadian 'self-creation' – is the ceaseless process of ethically training one's emotions, eliminating the selfish ones and cultivating those fostering harmony and interdependence, Whitehead's self-creation of the 'new creature' (note here implicitly present the idea of the Creator creating the human, working through the creature) is another process – an active enjoyment of emotions:

> If we stress the role of my immediate pattern of active enjoyment, this process is self-creation. If we stress the role of the conceptual anticipation of the future whose existence is a necessity in the nature of the present, this process is the teleological aim at some ideal in the future. This aim, however, is not really beyond the present process. For the aim at the future is an enjoyment in the present. It thus effectively conditions the immediate self-creation of the new creature.⁹⁷

Moreover, as mentioned earlier, in the Whiteheadian perspective, ethics or morality is not an omnipresent dimension of life but only a limited species among others (logic, religion, art, etc.) of an abstract genus, already introduced in the previous quotations ('important experience') – the generic notion of 'importance' (i.e. of great value). The latter embodies an axiological perspective, which enquires into values. In the following quotation, the philosopher brings sharply into focus the fact that 'there are perspectives of the universe to which morality is irrelevant'. This is not the case for the Song dynasty philosophico-religious thoughts of Qisong and Zhu Xi. Note that, aside from the explicit Western presuppositions illustrated above – classification and generalization – Whitehead's concept also embodies an axiological assumption. As part of the abstract 'importance', his conceptual ethics/morality is not concerned with the practice of specific good deeds or individual ethical transformation as in the Chinese context but focuses on value judgements and implicitly refers to norms. Whitehead is involved in defining general, generic (see next quotation), abstract, impersonal notions (i.e. emotions, importance, process, morality, etc.) and not with the process of individual, concrete life and one's inner and outer life as ethical practice:

> Importance is a generic notion which has been obscured by the overwhelming prominence of a few of its innumerable species. The terms *morality, logic, religion, art*, have each of them been claimed as exhausting the whole meaning of importance. Each of them denotes a subordinate species. But the genus stretches beyond any finite group of species. There are perspectives of the universe to which morality is irrelevant, to which logic is irrelevant, to which religion is irrelevant, to which art is irrelevant. ... No one of these specializations

exhausts the final unity of purpose in the world. The generic aim of process is the attainment of importance, in that species and to that extent which in that instance is possible.⁹⁸

Let us observe that in his text, each of the subjects of the sentences is an abstraction. In this context, morality is not a training to learn how to become sensitive to the naturally ethical course of events and to follow this same way in the social sphere, but it 'consists in the control of process so as to maximize importance'.⁹⁹ What is then, briefly, his process, when compared with the continuous breathing of the complete sincerity of the heaven-earth (至誠無息)?

In his landmark book *Process and Reality*, Whitehead defines the process using other connected concepts – feeling, feeler, subject, object, subjective experience. The next quotation proposes his generalization of the notion of process and presents his philosophy of organism in a way that most closely resembles a mathematical exercise in propositional logic, a propositional negation of the attributes of Kant's theory. Again, his notion of process relies on lifeless, general concepts; has at the starting point objective data and not distinct feelings; and embodies the Western dichotomy of subject and object:

> The philosophy of organism seeks to describe how objective data pass into subjective satisfaction, and how order in the objective data provides intensity in the subjective satisfaction. For Kant, the world emerges from the subject; for the philosophy of organism, the subject emerges from the world-a 'superject' rather than a 'subject'. The word 'object' thus means an entity which is a potentiality for being a component in feeling; and in the word 'subject' means the entity constituted by the process of feeling, and including this process. The feeler is the unity emergent from its own feelings; and feelings are the details of the process intermediary between this unity and its many data. The data are the potentials for feeling; that is to say, they are objects. The process is the elimination of indeterminateness of feeling from the unity of one subjective experience.¹⁰⁰

One does not perceive in these quotations the trace of the process of life, something similar to the process of the *Zhongyong*'s sincerity-breathing, but a creative exercise in mathematical logic and philosophy of science. From this paragraph, the process of 'feeling' emerges not as a living continuum but as an abstract unity of data as potentials, details and components. Whitehead focuses on the abstract movement of these data, components of the notion of feeling, outside an ethical perception of their content. In the Song dynasty context, as we have seen, the ceaseless movement of completion of sincerity comprises a constant concentration on the ethical content of those feelings, on the deeds they trigger – egotistic or strengthening interrelatedness – and on the training aimed at abandoning or transforming the first type in order to purify the heart-mind. In other words, while the Whiteheadian process of feeling is ontologically envisaged, the completion of sincerity is morally, socially and behaviourally regarded. On this difference, the next quotation and its use of the verb 'to be' are enlightening.

The compartmentalization of the abstract process is also highlighted, using temporal constituents (future, present, past) and successive degrees (composition, gradation, elimination):

> Thus the data consist in what has been, what might have been, and what may be. And in these phrases the verb *to be* means some mode or relevance to historic actualities. Such are the data; and from these data there emerges a process with a form of transition. This unit of process is the 'specious present' of the actuality in question. It is a process of composition, of gradation, and of elimination.[101] (italics in original)

Notice that, in this process, Whitehead highlights two Western presuppositions of creativity – the universalizing tendency and the creation of novelty:

> 'Creativity' is the universal of universals characterizing ultimate matter of fact. It is that ultimate principle by which the many, which are the universe disjunctively, become the one actual occasion, which is the universe conjunctively. It lies in the nature of things that the many enter into complex unity. ... 'Creativity' is the principle of novelty. An actual occasion is a novel entity diverse from any entity in the 'many' which it unifies. Thus 'creativity' introduces novelty into the content of the many, which are the universe disjunctively.[102]

This ultimate is in fact a highest abstraction: 'In all philosophic theory there is an ultimate which is actual in virtue of its accidents. It is only then capable of characterization through its accidental embodiments, and apart from these accidents is devoid of actuality. In the philosophy of organism this ultimate is termed 'creativity'; and God is its primordial, non-temporal accident.'[103]

It is this concrete example of a Western extremely abstract creativity that allows us to concretely and comparatively realize a different type of creativity: the Confucian sincerity as creativity, simultaneously real and metaphysical, a metaphysical corporeality. The next paragraph from Zhu Xi's commentary *Zhongyong zhangju* 26 provides conclusive evidence in this regard. The Song dynasty thinker explains what is meant by saying the complete sincerity is ceaseless:

> The sincerity does not have the smallest falsity, it is naturally without interruption. It is 'long-lasting' (*jiu* 久): namely, permanently inside the human. It has 'early signs' (*zheng* 徵): that is, visible in the outside world. ... When it remains within for a long time, the sincerity becomes visible outside, very far away, and therefore inexhaustible. 'Far away': in other words, it accumulates and becomes a vast expanse and a great depth. When it becomes vast and deep, its effects are great, high, bright, and pure. 'Long-standing': that is durably manifest. In this context, the inside and the outside are discussed together. Starting from the root, the movement of the sincerity is durably manifest and highly solid; being highly solid, it is more and more long-lastingly visible. This explains how the sage and the heaven-earth are functioning in the same way, and also how they have

the same metaphysico-corporeality. Perceptible: that is, is seen. Imperceptible but manifest: in other words, the sincerity is like the earth. Without moving, it transforms the realities: that is, it is like the heaven. Without acting, it completes everything: this means it is endless and limitless. 既無虛假，自無間斷。久，常於中也。徵，驗於外也。… 存諸中者既久，則驗於外者益悠遠而無窮矣。悠遠，故其積也廣博而深厚；博厚，故其發也高大而光明。悠久，即悠遠，兼內外而言之也。本以悠遠致高厚，而高厚又悠久也。此言聖人與天地同用。此言聖人與 天地同體。見，音現。見，猶示也。不見而章，以配地而 言也。不動而變，以配天而言也。無為而成，以無疆而言也。[104]

Despite their different cultural substrata, Whitehead's perspective on process and creativity and that of Zhu Xi on sincerity have something that brings them together – and this represents a major innovation of Whitehead included in one of his last works, *Modes of Thought* – a realization of the distinction between nature lifeless and nature alive, which results in his effort to build awareness of the importance to go beyond the Western dualism between mind and nature or mind and body, discussed in this book as the dichotomy of nature and culture:

Science can find no individual enjoyment in nature: Science can find no aim in nature: Science can find no creativity in nature: it finds mere rules of succession. The disastrous separation of body and mind which has been fixed on European thought by Descartes is responsible for this blindness of science.[105]

Also:

We are in the world and the world is in us. Our immediate occasion is in the society of occasions forming the soul, and our soul is in our present occasion. The body is ours, and we are in activity within our body. This fact of observation vague but imperative, is the foundation of the connexity of the world, and of the transmission of its types of order.[106]

However, note in the quotation above the abstract, ontological and cosmological character of the 'occasion' as the central notion in Whitehead's approach. Through this concept, the philosopher intends to build the unity of body and soul and to go beyond their Western dichotomy. To that end, he refers to the 'society of occasions' as forming the human soul. In an effort to structure a philosophy from the cosmical and not the human perspective, Whitehead concentrates on the occasion as a humanly 'neutral' element. Nevertheless, as a 'society of occasions', the latter implicitly point to the human and social context. Therefore, faithful to his 'world' perspective, for him, the 'unit' in creative activity is the actual occasion, that is, 'a novel entity diverse from any entity in the "many" which it unifies'.[107] Its creative activity is what is involved in his concept of process. The latter involves the occasions as successive and punctual events of novelty within the time.

This presentation of his articulation of the idea of process serves as introduction of a last issue that deserves comparative consideration: the notion of 'concern' as common philosophico-religious theme of Whitehead and Neo-Confucian thought. The first focus is on the 'concerned' character of the humanly neutral occasion. This reminds us of another type of concern: the Confucian 'concerned consciousness'. The following part uncovers their specific cultural presuppositions which determine their different functioning.

Let us look first at the Chinese context. It will be recalled that the Confucian concern suggests the metaphysico-ethical practice: a concern naturally existing within human nature, bestowed by the heaven, that is, hidden original complete goodness and sincerity which resonate with the natural (heaven-earth's) complete goodness and sincerity and induces a response. This is the individual's concern that they are entirely responsible for their acts. One might translate this concern as practical vigilance or commitment to increasingly complete their sincerity or honesty – one might say, ethical efficacy – so that it increasingly resembles the natural ethical efficacy, without the slightest trace of insincerity or dishonesty.

How about Whitehead's concern not of the individual but of the occasion, of the activity of concern? The philosopher invokes its Quaker meaning and the dichotomy transcendence/immanence:

> Each occasion is an activity of concern, in the Quaker sense of that term. It is the conjunction of transcendence and immanence. The occasion is concerned, in the way of feeling and aim, with things that in their own essence lie beyond it: although these things in their present functions are factors in the concern of that occasion. Thus each occasion, although engaged in its own immediate self-realization, is concerned with the universe.[108]

The Neo-Confucian is concerned first of all with the ethical qualities of their deeds for which they are entirely responsible; the individual is concerned about making their sincerity complete, that is, their heart-mind purified of its personal, biased and interested emotions/feelings. This personal concern is therefore ethical vigilance and resonant response to one's metaphysical corporeality. The Whiteheadian impersonal occasion is concerned with the whole of which it is a part – the universe – and with the Western metaphysical essence of things which participate in the concern of a particular occasion. Thomas Raymond Kelly (1893–1941) was a Quaker scholar who studied with Whitehead in 1931–2 while preparing for his doctorate at Harvard.[109] He defines the social concern referred to in the quotation above, which structures the Quaker concern-oriented life, ordered and organized from within:

> Social concern is the dynamic Life of God at work in the world, made special and emphatic and unique, particularized in each individual or group who is sensitive and tender in the leading-strings of love. A concern is God-initiated, often surprising, always holy, for the Life of God is breaking through into the world. Its execution is in peace and power and astounding faith and joy, for in unhurried

serenity the Eternal is at work in the midst of time, triumphantly bringing all things up unto Himself.[110]

Note that, as with the Confucian concern, its Quaker counterpart embodies an inner responsibility, 'a special responsibility experienced in a concern'.[111] However, the similarity between the two culturally different concerns stops here. If the Chinese one is focused on the individual's ethical interrelationships and has an inner and natural metaphysico-organic root, the Quaker concern is God-initiated, 'a particularization of the Divine concern of God for all creation'.[112] Their natures are dissimilar, too. The dichotomy is the Quaker concern's major presupposition: as reflection of the separate God, of its participation within the world, it is holy, therefore of another quality than the ordinary secular life, the manifestation of the Eternal at work in the midst of time. As demonstrated, the categorical continuity is the cultural assumption of the Confucian concern.

This section equally suggests that, beyond their different cultural roots and aims, the culturally specific content of these notions – creativity, process, concern, responsibility, etc. – represents particular responses to an omnipresent issue: thinking about the interrelatedness and its multiple depths. When taking the time to interculturally examine their particular presumptions, I learn from the other culturally different from me. Such comparative analyses of cultural presuppositions are aimed to contribute to intercultural pluralism in philosophy, to prompt it towards becoming not only non-ontologically inclusive but also more culturally inclusive and diverse.

Conclusion

The starting point of the present intercultural study on the classical Chinese religious traditions is the following assumption: there is no question that we belong to a Westernized world that continues to globally reinforce the Western domination and its way of thinking inherited from the Enlightenment era. This is evident in the academic field, including the area of religious studies, where the theoretical instruments used for assessing and interpreting non-Western forms of spirituality are research methods arising from Western Enlightenment thought. Its universal reason and technical rationality continue to oppress and 'attack at the source', to use Heidegger's term from *On the Way to Language*, 'everything that is of an essential nature' (see Introduction, Section 3.3).

This work suggests that one powerful cultural tool that might be effective in raising awareness about our responsibility to acknowledge, counteract and remedy this corrosive effect is to promote intercultural and interreligious sensibility through education. One of the keys to achieving that goal is through expanding, upgrading and diversifying the academic space (the field of science of religions, philosophy of religion included), its multicultural, intercultural and transcultural dimensions, by means of multiplying the ethical approaches.

The latter refer to culturally sensitive methods and are inspired by the Levinasian idea of non-indifference to alterity (see Chapter 2, Section 3.4): it is essential that instead of building universalizing theories, the focus should be set on uncovering specific cultural presuppositions of each particular culture. This would allow one to further elaborate interpretive tools explicitly designed for those studying the realities belonging to that particular area and their peculiarities. It might be said that such an endeavour would be an effective way to learn to think on a large scale, as Gadamer has put it, that is, beyond the Western religious/spiritual habits of thinking. In other words, one could say, inspired by Levinas, that expanding our own scale of assessment is nothing less than learning to ethically approach the otherness of the culturally other, while explaining it in terms of similarities and differences as usual, would be continuing to think on the same Western scale and reduce the non-Western to it.

This book develops this type of ethical approach in a particular domain – the academic field of religious studies and philosophy of religion, in the special case of classical Chinese religious traditions. In this area of research, scholarship committed to the values of the Enlightenment perseveres in developing the old project of universal theories. As demonstrated here, although the latter aspires to be culturally neutral, it inevitably continues to be based on Western presuppositions, therefore unable to accurately account for the specificity of the religiousness of non-Western cultures like the classical Chinese that do not share a family resemblance with the Western. The ethical approach used in this study enables us, Westerners and non-Westerners, not only to moderate the adverse, universalizing effect of the Westernization in academic as well as sociopolitical and cultural areas but also to build intercultural pluralism into them. In the specific sphere of the disciplines of religious studies and philosophy of religion, this translates into the challenge of constructing not universal but very specific 'theories' – interpretive and guiding tools, able to uncover and convey the deep particularity of individual religious traditions, as embedded in their unapparent but meaningful cultural assumptions. That is to say, theory does not have in this book the Western meaning rooted in modern science – a universalizing tool that enables the student to master the object of their research – but the Chinese connotation grounded in graphic etymology, discussed in Chapter 1, Section 2.2: a theory-practice of the naturally ethical, which involves becoming aware of our interrelatedness and learning how to follow it.

It is worth highlighting that such theory focuses on determining what this study calls particularly 'cultural presuppositions' and comparatively analysing them in relation to Western presuppositions. As this work shows, the latter are embedded in classical and contemporary theories; therefore, the scholars need to be both familiar with them and vigilant to ensure that they do not introduce them implicitly when interpreting non-Western cultures (texts, societies, ways of thinking, specific coherences of non-Western languages etc.). Only such interculturally comparative research can yield insight into the authentic features of a culture and prevents bias in interpretation of the researcher's findings. As discussed in Chapter 2, Section 5, which takes its inspiration from the ideas of Levinas, this special type of comparison involves building an ethical relationship with the culturally other. This approach allows the scholar to be both: able to avoid the distortions and misunderstandings that inevitably arise when one considers a foreign culture in a disconnected way, as isolated, and capable of ethically (in the sense discussed in this study) connecting with the other culture.

This book, dedicated to ethical interrelatedness, builds such a tailored interpretive theory, directly related with the classical Chinese religious traditions. It consists in identifying and comparatively examining their Chinese-specific presumptions. Its interculturally comparative dimension is rooted in the philosophical translation of Chinese texts and in philosophic comparative 'etymology' (alphabetic and graphic). In concrete terms, this ethical approach is built on three lines of enquiry – religion, transcendent and theory. The major results of ethical interrelatedness as theory include the following: first, it provides a basis for developing a new understanding of the ideas of 'religion' and 'Chinese religions' culturally and linguistically appropriate to the Chinese context; next, within this 'theoretical' framework, it comparatively (Chinese/Western) demonstrates that the concept of 'transcendent' is language-dependent and explains as well as interprets it in the domain of Chinese religious traditions, thus building a new, Chinese signification of this term, different from its Western counterpart; finally, in this field of religious studies, it engages in a systematic philosophical effort to rethink the notion of 'theory', taking into account its underlying cultural assumptions (Chinese/Western) and proposes a specific, non-Western meaning of this term arising from the coherence of the Chinese language and its particular way of thinking. Therefore, each of these above-mentioned lines of enquiry (further detailed below) of the interrelatedness as theory for the classical Chinese religious traditions has an assigned purpose: developing new intercultural knowledge and new meanings for terms such as religion, transcendent and theory, with an eye to diversifying and opening the academic fields (philosophy, religious studies), prompting them towards becoming interculturally pluralistic.

First, the study argues that in the Chinese area, 'religion' and 'Chinese religions' are equivalent with what might be called a 'philosophico-religious' or 'ethico-religious' thought and interprets its particularities. Specifically, it shows that this perception of religion concretizes a live process of orderly exchange, an interactive practice of teaching and learning between living individuals and between individuals and the 'traces' of those who lived before. Consequently, religion as Chinese teaching does not embody the idea of the belief in God or the effort of reading and understanding the divine essence but focuses on the interrelatedness between individuals as transformative foundation, as ethical and spiritual guidance for everyday living.

The second component of the ethical approach developed in this book is a new understanding of the transcendent of divinatory origin that lies at the heart of this interrelatedness as theory: as metaphysico-spiritual corporeality and ethical transcendent. It is of particular relevance to the domains of philosophy of religion and ethics.

Third, the Chinese idea of theory built in this work is directly linked to these Chinese notions of philosophico-religious and transcendent. It conveys the inseparability of theory and practice and implicitly carries the meaning of order as well as of effort to become aware of the naturally moral order in an attempt to spontaneously respond and heed it. It might be called a 'theory-practice of the naturally ethical'; a holistic approach aimed to strengthen the ethical human interactions emerging from the awareness of the metaphysico-spiritual interrelatedness of individuals. The study demonstrates that the latter refers to one's capacity to foresee or know beforehand the course of the unfolding of the natural ethical order and continuous change of events: that means the ability to detect and ethically interpret, at the very first moment of their appearance, the imperceptible signs of a new change in this continuous process. This quality allows humans to orient their behaviour in advance in an ethical direction, so the course of their social actions and exchanges will maintain and preserve its harmony and goodness for all.

Following this meaning, the book constructs interrelatedness itself as a theoretical tool for the examination of Chinese religious traditions, as a systematic way of approaching them based on their specific presuppositions: looking for and engaging with them at a deep level. When applying it in the Chinese context from where it emerges, the scholar of religious studies and the philosopher learn to put into practice a new manner of thinking, different from the scientific application of universalizing theories forged by the Western Enlightenment. Thus, the impact of this intercultural theoretical instrument that concentrates on determining the particularity of Chinese cultural assumptions goes beyond the area of Chinese culture, since by using it, instead of applying their own universalizing theoretical tools, the students may expand their own scale of assessment and discover different ways of thinking.

As illustrated in this study, the interrelatedness as theory used to examine Chinese philosophico-religious thought involves two key components: first, identifying and examining particular forms that the Chinese cultural presuppositions – rooted in divinatory thinking and graphic language – take on within the context of Chinese traditions; second, interpreting these various forms of cultural assumptions in a comparative intercultural (Chinese/Western) perspective – the book is an example of this kind of research enterprise in the philosophical field.

The first constituent relates to the major cultural assumptions pinpointed and articulated in this work: the emphasis on a special notion of ethico-religious, on ethical relationships, that is, tangible social life, the meaning of the good and the transformative character of its practice; on the identity between culture and nature; on the metaphysico-spiritual source of the everyday ethical interrelationships; on the non-duality of these two features; on a Chinese notion of 'ethical transcendent' of divinatory origin. Many more remain to be hereafter discovered. This exploratory dimension of the theory involves determining and addressing the specific forms of these foundational assumptions that grow out of the particular Chinese research content of the scholar.

As for its comparative dimension consisting in a parallel interpretation of these newly identified Chinese cultural presuppositions and their Western counterparts, as mentioned above, this endeavour opens up the possibility for scholars to interculturally communicate, that is, to embrace a special relationship with the Chinese religious tradition studied: not only as a cross-cultural and therefore cognitive but also as intercultural, ethical and transformative relationship. The latter implies realizing the interrelatedness of the researcher and the subject of their research. This method that focuses on analysing the above-mentioned cultural presuppositions and the specific forms they take in various areas of study in relation with the Chinese culture (philosophy, religious studies, sociology, political science etc.) is nothing less than finding and actively engaging in new ways of thinking beyond one's own habits of theorizing.

Concretely, within these pages, the student interculturally approaches the Song dynasty Chan Buddhist and Neo-Confucian ideas with a view to learning from their particular cultural assumptions embedded in the graphic language of divinatory origin. It must be stressed that, as determined in this analysis, the Chinese notion of divination has a specific meaning, significantly different from its Western counterpart. The investigation of the connections between divination, language, way of thinking and religious traditions in the Chinese area constitutes a further contribution of this book. To that end, the study equally develops a specific intercultural relationship between the cultural presumptions of Chinese and Western religious traditions. Therefore, this interpretation may prove useful not only for students interested in Chinese culture, in search for a theoretical tool that reflects its specificity, but also as a learning vehicle promoting diversity awareness in multicultural societies where Western and Chinese cultures live together. Other intercultural learning situations are just as important: for example, learning from the traditions of First Nations.

The training process pursued throughout this book in company with the classical Chinese ethico-religious traditions has several outcomes: the opportunity to interrelate with another perception, non-Western, of religiosity (philosophico-religious sensibility), transcendence and ethics; the occasion to become aware of a specific form of practising religion and religiousness – as ethical interrelatedness. The findings from this study provide several insights into the above-mentioned Song dynasty ethico-religious traditions.

First, the analysis demonstrates the profound link between Qisong's Chan Buddhism and Zhu Xi's Neo-Confucianism: their common distinguishing feature, which one does not find in the Western context, is the idea that *profoundly connecting with oneself, nourishing one's ethical, metaphysical and spiritual substratum, means in fact becoming aware of one's connection with all others at a non-substantial, profound level.*

Next, the book also uncovers and examines a specific perception of the transcendent that serves as foundation of this vision: a metaphysico-spiritual corporeality, perceived not as an abstract but as a subtle living body that needs to be constantly nourished through constant, simultaneously inward and outward training. This presence of the *dao* (transcendence) in things is considered as a form of interrelatedness.

Equally, the intercultural interpretation uncovers a new meaning of religion, based on the classical Chinese traditions: as profound ethical interrelatedness between individuals in their everyday reactions and interactions, built not as ontological knowledge but as ethical knowledge and practice; as connection between unique individuals by virtue of their deep sameness, that is, their original goodness. Interconnectedness means, of course, focusing on peace, harmony, order and metaphysico-spiritual sameness. This type of transcendence is not intangible but can be practised and demonstrates its efficacy within everyday interrelatedness – as subtle proximity of ethically living together. Such an education is transformative. From the works of the two Song thinkers, one learns that this transformation not only is self-transformation but at the same time manifests itself as a transformative resonance or echo between organically interconnected levels: the human self, the wider society and the environing nature. One of the major Chinese cultural presuppositions uncovered and highlighted in this book, which lies at the root of this particular idea of transcendence, is the identity or continuity between culture and nature.

Finally, and importantly, this ethical training is what classical Chinese religious traditions could instruct the West and the contemporary Westernized world; thus, it could help it to correct certain adverse effects of the Enlightenment which became globally widespread in the form of the religion of the global economy, like the universalism which does not recognize the other, and its individualist tendencies.

Notes

Introduction: Intercultural philosophical approach and cultural presuppositions

1. See, for example, Arghiresco/u, *De la continuité dynamique dans l'univers confucéen*; Arghirescu, *Building Bridges between Chan Buddhism and Confucianism*; Arghirescu, 'Confluences between Neo-Confucian and Chan Practical Methods of Self-Cultivation'; Arghirescu, 'Spiritual Discipline, Emotions and Behavior during the Song-Dynasty'; Arghirescu, 'Song Neo-Confucian Conceptions of Morality and Moral Sources (Zhu Xi)'; Arghirescu, 'Between Heart-mind and Names'.
2. Müller, *Chips from a German Workshop I*, 21. Cited by Sharpe, *Comparative Religion*, 148.
3. Smith, *Imagining Religion*, 104.
4. Patton, 'The Magic in Miniature, Etymological Links in Comparative Religions', 196.
5. See Derrida, 'Foi et savoir', 47–8. Translation from French by D. Arghirescu.
6. Derrida, 'Faith and Knowledge', 29.
7. Xu, *Shuowen jiezi zhu*, 128.
8. Abe, *A Study of Dogen*, 11.
9. Gadamer, 'Dialogues de Capri', 225. Translation from French by D. Arghirescu.
10. Gadamer, *Truth and Method*, 306.
11. Ricoeur, *Du texte à l'action*, 378.
12. Ibid., 109.
13. Gadamer, *Truth and Method*, 316–17.
14. Granet, *Études sociologiques sur la Chine*, 150–1. Translation from French by D. Arghirescu.
15. Neville, *Ritual and Deference*, 1.
16. Gadamer, *Truth and Method*, 306.
17. Ricoeur, *Du texte à l'action*, 33.
18. Ibid., 57. Translation from French by D. Arghirescu.
19. Neville, *Defining Religion*, 98.
20. Ibid., 19.
21. Ibid., 101.
22. Derrida, *La dissémination*, 136.
23. Saussure, *Cours de linguistique générale*, 25.
24. Vandermeersch, 'Écriture et divination en Chine', 66. Translation from French by D. Arghirescu.
25. Ibid., 67.
26. Gadamer, 'Dialogues de Capri', 204.
27. Hall and Ames, *Anticipating China*, xiv.
28. Heidegger, *On the Way to Language*, 16.
29. Gadamer, 'Dialogues de Capri', 223.

30. Ibid., 226. Translation by D. Arghirescu.
31. Ibid., 225.
32. Ibid., 226.
33. Merleau-Ponty, *La Nature*, 19. Translation by D. Arghirescu.
34. Xu, *Shuowen jiezi zhu*, 429.
35. Berthrong, *All under Heaven*, 182.
36. For a detailed study of their interaction, see Arghirescu, *Building Bridges between Chan Buddhism and Confucianism*.
37. Zhou Dunyi 周敦頤 (1017–1073); the Cheng brothers, Cheng Hao 程顥 (1032–1085), Cheng Yi 程頤 (1033–1107) and their uncle, Zhang Zai 張載 (1020–1077).
38. See Granet, *La pensée chinoise*, and *Études sociologiques sur la Chine*.
39. See Schwartz, *The World of Thought in Ancient China*.
40. See Graham, *Yin-yang and the Nature of Correlative Thinking*, *Disputers of the Tao* and *Studies in Chinese Philosophy and Philosophical Literature*.
41. See Hall and Ames, *Thinking through Confucius*, *Anticipating China* and *Thinking from the Han*.
42. Neville, *Ritual and Deference*.
43. Lee, *Confucianism*, 28–9.
44. Ibid., 29.
45. See Tang, *Tang Junyi quanji*, vol. 2, 49–50, and Huang, *Xu Fuguan in the Context of East Asian Confucianisms*, 116–17.

1 Classical theories of Western philosophy of religion (Durkheim and Weber): An analysis of their presuppositions from a Chinese perspective

1. See Qisong, the essay *Yuanjiao* 原教 (*Inquiry into the Teachings*) 0650b20-5, CBETA T52n2115_001 (tripitaka.cbeta.org) included in the anthology *Essays on Assisting the Teaching* (*Fujiao bian* 輔教編), CBETA T52n2115_001, Chinese Electronic *Tripitaka* Collection, released by the Chinese Buddhist Electronic Text Association (CBETA): *Zhonghua dianzi fodian xiehui* 中華電子佛典協會, Taibei: Zhonghua dianzi fodian xiehui, 2016 (see Bibliography, Primary Sources, Qisong). For an extensive analysis of Qisong's anthology, see Arghirescu, *Building Bridges*.
2. Qisong, *Yuanjiao* (*Inquiry into the Teachings*), 0649a17-3, in *Essays on Assisting the Teaching* (*Fujiao bian* 輔教編), CBETA T52n2115_001. All translations from classical Chinese (Qisong and Zhu Xi) and contemporary Chinese (Mou Zongsan, etc.) are the author's, unless otherwise noted.
3. Ibid., 0648c25.
4. Also see Qisong, the essay *Quanshu* 勸書 (*Letter of Advice*), 0652c24 (天下之教化者善而已矣), included in the same anthology *Essays on Assisting the Teaching* (*Fujiao bian* 輔教編), CBETA T52n2115_001.
5. Zhu Xi, *Zhongyong zhangju* 中庸章句 1 (ZZQS 6: 32) in *Zhuzi quan shu* 朱子全書 (*The Collected Works of Master Zhu*), vol. 6, here abbreviated as ZZQS 6 (see Bibliography, Primary Sources, Zhu Xi). The reference ZZQS 6: 32 means volume 6 of the ZZQS, p. 32.
6. See ibid. (ZZQS 6: 32-3), and Arghiresco/u, *De la continuité dynamique*, 45–62.
7. Qisong, *Yuanjiao*, 0651c18-1, CBETA T52n2115_001.

8. Zhu Xi, *Zhongyong zhangju* 1 (*ZZQS* 6: 33–4).
9. Ibid., 21 (*ZZQS* 6: 49).
10. Zhu Xi, *Lunyu jizhu* 4: 16 (*ZZQS* 6: 96). Zhu Xi's commentary to the *Analects, Lunyu jizhu*, is included in *Zhuzi quan shu* (*The Collected Works of Master Zhu*), vol. 6. See Bibliography, Zhu Xi, ZZQS). The reference *Lunyu jizhu* 4: 16 means Zhu Xi's annotation to the paragraph 16, section 4 of the *Analects*.
11. Qisong, *Guang yuanjiao*, 0655b18, in *Essays on Assisting the Teaching* (*Fujiao bian* 輔教編), CBETA T52n2115_002.
12. Qisong, *Yuanjiao*, 0649b28-10, CBETA T52n2115_001.
13. See Laozi, *The Way of Laozi* 老子, 30–1.
14. See the ancient *Analects* 7:21 (section 7, paragraph 21) in *Zhuzi quan shu* (*The Collected Works of Master Zhu*), vol. 6, ZZQS 6: 126.
15. Qisong, *Yuanjiao*, 0650b24-12, CBETA T52n2115_001.
16. Zhu Xi, *Lunyu jizhu* 4: 11 (*ZZQS* 6: 95).
17. Durkheim, *Les formes élémentaires de la vie religieuse*, 602.
18. This essay of Qisong, *Encomium of the Platform Sutra*, is included in his anthology *Essays on Assisting the Teaching* (*Fujiao bian* 輔教編), CBETA T52n2115_003. It is also the permanent introductory part of the mature version of the *Platform Sutra of the Sixth Patriarch* (*Liuzu Tanjing* 六祖壇經), the major Chan text attributed to Huineng 惠能 (638–713): *Platform Sutra of the Dharma Treasure of the Great Master, the Sixth Patriarch* (*Liuzu dashi fabao tan jing* 六祖大師法寶壇經), edited by Zongbao 宗寶 in 1291, CBETA T48n2008_001 (Chinese electronic *Tripitaka*).
19. Qisong, *Tanjing zan* in *Platform Sutra of the Dharma Treasure of the Great Master*, 0346a14-12, CBETA T48n2008_001.
20. Ibid., 0346b14-13.
21. Qisong, *Guang yuanjiao*, 0654c28-2, CBETA T52n2115_002.
22. Mou, *Zhongguo zhexue shijiu jiang*, 78.
23. Zhu Xi, *Zhongyong zhangju* 1 (*ZZQS* 6: 33).
24. I translate *qi* as 'vital breath' because this term emphasizes the dynamism of natural life, the holistic character of the substrate of the world, neither matter nor spirit, but both, and it suggests the interconnectedness of all things, which in Zhu's thought is effectively realized through sharing a common coherence principle of heaven.
25. Yin Tun (尹焞; 1061–1132), Cheng Yi's disciple and one of the four masters of the Cheng Brothers' school.
26. Zhu Xi, *Lunyu jizhu* 13: 23, in *Zhuzi quan shu* (*The Collected Works of Master Zhu*), vol. 6 (*ZZQS* 6: 185).
27. Ibid., 14: 45 (*ZZQS* 6: 199).
28. Zhu Xi, *Yulei* 1, in *Zhuzi quan shu* (*The Collected Works of Master Zhu*), vol. 14, (*ZZQS* 14: 116).
29. Bergson, *L'énergie spirituelle*, 39.
30. Hall and Ames, *Anticipating China*, 269.
31. Bailly, *Dictionnaire grec-français*, 933.
32. Weber, *The Religion of China*, 123.
33. Smith, *Drudgery Divine*, 51.
34. Smith, *Imagining Religion*, xi.
35. Levinas, *Humanisme de l'autre homme*, 40. Translated from French by the author.
36. Smith, *Imagining Religion*, 21.
37. Xu, *Shuowen jiezi*, 225.
38. See also Ricci, *Dictionnaire Ricci*, vol. 2, 2246.

39. Harbsmeier, *Science and Civilisation in China*, vol. 7, 142–3.
40. See Vandermeersch, 'Écriture et divination en Chine', 67.
41. Durkheim, *Les formes élémentaires de la vie religieuse*, 6. Translated from French by the author.
42. Ibid., 13.
43. Ibid.
44. Ibid., 55.
45. Smith, *To Take Place*, 105.
46. Durkheim, *Les formes élémentaires de la vie religieuse*, 602.
47. Qisong, *Guang yuanjiao*, 0654b24, CBETA T52n2115_002.
48. Thich, *Being Peace*, 39.
49. Abe, *Zen and Comparative Studies*, 126.
50. Abe, *Zen and Western Thought*, 181.
51. Tsai, 'Zhuzi dui fojiao de lijie ji qi xiangzhi', 177–213.
52. Chen, *Douguanji*, 16.
53. Tsai, 'Zhu Xi's Grasp of Buddhism and its Limitations', 186–7. Translation by Daniel Coyle, slightly modified.
54. Durkheim, *Les formes élémentaires de la vie religieuse*, 6.
55. Zhu Xi, *Lunyu jizhu* 2: 4, in *Zhuzi quan shu* (*The Collected Works of Master Zhu*), vol. 6 (ZZQS 6: 76).
56. Paden, *New Patterns for Comparative Religion*, 20.
57. Ibid., 23.
58. Durkheim, *Les formes élémentaires de la vie religieuse*, 56.
59. Ibid.
60. See Arghirescu, 'Zhu Xi's Ideal of Moral Politics: Theory and Practice', 482–8.
61. Qisong, *Tanjing zan*, 0346c27, CBETA T48n2008_001.
62. Ibid.
63. Zhu Xi, *Lunyu jizhu* 12: 1 in *Zhuzi quan shu* (*The Collected Works of Master Zhu*), vol. 6 (ZZQS 6: 167).
64. See also Sharpe, *Comparative Religion*, 85.
65. See Platvoet, *Comparing Religions*, 16; Freiberger, *Considering Comparison*, 46.
66. Hick, *Philosophy of Religion*, 31.
67. Qisong, *Yuanjiao*, 0650b24-12, CBETA T52n2115_001.
68. Zhu Xi, *Zhongyong zhangju* 29 (ZZQS 6: 55).
69. Paden, *New Patterns for Comparative Religion*, 21.
70. Merleau-Ponty, *La Nature*, 19. Translated from French by the author.
71. Ricoeur, *Du texte à l'action*, 332. Translated from French by the author.
72. *Zhongyong* 17, in *Zhuzi quan shu* (*The Collected Works of Master Zhu*), vol. 6 (ZZQS 6: 42).
73. Zhu Xi, *Zhongyong zhangju*, ZZQS 6: 42.
74. *Zhongyong* 17, in *Zhuzi quan shu* (*The Collected Works of Master Zhu*), vol.6 (ZZQS 6: 42).
75. Qisong, *Guang yuanjiao*, 0656a01, CBETA T52n2115_002.
76. Ricoeur, *Du texte à l'action*, 329; Weber, *Économie et société*, §1. Translated from French by the author.
77. See Weber, *Économie et société*, 7.
78. Ricoeur, *Du texte à l'action*, 329.
79. Ibid., 329; Weber, *Économie et société*, 20. Translated from French by the author.
80. Ricoeur, *Du texte à l'action*, 329.

81. Ibid., 330.
82. Parsons, 'Introduction', xxi.
83. Sharpe, *Comparative Religion*, 178.
84. Parsons, 'Introduction', xxx.
85. See Yang, 'Introduction', xiv.
86. See Weber, *L'éthique protestante*, 47–8.
87. Ibid., 222.
88. Ibid., 66.
89. Ibid., 211. Also Weber, *The Religion of China*, 104, 111.
90. Weber, *The Religion of China*, 231.
91. Weber, *L'éthique protestante*, 49-50. Translated from French by the author.
92. Weber, *The Religion of China*, 240.
93. Ibid., 236.
94. Ibid., 240–1.
95. Levinas, *Humanisme de l'autre homme*, 120. Translated from French by the author.
96. Weber, *The Religion of China*, 241.
97. Weber, *L'éthique protestante*, 136. Translated from French by the author.
98. Lee, *Confucianism*, 28–9.
99. Weber, *The Religion of China*, 248.
100. Ibid., 28.
101. Ibid., 240.
102. Ibid., 248.
103. See ibid., 23–7.
104. Derrida, *La dissémination*, 175.
105. Ibid., 77–213.
106. Weber, *The Religion of China*, 27.
107. Ibid., 168.
108. Ibid., 123.
109. Ibid., 125.
110. Ibid., 127.
111. Ibid., 152.
112. Zhu Xi, *Lunyu jizhu* 12: 1 (*ZZQS* 6: 167).
113. See also Arghirescu, 'Zhu Xi's Ideal of Moral Politics', 482–8.
114. Weber, *The Religion of China*, 170.
115. Zhu Xi, *Zhongyong zhangju* 22 (*ZZQS* 6: 50).
116. Ibid.
117. Weber, *The Religion of China*, 227.
118. Ibid., 235.
119. Ibid., 247.
120. Ibid., 160.
121. Weber, *L'éthique protestante*, 74.
122. Weber, *L'éthique protestante*, 193.
123. Weber, *The Religion of China*, 247.
124. Ibid., 246.
125. Zhu Xi, *Lunyu jizhu* 2: 12 (*ZZQS* 6: 78).
126. Zhu Xi, *Reply to Huang Daofu* (*Da Huang Daofu* 答黃道夫), 58, under *Huian xiansheng Zhuwengong wenji* (4), 晦庵先生朱文公文集(四), in *Zhuzi quan shu* (*The Collected Works of Master Zhu*), vol. 23 (*ZZQS* 23: 2755–6).
127. Weber, *The Religion of China*, 160.

128. Ibid., 248.
129. Hall and Ames, *Thinking through Confucius*, 283–4.
130. Weber, *The Religion of China*, 236.
131. Ibid., 247.
132. Weber, *L'éthique protestante*, 209.
133. Weber, *L'éthique protestante*, 66.
134. Gadamer, 'Dialogues de Capri', 225.
135. Polanyi, *Essais*, 459. Translated from French by the author.
136. Ibid.
137. Ibid., 459.

2 Contemporary theories of Western religious studies and philosophy of religion (John Hick, Ninian Smart, Jonathan Z. Smith): An analysis of their presuppositions from a Chinese perspective

1. Kitagawa, 'The History of Religions in America', 15.
2. Ibid., 17.
3. Vandermeersch, *Ce que la Chine nous apprend*, 16.
4. About the oracle-bone inscriptions of Shang dynasty, see Keightley, *Sources of Shang History*.
5. Vandermeersch, *Ce que la Chine nous apprend*, 16–17. Translated from French by the author.
6. About May Fourth Movement, see Chow, *The May Fourth Movement*, 1, and Huang, *Xu Fuguan in the Context of East Asian Confucianisms*, 72–3.
7. Vandermeersch, *Les deux raisons de la pensée chinoise*, 192. Translated from French by the author.
8. Kitagawa, 'The History of Religions in America', 24.
9. Hick, *An Interpretation of Religion*, 371.
10. Ibid., 4.
11. Smart, *Buddhism and Christianity*, 111.
12. Ibid., 83.
13. About the interactions among Chinese religions and 'the unity of the three teachings' (a notion established around the fourteenth century) in the Ming time (1368–1644) and in the Ming-Qing popular texts, see Brook, 'Rethinking Syncretism'.
14. Leibniz (1646–1716) already expressed such an interest for the religions of the East wishing (note his Christian pattern of thinking) that they send missionaries to us (*Introduction* to his *Novissima Sinica*, 1699): see Heiler, 'The History of Religions', 157 and Leibniz, *Writings on China*, 45.
15. Smart, *Buddhism and Christianity*, 83.
16. Hick, *An Interpretation of Religion*, 7.
17. Vandermeersch, *Les deux raisons de la pensée chinoise*, 12.
18. Hick, *An Interpretation of Religion*, 6.
19. Ibid., 1.
20. See ibid., 151.

21. The concept of epistemology of religion is not new. The previous perspective was that of an epistemology of the Western idea of 'truth', therefore connected with another Western notion, that is, the faith. Friedrich Heiler formulates it clearly: 'One of the most important tasks of the science of religion is to bring to light this unity of all religions. It thereby pursues only one purpose, that of pure knowledge of the truth' (Heiler 1959: 155). Hick's new epistemological approach advocates an epistemology of religion in the form of critical realism. 'Critical realism', he glosses, 'holds that the realm of religious experience and belief is not in toto human projection and illusion but constitutes a range of cognitive responses, varying from culture to culture, to the presence of a transcendent reality or realities. It would be possible to call this position "transcendentalism" or "super- or supra-naturalism"' (Hick, *An Interpretation of Religion*, 175).
22. Smart, *Buddhism and Christianity*, 61.
23. Qisong, *Exegesis of the Mean* 3 (*Zhongyong jie* 中庸解 3), 0666b25-4.
24. Zhu Xi, *Zhongyong zhangju* 1 (*ZZQS* 6: 32) in *Zhuzi quan shu* 朱子全書 (*The Collected Works of Master Zhu*), vol. 6, here abbreviated as *ZZQS* 6 (see Bibliography, Primary Sources, Zhu Xi). The reference *ZZQS* 6: 32 means volume 6 of the *ZZQS*, p. 32.
25. Hick, *An Interpretation of Religion*, 240–1.
26. Ibid., 175.
27. See Calame, 'What Is Religion?' 287. For him, an example of this contemporary cognitivist approach is the work of the cognitive anthropologist Pascal Boyer who gave the following title to a synthesis of his work – 'Religious thought and behavior as by-products of brain function': religious notions thus arise from our capacity for cognition – from what Boyer terms 'our mental machinery', which he considers to be shared by all human beings. The scientific approach is obviously universalizing.
28. Hick, *An Interpretation of Religion*, 1.
29. Ibid., 6.
30. Ibid., xiii.
31. Ibid., 1, 338.
32. Qisong, *Guang yuanjiao*, 0655c02-1, in *Essays on Assisting the Teaching* (*Fujiao bian* 輔教編), CBETA T52n2115_002.
33. Zhu Xi, *Lunyu jizhu* 6: 2, in *Zhuzi quan shu* 朱子全書 (*The Collected Works of Master Zhu*), vol. 6 (*ZZQS* 6: 109–10).
34. Hick, *An Interpretation of Religion*, 202.
35. Smart, *Buddhism and Christianity*, 100–1.
36. Ibid., 73–4.
37. Hick, *An Interpretation of Religion*, 240–1.
38. Smith, *Relating Religion*, 32.
39. Ricoeur, *Du texte à l'action*, 29.
40. Hick, *An Interpretation of Religion*, 12.
41. Smart, *Buddhism and Christianity*, 137.
42. Ibid., 338.
43. Smart, *Worldviews*, 5.
44. Smart, *Buddhism and Christianity*, 4.
45. Smart, *Worldviews*, 4.
46. Smart, *Buddhism and Christianity*, 4.
47. Ibid., 6.
48. Smart, *Worldviews*, 2.

49. Ibid., 5.
50. Smart, *The World's Religions*, 11.
51. Smith, *Drudgery Divine*, 143.
52. Smith, *Relating Religion*, 204.
53. Smart, *Worldviews*, 13.
54. See Ricoeur, *Du texte à l'action*, 30–5.
55. Ibid., 49.
56. Ibid., 57.
57. Smart, *Worldviews*, 13–14.
58. Ibid., 161.
59. Ibid., 14.
60. Ricoeur, *Sur la traduction*, 19.
61. Smart, *Buddhism and Christianity*, 112.
62. Billeter, *Chine trois fois muette*, 78–9. Translated from French by the author.
63. Smith, *Imagining Religion*, xi.
64. Calame, 'What Is Religion?' 296.
65. Urban, 'Making a Place', 342.
66. Calame, 'What Is Religion?' 298.
67. Smith, *Imagining Religion*, 197.
68. Smith, *Relating Religion*, 241.
69. See also Smith, *Drudgery Divine*, 51.
70. Derrida, *La dissémination*, 198.
71. Ibid., 206.
72. Knepper, 'The End of Philosophy of Religion?' 138.
73. Similar perspectives about the connection between the disciplines of anthropology and history of religion and political, cultural and economic colonialism can be found in Urban, 'Making a Place to Take a Stand' and Asad, *Genealogies of Religion*. Hewitt, Asad, Urban and Freiberger (Freiberger, *Considering Comparison*, 57) highlight the political nature of the comparativism in the academic study of religion. This study adds another element of its nature: the intercultural, rooted in cultural presuppositions.
74. Hewitt, 'How New Is the "New Comparativism"?' 16.
75. Calame, 'What Is Religion?' 288.
76. Another perspective is that of Arvind Sharma who uses the expression 'reciprocal illumination' to refer to occasions when our knowledge of another tradition enables us to gain a better understanding of some aspect of our own tradition and vice versa (Sharma, *Religious Studies*, 11).
77. Patton and Ray, 'Introduction', 8–9.
78. Claude Calame draws attention to the fact that the anthropological enterprise 'can only function through (instrumental) concepts that bear the mark of our own culture' (Calame, 'What Is Religion?' 295).
79. Levinas, *Totalité et infini*, 212. Translated from French by the author.
80. See Smith, *Relating Religion*, 204.
81. Smith, *Imagining Religion*, 8–9.
82. As Friedrich Heiler (1892–1967) discusses them, the roots of the Babel myth perspective are to be found in the initial tendency to situate the Christian religion and its specific concepts at the core of religious studies and consider the non-Christian religions, as well as pre-Christian world as providing analogies with the Christian notions. Heiler calls it a preparation for the cooperation of religions and

illustrates this perception using Schleiermacher's idea of the unity of religions ('The deeper one progresses in religion, the more the whole religious world appears as an indivisible whole'), as well as Max Müller's conception of an 'universal religion' ('There is only one eternal and universal religion standing above, beneath, and beyond all religions to which they all belong or can belong.') (see Heiler, 'The History of Religions', 141).

83. Smith, *Imagining Religion*, 21.
84. Smith relates: 'My two bedside books during high school were the seventh edition of Asa Gray's *New Manual of Botany* and A.S. Hitchcock's *Manual of the Grasses of the United States*, soon replaced by the second edition, revised by Agnes Chase. This interest remains today; taxonomic journals are the only biological field I still regularly read in' (Smith, *Relating Religion*, 2).
85. See Smith, *Relating Religion*, 187.
86. Ibid., 20.
87. Smith, *To Take Place*, 13–14.
88. Freiberger, *Considering Comparison*, 59.
89. Knepper, 'The End of Philosophy of Religion?' 134.
90. Hick, *An Interpretation of Religion*, 36–50.
91. Streng, *Understanding Religious Life*, 2–3.
92. Lawrence, 'Transformation', 338.
93. Hick, *An Interpretation of Religion*, 22.
94. *Daxue* 大學 (*The Great Learning*), in *Zhuzi quan shu* 朱子全書 (*The Collected Works of Master Zhu*), vol. 6 (ZZQS 6: 16 and 20).
95. Qisong, *Guang yuanjiao*, 0655a19.
96. Ibid., 0657b12-6.
97. Ibid., 0657b11-16.
98. See Csikszentmihalyi, *Material Virtue*, 27.
99. Zhu, *Zhongyong zhangju* 1, in *Zhuzi quan shu* 朱子全書 (*The Collected Works of Master Zhu*), vol. 6 (ZZQS 6: 33).
100. Hick, *An Interpretation of Religion*, 41.
101. Ibid., 44.
102. Ibid., 51.
103. See ibid., 278–9.
104. Hick, *An Interpretation of Religion*, 371.
105. Ibid., 309.
106. Smart, *Buddhism and Christianity*, 102.
107. Levinas, *Entre nous*, 119–20.
108. See William James's 1902 most famous book, *The Varieties of Religious Experience* and Charles Taylor's 2002 idiosyncratic and selective exchange with James in his *Varieties of Religion Today*; Hick's 1989, *An Interpretation of Religion*; and Smart's 1970, *The Philosophy of Religion*.
109. See James Bisset Pratt's (1875–1944) presentation by Eric Sharpe in *Comparative Religion*, 114.
110. See Sharpe, *Comparative Religion*, 144.
111. Otto, *The Idea of the Holy*, 12–13.
112. Hick, *An Interpretation of Religion*.
113. See Platvoet, *Comparing Religions*, 16; Freiberger, *Considering Comparison*, 46.
114. Patton and Ray, 'Introduction', 1.
115. Ibid., 18.

116. Smith, *Drudgery Divine*, 14.
117. Doniger, 'Post-Modern and -Colonial -Structural Comparisons', 68.
118. Knepper, 'How to Philosophize', 59.
119. McCutcheon, *Studying Religion*, 17.
120. McCutcheon, *The Discipline of Religion*, 79.
121. Paden, *New Patterns for Comparative Religions*, 3.
122. Ibid., 109.
123. Ibid., 122.
124. Ibid., 95–6.
125. Hewitt, 'How New Is the "New Comparativism"?', 16.
126. Paden, *New Patterns for Comparative Religions*, 63.
127. Freiberger, *Considering Comparison*, 35–6.
128. Levinas, *Entre nous*, 186.
129. Levinas, *Humanisme*, 40.
130. Smart, *Worldviews*, 161.
131. Levinas, *Totalité et infini*, 70. Translated from French by the author.
132. Freiberger, *Considering Comparison*, 55–6.
133. Ibid., 146.
134. Ibid., 96.
135. Levinas, *Is It Righteous to Be?*, 118.

3 Ethico-spiritual interrelatedness: The meaning of ethico-religious practice in the Chan scholar-monk Qisong's writings

1. This chapter emerged from an initial article 'Between Heart-Mind and Names: Interrelatedness in the Chan Scholar-Monk Qisong's Thought', published in *Comparative and Continental Philosophy* 13, no. 3 (2021): https://www.tandfonline.com/doi/full/10.1080/17570638.2021.2017249
2. Wang, 'Introduction', xxxiii.
3. For a detailed analysis of the essays included in Qisong's collection *Essays on Assisting the Teaching*, see Arghirescu, *Building Bridges*.
4. Tsai, '*Zhuzi dui fojiao de lijie ji qi xiangzhi*', 177–8.
5. See *Guang yuanjiao* (*Extensive Inquiry into the Teachings*), 0654b07, in *Essays on Assisting the Teaching* (*Fujiao bian* 輔教編), CBETA T52n2115_002.
6. One could also say that this inclusive feature of his thought is inspired by the previous work of the tenth-century Chan monk Yongming Yanshou 永明延壽 (904–975). Yanshou's thought has been extensively examined by Albert Welter (Welter, *The Meaning of Myriad Good Deeds*; Welter, *Yongming Yanshou's Conception*; Welter, 'Confucian Monks and Buddhist Junzi'). In a sense, Qisong follows Yanshou's perspective and further develops it in a new direction.
7. See Bol, '*This Culture of Ours*', 176–211.
8. Qisong, *Guang yuanjiao*, 0654b24.
9. Han, 'Han Yu and the Confucian "Way"', 569–73. About Buddhism as an 'illness' of the Chinese society, and the defeat of Buddhism with the help of developing the rites, see Liu, 'Rationalism and Religion', 156–65.

10. Qisong, *Yuanjiao* (*Inquiry into the Teachings*), 0649b28-10 in *Essays on Assisting the Teaching* (*Fujiao bian* 輔教編), CBETA T52n2115_001.
11. *Mencius* 6.A.2 included in *Gaozi zhangju shang* 告子章句上, in *Zhuzi quan shu* 朱子全書 (*The Collected Works of Master Zhu*), vol. 6 (ZZQS 6: 396).
12. His Confucian contemporary and Vice Minister Ouyang Xiu 歐陽修 (1007–1072) has a different opinion. In his 'Essay on Fundamentals', Ouyang states that in the ancient times of Yao, Shun and the Three Dynasties, ritual and behavioral rectitude (禮義) flourished in the world and thus prevented Buddhism from entering into China (Ouyang Xiu, 'Essay on Fundamentals', 593).
13. Qisong, *Quanshu* (*Letter of Advice*), 0653a02-3, in *Essays on Assisting the Teaching* (*Fujiao bian* 輔教編), CBETA T52n2115_001.
14. Qisong, *Yuanjiao*, 0648c25, in *Essays on Assisting the Teaching* (*Fujiao bian* 輔教編), CBETA T52n2115_001.
15. See Arghirescu, 'Spiritual Discipline', 1–26.
16. Qisong, *Yuanjiao*, 0650a1-15.
17. Qisong, *Quanshu*, 0652b02-16.
18. Qisong, *Yuanjiao*, 0649c19-15.
19. See Arghiresco/u, *De la continuité dynamique*, 279–301.
20. The *Great Learning* (canonical section *jing*), *Daxue, jing* 大學, 經, included in Zhu Xi's *Daxue zhangju* 大學章句, in *Zhuzi quan shu* 朱子全書 (*The Collected Works of Master Zhu*), vol. 6 (ZZQS 6: 17).
21. See *Zhongyong* 1 interpreted in Arghiresco/u, *De la continuité dynamique*, 45–6.
22. See Streng, *Understanding Religious Life*, 64–82.
23. Zhu Xi, *Lunyu jizhu* 14: 45, in *Zhuzi quan shu* 朱子全書 (*The Collected Works of Master Zhu*), vol. 6 (ZZQS 6: 199).
24. Qisong, *Yuanjiao*, 0650a16-3.
25. *Jinsilu* 近思錄 13: 6 (chapter 13, paragraph 6), included in Zhu Xi's *Zhuzi quan shu* 朱子全書 (*The Collected Works of Master Zhu*), vol. 13 (ZZQS 13: 278); in Wing-tsit Chan's translation – Zhu Xi and Lü Zuqian, *Reflections on Things at Hand; the Neo-Confucian Anthology Compiled by Chu Hsi and Lü Tsu-ch'ien*, 284.
26. Qisong, *Yuanjiao*, 0650a13-5.
27. Hsiao, *A History of Chinese Political Thought*, 23–4.
28. Qisong, *Yuanjiao*, 0650b01-4.
29. Ibid., 0651a18.
30. Qisong, *Guang yuanjiao*, 0660a07-8.
31. Ibid., 0660a03-13.
32. See ibid., 0654b24.
33. Ibid., 0655a19.
34. In his translation *The Complete Works of Zhuangzi*, Chapter 27, *Imputed Words*, 440, Burton Watson renders *damiao* as 'great mystery'; Wing-tsit Chan, in his translation of the Laozi, *The Way of the Lao Tzu*, 147, renders *yaomiao* 要妙 of the Laozi 27 as 'essential mystery'.
35. Qisong, *Guang yuanjiao*, 0656c21.
36. Ibid., 0654c29.
37. Ibid., 0655a26-1.
38. Qisong, *Quanshu*, 0652a08-12.
39. Zhu Xi, *Zhongyong zhangju* paragraph 13, in Zhu Xi's *Zhuzi quan shu* 朱子全書 (*The Collected Works of Master Zhu*), vol. 6 (ZZQS 6: 39). See also its interpretation in Arghiresco/u, *De la continuité dynamique*, 219–22.

40. Qisong, *Tanjing zan* in *Platform Sutra of the Dharma Treasure of the Great Master, the Sixth Patriarch*, 0346a13. This essay is equally included in his anthology *Fujiao bian* (*Essays on Assisting the Teaching*).
41. Qisong, *Guang yuanjiao*, 0655a26-1.
42. Ibid., 0654b24.
43. Ibid., 0657b18.
44. Ibid., 0656c16-11.
45. Ibid., 0656c10.
46. Ibid., 0659b01.
47. Ibid., 0659b12-16.
48. Ibid., 067b18.
49. Ibid., 0654b24.
50. Ibid.
51. Qisong, *Quanshu*, 0652a07-11.
52. Ibid., 0652a13-11.
53. Zhu Xi, *Zhuzi quan shu* 朱子全書 (*The Collected Works of Master Zhu*), vol. 13 (ZZQS 13: 276–81); in Wing-tsit Chan's translation – Zhu Xi and Lü Zuqian, *Reflections on Things at Hand*, 279–88.
54. Qisong, *Guang yuanjiao*, 0654b19-2.
55. Zhou Dunyi 周敦頤 (1017–1073), Cheng Hao 程顥 (1032–1085), Cheng Yi 程頤 (1033–1107), Zhang Zai 張載 (1020–1077).

4 Ethico-organic interrelatedness: The meaning of ethico-religious practice in the Neo-Confucian scholar Zhu Xi's writings

1. I am profoundly grateful to James D. Sellmann who so generously offered specific comments and suggestions that enabled me to improve this chapter. The remaining faults are entirely mine.
2. Joseph A. Adler has examined Zhu Xi's 'personal religious practice'. He argues that the three types of practice that Zhu Xi emphasized, that is, 'intellectual cultivation', 'spiritual cultivation' and 'putting into effect in social relations and formal rituals what one has learned', constitute Zhu Xi's religious practice (Adler, *Reconstructing the Confucian Dao*, 142). Although my approach is different, I share Adler's view on the three-dimensional meaning of practice in Zhu's thought.
3. Gadamer, *Truth and Method*, 203.
4. In the present context, the term 'Neo-Confucianism' designates Zhu Xi's school, the *daoxue* 道學 tradition. About 'the quest to revive and transmit the *dao*' representing a fellowship and about Zhu Xi 'as the symbol of the fellowship', see Tillman, *Confucian Discourse*, 138.
5. On heart-mind in Neo-Confucian spirituality equivalent to the seat of refined vital breath (*qi* 氣), and the space where the communication between heaven and human is established, where their unity effectively occurs, see Yü, *Lun tian ren zhi qi*, 171–218.
6. See the previous chapters; also, Tillman, *Confucian Discourse*, 17; Yü, 'Daoxue jia', 116.
7. Fu, 'Chu Hsi on Buddhism', 390–1.

8. See Hsiao, *A History of Chinese*, 19–24.
9. I want to thank James D. Sellmann for pointing out these new Neo-Confucian significations of interrelatedness.
10. See this idea of rectifying the heart-mind in Qisong's articulation of the heart-mind and names (Chapter 3, Section 3.2).
11. The issue of 'correcting the heart-mind' concerns an essential stage in the education of the exemplary person, addressed in the classic *Great Learning* (*Daxue, jing* 大學, 經), see Zhu Xi, *Daxue zhangju* (*ZZQS* 6: 17). 'Keeping individual's heart-mind present' and 'nourishing individual's nature' are ideas developed by Mencius in *Jinxin zhangju shang* 盡心章句上, paragraph 1, included in Zhu Xi's commentary *Mengzi jizhu* 孟子集注; in Zhu Xi, *Zhuzi quan shu* 朱子全書 (*The Collected Works of Master Zhu*), vol. 6, p. 425 (*ZZQS* 6: 425).
12. See Arghiresco/u, *De la continuité dynamique*, 289–301.
13. Zhu Xi, *Zhongyong zhangju* 20; in Zhu Xi, *Zhuzi quan shu* 朱子全書 (*The Collected Works of Master Zhu*), vol. 6, p. 49 (*ZZQS* 6: 49).
14. I thank Kirill Thompson for his observation about the 'deep ethico-moral holism' of these Song dynasty traditions as it emerges from this book.
15. About the idea of *li* 理 understood to mean principle, see Chan 1964: 124–42. The translation of *li* as 'principle of coherence' in the context of Zhu Xi's thought is complementary to its translation as 'pattern' or 'patterning' (see Thompson, 'Opposition and Complementarity', 149–51 and Thompson, 'Li and Yi as Immanent', 30–46). 'Coherence' emphasizes the capacity of constituting a unified whole, while 'pattern' stresses the idea of regular form. The two translations are correlative and focus on different perspectives: pattern relates to a cosmological and logical awareness of *li* and coherence principle to an awareness related to human spirit and morality. For a comparative philosophical analysis of the Greek notion of *principle* (Plato and Aristotle) and the notion of *li* in Zhu Xi's thought, see Arghiresco/u, *De la continuité dynamique*, 45–95. See also Zhang, 'Zhu Xi's Metaphysics', 15–45.
16. Zhu Xi, *Mengzi jizhu*, chapter *Gaozi zhangju shang* 告子章句上 paragraph 6; in Zhu Xi, *Zhuzi quan shu* 朱子全書 (*The Collected Works of Master Zhu*), vol. 6, p. 400 (*ZZQS* 6: 400).
17. Song dynasty local elites and imperial officials.
18. Zhu Xi, *Zhongyong zhangju* 22 (*ZZQS* 6: 50).
19. Arghirescu, 'The Neo-Confucian Transmoral Dimension', 54–8.
20. See Zhu Xi, *Lunyu jizhu* 6: 21; in Zhu Xi, *Zhuzi quan shu* 朱子全書 (*The Collected Works of Master Zhu*) (*ZZQS* 6: 115).
21. Zhu, *Daxue zhangju jing*; in Zhu Xi, *Zhuzi quan shu* 朱子全書 (*The Collected Works of Master Zhu*) (*ZZQS* 6: 16).
22. About this intellectualist dimension, see also Yü, 'Morality and Knowledge', 231–2.
23. Zhu Xi, *Daxue zhangju jing*; in Zhu Xi, *Zhuzi quan shu* 朱子全書 (*The Collected Works of Master Zhu*) (*ZZQS* 6: 17).
24. Mencius, *Gaozi shang* 6; in Zhu Xi, *Mengzi jizhu*, chapter *Gaozi zhangju shang* 告子章句上; in *Zhuzi quan shu* 朱子全書 (*The Collected Works of Master Zhu*) (*ZZQS* 6: 399).
25. Zhu Xi depicts the vital breath that 'which can be gradually refined, solidified, and concentrated, in order to give birth to all the things (氣則能醞釀凝聚生物也)' including feelings. (Zhu Xi, *Zhuzi yulei, juan* 4, in *Zhuzi quan shu* 朱子全書 (*The Collected Works of Master Zhu*), vol. 14, p. 185 (*ZZQS* 14: 185)). About *qi* 氣 as the

root of East Asian spirituality, see Okada, 'Practical Learning in the Chu Hsi School', 315–18.
26. Zhu Xi, *Mengzi jizhu, Gaozi zhangju shang* 6; in Zhu Xi, *Zhuzi quan shu* 朱子全書 (*The Collected Works of Master Zhu*) (ZZQS 6: 400).
27. Mencius, *Gaozi zhangju shang* 2; *in* Zhu Xi, *Mengzi jizhu* 孟子集注 (ZZQS 6: 295).
28. Zhu Xi, *Zhongyong zhangju* 20; in Zhu Xi, *Zhuzi quan shu* 朱子全書 (*The Collected Works of Master Zhu*) (ZZQS 6: 49).
29. Zhu Xi, *Daxue zhangju* 10; in Zhu Xi, *Zhuzi quan shu* 朱子全書 (*The Collected Works of Master Zhu*) (ZZQS 6: 26).
30. Thich, *Being Peace*, 39.
31. Chan, 'The Evolution of the Confucian Concept Jên', 314.
32. For a different perspective on *jing* 敬 translated as seriousness, see Yü, 'Morality and Knowledge', 230.
33. Chen, Guying and Zhao Jainwei, *Zhouyi zhushi yu yenjiu* 周易註釋與究, 41.
34. See also Arghiresco/u, *De la continuité dynamique*, 365–6.
35. *Zhongyong* 30, in Zhu Xi, *Zhongyong zhangju* (ZZQS 6: 55).
36. *Zhongyong* 31, in Zhu Xi, *Zhongyong zhangju* (ZZQS 6: 56).
37. Zhu Xi, *Zhongyong zhangju* 31 (ZZQS 6: 56).
38. Ching, 'The Problem of Evil', 174.
39. Mencius, *Gaozi shang* 6; in Zhu Xi, *Mengzi jizhu* 孟子集注, *Zhuzi quan shu* 朱子全書 (*The Collected Works of Master Zhu*) (ZZQS 6: 399).
40. See *Daxue jing* 大學, 經 interpreted in Arghirescu, 'Zhu Xi's Spirituality', 272–89.
41. Confucius, *Lunyu* 7:27; in Zhu Xi, *Lunyu jizhu, Zhuzi quan shu* 朱子全書 (*The Collected Works of Master Zhu*), vol. 6 (ZZQS 6: 127).
42. Mencius, *Gaozi shang* 6; in Zhu Xi, *Mengzi jizhu* 孟子集注 (ZZQS 6: 399).
43. Mencius, *Gongsun Chou shang* 公孫丑上 2; in Zhu Xi, *Mengzi jizhu, Zhuzi quan shu* 朱子全書 (*The Collected Works of Master Zhu*), vol. 6 (ZZQS 6: 281).
44. See also Okada, 'Practical Learning in the Chu Hsi School', 243.
45. Zhu Xi, *Lunyu jizhu* 6:2 (ZZQS 6: 109–10).
46. Zhu Xi, *Huian xiansheng Zhu wengong wenji (4)* 朱文公文集, *Da Huang Daofu* 答黃道夫; in Zhu Xi, *Zhuzi quan shu* 朱子全書 (*The Collected Works of Master Zhu*), vol. 23 (ZZQS 23: 2755).
47. See Arghirescu, 'Spiritual Discipline, Emotions and Behavior', 1–26.
48. Zhu Xi, *Zhongyong zhangju* 1 (ZZQS 6: 33–4).
49. Zhu Xi, *Zhongyong zhangju* 20 (ZZQS 6: 49).
50. Arghirescu, 'Zhu Xi's Ideal of Moral Politics', 468–74.
51. Ibid.
52. Zhu Xi, *Zhongyong zhangju* 1 (ZZQS 6: 33).
53. Ibid.
54. Zhu Xi, *Lunyu jizhu* 4: 11 (ZZQS 6: 95).
55. Zhu Xi, *Daxue zhangju jing* (ZZQS 6: 17).
56. Zhu Xi, *Daxue zhangju* 7 (ZZQS 6: 22).
57. Ibid.
58. Zhu Xi, *Daxue zhangju jing* (ZZQS 6: 17).
59. Zhu Xi, *Daxue zhangju* 7 (ZZQS 6: 22).
60. Ibid. 6 (ZZQS 6: 20–1).
61. Zhu Xi, *Daxue zhangju jing* (ZZQS 6: 17).
62. Zhu Xi, *Mengzi jizhu, Gaozi zhangju shang* 8 (ZZQS 6: 402).
63. Zhu Xi, *Daxue zhangju* 10 (ZZQS 6: 26).

64. Zhu Xi, *Mengzi jizhu, Gaozi zhangju shang* 8 (ZZQS 6: 402).
65. Mencius, *Jinxin xia* 35, 盡心下 35, in Zhu Xi, *Mengzi jizhu*, in *Zhuzi quan shu* 朱子全書 (*The Collected Works of Master Zhu*), vol. 6 (ZZQS 6: 455).
66. Zhu Xi, *Mengzi jizhu, Gaozi zhangju shang* 8 (ZZQS 6: 402).
67. *Daxue jing*, in Zhu Xi, *Zhuzi quan shu* 朱子全書 (*The Collected Works of Master Zhu*) (ZZQS 6: 16).
68. Zhu Xi, *Lunyu jizhu* 12.1 (ZZQS 6: 167).
69. See *Great Master Bodhidharma's Essential Discourse on Entering the Mahayana Path* 菩提達磨大師略辨大乘入道四行觀, X63n1217-1, 0001a06.

5 Ethical interrelatedness: An interpretive theory for Chinese religious traditions

1. Fingarette, *Confucius*, ix.
2. Arghiresco/u, *De la continuité dynamique*.
3. Arghirescu, *Building Bridges*.
4. Braithwaite, *An Empiricist's View*, 23.
5. Ching, *The Religious Thought of Chu Hsi*, 105.
6. Ibid.
7. Berthrong, *All under Heaven*, 11.
8. Saussure, *Cours de linguistique générale*, 98–101.
9. Ibid., 101.
10. Harbsmeier, *Science and Civilisation*, 207.
11. Ibid., 137, 142.
12. Smart, *Worldviews*, 5.
13. Harbsmeier, *Science and Civilisation*, 150.
14. Vandermeersch, *Ce que la Chine nous apprend*, 20.
15. Vandermeersch, *Les deux raisons de la pensée chinoise*, 169.
16. According to Julia Ching, the terms *ti* 體 (corporeality, body, substance, latent) and *yong* 用 (function, use, manifest) come from the Neo-Daoist philosopher Wang Bi (226–249). In his commentary on *Laozi* 4 ('The Dao is empty, yet use (*yong*) will not drain it.'), he uses the notion *ti* 體 when referring to Dao (see Ching, *The Religious Thought of Chu Hsi*, 11; and Laozi, annotated by Wang Bi 王弼, 19).
17. Zhu Xi, *Huian xiansheng Zhuwengong wenji* (4), 晦庵先生朱文公文集(四), (*Answering to Huang Daofu* (*Da Huang Daofu* 答黃道夫); in Zhu Xi, *Zhuzi quan shu* 朱子全書 (*The Collected Works of Master Zhu*), vol. 23, p. 2755 (ZZQS 23: 2755).
18. Yü, 'Between the Heavenly and the Human', 6.
19. Zhu Xi, *Zhongyong zhangju* 1; in Zhu Xi, *Zhuzi quan shu* 朱子全書 (*The Collected Works of Master Zhu*), vol. 6, p. 32 (ZZQS 6: 32).
20. Qisong, *Exegesis of the Mean* 3 (*Zhongyong jie* 中庸解), 666c18-1.
21. Qisong, *Inquiry into the Teachings* (*Yuanjiao*), 0650b18-14; in *Essays on Assisting the Teaching* (*Fujiao bian* 輔教編), CBETA T52n2115_001.
22. Ibid., 0649b02-1.
23. Thich, *Being Peace*, 45–6.
24. Vandermeersch, *Les deux raisons de la pensée chinoise*, 108. Translated from French by the author.
25. Huang, *Xu Fuguan in the Context*, 185.

26. Mou, *Mou Zongsan xiansheng quanji*, 12.
27. Arghirescu, 'Translator's Introduction', xiii–vii.
28. Streng, *Understanding Religious Life*, 124–5.
29. See Huang, *Xu Fuguan in the Context*, 24.
30. Zhu Xi, *Lunyu jizhu* 3: 25; in Zhu Xi, *Zhuzi quan shu* 朱子全書 (*The Collected Works of Master Zhu*) (ZZQS 6: 92).
31. See Zhu Xi's commentary to the *Zhongyong* 33, interpreted in Arghiresco/u, *De la continuité dynamique*, 380–4.
32. Mou, *Mou Zongsan xiansheng quanji*, 16; quoted in Huang, *Xu Fuguan in the Context*, 156.
33. Quoted in Huang, *Xu Fuguan in the Context*, 46.
34. Lindqvist, *China: Empire of the Written Symbol*, 18.
35. Couvreur, *La chronique*, 657–60; quoted in Vandermeersch, 'Écriture et divination en Chine', 66. Translated from French by the author.
36. Chen and Zhao, *Zhouyi zhushi yu yenjiu*, 41. See the interpretation of this paragraph in Chapter 4, Section 3.1.
37. Qisong, *Guang yuanjiao* (*Extensive Inquiry into the Teachings*), 0655c21-12, in *Essays on Assisting the Teaching* (*Fujiao bian* 輔教編), CBETA T52n2115_002.
38. Qisong, *Yuanjiao*, 0651b12-2.
39. *Zhongyong* 30 (ZZQS 6: 55). For a philosophical translation of this ancient paragraph 30 and of its Neo-Confucian commentary by Zhu Xi, see Arghiresco/u, *De la continuité dynamique*, 365–6.
40. Zhu Xi, *Zhongyong zhangju* 1 (ZZQS 6: 33).
41. Paden, *New Patterns for Comparative Religion*, 102.
42. Ibid., 95, 107–9, 122.
43. Ibid., 123.
44. Tweed, *Crossing and Dwelling*, 59, 71, 83, 136.
45. Paden, *New Patterns for Comparative Religion*, 124.
46. Hick, *An Interpretation of Religion*, 240–1.
47. Smith, *Imagining Religion*, xi.

6 A comparative perspective: Similarities and differences

1. Thompson, 'Lessons from Early Chinese Humanist Impulses', 83. In this context, the author also re-examines Mozi's (ca. 480–390 BCE) teaching of *jianai* 兼愛 (impartial regard, impartial affection) and identifies ways in which this 'could energize our ethical response to the problems of this age': see Thompson, 'Mozi's Teaching of *Jianai*', 848.
2. Thompson, 'Lessons from Early Chinese Humanist Impulses', 65.
3. Ibid., 66.
4. See Thompson, 'Zhu Xi's Completion of Confucius' Humanistic Ethics'.
5. About relational self, see also Thompson, 'Relational Self in Classical Confucianism'.
6. Thompson, 'Lessons from Early Chinese Humanist Impulses', 75.
7. Ibid.
8. Ibid., 84.
9. About Zhu Xi's 'particularistic approach in describing phenomena', his notions of transformation and change, and his practice of *gewu* (investigating things), see also Thompson, 'The Natural Philosophy of Chu Hsi', 168–74.

Notes 245

10. Thompson, 'Lessons from Zhu Xi's Views', 27.
11. Ibid., 33.
12. Thompson, 'Zhu Xi's Completion of Confucius' Humanistic Ethics', 614.
13. Ching, *The Religious Thought of Chu Hsi*, 5.
14. Ibid., 15.
15. Ching, *Chinese Religions*, 7.
16. Ching, *The Religious Thought of Chu Hsi*, 188.
17. See Yu, 'Ta-Hui Tsung-Kao and Kung-an Ch'an', 220–8.
18. Ching, *The Religious Thought of Chu Hsi*, 178.
19. Ibid., 188–9.
20. Yu, 'Ta-Hui Tsung-Kao and Kung-an Ch'an', 229.
21. Muller, *Korea's Great Buddhist-Confucian Debate*, 21.
22. Ibid., 6.
23. Ibid., 40.
24. Ch'en, *The Chinese Transformation of Buddhism*, 5.
25. Sharf, *Coming to Terms with Chinese Buddhism*, 1.
26. Ibid., 7.
27. Ibid., 98.
28. Ibid., 39.
29. Ibid., 37.
30. Ibid., 40.
31. Ibid., 76.
32. Ibid., 97.
33. Ibid., 115.
34. Ibid., 132.
35. Ibid., 137.
36. Ibid., 76.
37. Ibid., 98.
38. Ibid., 77.
39. Ibid., 81.
40. Qisong, *Exegesis of the Mean* 4 (*Zhongyong jie* 中庸解4), 0667a23-10.
41. Including the three classics on the rites *Sanli* 三禮.
42. Qisong, *Exegesis of the Mean* 3 (*Zhongyong jie* 3), 0666c08-1.
43. Qisong, *Guang yuanjiao* (*Extensive Inquiry into the Teachings*), 0655c16, in *Essays on Assisting the Teaching* (*Fujiao bian* 輔教編), CBETA T52n2115_002.
44. Thompson, 'Fox Koan and Dream: Dogen's New Light on Causality and Purity', 255.
45. Ching, 'The Problem of Evil', 174.
46. Qisong, *Guang yuanjiao*, 0656a01-6.
47. The chapter was elevated to part of the Song canon by Zhu Xi: See Csikszentmihalyi, *Material Virtue*, 98.
48. For a philosophical translation of the *Zhongyong*, including its commentary by Zhu Xi, *Zhongyong zhangju*, and an intercultural, comparative interpretation (Chinese/Western, Greek philosophy), see Arghiresco/u, *De la continuité dynamique*.
49. Ching, *The Religious Thought of Chu Hsi*, 3.
50. Ching, *Chinese Religions*, 158.
51. Ching, *The Religious Thought of Chu Hsi*, 94.
52. Ibid., 6.
53. Ibid., 105.
54. Ibid., 97–8.

55. Ibid., 111.
56. Ibid., 126.
57. Ibid., 127.
58. Tu, *Centrality and Commonality*, 12.
59. See Arghiresco/u, *De la continuité dynamique*, 106–8.
60. Tu, *Centrality and Commonality*, 116.
61. Ibid., 77.
62. Ibid., 70.
63. Ibid., 9.
64. Tu, *Confucian Thought: Selfhood as Creative Transformation*, 16.
65. Tu, *Centrality and Commonality*, 97.
66. Ibid., 101.
67. Ibid., 102.
68. Thompson, 'Opposition and Complementarity', 152.
69. Ibid., 154.
70. Tu, *Centrality and Commonality*, x.
71. Ibid., 113.
72. Ibid., 78.
73. *Zhongyong* 22, in Zhu Xi, *Zhongyong zhangju* 22; in Zhu Xi, *Zhuzi quan shu* 朱子全書 (*The Collected Works of Master Zhu*), vol. 6, p. 50 (ZZQS 6: 50).
74. Tu, *Centrality and Commonality*, 81.
75. *Zhongyong* 22 (ZZQS 6: 50).
76. *Zhongyong* 24 (ZZQS 6: 50-1).
77. This issue – 'the complete sincerity of the heaven-earth is ceaseless' – was taken up by Zhu Xi in his commentaries *Zhongyong zhangju* 11 (至誠無息), *Lunyu jizhu* 4: 15 (天地之至誠無息) and *Zhongyong zhangju* 26 (至誠無息).
78. Tu, *Centrality and Commonality*, 81.
79. Ching, *The Religious Thought of Chu Hsi*, 3.
80. Tu, *Centrality and Commonality*, 90-1.
81. Qisong, *Guang yuanjiao*, 0656a16-6.
82. Bellah, *Beyond Belief*, 95.
83. Lee, *Confucianism*, 28-9.
84. Thompson, 'Review', 323.
85. Berthrong, *Concerning Creativity*, viii.
86. Ibid., vii.
87. Ibid., 3, 10.
88. Berthrong, *All under Heaven*, 10.
89. Ibid., 162.
90. Thompson, 'Lessons from Early Chinese Humanist Impulses', 65; Bullock, *The Humanist Tradition*, 23-35.
91. Joubert, *Recueil des pensées*, 127-8. Translated from French by the author.
92. Ricoeur, *Philosophie de la volonté* 1, 108.
93. Whitehead, *Modes of Thought*, 13.
94. Billeter, *The Chinese Art of Writing*, 116.
95. Whitehead, *Modes of Thought*, 87.
96. Ibid., 167.
97. Ibid., 166.
98. Ibid., 11-12.
99. Ibid., 13.

100. Whitehead, *Process and Reality*, 123.
101. Whitehead, *Modes of Thought*, 89.
102. Whitehead, *Process and Reality*, 28.
103. Ibid., 9.
104. Zhu Xi, *Zhongyong zhangju* 26 (ZZQS 6: 51–2).
105. Whitehead, *Modes of Thought*, 154.
106. Ibid., 166.
107. Whitehead, *Process and Reality*, 28.
108. Whitehead, *Modes of Thought*, 167.
109. Steere, 'Biographical Memoir', 8.
110. Kelly, *A Testament of Devotion*, 111.
111. Ibid., 108.
112. Ibid.

Bibliography

Primary sources

Bodhidharma 菩提達磨 (?–535), *Great Master Bodhidharma's Essential Discourse on Entering the Mahayana Path* 菩提達磨大師略辨大乘入道四行觀, X63n1217-1 (www.cbeta.org).
Fazang 法藏 (643–712), *Essay on the Arousal of the Bodhi-Heart-Mind in the Huayan* (*Huayan fa puti xin zhang* 華嚴發菩提心章), T45n1878 (www.cbeta.org).
Huineng 惠能 (638–713), *Platform Sutra of the Dharma Treasure of the Great Master, the Sixth Patriarch* 六祖大師法寶壇經, T48n2008 (www.cbeta.org).
Laozi 老子 (6th century BCE), *The Way of Laozi* 老子, annotated by Wang Bi 王弼 (226–49). Taipei: Jinfeng chubanshe, 1992.
Laozi, *The Way of Lao Tzu*. Translated with introductory essays, comments and notes by Wing-tsit Chan. Upper Saddle River, NJ: Prentice Hall, 1963.
Qisong 契嵩 (1007–1072), *Essays on Assisting the Teaching* (*Fujiao bian* 輔教編). In *Collected Works of Qisong* (*Tanjin wenji* 鐔津文集),vols. 1, 2, 3, 鐔津文集卷一, 二, 三). T52n2115 (www. cbeta.org).
Qisong契嵩 (1007–1072), *Exegesis of the Mean* (*Zhongyong jie* 中庸解). In *Collected Works of Qisong Qisong* (*Tanjin wenji* 鐔津文集), vol. 4. CBETA T52n2115_004. Chinese Electronic Tripitaka Collection. tripitaka.cbeta.org.
Xu Shen 許慎 (ca. 55–ca. 149). *Shuowen jiezi zhu* 說文解字注, annotated by Duan Yucai 段玉裁 (1735–1815). Taipei: Hung Yeh Publishing House, 1998.
Zhu, Xi 朱熹 (1130–1200). *Zhuzi quanshu* 朱子全書 (*The Collected Works of Master Zhu*). 27 vols. Shanghai: Shanghai gu ji chubanshe, 2002. Cited as ZZQS.
Zhu, Xi, and Lü Zuqian 呂祖謙 (1137–1181). *Reflections on Things at Hand; the Neo-Confucian Anthology Compiled by Chu Hsi and Lü Tsu-ch'ien*. Translated by Wing-tsit Chan 陳榮捷 (1901–1994). New York: Columbia University Press, 1967.
Zhuangzi 莊子 (4th century BCE). *The Complete Works of Zhuangzi*. Translated by Burton Watson. New York: Columbia University Press, 2013.

Secondary sources

Abe, Masao. *Zen and Western Thought*. Edited by William R. Lafleur. London: Macmillan, 1985.
Abe, Masao. *A Study of Dogen: His Philosophy and Religion*. Albany: State University of New York Press, 1992.
Abe, Masao. *Zen and Comparative Studies*. Edited by Steven Heine. Honolulu: University of Hawai'i Press, 1997.
Adler, Joseph A. *Reconstructing the Confucian Dao: Zhu Xi's Appropriation of Zhou Dunyi*. Albany: State University of New York Press, 2014.

Arghirescu, Diana. 'Zhu Xi's Spirituality: A New Interpretation of the Great Learning.' *Journal of Chinese Philosophy* 39, no. 2 (2012): 272–89.

Arghiresco/u, Diana. *De la continuité dynamique dans l'univers confucéen: Lecture néo-confucéenne du Zhongyong* 中庸. Paris: Éditions du Cerf, 2013.

Arghirescu, Diana. 'Confluences between Neo-Confucian and Chan Practical Methods of Self-Cultivation: The Anthology *Reflections on Things at Hand* and the *Platform Sutra* in Comparative Perspective'. *Comparative and Continental Philosophy* 11, no. 3 (2019): 265–80.

Arghirescu, Diana. 'The Neo-Confucian Transmoral Dimension of Zhu Xi's Moral Thought'. *Philosophy East and West* 69, no. 1 (2019): 52–70.

Arghirescu, Diana. 'Translator's Introduction'. In *Xu Fuguan in the Context of East Asian Confucianisms* by Chun-chieh Huang, translated by Diana Arghirescu, xiii–xvii. Honolulu: University of Hawai'i Press, 2019.

Arghirescu, Diana. 'Chapter 21 "Zhu Xi's Ideal of Moral Politics: Theory and Practice"'. In *Dao Companion to Zhu Xi's Philosophy*, edited by Kai-chiu Ng and Yong Huang, 465–97. Cham: Springer Nature Switzerland, 2020.

Arghirescu, Diana. 'Song Neo-Confucian Conceptions of Morality and Moral Sources (Zhu Xi): Connections with Chan Buddhism'. *Journal of Chinese Philosophy* 47, nos 3–4 (2020): 193–212.

Arghirescu, Diana. 'Spiritual Discipline, Emotions and Behavior during the Song-Dynasty: Chan Monk Qisong's and Zhu Xi's Commentaries on the *Zhongyong* in Comparative Perspective'. *Philosophy East and West* 70, no. 1 (2020): 1–26.

Arghirescu, Diana. 'Between Heart-mind and Names: Interrelatedness in the Chan Monk-scholar Qisong's Thought'. *Comparative and Continental Philosophy* 13, no. 3 (2021): 220–34.

Arghirescu, Diana. *Building Bridges between Chan Buddhism and Confucianism: A Comparative Hermeneutics of Qisong's 'Essays on Assisting the Teaching'*. Bloomington: Indiana University Press, 2022.

Asad, Talal. *Genealogies of Religion: Discipline and Reasons of Power in Christianity and Islam*. Baltimore: John Hopkins University Press, 1993.

Bailly, Anatole. *Dictionnaire grec-français*. Paris: Hachette, 1950.

Bellah, Robert. *Beyond Belief: Essays on Religion in a Post-Traditional World*. New York: Harper & Row, 1976.

Bergson, Henri. *L'Énergie Spirituelle: Essais et Conférences*. Paris: Presses Universitaires de France, 1919.

Berthrong, John H. *All under Heaven: Transforming Paradigms in Confucian-Christian Dialogue*. Albany: State University of New York Press, 1994.

Berthrong, John H. *Concerning Creativity: A Comparison of Chu Hsi, Whitehead, and Neville*. Albany: State University of New York Press, 1998.

Billeter, Jean François. *The Chinese Art of Writing*. New York: Rizzoli, 1990.

Billeter, Jean François. *Chine trois fois muette. Essai sur l'histoire contemporaine et la Chine*. Paris: Allia, 2000.

Bodde, Derk. 'Types of Chinese Categorical Thinking'. *Journal of the American Oriental Society* 59, no. 2 (1939): 200–19.

Bol, Peter K. *'This Culture of Ours': Intellectual transitions in T'ang and Sung China*. Stanford: Stanford University Press, 1992.

Braithwaite, Richard Bevan. *An Empiricist's View of the Nature of Religious Belief*. Folcroft, PA: Folcroft Library Editions, 1974.

Brook, Timothy. 'Rethinking Syncretism: The Unity of the Three Teachings and Their Joint Worship in Late-imperial China'. *Journal of Chinese Religions* 21, no. 1 (1993): 13–44.
Bullock, Alan. *The Humanist Tradition in the West*. New York: W.W. Norton, 1985.
Calame, Claude. 'What Is Religion? Between Christianocentric Paradigm and Anthropological Relativism'. Translated by Erik Nesse. In *Irreverence and the Sacred: Critical Studies in the History of Religions*, edited by Hugh B. Urban and Greg Johnson. New York: Oxford University Press, 2019.
Chan, Wing-tsit. 'The Evolution of the Confucian Concept Jên'. *Philosophy East and West* 4, no. 1 (1955): 295–319.
Chan, Wing-tsit. 'The Evolution of the Neo-Confucian Concept *Li* 理 as Principle'. *Tsing Hua Journal of Chinese Studies* 4, no. 2 (1964): 123–48.
Ch'en, Kenneth K. S. *The Chinese Transformation of Buddhism*. Princeton: Princeton University Press, 1973.
Chen, Guying陳鼓應 and Zhao, Jianwei趙建偉. *Zhouyi zhushi yu yenjiu*周易註釋與究. Taipei: Shangwu Yinshuguan, 1999.
Chen, Shunyu陳舜俞. *Douguanji: Minjiao dashi hangye ji* 都官集：明教大師行業記. Taipei: The Commercial Press, 1972.
Ching, Julia. 'The Problem of Evil and a Possible Dialogue between Christianity and Neo-Confucianism'. *Contemporary Religions in Japan* 9, no. 3 (1968): 161–93.
Ching, Julia. *Chinese Religions*. Maryknoll, NY: Orbis Books, 1993.
Ching, Julia. *The Religious Thought of Chu Hsi*. New York: Oxford University Press, 2000.
Chow, Tse-tsung. *The May Fourth Movement: Intellectual Revolution in Modern China*. Stanford: Stanford University Press, 1967.
Couvreur, Séraphin. *La chronique de la principauté de Lou*. Vol. 3, reprint. Paris: Cathasia, 1951.
Csikszentmihalyi, Mark. *Material Virtue: Ethics and the Body in Early China*. Leiden: Brill, 2004.
Derrida, Jacques. *La dissémination*. Paris: Seuil, 1972.
Derrida, Jacques. 'Foi et savoir: Les deux sources de la "religion" aux limites de la simple raison'. In *La religion*, edited by Jacques Derrida and Gianni Vattimo, 9–86. Paris: Seuil, 1996.
Derrida, Jacques. 'Faith and Knowledge: The Two Sources of "Religion" at the Limits of Reason Alone'. Translated by S. Weber. In *Religion*, edited by Jacques Derrida and Gianni Vattimo, 1–78. Stanford: Stanford University Press, 1998.
Doniger, Wendy. 'Post-Modern and -Colonial -Structural Comparisons'. In *A Magic Still Dwells: Comparative Religion in the Postmodern Age*, edited by Patton Kimberley C. and Benjamin C. Ray, 63–74. Berkeley: University of California Press, 2000.
Durkheim, Emile. *Les formes élémentaires de la vie religieuse; le système totémique en Australie*. Paris: Presses Universitaires de France, 1960.
Fingarette, Herbert. *Confucius: The Secular as Sacred*. New York: Harper Torchbooks, 1972.
Freiberger, Oliver. *Considering Comparison: A Method for Religious Studies*. New York: Oxford University Press, 2019.
Fu, Charles Wei-hsun. 'Chu Hsi on Buddhism'. In *Chu Hsi and Neo-Confucianism*, edited by Wing-tsit Chan, 377–407. Honolulu: University of Hawai'i Press, 1986.
Gadamer, Hans-Georg. 'Dialogues de Capri'. Translated by P. Fruchon. In *La religion*, edited by Jacques Derrida and Gianni Vattimo, 221–33. Paris: Seuil, 1996.

Gadamer, Hans-Georg. *Truth and Method*. Translated and revised by Joel Weinsheimer and Donald G. Marshall. London: Bloomsbury Academic, 2013.
Gimello, Robert M. 'Marga and Culture: Learning, Letters, and Liberation in Northern Sung Ch'an'. In *Paths to Liberation: The Marga and Its Transformations in Buddhist Thought*, edited by Robert E. Buswell Jr. and Robert M. Gimello, 371–437. Honolulu: Kuroda Institute, 1992.
Graham, Angus C. *Yin-yang and the Nature of Correlative Thinking*. Singapore: The Institute of East Asian Philosophies, 1986.
Graham, Angus C. *Disputers of the Tao: Philosophical Argument in Ancient China*. La Salle: Open Court, 1989.
Graham, Angus C. *Studies in Chinese Philosophy and Philosophical Literature*. Albany: State University of New York Press, 1990.
Granet, Marcel. *La pensée chinoise*. Paris: Albin Michel, 1934.
Granet, Marcel. *Études sociologiques sur la Chine*. Paris: Presses Universitaires de France, 1953.
Hall, David L., and Roger T. Ames. *Thinking through Confucius*. Albany: State University of New York Pres, 1987.
Hall, David L., and Roger T. Ames. *Anticipating China: Thinking through the Narratives of Chinese and Western Culture*. Albany: State University of New York Press, 1995.
Hall, David L., and Roger Ames. *Thinking from the Han: Self, Truth, and Transcendence in Chinese and Western Culture*. Albany: State University of New York Press, 1998.
Han Yu. 'Essentials of the Moral Way'. Translated by Charles Hartman. In *Sources of Chinese Tradition*, vol. 1, edited by Wm. Theodore de Bary and Irene Bloom, 569–73. New York: Columbia University Press, 1999.
Harbsmeier, Christoph. *Science and civilisation in China. Vol. 7, Part 1: Language and Logic*. Edited by Joseph Needham. Cambridge: Cambridge University Press, 1998.
Heidegger, Martin. *On the Way to Language*. New York: Harper & Row, 1971.
Heiler, Friedrich. 'The History of Religions as a Preparation for the Co-operation of Religions'. In *The History of Religions: Essays in Methodology*, edited by Mircea Eliade and Joseph M. Kitagawa, 132–60. Chicago: University of Chicago Press, 1959.
Hewitt, Marsha A. 'How New Is the "New Comparativism"? Difference, Dialectics, and World-making'. *Method & Theory in the Study of Religion* 8, no. 1 (1996): 15–20.
Hick, John. *Philosophy of Religion*. Englewood Cliffs: Prentice Hall, 1963.
Hick, John. *An Interpretation of Religion: Human Responses to the Transcendent*. New Haven, CT: Yale University Press, 1989.
Hsiao Kung-chuan 蕭公權. *A History of Chinese Political Thought*. Translated by F. W. Mote. Vol. 1. Princeton: Princeton University Press, 1979.
Huang, Chi-chiang 黃啓江. 'Experiment in Syncretism: Ch'i-sung (1007–1072) and Eleventh-Century Chinese Buddhism'. PhD. diss. University of Arizona, 1986.
Huang, Chun-chieh. *Xu Fuguan in the Context of East Asian Confucianisms*. Translated by Diana Arghirescu. Honolulu: University of Hawai'i Press, 2019.
James, William. *The Varieties of Religious Experience*. Harmondsworth: Penguin, 1982.
Joubert, Joseph. *Recueil des pensées de M. Joubert*. Paris: Imprimerie le Normant, 1838.
Keightley, David N. *Sources of Shang History: The Oracle-Bone Inscriptions of Bronze Age China*. Berkeley: University of California Press, 1978.
Kelly, Thomas R. *A Testament of Devotion*. New York: Harper and Brothers Publishers, 1941.

Kitagawa, Joseph M. 'The History of Religions in America'. In *The History of Religions: Essays in Methodology*, edited by Mircea Eliade and Joseph M. Kitagawa, 1–30. Chicago: University of Chicago Press, 1959.

Knepper, Timothy D. 'The End of Philosophy of Religion?' *Journal of American Academy of Religion* 82, no. 1 (2014): 120–49.

Knepper, Timothy D. 'How to Philosophize about Religion Globally and Critically...with Undergraduates'. *Religious Studies* 56 (2014): 49–63.

Lawrence, Bruce B. 'Transformation'. In *Critical Terms for religious Studies*, edited by Marck C. Taylor, 334–48. Chicago: University of Chicago Press, 1998.

Lee, Ming-huei. 2017. *Confucianism: Its Roots and Global Significance*. Edited by David Jones. Honolulu: University of Hawai'i Press, 2017.

Leibniz, Gottfried W. *Writings on China*. Translated with an Introduction, Notes, and Commentaries by Daniel J. Cool and Henry Rosemont, Jr. Chicago: Open Court, 1994.

Levinas, Emmanuel. *Totalité et infini: essai sur l'extériorité*. Leiden: Martinus Nijhoff, 1971.

Levinas, Emmanuel. *Humanisme de l'autre homme*. Montpellier: Fata morgana, 1972.

Levinas, Emmanuel. *Entre nous – Essais sur le penser-à-autre*. Paris: Grasset & Fasquelle, 1991.

Levinas, Emmanuel. *Is It Righteous to Be?* Edited by Jill Robbins. Stanford: Stanford University Press, 2001.

Lindqvist, Cecilia. *China: Empire of the Written Symbol*. Translated by Joan Tate. Cambridge, MA: Da Capo Press, 2008.

Liu, James T. C. *Ou-Yang Hsiu, an Eleventh-Century Neo-Confucianist*. Stanford: Stanford University Press, 1967.

McCutcheon, Russell T. *The Discipline of Religion*. London: Routledge, 2003.

McCutcheon, Russell T. *Studying Religion: An Introduction*. London: Equinox, 2007.

Merleau-Ponty, Maurice. *La Nature: Notes du Collège de France*. Paris: Seuil, 1994.

Mou, Zongsan 牟宗三. *Zhongguo zhexue shijiu jiang* 中國哲學十九講. Taipei: Xuesheng shuju, 1983.

Mou, Zongsan 牟宗三. *Mou Zongsan xiansheng quanji* 牟宗三先生全集. 28. Taipei: Lianjing, 2003.

Muller, Charles. '*Tiyong* and Interpenetration in the *Analects* of Confucius; The Sacred as Secular'. *Bulletin of Toyo Gakuen University* 8 (2000): 15–29.

Muller, Charles. *Korea's Great Buddhist-Confucian Debate: The Treatises of Chong Tojon (Sambong) and Hamho Tuktong (Kihwa)*. Honolulu: University of Hawai'i Press, 2015.

Muller, Charles. 'The Emergence of Essence-Function (*ti-yong*) 體用 Hermeneutics in the Sinification of Indic Buddhism: An Overview'. *Critical Review for Buddhist Studies* 19 (2016): 111–52.

Müller, Max. *Chips from a German Workshop I: Essays on the Science of Religion*. London: Longmans, Green, and Co, 1867.

Needham, Joseph. *Science and Civilisation in China, Vol.2: History of Scientific Thought*. Cambridge: Cambridge University Press, 1956.

Neville, Robert Cummings. *Ritual and Deference: Extending Chinese Philosophy in a Comparative Context*. Albany: State University of New York Press, 2008.

Neville, Robert Cummings. *Defining Religion: Essays in Philosophy of Religion*. Albany: State University of New York Press, 2018.

Okada, Takehiko 岡田武彦. 'Practical Learning in the Chu Hsi School: Yamazaki Ansai and Kaibara Ekken'. In *Principle and Practicality: Essays in Neo-Confucianism and Practical Learning*, edited by Wm. Theodore de Bary and Irene Bloom, 231–305. New York: Columbia University Press, 1979.

Okada, Takehiko 岡田武彦. 'Mastery and the Mind'. In *Meeting of Minds: Intellectual and Religious Interaction in East Asian Traditions of Thought*, edited by Irene Bloom and Joshua A. Fogel, 297–340. New York: Columbia University Press, 1997.

Otto, Rudolf. *The Idea of the Holy: An Inquiry into the Non-Rational Factor in the Idea of the Divine and Its Relation to the Rational*. Translated by John W. Harvey. London: Humphrey Milford, 1923.

Ouyang Xiu. 'Ouyang Xiu: Essay on Fundamentals'. Translated by Wm. Theodore de Bary. In *Sources of Chinese Tradition*, vol. 1, edited by Wm. Theodore de Bary and Irene Bloom, 590–6. New York: Columbia University Press, 1999.

Paden, William E. *New Patterns for Comparative Religion: Passages to an Evolutionary Perspective*. London: Bloomsbury Academic, 2016.

Parsons, Talcott. 'Introduction'. In *The Sociology of Religion*, by Max Weber. Translated by Ephraim Fiscoff, xix–lxvii. Boston: Beacon Press, 1967.

Patton, Laurie L. 'The Magic in Miniature, Etymological Links in Comparative Religions'. In *A Magic Still Dwells: Comparative Religion in the Postmodern Age*, edited by Patton Kimberly and Benjamin Ray, 193–205. Berkeley: University of California Press, 2000.

Peirce, Charles. *Collected Papers of Charles Sanders Peirce*. Edited by Charles Hartshorne and Paul Weiss, vol. 2. Cambridge, MA: Harvard University Press, 1932.

Platvoet, Jan G. *Comparing Religions: A Limitative Approach: An Analysis of Akan, Para-Creole, and IFO-Sananda Rites and Prayers*. The Hague: Mouton, 1982.

Polanyi, Karl. *Essais*. Translated by Françoise Laroche and Laurence Collaud. Paris: Seuil, 2008.

Ricci Association. *Dictionnaire Ricci de caractères chinois; préparé par les Instituts Ricci (Paris-Taipei)*. Vols. 1 and 2. Paris: Desclée de Brouwer, 1999.

Ricoeur, Paul. *Philosophie de la volonté*. Vol. 1. Paris: Aubier, 1949.

Ricoeur, Paul. *Du texte à l'action: Essais d'herméneutique II*. Paris: Seuil, 1986.

Ricoeur, Paul. *Sur la traduction*. Paris: Bayard, 2004.

Saussure, Ferdinand de. 1916. *Cours de linguistique générale*. Paris: Payot, 1971.

Schwartz, Benjamin I. *The World of Thought in Ancient China*. Cambridge: Belknap Press of Harvard University Press, 1985.

Sharma, Arvind. *Religious Studies and Comparative Methodology: The Case for Reciprocal Illumination*. Albany: State University of New York Press, 2005.

Sharpe, Eric J. *Comparative Religion: A History*. London: Duckworth, 1975.

Smart, Ninian. *The Philosophy of Religion*. New York: Oxford University Press, 1970.

Smart, Ninian. *Buddhism and Christianity: Rivals and Allies*. Honolulu: University of Hawai'i Press, 1993.

Smart, Ninian. *The World's Religions*. 2nd edn. Cambridge: Cambridge University Press, 1998.

Smart, Ninian. *Worldviews, Crosscultural Explorations of Human Beliefs*. 3rd edn. Upper Saddle River, NJ: Prentice Hall, 2000.

Smith, Jonathan Z. *Imagining Religion: From Babylon to Jonestown*. Chicago: University of Chicago Press, 1982.

Smith, Jonathan Z. *To Take Place: Toward Theory in Ritual*. Chicago: University of Chicago Press, 1987.

Smith, Jonathan Z. *Drudgery Divine: On the Comparison of Early Christianities and the Religions of Late Antiquity*. Chicago: University of Chicago Press, 1990.

Smith, Jonathan Z. *Relating Religion: Essays in the Study of Religion*. Chicago: University of Chicago Press, 2004.

Steere, Douglas V. 'Biographical Memoir'. In *A Testament of Devotion*, by Thomas R. Kelly. New York: Harper & Brothers Publishers, 1941.

Streng, Frederick J. *Understanding Religious Life*. 3rd edn. Belmont: Wadsworth Inc. 1985.

Taylor, Charles. *Varieties of Religion Today: William James Revisited*. Cambridge, MA: Harvard University Press, 2002.

Tang, Junyi. *Tang Junyi quanji* II 唐君毅全集, 二 (The Complete Works of Tang Junyi, vol. 2). Taipei: Student Book Co, 1991.

Thich, Nhat Hanh. *Being Peace*. Edited by A. Kotler. Berkeley: Parallax Press, 1987.

Thompson, Kirill O. 'Review: Confucian Thought: Selfhood as Creative Transformation by Tu Wei-ming'. *Philosophy East and West* 37, no. 3 (1987): 323–5.

Thompson, Kirill O. 'Li and Yi as Immanent: Chu Hsi's Thought in Practical Perspective'. *Philosophy East and West* 38, no. 1 (1988): 30–46.

Thompson, Kirill O. 'The Natural Philosophy of Chu Hsi 1130–1200 (Review)'. *China Review International* 9, no. 1 (2002): 165–80.

Thompson, Kirill O. 'Fox Koan and Dream: Dogen's New Light on Causality and Purity'. *Asian Philosophy* 21, no. 3 (2011): 251–6.

Thompson, Kirill O. 'Lessons from Early Chinese Humanist Impulses'. In *Exploring Humanity: Intercultural Perspectives on Humanism*, edited by Mihai I. Spariosu and Jörg Rüsen, 65–84. Taipei: National Taiwan University Press, 2012.

Thompson, Kirill O. 'Mozi's Teaching of *Jianai* (Impartial Regard): A Lesson for the Twenty-first Century?' *Philosophy East and West* 64, no. 4 (2014): 838–55.

Thompson, Kirill O. 'Opposition and Complementarity in Zhu Xi's Thought'. In *Returning to Zhu Xi- Emerging Patterns within the Supreme Polarity*, edited by David Jones and Jinli He, 149–75. Albany: State University of New York Press, 2015.

Thompson, Kirill O. 'Zhu Xi's Completion of Confucius' Humanistic Ethics'. *International Communication of Chinese Culture* 3, no. 4 (2016): 605–29.

Thompson, Kirill O. 'Lessons from Zhu Xi's Views on Inquiry and Learning for Contemporary Advanced Humanities Education and Research'. *Azijske študije/Asian Studies* 5, no. 2 (2017): 11–42.

Thompson, Kirill O. 'Relational Self in Classical Confucianism: Lessons From Confucius' Analects'. *Philosophy East and West* 67, no. 3 (2017): 887–907.

Tillman, Hoyt Cleveland. *Confucian Discourse and Chu Hsi's Ascendency*. Honolulu: University of Hawai'i Press, 1992.

Tsai, Chen-feng 蔡振豐. '*Zhuzi dui fojiao de lijie ji qi xiangzhi*' 朱子對佛教的理解及其限制 (Zhu Xi's Understanding of Buddhism, and Its Limitations). In *Dongya Zhuzixue de quanshi yu fazhan* 東亞朱子學的詮釋與發展, edited by Tsai Chen-feng, 177–213. Taipei: Taiwan daxue chuban zhongxin, 2009.

Tsai, Chen-feng 蔡振豐. 'Zhu Xi's Grasp of Buddhism and Its Limitations'. Translated by Daniel Coyle. *Contemporary Chinese Thought* 49, nos. 3–4 (2018): 186–206.

Tu, Weiming. *Confucian Thought: Selfhood as Creative Transformation*. Albany: State University of New York Press, 1985.

Tu, Weiming. *Centrality and Commonality: An Essay on Confucian Religiousness*. Albany: State University of New York Press, 1989.

Tweed, Thomas. *Crossing and Dwelling: A Theory of Religion*. Cambridge, MA: Harvard University Press, 2006.
Urban, Hugh B. 'Making a Place to Take a Stand: Jonathan Z. Smith and the Politics and Poetics of Comparison'. *Method & Theory in the Study of Religion* 12, no. 3 (2000): 339–78.
Vandermeersch, Léon. 'Écriture et divination en Chine'. In *Espaces de la lecture*, edited by Christin Anne-Marie, 66–73. Paris: Éditions Retz, 1988.
Vandermeersch, Léon. *Les deux raisons de la pensée chinoise: divination et idéographie*. Paris: Gallimard, 2013.
Vandermeersch, Léon. *Ce que la Chine nous apprend: sur le langage, la société, l'existence*. Paris: Gallimard, 2019.
Wang, Youru. 'Introduction'. In *Historical Dictionary of Chan Buddhism*, by Youru Wang. London: Rowman & Littlefield, 2017.
Weber, Max. *The Religion of China: Confucianism and Taoism*. Translated and edited by Hans H. Gerth. New York: Free Press, 1964.
Weber, Max. *Économie et Société*. Paris: Plon, 1971.
Weber, Max. *L'éthique protestante et l'esprit du capitalisme*. Paris: Pocket, 1994.
Welter, Albert. *The Meaning of Myriad Good Deeds: A Study of Yung-ming Yen-shou and the Wan-shan t'ung-kuei chi*. New York: Peter Lang, 1993.
Welter, Albert. *Yongming Yanshou's Conception of Chan in the Zongjing lu: A Special Transmission within the Scriptures*. Oxford: Oxford University Press, 2011.
Welter, Albert. 'Confucian Monks and Buddhist Junzi: Zanning's Topical Compendium of the Buddhist Clergy (*Da Song seng shi lüe*) and the Politics of Buddhist Accommodation at the Song Court'. In *The Middle Kingdom and the Dharma Wheel: Aspects of the Relationship between the Buddhist Samgha and the State in Chinese History*, edited by Thomas Jülch, 222–77. Leiden: Brill, 2016.
Whitehead, Alfred North. *Process and Reality: An Essay in Cosmology*. Cambridge: Cambridge University Press, 1929.
Whitehead, Alfred North. *Modes of Thought*. New York: Free Press, 1966.
Yang, Ch'ing-k'un. 'Introduction'. In *The Religion of China: Confucianism and Taoism*, by Max Weber. Translated by Hans H. Gerth, xiii–xliii. New York: Free Press, 1951.
Yu, Chun-Fang. 'Ta-Hui Tsung-Kao and Kung-an Ch'an'. *Journal of Chinese Philosophy* 6, no. 2 (1979): 211–35.
Yü, Ying-shih 余英時. 'Morality and Knowledge in Chu Hsi's Philosophical System'. In *Chu Hsi and Neo-Confucianism*, edited by Wing-tsit Chan, 228–54. Honolulu: University of Hawai'i Press, 1986.
Yü, Ying-shih 余英時. 'Daoxue jia 'pifo' yu songdaifojiao de xindongxiang 道學家「闢佛」與宋代佛教的新動向'. In *Zhu Xi de lishi shijie: Song dai shi da fu zheng zhi wenhua de yanjiu*, vol. 1, 103–59. Taipei: Yunchen wenhua, 2003.
Yü, Ying-shih 余英時. *Lun tian ren zhi qi: zhongguo gudai sixiang qi yuan shi tan* 論天人之際: 中國古代思想起源試探. Taipei: Lianjing chuban gongsi, 2014.
Yü, Ying-shih余英時. 'Between the Heavenly and the Human'. In *Chinese History and Culture: Sixth Century B.C.E. to Seventeenth Century*, Vol. 1, Yü Ying-shih, edited by Josephine Chiu-Duke and Michael S. Duke, 1–19. New York: Columbia University Press, 2016.
Zhang, Liwen. 2015. 'Zhu Xi's Metaphysics'. Translated by A. Lambert. In *Returning to Zhu Xi: Emerging Patterns within the Supreme Polarity*, edited by David Jones and Jinli He, 15–49. Albany: State University of New York Press, 2015.

Index

Abe Masao 5, 20, 48
Ames, Roger T. and David L. Hall 11, 18, 36–7, 72
Analects
  emotions 29
  exemplary man 70, 118
  good 31
Aristotle 14, 37–8, 78
authentic nature (*xing* 性)
  bestowed 30, 34, 206
  Chan 99–100, 199–200
  metaphysical 175
  Neo-Confucian 71, 83–4, 133–7, 144–7, 167–8, 209

behavioral rectitude (*yi* 義) 35, 80, 115–16, 139, 141–4, 154–5, 200
belief. *See also* faith
  Durkheimian 50, 52
  in God 4, 26, 225
  Hick's 81–2
  Smart's 89–90, 103
  system of 105
  totemic 45
  Weberian 59–61
  Western, 11, 181
body (*ti* 體). *See also* functioning
  ethical 32–3, 35, 70
  graph for 36
  metaphysical 34, 46, 55, 59, 145, 160, 171, 204, 219–20
  Neo-Confucian, 32, 50, 148, 195, 208
Bodhisattva 19, 52, 169
Book of Rites 30, 40
Buddha-nature 36, 48, 117, 121, 161, 171, 182
  theory of 132
Buddhism (Chinese) 4–5, 27, 29, 54, 84, 145, 150, 191
  Chan 16–18, 26, 48–9, 80, 102–3, 113–17, 120–1, 124, 127–8, 155–6, 161, 182, 200

Huayan 126
Korean Chan 195
medieval, 196–8
Song 118–19, 132, 202–3
Zhu Xi and 192–3

capitalism/capitalist 4, 12, 21
  global 97
  modern 62–3, 69, 80
  rational 72–3
  society 74
  Western 60–1
categorical/categorization/category 60, 79, 82, 85, 96–7, 162, 165
  Aristotle's 78
  continuum 208, 222
  grammatical 78, 166
  metaphysical 195
  permeability 207–8
  theoretical 7, 51, 105, 199
  universal 11, 180–2
  Western 91–4, 108–9
Chan 5, 17–18, 193
  Buddha-nature 36, 60–1
  Confucianized 113, 132
  Korean 194–5
  'lettered' 27
  Linji 160–1, 191–2, 194
  non-duality 47, 119, 139, 168–9
  sameness 120–5
  Song dynasty 27–9, 35, 52
  transformation 99–101, 115
  Yunmen 26–7, 128, 160–1, 193
Chineseness 19, 21, 78, 172
Ching, Julia 141, 149, 160–1, 191–3, 195, 202–6, 209–10
Christian/Christianity 14, 48, 77, 85, 91, 98, 101, 181
  asceticism 62–5
  Enlightenment 5

faith 91, 102–3
  Judeo- 14
  liberal 2
  monotheistic 80
Classic of Changes (Yijing 易經) 15, 78, 132, 165, 174, 176–7
classification 45, 60, 78–9, 85–6, 96, 104, 106–7, 110, 161–2, 165–6, 180–3, 199, 217
Classic of Songs (Shijing 詩經) 57–8
comparative
  Chinese/Western 18, 19, 226
  etymology 44, 224
  interpretation 1, 39, 69, 162
  method 40, 72, 76, 88, 90–2, 106–10, 116, 127–8, 131
  religion 77, 94, 161, 173
  study 2, 10, 17, 25, 37–8, 54, 67, 91, 97–8, 104, 160, 182–4, 205–6, 212
  theology 213–14
  theory 56, 60–2, 66, 81, 107–9 180
comparison 2, 39–40, 92–3, 96–7, 104, 106–7, 224
  cross-cultural/transcultural 64, 94, 106
  intercultural 1–3, 106–9, 224
  Western-centred 67, 104, 107
concern/concerned
  consciousness 172–6, 178, 184, 189, 215, 221–2
  ethical 79, 89
  Neo-Confucian 222
  Quaker 221–2
  ultimate 207
Confucianism 4–5, 64, 113–16, 127–8, 212–13
  ancient 17–18, 53, 118, 132, 156, 199
  Mencian 115, 131–2, 142–3
  Neo- 43, 84, 101–2, 118, 126, 131, 155–6, 191–4, 209, 214, 227
  New 20–1, 161, 174
  pre-Song 119–20, 129
  Weberian 68–9, 80
Contemporary New Confucians 19–20, 64, 172
consciousness 36, 89, 98–9, 123, 135, 155, 195, 201
  collective 55
  concerned 172, 174–6, 178, 184, 189, 215, 221
  interpreter's 8
  religious 104
  self- 86–7, 122
corporeality
  ethico-metaphysical 31, 37, 70–1, 81–3, 170–1
  intangible 46–7, 182
  metaphysico-spiritual 32–6, 43–4, 46, 50–3, 55, 59, 61, 64, 66–7, 84–5, 87–8, 145, 147, 160, 165–8, 179, 195, 204, 206–8, 210–11, 215, 219–21, 225, 227
cosmology 140, 192, 196–7, 211, 214
  ethical 138, 151
  metacosmology 170
  organic 141, 150
  philosophical 7
creativity/creative 151, 188, 205, 213–15
  ceaseless 210, 219
  cosmic 208–9
  as ethical vitality 209
  etymology of 213–15
  as novelty 209, 214–15, 219–20
  as sincerity 215–17
  transformation 209, 211–12
  Whiteheadian 219–20
cross-cultural 2, 19, 75, 87–8, 94–5, 104, 106–9, 187, 198, 226
cultivation (*xiu* 修) 53, 72, 103
  Chan 54, 84, 118, 183
  Neo-Confucian 29, 55, 190, 192
  self- 85, 87, 99, 101, 193, 203, 206, 208–9
culture 2, 7–8, 42, 51, 60, 74
  Confucian 99, 114, 116, 119, 124, 127, 137, 196, 212
  nature and 13–14, 16, 42, 56–8, 63–4, 67, 78, 85, 105, 164, 189–90, 195, 204, 208, 210, 220, 226
  other 94, 106, 166, 168, 223–4
  Song dynasty 46, 49, 52, 117, 128, 192–3, 202
  wen 文 (Chinese) 15, 17–20, 25–7, 35, 37, 61, 65, 75, 81, 132, 159, 162, 172–3, 178, 187–8, 191, 197–8
  Western 5, 10, 21, 29, 31, 38–9, 62, 90–1, 170–1, 181–2

cultural assumption/presupposition/
   supposition/presumption 1–4, 6,
   9–11, 13–14, 16–18, 26–7, 36–7, 42,
   51, 55–7, 62–4, 67–9, 75–6, 79, 90,
   93, 97, 107–10, 113, 127, 131, 159–60,
   180, 187, 209, 212–14, 224–6 (*see also*
   prejudice)

Dahui Zonggao 192, 194
Daoism 4, 18, 80, 189, 195, 197
Daxue 大學 (*Great Learning*) 82, 99, 118,
   125, 132, 134, 138, 148–9, 155
Derrida, Jacques 3–4, 10, 12, 65–6, 74,
   93–4, 108
destiny/mandate (*ming* 命), 56–8
   of heaven (*tian ming* 天命) 118, 168,
   200
dichotomy 10, 14, 31, 44, 63, 69, 103–4,
   204, 222
   God-world 20, 26, 63, 66, 221–2
   good-bad 10–11, 28, 31, 44, 52, 58, 83,
      88, 116–17, 178, 197, 201–2
   nature-culture 13–16, 42, 56–8, 63–5, 67,
      78, 85, 105, 181, 189, 190, 195, 220
   sacred-profane 4, 26–7, 33, 44–6, 51–2
   subject-object 107–8, 204, 218
   transcendence-immanence 47, 206–7,
      221
difference 5, 93–7, 106, 117, 180
   cultural 17–19, 48, 61, 68, 74
   intercultural 95
   relative 94, 99, 109
   religious 80
distanciation/distancing 8–9, 90, 109
divination/divinatory 10–11, 66–7, 78, 85,
   99, 173–4, 177–8
   diagrams 11, 43–4
   process of 41, 43–4, 138, 164,
      166, 169–71
   as thinking 161, 176, 165, 176, 190,
      203, 209–10, 226 (*see also* written
      language)
dualism 14, 16, 220
Durkheim, Émile/Durkheimian 7, 25,
   33, 37
   sacred 45–6, 50–2, 55
   society 46–7, 51, 56
   theory of religion 44–5, 47, 53–4,
      60–1, 74–5

emotions/feelings 28–30, 71, 99, 121–4,
   135, 144–8, 160–1, 168, 172, 178,
   199, 217
   self-interested 59, 66, 68, 82–4, 87, 100–1
emptiness 103, 118, 121–2, 125, 127, 172,
   183, 201
Enlightenment 2, 5, 7, 11–14, 15, 17, 33,
   39, 40, 56, 62, 65, 67, 74–5, 77, 79, 92,
   96–7, 125, 180, 188, 223, 225
epistemology 20, 81–3, 87, 89, 93
ethico-organic 32, 36–7, 44, 46, 57, 68, 101,
   131, 165, 177, 206, 211, 215
ethico-religious 27–8, 31–2, 37,
   45, 131, 143–4, 149–1, 171–2,
   198, 202–5, 225–7 (*see also*
   philosophico-religious)
ethico-transcendent 205–6
ethics/ethical
   action 28, 30–2, 34, 43, 51, 56, 58–60, 66,
      78, 84, 160, 174, 210
   completely 175
   corporeality 70–1, 81, 83, 171
   growth 56–7, 59, 68, 118, 153–4, 216
   harmony 20, 122, 137
   interaction 32–4, 47, 52, 55, 100, 121–2,
      172, 174, 216, 225
   metaphysical ethical (ethico-
      metaphysical) 32, 34, 36, 56, 68, 70–1,
      83, 132, 134, 166, 183, 221
   of perfectibility 203–5
   practice 26–7, 31, 34, 42, 72, 82, 86–90,
      101, 161, 171–3, 178, 191, 217, 227
   organicity 37, 43
   performative 31–2, 171
   Protestant/Puritan 25, 45, 56, 61–5, 73
   relationships 30, 32–3, 51, 58, 82, 100,
      114, 122, 160–1, 222
   two-levelled 33, 35–6, 46, 50
   understanding/knowledge 20, 135
etymology
   graphic 4, 11, 30, 32, 34, 36, 40, 42–4,
      63–4, 72, 105, 164, 204, 208, 210
   Western 3, 38–9, 92, 170
exemplary man (*junzi* 君子) 35, 58, 68–9,
   70–2, 100, 103, 118, 122, 126–7, 131,
   134, 139, 146, 148–9, 179

faith (*see also* belief)
   Christian 91, 102–3

in God 4–5, 26, 63, 86
Western 60, 81, 85
Five elements/phases 83, 144, 197, 199–200, 207
Five Permanencies 41, 63, 116, 118–19, 122, 160, 192, 211
Five Precepts and Ten Good Deeds 115–16, 118, 160, 192
functioning (*yong* 用) (*see also* body)
  of the body 32, 37
  ethico-organic 44, 153
  great 33–4
  of the language 93, 97, 105, 107, 110, 162–5, 167, 180
  socio-ethical 32–3, 35, 46–7, 50, 60–1, 70, 72, 171, 182, 206, 210

Gadamer Hans-Georg 5–6, 8, 11–14, 16, 19, 21, 37, 62, 65, 73–4, 76, 79–80, 87, 95, 182, 188, 223
God 2–4, 10, 20–1, 26, 48, 54, 62–6, 69, 71–3, 81–2, 86, 90, 101, 103, 163, 166, 174, 214, 219, 221–2, 225
gongan 192–4
good (*shan* 善)
  complete 88, 99, 135, 139
  deeds 28–30, 52, 57–8, 100, 102–3, 133, 142–3, 171
  etymology of 30–1
  homogenous 133–4
  intrinsic 53
  making people 114–17
  Neo-Confucian nature of 135–7
  as sameness 137–8
goodness 132, 136, 140, 145–6, 148, 152, 154–6, 160–1
  original 29–32, 50, 155, 172, 204, 215, 221, 227
Granet, Marcel 7, 18, 67
graphs/graphic (Chinese) 4, 9–10, 15, 32, 67, 165–7, 169–70
  divinatory origin of 44, 176, 208
  etymology 41–4, 63–6, 72, 77–8, 105, 204, 210
  language 81, 85, 91, 106, 109–10, 138, 161–4, 173, 198, 226
  simplification of 78
Greek thought 6, 14, 20, 164, 166, 170

growth 59
  ethical 66, 68, 88, 118, 153–4, 216
  organic 40, 56–8, 140, 149, 151–3, 202, 215
  spiritual 2, 58–9, 208
guwen 古文 27, 30, 49, 113–14, 125, 127–8, 131, 159–60, 168, 191, 194, 198, 202

harmony (*he* 和), 35, 118, 180, 211
heart-mind (*xin* 心) 144–9
  Chan 27, 31, 33, 47–50, 58, 83, 98–9, 117–18, 120–7
  marvelous 99
  Neo-Confucian 35, 53, 81, 150–2
  no-heart-mind 154
  original 68, 84, 153, 155
  present 147–9, 156
Heidegger, Martin 12, 90, 223
hermeneutics
  intercultural 6, 132–3
  of Sinification 195, 197–8
  Western 87, 90
hexagram 15, 139, 155, 165, 170, 176–7
Hick, John 53–4, 75–6, 79–88, 98–9, 101–2, 147
Huayan Buddhism 114, 126, 136
humaneness (*ren* 仁) 83, 116, 190, 195, 200 (*see also* kindness)

immanent 20, 26, 31, 47, 81, 90, 204, 206 (*see also* transcendent)
individualism 59, 85, 188
intercultural/interculturalism
  analysis 9, 11, 17–19, 25, 51, 62, 76, 108, 205, 214, 223
  comparison 109, 159, 187, 226
  dialogue/encounter 1–2, 5–7 16, 94–5, 97–8, 106–7, 171
  interpretation 26, 59, 72, 127–8, 227
  pluralism 222, 224–5
  translation 3, 36, 110
  understanding/knowledge 20, 55, 91, 225
interdependency/interdependent 5, 20, 28, 33, 35, 41, 57, 68, 132, 198, 169, 198, 206, 217
  ethical 1, 46, 55, 57, 61, 136
  feeling 145

individual/human/self 10, 15, 44, 46, 59, 63, 71, 116, 143–4, 151, 172, 175, 179, 211
interpretation
  of Buddhism/Chan (Qisong) 27, 49, 52, 113, 115, 119–20, 124, 127–8, 201
  comparative 161, 173–4, 226
  Confucianized 18, 27, 50, 113, 127–8, 132, 162
  of cultural presuppositions 1–3, 7, 9, 21, 213
  divinatory 43, 176–8
  of graphs 15, 63
  Neo-Confucian (Zhu Xi) 29, 33, 44, 59, 71, 137–8, 143–5, 149, 152–3, 159, 183, 190
  of religion 53–4, 81, 86
  Western 65, 70, 76, 87, 96, 182
interrelatedness
  ancient 139–43
  Chan (Qisong) 29, 52, 58, 123
  divinatory 176–8
  ethical 159–62, 171–2, 178–80, 191–5, 224–7
  ethico-organic 78, 85, 103, 114, 116–17, 131, 139–42, 150
  ethico-spiritual 18, 20, 98
  experiencing 117–19, 127
  karmic 166
  metaphysico-spiritual 165–70
  moral 210
  Neo-Confucian (Zhu Xi) 55, 82, 118, 122, 129, 133–4, 144–8, 153–6
  notion of 11, 110, 113, 126, 128, 197, 214–15
  as sameness, 119–21, 124, 137–8, 152, 180–4
interrelationships
  ethical/ethico-organic 36, 51, 58, 64, 82–4, 114, 226
  social 46, 61, 120, 134, 137, 193, 222
intracultural 1, 6, 8, 198 (*see also* intercultural interpretation)

karma/karmic
  action of 142, 202
  causes and effects 58, 122, 172, 201
  resonance 28, 45, 197
  retribution 55

kindness (*ren* 仁) 83, 116, 141–4, 152, 154, 188, 200, 211 (*see also* humaneness)
knowledge 2, 8, 77, 85–7, 92–4, 105–8, 110
  cosmological 43
  intellectual 38–9, 89
  intercultural 225
  moral/ethical 83, 116, 133–5, 141–4, 150, 205, 227
  object of 97
  ontological 20–1

language 3, 7, 38, 90, 92, 95, 97, 182–3
  alphabetical 37, 41–2, 65–6, 107
  Chinese classic 78, 85, 170, 207, 225
  common origin of 77
  Confucian 49, 117 (see also *guwen*)
  graphic 78, 91, 109–10, 138, 165–7, 173–4, 191, 208, 226
  hospitality 91
  phonetic 91, 162–5, 169
  spoken
  Western 9, 10, 12, 78, 80, 94, 105, 108, 180
  written 10, 17, 67, 81, 96, 198
Laozi 31, 121, 137, 189, 196
learning 7, 19, 26, 47, 74, 90–1, 95, 97, 107, 182, 188, 225–7
  of changes 78
  ethical 137, 146
  Song dynasty 27–30, 32, 34
  transformative 172
letter 65–6, 74, 78, 93–4, 163–4
Levinas, Emmanuel 39–40, 64, 95, 103–4, 106–7, 109–10, 173, 182, 223–4
Liji 禮記 (*Record of Rites*) 30, 40, 203
Lunyu jizhu 35, 50, 155–6

marvellous/supernatural (*miao* 妙) 33, 47, 98–9, 101, 121–3
May Fourth Movement 78
Mencius 18, 115–16, 132, 136–8, 142–3, 145, 147–8, 151, 154, 156, 195, 199
Merleau-Ponty, Maurice 14, 56, 63
metaphysics 145, 170, 206
  moral 43, 68
  Neo-Confucian ethical 33, 167, 192–3, 206, 211

moral/ethical (ethico-moral) quality (*de* 德)
   Chan (Qisong) 47–50, 124, 126–7, 171, 201
   Chinese 52, 56–9, 68, 73, 168, 173, 178–9, 198, 210, 214–15
   Neo-Confucian (Zhu Xi) 31, 70, 81, 141, 146–7, 149, 175
Mou Zongsan 牟宗三 19, 33, 68, 172–4, 178, 213, 215
Müller, Max 2, 76–7, 81, 104
multiculturalism 5, 19

name/reputation (*ming* 名) 57, 120 124–7
nature
   Chan original/universal 28, 30, 33, 36, 48–9, 61, 83–4, 99–100, 114, 117, 121–4, 126, 178, 194, 199–200
   -emptiness 122, 172
   heaven- (*tian* 天) 31, 40, 45, 55, 57–8, 68, 134, 149, 152–3
   Mencian human 115, 142–3, 199
   Neo-Confucian authentic 27, 34, 61, 71, 84, 133–8, 144–9, 167–8, 175
   Western 65–6, 216, 219–20
Neville, Robert 7, 9, 18
no-heart-mind (*wu xin* 無心) 121
non-duality 30, 33, 35, 47–9, 52, 61, 65, 101, 119, 121–2, 124–5, 128, 154, 168, 172, 226
nothingness 52

ontology/ontological
   disconnect/division 32, 78, 166
   ethico- 64, 204
   knowledge 20, 227
   perspective 81–2, 170
organic
   ethico- 32–3, 35–6, 43–4, 46, 59, 68, 81, 98, 101, 118, 131–4, 138-2, 145–7, 149–5, 165, 171, 177, 179, 206–8, 215
   life 31, 56–8, 202
   metaphysico- 138, 145–6, 154, 156, 167–8, 172, 222
   Western 36–7, 63–4
organism
   living 151, 153
   metaphor of 36–7, 42–3, 56
   Neo-Confucian 179
   Western 165, 218–19

other(ness) 1, 11–12, 93
   Chan 125–6
   comprehension of 91
   learning from 19, 74, 79, 95, 97, 107, 110
   culturally 7–8, 13–14, 17, 19, 37, 39, 48, 62, 73–7, 93–4, 97, 106–10, 188
   -oriented 59–60
   Neo-Confucian 143, 152–3
   of the past 6

Pascal, Blaise 14, 56, 63
Peirce, Charles 9–10, 15
philosophical hermeneutics 1, 13, 187
philosophico-religious 3, 5, 7–9, 11, 17, 19, 51, 72, 76–9, 82–3, 91, 102, 162–3, 178–9, 225–7 (*see also* ethico-religious)
Plato
   Meno 106
   Phaedro 106
   Phaedrus 10, 93–4, 106, 163
   Philebus 93–4
   Republic 38, 89
   Sophist 94
pluralism
   intercultural 224
   philosophical 213, 222
   religious 5, 79–80, 173
Polanyi, Karl 73–4
precepts (Chan) 28, 160, 169 (*see also* Five Precepts and Ten Good Deeds)
   no-form 52–3, 59
   non-dual 101
prejudice 6–8, 10, 20 (*see also* cultural presupposition)
principle of coherence (Neo-Confucian) (*li* 理) 27, 33–4, 36, 52, 56, 58, 61, 71, 81, 83–4, 100, 117, 133–5, 145–8, 153, 167–8, 172, 183, 214
   of heaven (*tian li* 天理) 50, 53, 68, 70, 122, 134
process
   continuous 15, 17, 42, 153, 225
   divinatory 10, 41, 43–4, 138, 164, 170, 173, 176, 210
   etymology of 85
   thought 3, 37–8, 213
   transformation 99, 101, 166, 177, 205

Western 84–5, 161
Whiteheadian 213–14, 218–19
Puritanism 12, 62–5, 69, 73, 212

Qisong
  Confucianized Chan thought 49–50, 115–20, 122–4, 131–3, 159–2, 191–2
  life and work 18, 26, 113–14
  teaching 27–30, 31, 33, 46–9, 52, 73, 81, 84, 99–100, 120–2

relationship
  ethical 33, 36, 51, 100, 107–8, 110, 114, 122, 160–1, 182, 193, 222, 226
  five generic (*lun* 倫) 63, 116, 118–19
  human (*lun* 倫) 41–2, 46, 52–3, 56, 82–5, 98, 124, 140–1
  graphic etymology of 41
religion
  Chinese 4–5, 8–9, 10–11, 16, 32, 131, 225
  epistemology of 81–3
  as 'family-resemblances' 80, 86, 92, 96–7
  of the global economy 12, 14, 73
  history of 39, 77
  Latin etymology of 3–4
  science of 13, 45
  theory of 18, 21, 25–6, 37–8, 40, 46, 51, 54, 56, 59, 74, 75, 159, 163, 180–1, 187
  as worldview 88–9
religious
  belief 52, 82, 181
  duty 63
  philosophico- 7–9, 11, 17, 25–7, 31, 46, 51, 53, 72, 74–9, 91, 93, 98–9, 108, 113, 133, 162–3, 173–4, 182–4, 198, 209, 225–6
  pluralism 79–80
religiousness
  Chinese 9–10, 20, 26, 32, 55, 224, 227
  Confucian 205–7
  Western 107
resonance (stimulus-response, *gan ying* 感應)
  karmic 28, 45, 58
  natural 177–9
  process of 178
  sympathetic 196–7, 199–2

responsibility 61, 140, 173–8, 184, 189–90, 193, 222
retribution 55, 178
reverence (*jing* 敬) 55, 60, 101, 139, 142
  ethical 61
  as responsibility 190
  teaching of 204–5
Ricoeur, Paul 6, 8–9, 56, 59–60, 86–7, 89–91, 109, 182, 215
ritual (*li* 禮) 53, 68, 83, 115–16, 120, 141–4, 200

sacred
  Chinese 47–8, 50, 54–5
  Durkheimian 45–7, 50–4
  and profane 4, 26–7, 33, 44–6, 51–2
sage
  Chan 28–30, 47, 58, 100, 121–3, 125, 127, 200, 202
  etymology of 54
  Neo-Confucian 50, 141, 175, 219–20
sameness (*tong* 同)
  Chan 47–8, 119–21, 125–7
  Confucian 126, 132–3, 137, 146–7, 151–2, 219–20
  metaphysical idea of 126
  of teachings 30, 115, 117, 124
Saussure, Ferdinand de 9–10, 163–4
scientific
  rationality 11, 33, 53
  spirit 7
  study of religions 2, 75, 77, 104, 225
School of Principle 18, 117, 126, 128–9, 155
self
  -creation 213, 217
  -cultivation 85, 87, 99, 101, 193, 206, 208–9, 214
  -enjoyment 217
  -immanence 90
  individual 30, 59, 85–6, 100–2, 118–19, 127, 139, 144, 148, 150, 156, 183, 188–9
  interdependent 5, 59, 83, 132, 143–4, 151, 179
  Mencian 142–3
  no- 83, 100, 122, 126, 154, 172, 211
  -transcendence 203–4, 208
  -transformation 98, 109, 121, 172, 205, 207, 210

Shuowen Jiezi 說文解字 4, 40–1, 164 (see also *Xu Shen*)
sign
  graphic 66, 165
  imperceptible (*ji* 幾) 41–4, 66, 85, 99, 163, 166–7, 170, 176, 210, 219–20
  theory of 9–10, 15, 108 (*see also* Peirce, Charles and Saussure, Ferdinand de)
sincere/sincerity (*cheng* 誠)
  Chan 116
  complete 209–10, 215, 218, 221
  Confucian 149–1, 155–6, 183, 208–13, 219–20
Sinification 195, 197–8
Smart, Ninian 76, 80–1, 84–5, 87–1, 96, 102, 165
Smith, Jonathan Z. 39–40, 46, 51, 75–9, 86, 92–6, 104, 106
spirit (*shen* 神)
  Chan 31, 47, 54, 84, 100, 117, 121, 199, 200
  Confucian 154, 210
  way of 28, 124, 126
Streng, Frederick 98, 118, 147, 173–4
suchness/ultimate reality (*shi* 實) 103, 111, 120–5, 183 (*see also* thusness)

teaching (*jiao* 教) 4, 28–30, 33–4, 47, 50, 125, 200
text 3, 8–10, 15, 91, 95
theory
  Chinese etymology of 40–4
  interpretive 18, 110, 159, 162, 183–4, 187, 224–6
  of religion 45–6, 51–5, 56, 59–60, 69, 72–3, 75, 77, 81–2, 84, 86, 88–9, 92–7, 101
  of signs 9–10
  Western etymology of 38–40
Thompson, Kirill 188–90, 195, 201, 205, 207, 212, 214
thusness (*ru* 如) 119, 121, 123 (*see also* suchness)
Tillich, Paul 48, 207
Tower of Babel 75, 77, 79–81, 91–2, 94, 97, 108
transcendent 31–2, 47, 69, 81–4, 104, 166–7, 206, 224–5 (*see also* immanent)
  comprehension of 86–8, 90, 207
  deity 5, 26, 62–3, 65–6, 71
  of divinatory origin 170–1, 174
  ethical 178, 184, 202–4, 226
  feeling 20, 64, 212
  presence 53, 68, 101, 192
transcultural 2, 4, 17, 19, 64, 223
transformation
  Chan 54, 99–100, 118–19, 121–3
  Confucian 116, 140, 190
  continuous 99–101, 179, 215
  ethical 102–3, 115, 169, 171, 204, 207, 210, 217
  of the heart-mind 99
  human 98, 102
  inner 100, 146, 172
  salvific 101–2
  self- 98, 109, 172, 205, 207, 210
  ultimate 147, 205
transformative
  exchanges 2–3, 7–8, 107, 226
  teaching 26, 39, 100, 115–20, 171–2, 226–7
translation
  hermeneutical 8, 10–11, 97, 110, 128, 161
  intercultural 36
  philosophical 2, 9, 72, 91, 109, 159, 183, 224
  transcultural 4

universal principle (Chan) (*li* 理) 125–6, 136, 145, 153–4, 168, 171
universalist
  assumption 16, 60, 81
  way of thinking 7, 13, 16, 19, 39, 60–1, 80
  Weber's meaning 71–2

Vandermeersch, Léon 11, 43–4, 78, 81, 166, 170, 177
vital breath (*qi* 氣)
  movement of 34–6, 47, 54–5, 57–8, 70–1, 132, 145–7, 164–5, 167, 215
  practice of 84, 118, 151–5, 136
vocation 62, 69, 71–2

way (*dao* 道) 28–30, 52, 60, 84, 101
  Buddhist 33, 47, 100
  ethical 59, 81–3, 120

of humans 126
metaphysical 145–6, 207, 227
Neo-Confucian 34, 49–50, 68, 70–1
of spirit 124, 126, 167–8
Weber, Max 12, 25, 37–8, 41, 45, 55–6, 59–60, 61–7, 69, 73
Whitehead, Alfred North 37, 213–20
writing
alphabetic 10–11, 96
meaning of 65
myth of 15, 94, 163
phonetic (Western) 3
graphs (Chinese) 78, 216

Xu Fuguan 徐復觀 19, 172–6, 178, 189, 215

Xu Shen 許慎 4, 15, 30, 40 (see also *Shuowen Jiezi*)

Zhongyong
ancient 54, 57, 140–2, 178–9, 208–10, 212
Chan interpretation of 81, 168
Neo-Confucian interpretation of 34, 81, 100, 122, 133–4, 146, 168, 179–80, 203–6, 219–20
Zhu Xi
biography and works 18, 29–4
thinking 36–7, 53, 55–7, 68, 70–1, 81, 83, 122, 131–9, 141–9, 150–6, 159–60, 167–8, 172–3, 175, 211–13, 219–20
Zhuangzi 121, 189, 196

www.ingramcontent.com/pod-product-compliance
Lightning Source LLC
Chambersburg PA
CBHW062126300426
44115CB00012BA/1831